DISCARD

NEW RIGHT, NEW RACISM

Also by Amy Elizabeth Ansell

UNRAVELING THE RIGHT: The New Conservatism in American
Thought and Politics (*editor*)

New Right, New Racism

Race and Reaction in the United States and Britain

Amy Elizabeth Ansell
Assistant Professor of Sociology
Director of International Programs
Bard College

NEW YORK UNIVERSITY PRESS
Washington Square, New York

First published in the U.S.A. in 1997 by
NEW YORK UNIVERSITY PRESS
Washington Square
New York, N.Y. 10003

This book is printed on paper suitable for recycling and
made from fully managed and sustained forest sources.

Library of Congress Cataloging-in-Publication Data
Ansell, Amy Elizabeth, 1964–
New right, new racism : race and reaction in the United States and
Britain / Amy Elizabeth Ansell.
p. cm.
Includes bibliographical references and index.
ISBN 0–8147–0656–8
1. Racism—United States—History—20th century. 2. Racism—Great
Britain—History—20th century. 3. Conservatism—United States–
–History—20th century. 4. Conservatism—Great Britain–
–History—20th century. 5. Right and left (Political science)
6. United States—Race relations. 7. Great Britain—Race relations.
I. Title.
E185.A69 1997
305.8'00973—dc21   97–14583
                                                                    CIP

Printed in Great Britain

To my parents, Burton and Marjory Ansell

Contents

Acknowledgements

This book represents the end of the beginning of a long journey through different institutional, intellectual and personal terrains. It is my pleasure to acknowledge the many colleagues and friends who have helped make the trip possible.

It was at the University of Michigan that I first stumbled on to the terrain of the politicized. Buzz Alexander and a street theater troop called 'The Pinkertons' introduced me to the possibilities inherent in uniting creativity and playfulness with political commitment and activity. Carl Cohen (ironically, or perhaps not so ironically, a character in this book) nurtured my search for intellectual rigor and honesty. A Eugene Power Exchange Scholarship provided me the opportunity to pursue two years of graduate study at the University of Cambridge, England.

During my years studying in the Faculty of Social and Political Sciences at Cambridge, I benefited greatly through contact with Professors and lecturers (especially Anthony Giddens, John Thompson, Graham McCann, John Barber and Paul Ginsberg), as well as my peers (Carla Willig, Movindri Reddy and Mike Pace, amongst others). Generous support from the Cambridge Board of Graduate Studies, the Commonwealth Trust, the Overseas Research Scholarship and New Hall enabled me to pursue doctoral studies – of which this book is a product – under the useful guidance and thoughtful direction of my supervisor, Dr Gerard Evans. A fellowship awarded by the National Endowment for the Humanities enabled me to complete field work on the US front, while a Visiting Scholar appointment at New Hall, Cambridge, supported me in the completion of field work in Britain.

I would especially like to thank the efforts of numerous people and organizations with whom I came into contact during the course of field work, most importantly: Chip Berlet, Jean Hardisty and the late Margaret Quigly at Political Research Associates in Cambridge, Mass.; and Paul Gordon, Kenneth Leech, Paul Coleman, and Kaushika Amin at the

Runnymede Trust, London. I also would like to acknowledge
the library staff at the State Historical Society of Wisconsin at
Madison; the staff at the Institute of Race Relations, London;
and Carol Keys and her library staff at People for the American
Way in Washington, DC. Adam Meyerson at the Heritage
Foundation and Gerald Hartog at the Freedom Association
were particularly helpful and generous with their time. For this
and later stages of the project, I owe a particular debt of gratitude to Murry Edelman, Professor Emeritus of Political Science
at the University of Wisconsin – Madison, whose lifelong work
has provided a source of inspiration for my own. I value him as
a good friend as much as a teacher.

The experience of teaching sociology and directing international programs at Bard College in Annandale-on-Hudson,
New York, and in particular the free-thinking student body and
the intellectual excellence of the faculty, has contributed
greatly to the fine-tuning of my ideas. Also important in this
regard is a much-valued network of professional colleagues
that includes (in addition to the above): Sanjib Baruah, Ric
Brown, Ron Cox, Sara Diamond, Michele Dominy, the late
Ernest Gellner, Chip Gallagher, Susan Gillespie, Pete Green,
Allen Hunter, Jon Kahn, Walda Katz-Fishman, Matthew Lyons,
Nancy MacLean, Ellen Messer-Davidow, Robert Miles, Michael
Omi, Laurie Patton, Gillian Peele, Gennady Shkliarevsky, Anna
Marie Smith, Stephen Steinberg, Suzanne Vromen, Sarah
Willie, Howie Winant, Ann Withorn, and Richard Wolff.
Whether they realized it or not, each in their own way pushed
me ahead on the learning curve through their own intellectual
or other engagements; some read and commented on parts of
the manuscript. Carla Willig, a long-time friend as well as
transatlantic colleague, has been an important influence on
the honing of my ideas from start to finish. A special word of
thanks is due to Stephen Small, who provided me with invalu-
able feedback on the entire manuscript at different stages of its
incarnation.

Timothy Barlett, my editor, of New York University Press,
worked with me throughout the final stages of completion and
offered sober and incisive guidance. Credit is also due to
Annabelle Buckley and Keith Povey, at Macmillan, for guiding
me through the final stages of manuscript preparation and for
their general professional excellence.

Finally, I would like to thank family and good friends for their support and humor: Richard Ansell, Evie Ansell, Geri Garfinkle, Tanya Marcuse, Ellen Katzman Michaels, James Romm, Becky Shaw, Sergei Teplyakov, and Georgia Ward. A very special gesture of gratitude and appreciation is due to Loretta Oliva, whom over the past three and a half years, has taught me what it means to be a true friend.

Nearing the end of my journey, I have had the good fortune to meet my ideal travel partner, James M. Statman. As a first-rate intellectual, masterful collaborateur, champion editorial critic, and playmate, I look forward to the next chapter together. I thank him for refusing to read me as a script but instead demanding that I be present, with integrity and soul, in everything that I do.

Annandale-on-Hudson   AMY ELIZABETH ANSELL

Introduction: The New Right – Storm-Troopers in the Name of Liberty

> I could be over-interpreting but there's a paranoid smell in the air … something has shifted. They're [the extreme right] idealising the storm-trooper in the name of liberty.
>
> (Arthur Miller)[1]

Over the course of the last two decades, political opinion in the USA and the UK has drifted unmistakably to the right; a new 'smell in the air' is palpable. Yet, the extent to which new, albeit indirect forms of exclusion are being established and justified by a new breed of right-wing politicians often has gone undetected. The most extreme manifestations of the rightward shift have been publicly recognized and condemned, such as the anti-government activities of the militia movement in the United States or the moment when Vladimir Zhironovsky, an ultra-nationalist leader in Russia, congratulated Patrick Buchanan on winning the 1996 New Hampshire Presidential primary, referring to him as a comrade in arms in the struggle for national liberation. The public furor that surrounded events such as the Oklahoma City bombing and Buchanan's short-lived strength in the polls, following as they did in the wake of what was popularly regarded as the 1994 'Republican Revolution', served to draw a symbolic boundary between the sort of illiberalism espoused by the militias or Buchanan and the seemingly more benign rhetoric and policies of the Republican Right, the Reagan Democrats, and the Clinton Conservatives.

One of the contentions of this book is that such a boundary obscures the process by which liberalism itself is being highjacked by the so-called respectable right to serve an illiberal agenda; an agenda that is all the more poisonous because it is largely invisible or misrecognized. Liberal rhetoric and values are being mobilized against the very liberal legacy that

1

brought them into being, and all parts of the political spectrum are colluding in this boomerang effect to the degree that they are participating in the establishment and normalization of a more authoritarian form of democracy.

When people talk about the right turn, it is most often with regard to tax policy, welfare reform, or family values. It is a rare conversation that mentions civil rights policy, for it is commonly presumed that great strides have been made in the arena known as race relations. Racist prejudice has declined significantly in the post-war decades in both the United States and Britain, overt racism is no longer permissible except at the very fringes of political debate, and an emerging black middle class has demonstrated the rewards of a society increasingly freed of institutionalized forms of discrimination in education and the workplace. Moreover, politicians of all stripes, including John Major, the current British Prime Minister, express a commitment to non-racialism and promise to root out prejudice and discrimination wherever it appears. The 1996 Republican and Democratic Conventions in the United States were virtual spectacles of inclusion, with speakers of every color, disability, and creed paraded before the television cameras. Media commentators pronounced that the politics of the symbol had replaced that of the concrete, although none have noted the racialized nature of many of the symbols invoked and the way in which they are working to obscure the real effects of the ascendant authoritarian democratic policy consensus.

During the 1996 Republican Convention in San Diego, Colin Powell spoke eloquently about the color-blind American Dream while the battle waged against affirmative action by so-called angry white men was working its way on to the November ballot in California. A few days later, in an address before the National Association of Black Journalists, Republican-nominee Bob Dole tried to prove his race credentials by recounting an emotionally-laden story about a blood transfusion that occurred during an era when many people recoiled at the thought of mingling black and white blood, this after his party endorsed a platform so antithetical to the interests of people of color. The choice of Jack Kemp as running mate on the condition that the vice-presidential nominee renounce long-held civil rights positions did little to appease the worries of those in the anti-racism community. The next day, Newt Gingrich, Speaker of the House, appeared in a video surrounded by black kids and quoting Martin Luther King, Jr while the Dole–Cannady bill, intended to scrap all federal affirmative action programs, was being prepared as the Republican wedge issue par excellence in the run-up to the 1996 presidential election.

The Democratic Convention bode no better, as Al Gore performed his version of the macarena against the background beat of 'English Only' legislation being drafted by Republicans for a vote in the next Congressional session. Although the Democrats have promised to veto the legislation, Gore's wooden dance represented but one instance of the broader Democratic strategy of symbolically engaging in outreach activities with Hispanic and other communities of color while remaining silent and ineffectual in the face of policy-driven attacks on those very same communities. Bill Clinton invoked the flame atop the Statue of Liberty in moral protest against the flames that had recently destroyed more than thirty black churches in the American South, only weeks after he had signed a Republican-sponsored welfare bill that will deny health and welfare benefits to both legal and illegal immigrants. The fact that the impact of such a bill will fall disproportionately on the poor, people of color, and immigrants most certainly had something to do with President Clinton arranging to have three black former welfare mothers introduce him when he signed the welfare bill.

Transatlantic echoes of such camouflaged pageantry have reverberated in Britain in recent years. During the 1995 Conservative Party Conference in Blackpool, Party leaders condemned prejudice and bigotry while their members organized at fringe meetings to build support for racist immigration and law and order policies. Immigrants are having too many babies and are taking away 'our womenfolk', they argued, while down the hall stories were told of black landlords forcing out white tenants by hanging shrunken heads in the hallways. The public face of the Conservative Party celebrated a forward-looking and compassionate nation of opportunity and liberty while a significant nationalist wing organized in opposition to European unification, warning of the flood of immigrants that would result if Britain loses the power to police her own borders, and in step with a new Asylum Bill that effectively prevents refugee status applicants from claiming social security, housing benefits, free national health treatment, and student loans. Even the opposition – 'New Labour', led by Tony Blair – offers a rhetoric of inclusiveness while colluding with the Conservative Party on a whole range of policy fronts, particularly welfare reform, the deleterious effects of which will fall disproportionately on the poor and the British black population.

The above examples represent more than the politics of the symbol over that of the concrete, it is a showcase of a liberal culture of rhetorical inclusion in pursuit of an illiberal politics of indirect exclusion. Such symbolic showcases of tolerance and reconciliation divulge important clues as to the nature of the racialized fissures and conflicts that exist in contemporary US and British society. The potentially explosive racial fault lines that persist in both societies now lie deeper underground; they have become more hidden, subtle, gentle, even seemingly trivial. One misses the depth of the fault lines if sensors are focused only on obvious events such as the Los Angeles riots in the United States or the activities of the British National Party. Rather, the new politics of racism and reaction demands that our attention focus on more amorphous and complicated cultural events.

In the context of the United States, the competing interpretations surrounding the O.J. Simpson case, not simply regarding beliefs about his innocence or guilt but involving conflicting interpretative repertoires about exactly what was at issue, is a case in point. Approached as a social phenomenon rather than a court trial, the O.J. Simpson affair provides a unique and profound glimpse into the potentially explosive residues and reservoirs of racial animosity, resentment and blame, that continue to mark the US political and social landscape. Similar glimpses can be had for those watching manufactured brouhahas such as Clinton's condemnation of rap artist Sista Soulja, Colin Powell's meteoric rise to fame as black folk hero, or the public witch-hunts against black nominees of all political stripes such as Lani Guinier or Clarence Thomas, to public office.

In Britain, similar cultural indicators of the new politics of racism and reaction have been exposed in seemingly odd, out-of-the-way places. For example, in 1992, Conservative Party chairman Norman Tebbit, in the midst of heated debates around black immigration, proposed a 'cricket test' that would help decipher to whom black people and immigrants owe their loyalty – to Britain or their country of origin – by asking for which cricket team do they cheer. A myriad of other cultural events could be noted as examples of virtual Rorschach tests on to which various and competing meanings related to race and racism have been projected, including the now notorious protests surrounding the publication of *The Satanic Verses* by Salmon Rushdie and the controversy that came to be known as the Rushdie Affair. And, consonant with the therapeutic insights behind the use of Rorschach tests, the meanings attached to such cultural events reveal more about their audience than the 'objective' images or events to which the response ostensibly refers.

It is with respect to such cultural sites of political conflict that it is possible to ascertain not only the continued oppositional sentiments of the dominant society with regard to the pursuit of racial equality in an era where the expression of explicit racism is taboo, but also to recognize the persistent resistance sentiments on the part of communities of color, albeit often unacknowledged and misrecognized, ready to explode in the event of a strong cue. Studying the intersection of race and the right at the crossroads of democracy and the battle over the legacy of the civil rights era provides a unique vantage point from which to view this new politics of illiberalism with a liberal face.

THE NEW RIGHT ASCENDANCY

The shift toward a more authoritarian version of liberal democracy is not a result of the spontaneous combustion of the reactionary sentiments of a segment of the public; nor is it a product of what some regard as the inevitable rhythmic swings of the political pendulum. The emergence of new forms of racism, similarly, is not, as conventional wisdom would have us believe, a simple function of the expression of natural, ahistorical or tribal animosities held by people of different racial or ethnic identities. Rather, the politics of racism

and reaction at the heart of the shift toward a more authoritarian form of liberal democracy is the result of concerted
and conscientious social practice. It is a product of more than
twenty years of organization and struggle by new players on
the right-wing of the political landscape, what I refer to as the
New Right.

The New Right has succeeded in setting the ideological
agenda and influencing the development of government
policy formation in a conservative direction. The result has
been the constitution of a new climate of opinion deeply
hostile to the type of liberal egalitarianism that marked the
political climate of the post-war era. A new authoritarian
democratic consensus is emerging, organized around the New
Right defense of individual liberty, market freedom, traditional values, and white racial nationalism. And although
many counter-trends can be noted in both societies, the
manner in which the opposition expresses its voice – both
competing political parties and also institutionalized anti-
racism – is very much informed by the rightward lurch; people
from all parts of the political spectrum are being forced to
adapt or fail.

The emergence of this new consensus must be understood
in the context of the disintegration of the old one. The political formulas of the post-war era now appear bankrupt.
Though the promises of the dawn of the new millennium
abound, the dusk of the twentieth century seems mired in
confusion and crisis at almost every dimension of social and
political life. Government intervention in the economic arena
seems impotent in its efforts to return the respective national
economies to previous levels of prosperity. This decline in
economic confidence is matched by a feeling of crisis at the
social and even moral level as traditional two-parent families
break apart, crime and illegitimacy rates soar, education standards decline, and as nostalgia for a past wherein authority was
obeyed and tradition respected gives way to a new spirit of
social meanness. A sharply felt sense of political uncertainty
coalesces as traditional electoral coalitions break apart and the
so-called post-war consensus disintegrates, not yet replaced
with anything as coherent or compelling as a political vision of
the national community. As this book will attempt to demonstrate, these multiple levels of confusion and crisis have now,

in the context of the 1990s, snowballed into what could be thought of as a crisis of thinking or a crisis of symbolic representation, catapulting the definition of who 'we' are as a people and a nation to the very center of political debate.

It should come as no surprise that such an identity crisis is occurring at this time. While the post-war liberal consensus began to disintegrate near the middle of the 1970s due to a variety of material and political circumstances, the real break occurred in harmony with the first cracks in the Berlin Wall.[2] The absence of the Soviet enemy as an ordering principle of national political life has left an unintended symbolic vacuum in which the nation and its citizens are engaged in a collective search for a new anchor of meaning around which to rally. The Cold War helped to define and shape the boundaries of national communities: the West was about freedom versus oppression, democracy versus authoritarianism, individual rights versus duty and dogma. The collapse of communism, as well as a variety of other economic and socio-political factors, has required a symbolic redrawing of these moral boundaries so as to make them relevant in the context of a 'new world order'.

During such periods of 'moral panic', when politically dominant cultural and ideological frames have broken down, and new ones have yet to be established, there emerges a period of symbolic conflict regarding the meaning of contemporary events and the recipe for future well-being.[3] These periods are typically characterized by the symbolic construction of political problems, leaders, enemies, and solutions. Such 'construction of the political spectacle' often involves the attempt by social actors to rearticulate and contest the 'truths' dominant in a particular society for strategic and partisan advantage.[4]

The New Right has been a central player in the symbolic contest to define what will replace the consensus politics that characterized the relative stability of the post-war US and British scene. The New Right in both societies emerged in the mid-1970s as the leading entrepreneurs of contemporary moral panics around a variety of issues: from obscene art and the spread of HIV/AIDS; to inner-city crime and 'political correctness'; and against so-called welfare scroungers and underclass youth. In taking on such a broad range of old and new enemies, the New Right sees itself as engaged in a war of ideas, a war of ideology, to reshape the climate of opinion nationally and thus pave the way for a conservative revolution in the realm of policy formation.

For New Rightists, the battle lines are drawn: individualists versus tribalists, opponents of collectivism versus a 'new class' of liberal bureaucrats, God-fearing citizens versus secular humanists, productive versus unproductive citizens, and so on. Their strategy is to organize discontent and win the hearts and minds of the 'silent majority' of conservative citizens in order to save their nation from moral and economic decay. Theirs is largely a symbolic struggle over competing national myths; a struggle to reorientate national politics and culture away from social democracy and liberalism and toward more conservative values and principles. In the process, by defining the consensus politics of earlier decades as the new face of the enemy within, the New Right has challenged the liberal-democratic assumptions that have dominated US and British politics for the past half century.

We should recognize the potential dangers posed by such a challenge to previously hegemonic economic, socio-political, and cultural assumptions, even to Western-style democracy as we know it. Though it is extremely unlikely that democracy will 'fall' in the way that communism did, there is nevertheless a risk that the societies that the United States and Britain now represent are in the process of becoming more rigid and closed. It is ironic that concerns to safeguard participatory citizenship, free exchange of ideas, the popular extension of social rights, and respect for minorities and minority opinion are by no means irrelevant to the sociological study of the self-proclaimed 'winners' of the Cold War. Today the New Right is championing the growth of social inequality, accompanied by a new spirit of social meanness, which helps sustain the shift to a more authoritarian form of democracy. We are living through this shift today, with important implications for the kind of democracy we inherit for the future.

These implications include the question of how people differentiated by 'race' and ethnicity are either included within or excluded from the framework of the national community.[5] Race has been an important interpretive vehicle through which the New Right challenge to the post-war consensus has been orchestrated and around which contemporary debates about civil rights, social justice, citizenship, and the meaning of equality are expressed and amplified. Many controversies at the center of political debate today – immigration, affirmative action, law and order, welfare, multiculturalism, traditional/family values – invoke race as a kind of index of the disintegration of the social order. Ostensibly non-racial issues such as those listed above, linked as they are to other racially coded frames such as the deterioration of inner cities, bloated government, a culture of dependency, sexual licentiousness, and so on, become condensation symbols for the concern over national identity, economic vitality, and even cultural survival. Race serves as an ideological conductor for populist anxiety that the national 'way of life' is coming apart at the seams, and also helps bolster the credibility and power of those who promise to put it back together again.

RACE AND THE RIGHT TURN

Although there has been a plethora of attention to the New Right in both journalistic and academic accounts of the right turn, there has been a relative paucity of attention to the issue of race.[6] In the United States most studies of the New Right have tended to emphasize the importance of family and moral issues, status anxieties, intellectual response to the 1960s, religious mobilization, and a range of single-issue politics in which the New Right has been active.[7] In Britain there have been several important studies of race and the electoral right, racism and the press, and many studies focusing on the Far Right, yet very little in the academic literature specific to the influence of the New Right.[8]

There are, however, important exceptions to this general myopia. In the context of the United States, for example, Michael Omi and Howard Winant argue convincingly that race, racial formation, and racialization processes have been important to the New Right's brand of authoritarian populism.[9] Thomas and Mary Edsall richly document the conservative's strategic use of race, rights, and taxes to realign electoral blocs in the attempt to establish a governing Republican majority.[10] Stephen Steinberg analyzes what he terms the social science scholarship of backlash and links it to the retreat from racial justice in US thought and policy.[11] In the context of Britain, Gill Seidel usefully argues that the crucial significance of race as a defining issue for the New Right has been underestimated, and that the lack of direct emphasis on racial issues is deceptive.[12] Anna Marie Smith presents a highly sophisticated analysis of the role of new forms of racism, forms that disavow racist intent yet demonize and marginalize Commonwealth immigrants and lesbians and gays, in the political project popularly known as Thatcherism.[13] And writing in a comparative vein, Stephen Small rejects the notion of a 'new racism' but nevertheless highlights the continuing significance of what he calls the 'racialized barriers' that prevail in Britain and the United States, maintained and reinforced in part by the new forms of racialized language championed by the New Right.[14]

In various ways and to different degrees, the above authors argue that race-based symbolism was important to the emergence of the New Right in both the United States and Britain, and crucial still for its overall appeal. Tracing the historical roots of the New Right in each country to the racist ideologies and organizations of earlier decades would not be difficult, and has been done.[15] Several studies have demonstrated the continuing involvement of certain individual New Rightists in racist organizations.[16] Since race was central to the historical traditions out of which the New Right emerged (such as Powellism in Britain and the John Birch Society, the Wallace candidacy and the Goldwater campaign in the United States), and also to contemporary organizational networks, it would be astonishing if race did not play an important role in the workings of New Right ideology.

With that said, it is important to emphasize that my intention here is less to demonstrate a purported hidden racist agenda of the New Right than it is to understand the symbolic role of race in the so-called right turn of US and British politics. Less than a decade ago the thesis that race continues to be an important organizational theme for the right wing was controversial and required defense. At least in the context of the United States, many believed that so-called family issues such as abortion and homosexuality had replaced race as an organizing theme for the right wing. From the perspective of the 1990s, however, such a thesis is less prone to challenge as race-related issues are increasingly in the political spotlight. In the United States, issues such as affirmative action, welfare, and immigration, long championed by the New Right and infused with racial referents, emerged as hotly contested themes in the run-up to the 1996 presidential election. In Britain, issues such as multicultural/anti-racist education and criminality continue to resonate in domestic politics, while the racially-coded issue of immigration has been revived in recent debates over European integration.

More important than proving the relevance of race to the political project of the New Right, therefore, is the analysis of the role of race as a 'nodal point' in contemporary British and US politics.[17] The concept of nodal point suggests that race is best approached not from the perspective of single-issue politics, nor from the view that racial issues are now the central axis around which other issues are organized. Rather, the concept of race as a nodal point directs attention to the study of the process by which the New Right's discursive utilization of racial symbols has served to:

1. organize the disintegration of the post-war consensus and the New Right's attempt to construct a new hegemonic social bloc;
2. disorganize the opposition by stigmatizing political alternatives as unviable, tainted by 'special interests', and even silly; and
3. interpellate social subjects in a way that secures at least a degree of popular consent for the right turn in policy formation.

Understanding race as a nodal point reinforces the point made by many critical social theorists that race and racism are not pre-modern phenomena, existing somehow outside of the mainstream of liberalism as a strange residue of irrational prejudice. Rather, race and racism are constituent parts of liberal democracy, even modernity itself, and thus a study of race as a nodal point in the right turn of US and British politics is at the same time a study of the trials and transformations of liberalism in the two societies.[18] It is far too simplistic to think of racism as a product of tempestuous race relations or ancient hatreds frozen during the modern liberal era, peeping out only at times of thaw in enlightenment tolerance. Instead, this study will emphasize the process by which the organization of liberal democracy itself has enhanced the salience of race and racism, and how aspects of the current exit from the post-war consensus heighten their salience and popular appeal.[19]

Several features account for the increased salience of racial issues during this period of transition to a more authoritarian form of democracy. The first is the role of electoral politics. Contrary to the popular conception that a democratic polity serves to stifle race as an organizing theme of social life, political parties in both the United States and Britain, especially during this time of exit from consensus, are making use of the racial idea as they scramble to find a recipe to reconstitute political legitimacy. Conservative parties in particular – the Republican Party in the United States and the Conservative Party in Britain – are using race as one means by which to construct moral authority for themselves and to undermine that of opposition parties.

Though the New Right has not been alone in its use of racial symbols, it has been particularly adept at creating a political mood that is susceptible to the symbols inherent in racial appeals. For example, in the United States, conservative Republicans tied to the New Right have used racialized symbols such as Willie Horton, illegal immigrants, and 'welfare queens' to demonize the so-called permissiveness of the Democratic Party on racial issues. In Britain, right-wing media tabloids and political pundits associated with the New Right have exploited images of 'welfare scroungers' and 'bogus' asylum-seekers to argue that the development of ethnic pluralism could have potentially dangerous consequences for the social stability and cohesion of the nation. In both cases, opposition to so-called race liberalism appears in New Right discourse as a defense of national values. Such symbolic mobilization of racial issues in electoral politics is important because of its potential to appeal to a large number of people who feel that they are losing out; people who are looking for an easy explanation for why or, worse still, for somebody to blame.

The existence of such potential appeal is related to a second feature that accounts for the heightened salience of race and racism during this period of exit from consensus; their use in organizing and defending existing relations of class power and dominance. Although the organization of racial advantage is a significant concern in and of itself, this concern must be related to broader class strategies if we are to avoid reifying race as the 'real' concern of the right wing. For strategies of class domination to work within a liberal-democratic society, they must present themselves as representing a universal principle or as defense of the general/public/national interest. Yet the practical results of such strategies have systematically fallen on certain racialized groups of people. This is especially true in the United States, where the class system is racialized to a very great extent, and also in Britain as a function of the legacy of colonialism. The symbol of race has proven useful as a means of rendering the universal promise of the theory of liberal-capitalism consistent with its historic results.

This usefulness is heightened during moments of societal transition. In pursuing an aggressive class strategy that entails the return to neo-liberal forms of capitalism, the New Right has attempted to stigmatize social democracy/Great Society liberalism itself as the cause of present difficulties, thereby absolving the operation of the market from responsibility for rising social inequality. In doing so, the New Right has rhetorically conflated race with so-called liberal permissiveness in a way that deflects attention from complex structural sources of economic strain and at the same time offers a response that justifies the reorganization of material advantage in favor of capital. Consider the case of the ideological response to the 1992 Los Angeles disturbances: conservative politicians such as former Vice-President Dan Quayle attributed blame for the disturbances to liberal welfare programs (as well as television shows such as Murphy Brown) that supposedly have fostered indulgent and otherwise pathological social behaviors. Solutions of a more structural nature proposed some three decades before in the wake of the Watts riot were thereby foreclosed. Instead, race and the riots, not to mention single-mother households, became useful condensation symbols for conservatives interested in justifying the withdrawal of government from key functions related to the regulation of the market and the guarantee of social rights.

The final feature that accounts for the link between this period of exit from the post-war consensus and the appeal of racial issues is related to what was described above as the current identity crisis facing the two societies. With communism gone as the external enemy, there has been a search for a new internal enemy against which to rally. As any student of the sociology of deviance can attest, social identities are commonly defined in relation to an unacceptable 'other' whom one excludes from one's moral community. This is the 'them' versus 'us' theory of political discourse popularized by post-structuralism, suggesting that the definition of one's community revolves around the symbolic construction of insiders and outsiders. According to this theory, it should come as no surprise that the end of the Cold War has produced a crisis in self-conception for the West and a search for a new enemy around which to articulate the values for which the 'we' stands firm.

Racialized others are among those standing in for the once commanding communist threat. People of color and immigrants are offered as scapegoats in a long-effective political tactic to explain away social problems by identifying a certain group of individuals as personifying their cause. Pseudo-solutions to the economic problems facing each society are offered via the construction of racialized others presumed to be lacking a healthy work ethic and acting as a drain on scarce fiscal resources. Simplistic analyses of a variety of difficult political challenges are offered that present people of color and relevant governmental agencies as illegitimate 'special interests' demanding that they be treated more equally than others, thereby distorting the system of representative democracy. A myriad of social and cultural controversies are racialized as conservatives revamp 'culture of poverty' theories that explain rising negative social indicators in communities of color as a result of a deficit of functional values. As is usually the case, such racial symbolism reveals as much about the society that invokes it as about any objective social problems to which the symbol ostensibly refers. In this way, people of color have come to symbolize the chaos and confusion associated with the disintegration of consensus politics.

Understanding that the study of race and the New Right is also and inevitably a study of the trials and transformations of liberal democracy contributes to the view that race is above all a political symbol. This view lends itself to an approach that appreciates the role of symbolic politics over an economic-orientated or single-issue-based perspective on the right turn. Symbolic themes such as race, sexuality, and nation have been and continue to be crucial to the New Right's effort to construct a right-wing populist project. A cultural studies approach, or what will be labelled in Chapter 1 as a 'symbolic conflict' approach, offers the most promising framework within which to study the New Right's struggle to re-define the modes of signification, categories of assumptions, and cultural codes upon which the consensus politics of the post-war years was built.

A cultural studies approach allows one to bridge the theoretical bifurcation of structuralist versus ideological accounts of the role of the New Right in the right turn that characterizes the current literature. Structuralist accounts focus upon the novel political coalitions formed between certain sectors of the business and political elite, and the policies that they together advocated, during a period of economic contraction and political instability.[20] In the historical context under study, so the argument goes, both business and the state moved to the right in order to secure conditions for capital accumulation and restore the legitimacy of established institutions. According to the logic of the structuralist approach, the role of ideology is conceived as secondary or subordinate to the story of the right turn in policy formation. Survey research is presented to demonstrate that there exists much popular resistance to both the ideas and the policies advocated by the New Right.

In their analysis of both the 1980 and 1984 Presidential elections in the United States, Thomas Ferguson and Joel Rogers identify what they label the hidden or underlying sources of the right turn as the drastic restructuring of internal relations among US elites.[21] According to their argument, the real battle being waged is between different sectors of capital, and in no way represents a popular realignment to the right. More important than any shifts in public opinion was the movement of the Democratic Party to the right in 1980 in response to the failure of the Carter administration's economic policies, and in 1984 as a reaction in favor of Reagan's program for economic recovery (that is, lower taxes and higher military spending). Reagan's popular support in both elections, they argue,

turned almost entirely on economic issues, not a massive ideological conversion of the electorate.

Such an argument is echoed in various studies of
Thatcherism.[22] As above, these structural analyses of
Thatcherism criticize those (Stuart Hall in particular) who understand Thatcherism's success in ideological terms. Instead
the focus is on the nature and the limits of Thatcher's economic strategy, the disorganization of the resistance to
Thatcherism, and strategic errors of the Left. It is argued that
the view based on hegemony runs the 'risk of imposing a spu-
rious unity on Thatcherism' and that 'ideologies must not only
be transmitted; they must also be received, understood and
acted upon.'[23] As in Ferguson and Rogers' analysis, critical attention is focused on the lack of firm evidence that the ideology of the New Right has struck deep popular chords.
Thatcherism's populism is conceived of as being ventriloquist
in nature whereby 'the people' are invoked as part of the
struggle against institutional bases of opposition both within
and outside the Conservative Party. Thatcherism, in such an
analysis, is significant less in terms of the organization of positive support among the people or within the power bloc than
as a 'passive revolution' whereby the more pragmatic state
interests of lowering direct taxation, selling council houses,
lowering inflation, and so on are secured.

Structuralist accounts provide an important corrective to pluralist approaches that understand the right turn as the consequence of a set of popular demands placed upon the state that
effectively pulled it to the right. However, despite their contributions, structuralist accounts are insufficiently dynamic. That
is to say, though the reasons seem convincing for rejecting the
view that the right turn from below *caused* the right turn from
above (that is, the pluralist view), it does not follow that the
former was non-existent or irrelevant. Rather, it is important to
pay analytic attention to the right turn from below as both an
independent variable and an associated effect of the attempt
by the dominant social bloc to make the shift in a more conservative direction appear legitimate, even popular. Thus, structuralist accounts are not so much rejected here as modified to
take account of the significance of the symbolic dimensions of
the New Right political project in facilitating the rightward shift
in society and politics that was already under way.

Two assumptions guide such a thesis. The first is that public beliefs, as well as the policy preferences of governing elites, change along with transformations in social and material conditions. The set of structural factors that caused ruling elites to shift in a more conservative direction also exercised an impact upon the consciousness of relevant social groups. Second is the assumption that governing elites at least attempt, especially during periods of exceptional transformation, to mobilize popular support behind their policy goals. The degree to which elites succeed in this consensual project is usually not a decisive factor in politics, but nevertheless it is an important one, and one that is worthy of study. It is in relation to this consensual project that the role of New Right ideology in the right turn assumes critical importance.

A focus on the symbolic dimensions of the right turn need not require demonstration of the existence of a majoritarian consensus with regard to a set of shared dominant values.[24] There is no need to search for the factual recognition of dominant values or a coherent system of specific beliefs on particular topics. As Stuart Hall writes with regard to Thatcherism,

> Thatcherism has never been 'hegemonic' if by that we mean that it succeeded in unifying a major social bloc, 'winning the consent' of the great majority of the subordinate classes of society and other key social forces to a major task of social reconstruction. Especially if we conceive 'hegemony' as a permanent, steady state of affairs. What we have always argued is that it had a 'hegemonic project'. It was designed to renovate society as a whole. And, in doing so, it understood that it must organise on a variety of social and cultural sites at once, both in society and in the state, on moral and cultural, as well as economic and political terrain, using them all to initiate the deep reformation of society.[25]

In other words, without arguing that the New Right has succeeded in forging an alternative hegemonic consensus on a set of dominant values, it is important to challenge the structuralists' conception of the right turn as simply a set of strategic policy shifts to reinvigorate capitalism. In fact, the political project of the New Right is interesting precisely because it has attempted to translate the neo-liberal economic project into a populist moralism and common sense.

This modification of the structuralist account so as to make it more dynamic must be distinguished from those ideological accounts of the right turn that render the study of the New Right as an account of that political force that has succeeded in best articulating the popular. Ideological accounts often portray the New Right political project as one of grabbing the state and pulling it rightward. In this view, parents worried about the education of their children, politicians seeking to establish conservative electoral coalitions, citizens concerned about rising crime rates, business groups advocating decreased interference in the economy, religious leaders seeking to reassert the sanctity of the family and traditional values, and so on, all equally and successfully vied for state power. Such an account conceives of New Right ideology as autonomous from wider social relations and struggles for power and so empties the study of the ideology of the New Right of its critical content.

A cultural studies approach is perfectly suited to overcome this theoretical bifurcation between structuralist and ideological accounts of the role of the New Right in the right turn. Such an approach allows one to bring the socio-economic and cultural moments of the right turn together in one conceptual framework. As Stuart Hall reminds us in the above quote, a hegemonic project cannot be simply economic or ideological in orientation. A study of the racial ideology of the New Right would be severely limited if we were only to study the deleterious impact of free market policies on communities of color, as it would be if we were only to focus on the manipulation of racial rhetoric by conservative politicians concerned to construct a new majoritarian electoral bloc. The rejection of the post-war consensus on a whole range of policy matters, including racial ones, is about more than a set of economic imperatives or electoral arithmetic. It is fundamentally a symbolic project, and the New Right's attention to racial issues has been central to its attempt to create new national myths, articulate an alternative and compelling political imagination, and reinterpret previously hegemonic cultural codes. In this sense, the New Right has succeeded in shifting national, social and individual identities rightward – with significant implications for the politics of racial inclusion/exclusion.

A NEW RACISM

If race-based symbolism was important both in terms of the emergence and continuing appeal of the ideology of the New Right, and central to the practice of the right turn as a whole, how are we to explain the relative paucity of attention to the issue of race in the literature on the contemporary Right? One possible answer is that the New Right itself does not devote much explicit attention to the issue. But this is not the case. New Right headlines, journal articles, speeches and direct-mail materials are full of references to the racial 'problems' so prevalent in contemporary US and British society.

It is not blindness to the issues of race and racism, but rather lack of theoretical clarity as to their very definition – a definition which carries within it strong assumptions about society and how it operates – that accounts for the relative paucity of attention paid to racial issues in the literature on the New Right. Racial discourse has changed significantly in character in the last several decades, so much so that there are no longer any clear signposts or criteria (if there ever were) by which to characterize a particular political discourse or project as racist. Recent survey research suggests that views of racism are highly inconsistent and contradictory, and closely related to the racialized subject position of the interviewee.[26] It is to this change in the character of racial discourse and confusion over what constitutes racism that the second major theme of this book is addressed.

Attention to the manner in which racial discourse has changed in recent years is linked in various ways to the first theme of race as a nodal point in the right turn. This is so since the changes at the level of racialized discourse are not entirely semiotic in nature, but rather organized in response to the new realities and contradictions thrown up by social reality. New Rightists have acted as cultural entrepreneurs of what will be characterized in the following chapters as the 'new racism', but it is an entrepreneurial activism that is of more than a linguistic nature. The New Right has served as a catalyst in linking the racialized backlash sentiments of relevant social groups with the shifts at the level of policy formation characterized above as the right turn in US and British politics. In the process of mobilizing race as an ideological

articulator of the exit from consensus politics, the New Right
has altered the way in which contemporary debates about civil
rights, social justice, citizenship, and the meaning of equality
are expressed and amplified, in turn demanding an analysis
of the ways in which our very notions of racism require
theoretical revision.

The second main thematic thread running throughout this
book, therefore, is a comparative analysis of the changing
forms of racial discourse in the two societies, with a particular
focus on the critical role the New Right has played in the reorganization of key elements of right-wing racial discourse. An
understanding of recent shifts in the forms and uses of racialized political language is vital if we are to analyze better
contemporary policy debates about issues such as race relations, affirmative action, multiculturalism, welfare and crime.
Particular attention is paid to:

1.   the ways in which the new forms of racial discourse pro-
     duced and circulated by the New Right are distinct from
     the right-wing racial ideologies of the past;
2.   the role that political culture plays in shaping the chang-
     ing forms of racial discourse in the two countries; and
3.   the role of political language in the racialization of con-
     temporary US and British politics.

The forms of racial discourse produced and circulated by
the New Right are distinct from the right-wing racial ideologies of previous decades. Although none of the discursive
elements are entirely novel, and in fact draw on interpretative
repetoires established in earlier moments such as the George
Wallace candidacy in the United States and Powellism in
Britain, as an ensemble they represent a new form of racial
discourse, even a new racism, qualitatively distinct from more
traditional forms.

The new racism actively disavows racist intent and is
cleansed of extremist intolerance, thus reinforcing the New
Right's attempt to distance itself from racist organizations
such as the John Birch Society in the United States and the
National Front in Britain. It is a form of racism that utilizes
themes related to culture and nation as a replacement for the
now discredited biological referents of the old racism. It is

concerned less with notions of racial superiority in the narrow sense than with the alleged 'threat' people of color pose – either because of their mere presence or because of their demand for 'special privileges' – to the economic, socio-political, and cultural vitality of the dominant (white) society. It is, in short, a new form of racism that operates without the category 'race'. It is a new form of exclusionary politics that operates indirectly and in stealth via the rhetorical inclusion of people of color and the sanitized nature of its racist appeal.

Mainstream social science for the most part has failed to track the emergence of the new racism precisely because of its symbolic re-coding, and most importantly because of its apparently benign race-neutral form. For similar reasons, the new racism has penetrated popular ways of thinking on the part of social groups caught up in the confusion and chaos of the period and looking for answers, yet unresponsive to those who employ blatant tactics of scapegoating or explicitly express intolerant or exclusionary sentiments.

One reason why the new racism has not been obvious to either experts or its general audience is because it is couched within, and not against, both societies' civil religion – the vocabulary of equal opportunity, color-blindness, race-neutrality and, above all, individualism and individual rights. More than this, the new racism has operated by circumventing the vocabulary of the civil rights movement itself. As is evident from the California initiative on affirmative action that won voter approval in the 1996 Presidential elections in the United States, it is the New Right that currently champions the idea that people should be judged on the 'content of their character' and not the color of their skin. In Britain, racist anti-immigrant campaigns are organized around the multiculturalist demand for respect for cultural difference. Words and phrases such as color-blindness and equality of opportunity have been similarly highjacked and repackaged so as to service a different agenda, this time in favor of a politics that is, albeit indirectly, exclusionary rather than inclusionary in spirit. Accordingly, my study of the new racism has not been driven by a search for the irrational or the bizarre. Rather, it has traced the way in which the new racism has become a hegemonic discourse as a function of the New Right's successful attempt to center its discourses on race and normalize it in relation to other more mainstream political discourses and cultural codes.

In any comparative study of this sort it is important to acknowledge differences in the political cultures of the two societies. The New Right is an international phenomenon, albeit one with national peculiarities, yet most studies have been restricted to the analysis of a single country. Focusing on the issue of race allows for an exploration of the essential similarities shared by the New Right in the two countries in terms of the material roots and symbolic functions of its ideology. While dissimilarities owing to differences in the history of slavery, the origin and size of the respective communities of color, colonial history, the political system, and the position in the international political economy must be acknowledged, this study will emphasize the similar functions of New Right racial ideology in both societies to mobilize meaning in service of white privilege.

Finally, an attempt will be made to understand better the role of political language in the racialization of contemporary US and British politics. Race-related issues have been the subject of enormous public debate in recent years, and this has inevitably led to a number of changes in the use of racial symbols and language within political life. Most importantly, racialized political language has been reformulated around the concepts of cultural values and national identity. Such reformulation is made evident in this study of the New Right's manipulation of symbolic images of culture and nation to orchestrate fears about immigration, multiculturalism, and inner-city decay. An understanding of the role of New Right discourse in the racialization of contemporary politics is crucial if we are to appreciate and combat recent political debates that assume a non-racialist form but nevertheless serve to establish and maintain relations of racial inequality. In this respect, analysis of the new racism not only contributes to an understanding of the ways in which it is distinct from more traditional forms of racism, it is also fundamentally a challenge to contextualize accounts of the new racism within an analytic framework of the right turn that takes account of the impact of social relations on processes of racialization.[27]

THE STRUCTURE OF THIS BOOK

Taking this challenge seriously, I have analyzed New Right racial discourse along the fault line of the two thematic threads outlined above: the role of race as a nodal point in the right turn of US and British politics, and the new forms and uses of racialized political discourse mobilized by the New Right. In Chapter 1, I elaborate on the usefulness of a cultural studies approach to the study of race and the right turn by offering what I label a symbolic conflict model of politics. Rather than conceive New Right racial ideology as a simple expression of the dispositional needs of its supporters, the personal ambitions and/or electoral tactics of its leadership, or the interests of dominant social groups, the symbolic conflict approach examines the New Right's role as catalyst in linking popular backlash sentiments with right-wing solutions to contemporary issues and events.

My focus upon the specifically racial dimensions of the right-wing reaction against the post-war consensus allows for an analysis of the new forms of racial discourse that have emerged in the United States and Britain and the manner in which they have been shaped by and intersect with changing economic, social, and political relations. This is my aim in Chapter 2, where I survey the ways in which the forms of racial discourse mobilized by the New Right can be thought of as new, and explore the question of whether these new forms in actuality constitute a new *breed* of racism.

The comparative aspect of the book facilitates an examination of the role of political culture in shaping both the form and content of New Right racial discourse. Defining racism as a dynamic socio-historical symbol rather than a static and ahistorical set of prejudices implies the need to examine the internal forms of New Right racial ideology via critical discourse analysis. My aim in Chapters 3 and 4 is to do just that by deconstructing what I label the key categories of meaning that operate together to render New Right ideas on race coherent.[28] Toward this end, I collected hundreds of direct-mail letters, research papers, newspaper articles, and policy statements produced by the New Right. In addition, I systematically searched the official journals and books published by these organizations, as well as books and articles written by individuals associated with them, for material pertaining to race and related issues. Interviews were conducted with leading New Right personalities. Rather than restrict my search to those New Right organizations and individuals that I deemed pertinent from the start, every effort was made to ensure that the search was as inclusive as possible. Key assumptions were identified according to how often they appeared. Many more categories than are presented were originally identified. Their number was reduced as a result of combining categories that share a broader core assumption. Analysis of the key categories of meaning further generated a set of associated ideological mechanisms that are similarly identified and discussed. The interactions of these general ideological mechanisms are identified in Chapters 3 and 4 as forming the core of the New Right's new racism. In order to be fair to the category-users themselves, I use direct quotes in these chapters as much as possible.

The focus on political language provides a framework in which to analyze the complex ways by which the emergence of a new set of racial meanings and symbols has contributed to the racialization of contemporary US and British politics. In order to determine the extent to which the new racism of the New Right can be said to have become hegemonic, it is necessary to examine the impact of the key categories of meaning produced and circulated by the New Right on government policy formation. This is my aim in Chapter 5.

Finally, I offer some concluding remarks on the relationship between the New Right, the new racism, and the right turn of US and British politics. I argue that while the New Right may represent only one segment of political opinion in the two countries, a critical analysis of New Right symbolic conflict over racial meanings is essential if we are to understand and combat its role in reinforcing the potential, if not the reality, of a shift towards a more authoritarian form of democracy.

1 Race and the Right Turn: The Symbolic Conflict Approach

The role of race in the right turn of US and British politics is pivotal. Race is above all a political symbol that has helped organize, at the ideological and cultural level, the rightward shift in policy formation associated with the Reagan and Thatcher eras and beyond. Attention to the symbolic construction and political uses of race helps remind us that shifts at the level of policy formation are not only about elite economic strategies or the failure of the Left. Rather, such shifts point to the importance of the symbolic and cultural dimensions of political conflict and change. It is in this regard that the New Right's self-proclaimed revolutionary strategy to establish social conservatism as politically dominant assumes critical importance.

The New Right presents its strategy as a sort of 'Gramscianism of the Right'.[1] Antonio Gramsci was an Italian social theorist who, while imprisoned by the fascists in the 1920s, revised many key points of socialist strategy so that they might better apply to the political context of Western parliamentary democracy. Of key importance for Gramsci was the struggle in the realm of ideas, a struggle that he insisted must be won within civil society prior to the winning of state power. Ironically, it is the New Right that has emerged as the implicit champions of Gramsci's ideas. New Rightists insist that if the conservative policy revolution is to succeed, it must be complemented by a conservative revolution in the arena of culture and ideas. As Paul Weyrich writes, 'It's a war of ideas, a war of ideology, it's a war over our way of life.'[2]

As a political symbol, race serves for the New Right as a catalyst in rotating the kaleidoscope of social meanings that shape common sense understandings about a wide range of social phenomena. The newly-configured picture consists of the

25

same fragments of colored assumptions and ideological shapes as before, but this time in a new combination. This new conservative-tinted common sense, I will argue, carries potentially serious implications for the status of cultural pluralism and racial equality in the post-civil rights era.

More than a mere symptom of the retreat from racial justice in thought and policy that has been the subject of recent scholarship in the field of race relations, New Right discourse about race is more generally anti-radical, even anti-liberal, in effect.[3] Race is a symbol upon which a broad range of problems related to the disintegration of the post-war liberal consensus are being loaded. In the economic realm, liberal racial policies and understandings are blamed for declining economic indicators, rising (white) unemployment, and falling living standards. In the social and moral realm, these same policies and understandings are blamed for causing or at least worsening a whole host of problems: for example, welfare dependency, sexual promiscuity, family breakdown, and a culture of personal irresponsibility. Politically, the supposed unresponsiveness of the Democrat and Labour Parties to 'ordinary' citizens is blamed on their being captured by minority 'special interests'. A picture emerges of the good citizen betrayed by her government, of little old white ladies afraid to leave their homes for fear of being attacked by the dangerous dark forces left to roam on the streets, and unprotected by an impotent government unwilling to take on the worn-out dogmas of the civil rights establishment and the 'race relations industry'.[4]

My goal is not to prove that this picture is erroneous, but rather to link its production to the New Right's hegemonic project as a whole. The race problem has been symbolically constructed and politically used as part of a concerted effort by the New Right in both countries to organize consent for its own political project. In doing so, New Rightists have rearticulated dominant cultural frames in ways that respond to popular anxieties during this volatile period wherein no alternative consensus is yet clearly consolidated. However, it is important to emphasize that the New Right's response is not neutral, it is a response that itself shapes or interpellates this anxiety in a conservative and racialized form. It is a response that, at its broadest level, posits a causal relationship between the revival of traditional values or national 'ways of life' and

the reversal of economic decline. Not only is such an argument profoundly unsociological in that it reduces contemporary difficulties to a simple crisis of values, it is also racial to
the extent that blame for systematically asymmetrical relations
of racial and class inequality is shifted from white racism and
the structure of society to the supposed cultural or moral failings of people of color themselves.

If there is to be an effective counter-response, concern must
be paid not only to the reversals at the level of policy formation to which much of mainstream social science directs attention, but also to the symbolic reversals in the arena of social
thought more generally. In its attempt to reconstruct an alternative ideological bloc around a set of conservative assumptions and expectations, the New Right has succeeded in
winning a major ideological reversal: discrediting the currents
of thought and argument of the opposition and transforming
the underpinning ideologies of consensus politics to conservative advantage. This success is overlooked by those who study
the right turn on a narrow economistic basis and, as a consequence, deny its agency. And there is no more powerful agent
of the right turn than the New Right.

IS THERE A 'NEW RIGHT'?

Most people today agree that the recent rise in right-wing
ideas and policies represents something new and important in
US and British politics, yet differences of opinion emerge over
the application of the label 'New Right'. Rather than being
merely semantic, such differences indicate the need to clarify
our understanding of the relationship of today's conservative
forces with right-wing movements of the past, as well as with
other factions of the contemporary Right.

At one end of the continuum of opinion are those who
believe that the strategies and beliefs of the contemporary
Right are fundamentally consistent with the right wing of the
past. These authors point out that right wingers themselves
have not defined themselves as New Right since the 1970s, and
object that the term obscures the continuity between current
right-wing movements and their predecessors of the 1940s
and 1950s.[5] In this view, the term 'right-wing movements' is

preferred so as to avoid making an analytic distinction between post-war generations of the right wing.

Others believe that while there was something new about the New Right in the mid-1970s and early 1980s, it is not very revealing to continue to label these forces on the right of the political spectrum as 'new' in the 1990s.[6] Moreover, it is noted that many of the organizations of the New Right of the late 1970s and early 1980s are now defunct (for example, Moral Majority, Religious Roundtable, National Conservative Political Action Committee, to name a few). In this perspective, the term 'conservative movement' is preferred because the right wing of the 1990s is much more than a limited set of organizations or network of personalities and, as such, more deeply institutionally-embedded as a social movement as compared to the right wing of only a decade ago.

At the other end of the spectrum are those who believe that the right-wing of the last two decades is qualitatively distinct from the so-called Old Right and so continue to apply the label New Right. These authors argue that the New Right is populist in orientation, the product of a novel and distinct ideological synthesis of neo-liberalism and social conservatism, and/or focus on innovative strategies of communication or coalition-building between secular-political and religious conservatives.[7]

Each of these perspectives has merit and point to important questions for any student of right-wing movements: how long can a movement or ideology be defined as new? Can we speak of a coherent, singular movement when important differences exist between the religious, secular-political, and intellectual factions of the Right? Should a movement be defined by reference to a specific set of organizations and the individuals associated with them, or by reference to the content and style of its discourse and ideology?

I employ the term 'New Right' despite the disfavor into which it has fallen, because it remains analytically useful for a number of reasons. It emphasizes that which is distinct about the constellation of political forces on the Right of the political spectrum that emerged in both countries in the mid-1970s. Among the features that mark the New Right as distinct from right-wing movements of the past are: its populist and sometimes even revolutionary rhetoric; a hybrid ideological fusion of neo-liberalism and social conservatism; avoidance of extremism and the centering of its discourse as part of an aggressive bid for political power; mobilization of new blocs of voters around a broad range of social issues; and success at coalition building and attention to organizational detail.

Although I recognize the clarity that comes from restricting the term to a particular historical moment and/or set of organizations and the individuals associated with them, such clarity comes at the cost of obscuring the ideological continuities that exist between the New Right which emerged in the mid-1970s and the right wing of today, and the ways in which they together are distinct from right-wing movements of previous decades. The New Right is new because of its ideology, located in this specific historical juncture of breakdown in consensus politics, and should not be judged otherwise because this or that organization has become defunct. Specifically, the historical context in which the New Right emerged, marked as it is by the perceived failure of interventionist policies in both the economic and social realm and the demobilization of the popular struggles of the 1960s and early 1970s, has provided the opportunity for a revitalized right wing to re-frame its discourse in anti-government and even populist terms.

This point of view is especially relevant with concern to the study of race and the New Right. The New Right in both countries has mobilized, from the mid-1970s to today, new and sanitized forms of racialized political language organized around the theme of anti-anti-racism in its effort to displace the progressive racial understandings and policies ushered in during the civil rights era and, in so doing, to construct an alternative conservative social bloc. In this way the New Right aims to indict the failed pursuit of racial equality that marked the early post-war years for itself causing the current adverse state of race relations in the two societies. The result, as will be detailed below, represents a family of right-wing racial politics distinct from that of the early post-war period.

ORGANIZATIONS AND CURRENTS

The term 'New Right' is used here to denote the realignment of different political forces on the right-wing of the political spectrum that have set themselves the task of fracturing the so-called post-war consensus. This realignment has not been the product of a unified or homogeneous political tendency, but rather of the promulgation of a range of ideas, inter-pretations and opinions for which the term 'New Right' pro-vides a convenient shorthand.

In a narrow sense, the term refers to that aggregate of organizations, and the individuals associated with them, which emerged and coalesced in the mid-1970s. In both the United States and Britain, as will be detailed below, new right-wing organizations were born and older conservative net-works revitalized. Yet in a broader and more meaningful sense, the 'New Right' refers to a constellation of beliefs adopted and espoused by a wider range of people and institu-tions. The term is therefore used here to denote a particular worldview, and the organizational network that emerged as its political vehicle, to challenge both liberalism and mainstream conservatism.

The New Right represents that section of the right wing distinct from both traditional conservatism and from more extreme Far Right groupings. Its distinctiveness is most com-monly attributed to its emphasis on social issues – although its stress on free market economics has been crucial for its overall appeal. It is important to study the New Right since it, more than any other section of the contemporary right wing, has served as a catalyst in connecting popular backlash sentiments with the electoral strategies and policy goals of the Republican and Conservative Parties.

The New Right advocates its policy proposals through pres-sure groups, academic journals, think tanks, grassroot activist networks, and the media. Political pressure groups such as the Free Congress Foundation in the United States and The Freedom Association in Britain supply the political mechanics by which to take over government, one precinct at a time. Academic journals such as *Commentary* and the *Salisbury Review* provide a meeting ground for embittered neo-conservative in-tellectuals to apply their new ways of thinking to timely topics of political debate. Think tanks such as The Heritage Foundation and the American Enterprise Institute in the United States, and the Social Affairs Unit and the Centre for Policy Studies in Britain, prepare 'mandates for leadership' to help guide conservative administrations down the road to victory. Grassroot activist networks organized around a wide range of religious and social issues (abortion, education, gay rights, and so on) mobilize new groups of conservative voters and furnish ready-made SWAT teams to intervene in local controversies. Finally, right-wing radio and television personalities such as Rush Limbaugh in the United States and a group of media commentators writing for a whole variety of British right-wing newspapers cultivate the ground in civil society more generally to help make the unthinkable thinkable again.

Employing such a broad definition of the New Right carries the risk of overlooking the sometimes considerable differences that distinguish various New Right organizations from one another, especially with concern to the question of political style. For example, the academic tenor of the neo-conservative intellectuals writing for *Commentary* or *The Public Interest* in the United States is distinct from the populist and even rabble-rousing tone of Christian Coalition teach-ins. By the same token, in Britain, the Salisbury Group's intellectual focus on neo-conservative themes of authority and order differs significantly from The Freedom Association's concern for neo-liberal notions such as freedom and minimal state interference. Yet, importantly, such an inclusive definition allows one to focus less on organizational differences and more on the shared constellation of political beliefs that together define the New Right worldview.

The New Right worldview may be divided into two distinct yet overlapping ideological components: economic liberalism and social conservatism. Broadly speaking, the economic liberal strand concerns itself with the free market economy and individual freedom, while the social conservative strand focuses upon the need for authority, tradition, family, and a secure sense of national identity and pride.[8] Social conservatives share with economic liberals a general commitment to the free market, yet differ in their insistence that economic freedom alone will not be sufficient to reverse economic or social decline. Unless freedom operates within a social context of order, social conservatives argue, decline will not be reversed but advanced.

While it is important not to underestimate the degree of internal disagreement within New Right ideology, both strands do overlap considerably in practice. Many economic liberals recognize the need for a strong state to enable the market to be free, while many social traditionalists find the market a useful tool as regards conservative doctrines of order, discipline and hierarchy. Thus the difference between the two strands is more a difference of emphasis than kind. Though they are ideologically inconsistent, in terms of politics this inconsistency has been no handicap. In fact, the resonance of New Right ideology can convincingly be attributed to just such a fusion of ideas.

The potency of this particular fusion of themes reflects the social and material situation out of which the New Right emerged. The world economic recession of the mid-1970s made New Right free market policy initiatives appear more valid, while the social and political upheaval born from recession made the emphasis on discipline, tradition and authority seem more relevant. In this way, the paradoxical yet working combination of the 'free economy and the strong state' became the new basis for a conservative drive for hegemony.[9] Thus conceived, it becomes possible to understand the imposition of a more authoritarian style of politics from above as an elite attempt to re-establish conditions for profitable capital accumulation in a climate of economic decline, and the mobilization of popular consent from below as relevant social groups react to the worsening socio-economic climate, as happening together as part of the same transaction.[10]

The New Right's project has been to challenge many of the policies and key socio-political assumptions associated with the post-war consensus: Keynesian-orientated policies in the economic sphere, welfare programs in the social, and the whole range of collectivist, egalitarian values associated with this consensus in the cultural arena. In doing so, the New Right has rearticulated assumptions regarding, for example, the role of government (that it should be limited rather than interventionist), egalitarianism (that government should guarantee individual equality of opportunity, not enforce collective equality of outcome), and liberty (that we should be concerned with the negative freedoms from, not the positive freedoms to). In this way, the New Right has played a key role in challenging the so-called liberal consensus, even if it has failed to forge an alternative conservative consensus to take its place.

New Right ideology has aimed to organize the hearts and minds of popular forces in a more right-wing direction, and so arguably has helped to enable conservative socio-economic policies to go through relatively unhindered.

As a group of conservative ideologues, the New Right, intentionally or not, has aided dominant social groups in their search for a new set of ideological formulations with which to justify the right turn in policy formation. In their bid to explain contemporary realities in a popular idiom, the New Right has helped bring to the fore of the political landscape contested symbols related to race, gender, sexuality and nation. Right-wing interpretations of the meaning of such symbols often serve, especially during periods of instability or crisis, to deflect attention away from structural and historical factors (such as monetary policy, white racism, or institutional causes of inequality), and toward personal and moral ones (such as the disruptive influence of the black immigrants' 'way of life' or the 'pathological black family structure').[11] In this way, by imposing certain key categories of thought and meaning, the New Right has attempted to perform the crucial function of forging cross-class alliances in support of rather than in opposition to regressive policies and prevailing ideologies.

SYMBOLIC CONFLICT AND THE NEW RIGHT

> 'When I use a word,' Humpty Dumpty said in a rather scornful tone, 'it means just what I choose it to mean. Neither more nor less!' 'The question is' said Alice, 'Whether you can make words mean so many different things.' 'The question is,' said Humpty Dumpty, 'Who is to be master. That is all.'[12]

The model of politics that emerges from the above discussion is what I label the 'symbolic conflict model'. The symbolic conflict model is, in essence, a contribution to a sociology of the construction of worldviews. It seeks to understand how, in the battle between competing groups in society for one or another material or political interest, a struggle ensues over the power to dominate the ideological representations with which agents confront and apprehend their social worlds. The outcome of symbolic conflict secures, in effect, the power to impose the legitimate view of the world and the agents' position in it. The symbolic conflict model is therefore, in its largest sense, an examination of the struggle by different social groups to impose one interpretation of social reality over another.

This struggle over the construction of worldviews is inevitably a struggle over language, even the meaning of specific words, for as the so-called linguistic turn in the social sciences suggests, language does not merely reflect social reality but helps constitute it. Symbolic conflict is above all a political process that involves the discursive construction and deconstruction of cause and effect, blame and responsibility, support and opposition, even identity and memory. It is a process of struggle over competing public transcripts, contesting identities and meanings in the process, and foreclosing alternative cultures of ideas. It is in this sense that words and values such as equality, freedom, opportunity, justice – even racism – do not have one simple meaning attached to them and no inherent link to a particular political project; left, right or other. Rather, each political culture includes within it a range of such contested 'truths' that have ample scope to allow for a multiplicity of readings. Words such as equality and opportunity are examples of such contested 'truths', with the New Right interpreting them in a radically individualistic manner as opposed to the alternative radical democratic script. Or to take another example, the notion of group rights expressed by progressive activists for racial justice in the United States is currently opposed by the New Right as a challenge to the priority of the individual and the system of meritocracy in its apology for existing inequalities, while in countries such as Britain and South Africa, the New Right embraces the notion in its defense of the right to cultural exclusivity and white privilege in the face of challenge. This latter example emphasizes the point that the contest over meanings and public transcripts is not about right-wing words versus left-wing words, but primarily about the relation between word and context, or about the specific meanings attached to the words in the pursuit of particular political projects.

The term 'symbolic conflict' is employed to signify the ideological struggle between competing social groups to dominate the contested symbolic field, and the symbolic power that goes along with that domination. Symbolic conflict is not an abstract process at the level of ideas only, however, but one that is intimately linked with material and political struggles.[13] Symbolic conflict is forged in the midst of efforts by competing groups to secure particular policy outcomes that serve specific material and political interests. To do this, each group aims to present its worldview, with its particular interests inside, as the universal one, as representing the interests of the whole nation. Such an aim forms the basis of the New Right's struggle to forge a new conservative common sense.

The symbolic conflict model builds upon the work of otherwise quite diverse theorists – Stuart Hall, Murray Edelman, Pierre Bourdieu – who have drawn attention to the symbolic dimensions of politics.[14] The 'symbolic dimensions of politics' refers to those dimensions of political discourse and conflict that aim not towards purely instrumental goals, such as an increase or decrease in wages, but rather towards the power to impose the key categories of meaning, or implicit schemes of thought, with which agents confront and interpret their social world. That is, symbolic conflict does not directly involve the struggle over material or political resources, but rather the struggle over the set of meanings which helps to determine the mental criteria by which the distribution of such resources are perceived and judged.

Attention to the symbolic dimensions of politics allows for an analysis of the production and use of symbols with which dominant groups are able to explain what the trouble is, why it is so, and what to do about it. It allows for the analysis of the role of symbols to rationalize power and privilege via the articulation (and rearticulation) of the categories of meaning by which the politics of perception, interpretation and action are secured. Symbolic forms thereby exercise their own type of power and violence by producing a consensus on meanings that impedes the formation of alternative ideologies and practices. In this way, symbolic systems sometimes operate as instruments of domination.

The symbolic conflict model provides a useful approach to the study of the New Right. The symbolic conflict approach demands that an analysis of the role of New Right ideology in the right turn of US and British politics begin from an appreciation of the material context out of which it emerged and in which it is taking hold. Yet it challenges materialist analyses to go further and attempt to bring the agency of the right turn back in. Such an attempt is based upon the belief that while it is important to argue against ideological and pluralist interpretations of the New Right that give primacy to the role of ideas and social actors, and instead examine the objective social and material conditions that produced the right turn as a whole, it is essential nevertheless that structural analyses themselves be made more dynamic. This is achieved by reincorporating the symbolic dimensions of politics, and specifically the symbolic struggles of the New Right. Only then does the New Right assume importance as a movement in civil society that has worked to organize the hearts and minds of the 'silent majority' in a conservative direction – in the now notorious words of New Rightist Paul Weyrich, to 'organize discontent'.[15]

The symbolic conflict approach is concerned with the complex assemblage of symbolic themes that exist within the New Right worldview. It is orientated to the study of the ideological functioning of New Right symbols – to organize perception, interpret events, and justify certain courses of action over others. More specifically, it is orientated to the study of the New Right's endeavour to appropriate evocative symbols – such as those related to race, gender, morality and nation – to serve as ideological articulators of recent structural transformations. The primary booty of this struggle is the symbolic power to draft the legitimate ideological map of the social world; one which arguably conceals, and sometimes even contradicts, the instrumental effects of political action.

The political struggle over ideology and representation with which the symbolic conflict model is concerned is most commonly referred to in the sociological literature as having to do with *hegemony*, a term associated with Gramscian social theory that refers to the attempt to exercise power via the organization of consent rather than rule by coercion.[16] Although hegemony can have both material and ideological bases, it is usually associated with the employment of ideas and symbols to organize consent to a particular version of the social order. The goal is to render one particular version of social reality as the only credible one, as taken-for-granted, as natural or 'just

the way things are', and at the same time to delegitimize alternative political horizons.

To argue that the New Right is engaged in a hegemonic political project is not to imply the need to prove that subordinate social groups have become duped into subscribing to a
set of particular right-wing ideas and beliefs. Rather than conceive of hegemony as a *state* of positive consent, the symbolic
conflict model understands hegemony as a continual *process* of
struggle to link popular experiences and sentiments with
right-wing interpretations and solutions. This weaker view of
hegemony, importantly, allows ample room for contradictions
at the level of social consciousness, and in fact places these
contradictions at the center of analysis of the way in which
actors such as the New Right play on them, dislodge them
from alternative articulations, and represent them in a
manner consistent with the policies and class strategies of the
Right.[17]

The New Right hegemonic project aims to construct a new
social bloc by discrediting the old one, in the popular political
imagination as well as institutionally, so that its political
horizon becomes the only legitimate, thinkable and even
natural one. Race has been important to the normalization
strategies of the New Right, and has been employed symbolically to stigmatize alternatives and to construct political
enemies with labels such 'reverse racism' and the 'loony left',
thus furthering the disintegration of the post-war liberal consensus and its positive vision of the role of government in pursuing racial equality policies. Race has also been used, in a
more subtle way, to help forge a new political imagination and
right-wing consensus that links recipes for national revival to
racialized and often exclusionary images of the national community and its purported stock of cultural values.

It is this shift in the terrain of struggle that has created the
very subject positions which the New Right claims to represent. The New Right presents its political project as essentially
populist, with constant references to 'the people', the 'silent
majority' of conservative citizens, and 'ordinary people'.
Rather than accept these claims of representation at face
value, the symbolic conflict approach explores the extent to
which the New Right has itself created the subjectivities to
which its discourse refers. Far from claiming that the New

Right has tapped into a pre-discursive and latent popular racism or authoritarianism, the symbolic conflict model seeks to understand the process whereby such right-wing identity positions are constructed in and constituted by political discourses. With respect to epistemology, Pierre Bourdieu argues that people only know what they think when they recognize somebody else saying it.[18] A similar point can be made with respect to ontology: people only discover who they are when they recognize themselves in somebody else's discursive image. Thus, following the insights of Foucault, the study of the production of ideology is also, inevitably, a study of the creation of new subject positions.[19]

The New Right has been successful in its hegemonic project to the extent that it has succeeded in normalizing its political worldview in relation to others defined less legitimate, and to the degree that it has successfully linked this worldview to a broader social imaginary and identity position. This measure of success has not been prevalent in studies of the New Right which count legislative victories, but it is arguably the most significant victory in the sense that it is not easily reversed. Political acts are highly effective when they offer a framework of interpretation that can be applied to all policy areas, a framework that, if coherent, is not easily dislodged by empirical evidence that contradicts it. Categories of assumptions and modes of representation are highly resilient and powerful political weapons, especially in periods such as the present when people are looking for assurance and easy answers.

It is in this context that the New Right has achieved significant category reversals, or what Murray Edelman has termed 'category mistakes', by attributing responsibility for current difficulties to the problems and weaknesses of the old consensus politics itself, thereby supporting their push for radical rethinking.[20] With respect to race-related matters, the New Right has exploited the weaknesses of liberal anti-racism and turned it around so that anti-racism itself comes to be defined as the problem in need of addressing, thus positioning the New Right as the defenders of freedom and tolerance. This achievement owes less to a set of pre-constituted racist sentiments among the people to whom the New Right is trying to appeal than to the success of their struggle over ideology and representation to construct new social bases for its political project.

COMPETING CONCEPTUAL APPROACHES: A DIALOGUE

The distinctiveness of the symbolic conflict approach is especially evident when opposed to the alternative conceptual approaches to the sociological study of the New Right. The three
main competing approaches are what I label the 'status politics approach', the 'formalistic approach', and the 'elite politics approach'.

The status politics approach highlights the role of popular
discontent in the formulation and transmission of right-wing
ideology to the exclusion of its social effect. It was pioneered
in the United States in the 1950s by Richard Hofstadter,
Nathan Glazer, Daniel Bell, Seymour Martin Lipset and Peter
Viereck in their studies of the John Birch Society, and
McCarthyism.[21] Applied to the present US context, the status
politics approach attributes popular support for the New
Right to a sense of status vacuum in political life that fuels an
irrational, or paranoid, defence of traditional life-styles and
values. New Right politics is therefore conceived not as a
vehicle of conflict over a set of objectified interests, but as a
rear-guard action by certain status-threatened groups to halt
societies' acceptance of views and values more liberal than
their own.

For example, Alan Crawford, a former editor of the New
Right's *Conservative Digest* (now defunct) and of the Young
American for Freedom's *New Guard,* wrote one of the first critical studies of the contemporary New Right, entitled *Thunder
on the Right.* Crawford writes from the perspective of the Old
Right and distinguishes this position from what he labels the
'populist radicalism' of the New Right. Crawford conceives of
the New Right as obsessed with symbolic acts of social protest;
protest which he defines as often 'non-political'. 'Social
protest and not governing is the real interest of the New
Rightists.'[22] In this respect, Crawford's analysis shares much
affinity with the status politics approach. He writes, 'Status resentments frequently result in the appearance of right-wing
backlash groups which attempt to reestablish through formal
political processes, the social support that the group's values
once commanded.'[23] Such an analysis assumes that the New
Right is an exceptional form of politics based on irrational
status anxieties and largely peripheral to the larger political

culture and system. It thus allows traditional conservatives to distinguish themselves from the New Right without departing from prevalent conservative assumptions.

It is interesting to note that Crawford's analysis, written in the early 1980s, makes hardly any mention of race. It was more common then to draw attention to popular anxiety surrounding religious and family issues and to assume that race was no longer a compelling status issue. However, by the late 1980s, it became apparent that such an assumption was mistaken. In *Chain Reaction*, Thomas and Mary Edsall address Crawford's oversight by examining the role of what has become known as the 'angry white male' factor in US politics, and so highlight the racial dimensions of the kind of status politics practiced by the New Right.[24] While this correction is an important one, to understand the racial politics of the right wing as a form of status politics carries with it the danger of reifying the racist views of the public, as do the Edsalls, without examining how these views are constructed and even how the very subject position of the 'angry white male' is constituted in and through New Right discourse. Only then is it possible to avoid viewing the white backlash as an understandable or even natural response to the alleged injustices wrought by existing racial equality policies and focus instead on the sort of racism that renders these policies problematic to the status position of whites.

Another interpretation of the New Right, one that is commonly found in media treatments of the subject, focuses upon the personalities and electoral strategies of its leadership, an approach here labelled as the 'formalistic approach'. This approach attributes New Right visibility to effective leadership skills, organizational tactics, and the innovative use of political and media technologies. For example, US New Rightists and commentators alike have attributed the newness and relative success of the New Right to the organizational networks it has created between conservative political and religious leaders. The growth of New Right visibility is also often attributed to the impact of televangelism and computerized direct-mail solicitation techniques.

Gillian Peele's book entitled *Revival and Reaction: The Right in Contemporary America* is an example of the formalistic approach. Peele, a British political scientist at Oxford University, identifies five features which, in her view, distinguish the US

New Right from mainstream conservatism. These are its aggressive mood of determination, its attention to organizational detail, its hostility to the existing party structure, its special agenda of issues, and its populism.[25] Of key importance for Peele is the New Right's development of new techniques for campaigning, such as direct-mail solicitation and the creation of political action committees (PACs), as well as its use of family and moral issues to mobilize new groups of voters (for example, religious fundamentalists), and to realign older constituencies (for example, 'Reagan Democrats'). According to Peele, it is this set of features that accounts for the New Right's ascendancy in the mid-1970s.

Again it is interesting to note how little attention is paid to the issue of race. Those formalistic studies that do mention race to any significant degree tend to treat it as a single issue among many, or as a tool used to realign blocs of voters. Critical analysis of the role of race most often centers on exposing organizational connections between the New Right and more extremist, racist groups. This approach is premised upon an infiltration view of right-wing politics; that is, that the racism which exists within 'normal' or mainstream politics is conceived as being external, intruding only during periods of collapse or popular decline of nationalistic-racist parties. At these times, so the argument goes, racist Far Right elements decide that the best route to power and influence is to infiltrate other more mainstream political groupings.

The formalistic approach traces the past and continuing involvement of individual New Rightists in racist organizations. For example, writing about the United States, Russ Bellant has traced connections between New Rightist Paul Weyrich and racist Roger Pearson, and between New Rightist Robert Whitaker and neo-Nazi activist Robert Hoy.[26] In the same study Bellant discloses the racist practices and beliefs of one of the primary New Right financial donors – the Coors family. Other studies have exposed organizational connections between New Right organizations and, for example, the Reverend Moon and LaRouche networks, as another means of challenging the New Right's attempt to shun its image of extremism.[27] More recently, media attention has focused on the purported infiltration of neo-fascist and anti-semitic personalities in the 1996 Buchanan Presidential campaign.[28]

In Britain, studies have traced the involvement of certain New Right figures in racist organizations such as WISE (Wales, Ireland, Scotland, England), the National Front, Tory Action, and the British National Party. For example, the BBC Panorama program entitled 'Maggie's Militant Tendency' exposed links between several British New Rightists, most notably Harvey Proctor, and the racist organization Tory Action.[29] The media has also exposed links between the racist British National Party and two British New Right groups – the Federation of Conservative Students and the Monday Club.[30] It has been noted that Enoch Powell, the key figure in the renewed salience of racialist ideology in the late 1960s, is a frequent contributor to the British neo-conservative journal the *Salisbury Review*.[31]

Yet analysis of New Right symbolic conflict over the meaning of race would be overly restricted if it were limited to the tracing of individual and/or organizational connections between racist organizations and the more mainstream New Right. While such work is important and in many respects revealing, it wields little explanatory power. The fact that the New Right has had and still has connections with Far Right parties suggests that racism is more than likely an active ingredient in its politics, yet such revelations do not explain why this is so.

Other analysts are critical of formalistic studies and, while implicitly accepting the formalistic approaches' focus on organizations and the individuals associated with them, shift attention to a more critical analysis of New Right ideology. The result is a set of criticisms that inadequately treat New Right ideology as an expression of some other formal requirement to be elucidated (the personal and/or financial objectives of New Right leaders, or the logic of building lucrative organizational networks and increasing net assets), and so underestimates both the significance of the meanings produced and circulated in New Right discourse and the degree to which they correspond to supporters' real needs and experiences.

In relation to the study of the issue of race, this critical formalistic approach shifts attention away from organizational and inter-personal connections between the New Right and the more extreme, racist Right to an exploration of their discursive continuities. For example, in several different studies, Gill Seidel argues that the crucial significance of race as a defining issue for the British New Right has been underestimated, and that the lack of direct emphasis on racial issues is deceptive.[32] She sets herself the task of decoding the obvious euphemisms for race in New Right discourse. One such euphemism, Seidel notes, is the New Right's use of the rhetoric of cultural difference as a substitute for the more traditional racist belief in biological hierarchies of racial superiority/inferiority. She further directs attention to the importance of discursive constructions of 'us' and 'them', of 'Britishness' and the British 'way of life'.

Seidel's work is most notable for recognizing the potential such themes carry for provoking a popular mobilization behind racist ideas, even if New Right rhetoric does not itself demand, at this point, such a mobilization. This potential exists, Seidel insists, irrespective of the presence or absence of racist intent. Yet such an approach remains locked into describing how the New Right has rearticulated race via a series of discursive strategies, or what she labels 'semantic mythical reversals'. While it is important to understand how the New Right argument is constructed, and how the various identifications are made, such deconstruction devoid of an analysis of the historical and material conditions in which the discourse is produced and transmitted remains an abstract academic exercise.

Thus we can build upon Seidel's analysis of New Right racial discourse by relating it to the historical context in which it has developed. More importantly, we can shift the focus from how the discourse works to why it appeals by extracting and making explicit the key categories of meaning that constitute what Seidel terms the 'new cultural racism'. These categories are related to the New Right's general worldview of social conservatism, not to its verbal or semantic strategies operating to mask a supposed and underlying set of racist attitudes. By embedding New Right racial discourse in its historical context, and by extracting the general and pervasive ideological assumptions that underlie its discursive strategies, it becomes possible to build upon the conclusions of formal discourse analyses that merely describe New Right discourse on race without explaining why it appeals or who ultimately benefits from its transmission.

Whereas formalistic approaches reduce New Right ideology to the logic of the New Right organizational nexus, the elite politics approach reduces New Right ideology to an elite strategy; that is, one manufactured by the ruling class as a smokescreen for 'real' (class) politics. The New Right is understood here as a social movement created by the ruling class in order to maintain capitalist relations of production. In this view, the New Right mobilization is a symptom of capitalism in crisis, and more specifically, the weakness and desperation of a ruling class intent on maintaining its power.

Such an approach is perhaps most obvious in those studies that focus on New Right neo-liberal economic policies. Yet it is also evident within studies that focus on one or another of the New Right's so-called social issues. For example, certain studies have highlighted the alleged collusion between the New Right and capital in the mobilization of a backlash against the women's movement. The New Right's advocation of traditional gender roles and its insistence on the need for women to return to the home allows, according to this view, the ruling class to legitimate its withdrawal from crucial economic functions by returning responsibility to its 'natural' holder – the wife and mother – as opposed to the state. The values of the 'free market' and the 'nuclear family' are re-asserted simultaneously as part of the ruling class aim to reduce the costs of public sector activity. In this vein, Frankie Ashton concludes, '[F]or capital, especially in recession, women's low social status provides the perfect foil for the supra-exploitation of labor. The demand for cheap, less-organized sources of labor that might be hired and fired at will, such as the female population, has risen.'[33]

The elite politics approach is also evident in certain studies more directly pertaining to the issue of race. Racism is here related to shifts in the needs of the capitalist system of production itself. For example, A. Sivanandan, the Director of the Institute of Race Relations in London, explains the shifts in Britain's immigration policy under the Thatcher administration, and the renewed salience of racism more generally, as a reflection of the changed needs of capitalism – from a system that needed black labor during the period of economic growth in the 1950s and 1960s to a system desiring to expel their labor during the economic recession of the 1970s. Sivanandan concludes: 'The racist and anti-working class sentiments of Thatcher and Joseph reflect the anxieties and fears of a decaying bourgeoisie ... The strategy is to defeat the class, the tactic is to divide it – and they both stem from the ideology of outmoded capital.'[34]

Although the elite politics approach corrects for the afore-mentioned limitations of the formalistic approach by drawing out the social functions of New Right racial dis-course, it does so in a way that inadequately treats race as a smokescreen or inaccurate representation of 'real' (that is, class) politics. This view is problematic because it sidesteps the question of the link between meaning and power at the center of the symbolic conflict model and reduces the former to a straightforward reflection of the latter. Not only does such a view reduce race to false consciousness, but at a broader level it neglects one of the central insights of post-modernism, even the Althusserian insight, that there is no objective reality outside of language and ideology. If we extend this insight to the elite politics approach, it follows that we need an approach that understands racial ideology as not simply justifying economic disadvantage, but helping to constitute it.

The symbolic conflict critique, in summary, is threefold. It argues against:

1. the status politics view of the New Right as a rear-guard and irrational mobilization of the status frustrated – a con-ceptualization that understands New Right racial ideology as expressive of the psychological dispositions of the indi-viduals who take it up;
2. the formalistic approach to the New Right as an organiza-tional nexus that has successfully mobilized the resources at hand – a conceptualization that understands New Right racial ideology as created by the electoral interests and innovations of New Right leaders; and
3. the elite politics approach to the New Right as a tool of the ruling class – a conceptualization that understands New Right racial ideology as manufactured by dominant elites as a smokescreen for 'real' (that is, class) politics.

All three approaches are limited in the sense that they neglect the dialectic within New Right ideology of the expressive and the instrumental aspects of ideology.[35]

The symbolic conflict approach attempts to transcend the limitations of these competing conceptual approaches while building on their insights. It examines what I defined earlier as the New Right's most important role – as a catalyst in linking popular backlash sentiments to the electoral strategies and policy goals of the right-wing of the Republican and Conservative Parties. It follows from such a conceptualization that, to be adequate, an analysis of the New Right must incorporate three levels of analysis at once: popular dispositions, the New Right organizational nexus, and elite strategies.

The three conceptual approaches identified above each reduce the study of New Right ideology to only one of the analytic levels just mentioned, and so remain inadequate. The symbolic conflict approach, on the other hand, attempts to incorporate all three levels of analysis at once. The task facing the symbolic conflict approach is to posit a non-reductionist relationship between the three. Such a task requires rethinking the relationship between pluralist demands and official representations, the role of political leadership, and the nature of ideological effect.

First is the question of the role played by official representation. What is the relationship between popular dispositions (white racial anxieties, resentment, discontents, expectations) and New Right ideology? The mainstream assumption (that is, pluralism) is that popular dispositions are reflected in official representations, which in turn affect government policy formation. The status politics approach, for example, is largely based upon such an assumption. The symbolic conflict approach reverses – almost – this sequence by examining the processes by which government policy formation and official representations, situated within determinate material circumstances, themselves affect and shape popular dispositions.

By circulating an ideology that selects and favors certain aspects of reality over others, New Right ideology not only reflects but creates a public culture. To portray the New Right as populist is therefore to obscure the fact that populist rhetoric is as much a legitimating tool for elites as it is a factual description of a reality of popular support. In short, 'public discourse' and 'the public's discourse' coexist in a symbiotic yet asymmetrical relationship.[36] Public discourse reflects and responds to the public's discourse only after having first shaped it, a thesis that demands that the concept of representation itself (one that is at the heart of the pluralist approach) be put under scrutiny.[37]

Second is the question of the role played by political leadership. Proponents of the formalistic approach argue that the role of New Right leadership is crucial, and thus identify as a crucial task the discovery of their unstated and often illicit interests. They make the common mistake of slipping from an analysis of how New Right ideology is channelled and distorted by various action-orientated, personal and institutional interests to a view asserting that these interests are the origin, or creating element, of the ideology. The symbolic conflict approach focuses less on the innovations of the New Right leadership as the cause of its increased support than on its catalytic role of channelling and transforming prevailing ideologies, already free-floating and widespread in the political cultures under study, to meet new social realities, and to interpellate the popular dispositions to which these new realities give rise.

Right-wing leaders and opportunist politicians have been around for decades, espousing a worldview not so different from the one transmitted in New Right ideology. The phenomenon to be explained is not how such leaders or organizations have emerged in the political spotlight, but rather why such ideas, long in circulation, have gained prominence. Thus, the actions and innovations of the New Right organizational nexus, while worthy of analysis, are less important than the formalistic approach makes out. Focusing on the personalities and electoral activities of the New Right leadership deflects attention from the material circumstances, historical trends, and modes of signification that have created the followers that the New Right claims to lead. In this way, by recognizing that the unconventional belief that leaders create those in whose name they speak is as true as the reverse, the concept of political leadership (at the heart of the formalistic approach) becomes itself a reductionist symbol that needs to be viewed in a rather different light.[38]

Finally, the question of ideological effect offers the opportunity to rethink certain key tenets of the Marxist theory of ideology. The symbolic conflict approach rejects the simple mechanistic equation between ruling ideas and the ideas of the ruling class. Rather than positing the existence of a functioning and coherent dominant ideology already in place, the symbolic conflict model suggests a contested ideological field within which ideas have to struggle for ascendancy. Those ideas which do become dominant, moreover, are wrought with internal fissures and contradictions, and have to be constantly rearticulated and reorganized (so as to defend against challenge from below as well as from opposition within the state/power bloc) in a never-ending struggle to connect dominant ideological formulations with new popular and systemic realities.[39]

A focus on symbolic conflict ensures that due attention is paid to what is arguably most distinctive about New Right ideology – its attempt to address 'the people' and position them with, not against, the dominant social bloc. New Right ideology does not produce a set of illusions that swindle subordinate groups into believing what is not 'true', but rather map or classify the social world (that is, construct a worldview) so as to make the reasoning and calculation of particular social groups appear as universal. Dominant ideologies do not directly prescribe the informational content of *what* to think, but affirm and reinforce a range of meanings that influence *how* agents think about the social world: which categories of meaning are legitimate and which illegitimate, which ideas are thinkable and which unthinkable, which styles of expression are culturally acceptable and which taboo.

In summary, the symbolic conflict approach calls for an examination of the critical role New Right ideology has played in the reorganization of key elements of right-wing discourse. Rather than conceive of New Right ideology as a simple expression of the dispositional needs of its supporters, the personal ambitions and/or electoral tactics of its leadership, or the interests of the ruling class, the symbolic conflict approach examines the New Right's role as catalyst in linking popular backlash sentiments with right-wing solutions to contemporary issues and events. In this view, the New Right is most significant as a catalyst in mobilizing popular support behind, rather than in opposition to, the more authoritarian style of politics instituted by the Reagan and Thatcher administrations and beyond.

2 The New Right Racial Backlash: A New Racism

Although the idea of the biological inequality of different races has fallen largely into disrepute, race-based symbolism nevertheless remains an important explanatory framework for many of the changes and challenges people face around them, as well as a legitimating ideology for elites. Race serves as a lens through which a whole array of other crises in existing social relations are perceived and explained. Whereas the specific contents of the stereotypes and prejudices produced and circulated change over time and between different societies, the presence of a system of racial meanings, or ideologies, is a constant feature of liberal capitalist societies, indeed of modernity itself. In this chapter I focus on the context of reaction out of which the New Right racial backlash emerged, trace the changes in the system of racial meanings represented in New Right discourse, and explore the question of whether these changes in fact constitute a new form of racism.

THE CONTEXT OF REACTION

> In any assessment of what is happening in the so-called New Right ... it is important to remember that what is being observed is a 'reaction' to the 'action' begun by the liberals as they sought to dismantle our moral heritage.
>
> (Jerry Falwell)[1]

Analysis of New Right racial ideology must begin with the social and material environment out of which it emerged. Understanding the transformation of racial ideology as a function of changes in the socio-economic and political context implies that New Right racial ideology is more than a mere discursive cover for an old racism now in disrepute. Outlining

49

the context for reaction serves to remind us that social circumstances more often shape than are shaped by the symbolic uses of racism. New Right racial ideology was initially produced as a reaction to the civil rights movements in the United States and the burgeoning culture of black resistance in Britain, and the reformist actions of the liberal-capitalist state to contain them. Its transmission and reception was facilitated by subsequent developments; most importantly, the onset of world economic recession, the mobilization of business interests, and the unraveling of post-war electoral coalitions. The newness of New Right racial ideology arguably has more to do with these contextual factors than with the content (that is, discursive strategies or codewords) of what is communicated.

In the United States, the civil rights movement forced the expansion of the parameters of mainstream political debate to include the question of racial equality as never before. Resistance and struggle on the part of people of color and their allies supplied the necessary grassroots pressure to force new court orders and legislative acts. Their demands led to the passage of landmark legislation including the 1964 Civil Rights Act and the 1965 Voting Rights Act, thereby committing the Federal government to more involvement in protecting and expanding the rights of people of color. In 1965 President Johnson signed executive Order No. 11246 that mandated the sweeping adoption and application of affirmative action programs in nearly every sector of public and private activity.

The interpretation and enforcement of civil rights legislation became more radical in spirit as the civil rights movement itself radicalized during the mid-to-late 1960s. While the early phase of civil rights legislation restricted affirmative action to cases of known and intentional individual discrimination, Title VII guidelines of the 1964 Civil Rights Act were later interpreted in a way that sanctioned the use of quotas and time-tables as legitimate means for the pursuit of racial parity. President Johnson's speech at Howard University in 1965 first signalled the shift from the color-blind vision of an equal opportunity society to the color-conscious vision of justice based on equality of outcome:

Freedom is not enough. You do not wipe away the scars of centuries by saying: Now you are free to go where you want, do as you desire, and choose the leaders you please. You do not take a person who, for years, has been hobbled by chains and liberate him, bring him up to the starting line of a race and then say, 'you are free to compete with all the others', and still justly believe that you have been completely fair. Thus it is not enough just to open the gates of opportunity. All our citizens must have the ability to walk through those gates. This is the next and more profound stage of the battle for civil rights. We seek not just freedom but opportunity – not just legal equity but human ability – not just equality as a right and a theory but equality as a fact and as a result.[2]

A similar shift from a focus on intent to outcome occurred in the judicial realm as the Supreme Court interpreted the phrase from the *Brown* decision that schools be desegregated 'with all deliberate speed' as meaning that discrimination should be judged on the basis of unequal results (that is, dual school systems) rather than on discriminatory intent (Green *v.* County School Board of New Kent County, 1968); that busing was both a useful and legitimate means to achieve equal outcome (Swann *v.* Charlotte-Mecklenburg, 1971); and that court-ordered desegregation was also legitimate in the North where segregation was mostly *de facto* rather than *de jure* (Keyes *v.* School District No. 1, Denver, Colorado, 1973). The program of reform associated with the civil rights movement was thereby radicalized as the principle upon which it was based changed from that of equality of persons (that is, individual rights) to the more radical principle of collective equality (that is, group rights). It is precisely this shift in thinking – from color-blindness to color-consciousness, from a focus on intent to outcome, and from individual to group rights – that lay at the heart of the New Right racial backlash in the United States.

In Britain, there also emerged a burgeoning culture of black (Afro-Caribbean and Asian) resistance that similarly led to landmark legislation in the arena of civil rights.[3] The first generation of struggle in the 1950s and early 1960s was largely spontaneous and reactive in nature, aiming at those discriminatory practices (in housing, education, and the workplace) that denied both the Afro-Caribbean and Asian communities

basic needs and services. The activities of new black organizations created to manage the new-born sense of unity and
spirit of resistance included:

1. demanding the repeal of discriminatory legislation, es-
    pecially regarding immigration control;
2. struggling against the new forces of fascism (the British
    Union Movement, the League of Empire Loyalists, and
    the White Defence League); and
3. tackling class and community-related issues such as police
    brutality, housing and employment discrimination, and
    the discriminatory labelling of black children as low
    achievers in the nation's schools.

These struggles helped to create a common and burgeoning
black culture of active resistance to racism, and led to the
passage of a series of legislative acts, including the 1965 and
1968 Race Relations Acts, the creation of statutory bodies such
as the Race Relations Board and the National Committee for
Commonwealth Immigrants, and Section 11 of the 1966 Local
Government Act. In 1966 the official justification for such
state action was summed up by then Home Secretary Roy
Jenkins in a speech in which he called for integration of the
black community into the 'English way of life'; integration
seen 'not as a flattening process of assimilation but as equal
opportunity accompanied by cultural diversity, in an atmos-
phere of mutual tolerance'.[4]

The foci of black struggle shifted with the coming of age of
the second generation of New Commonwealth migrants. It
shifted from a more or less defensive stance regarding discriminatory practices and attitudes to a more pre-emptive attempt
to establish a social and educational infrastructure for the
black community. Projects were set up to teach skills to black
youth, to set up supplementary schools, community clubs,
youth centers, and an alternative black media. The 1970s were
dotted with battles waged by black youth against police harassment and brutality, indicating that racial struggles now centered more around the politics of black youth.[5] The foci of
state strategies shifted accordingly, away from the goal of integration and more toward addressing the sources of the urban
disturbances of the mid-1970s and early 1980s. Urban aid was

granted to areas designated as having 'special social problems'. Black community groups were funded. The 1976 Race
Relations Act set down anti-discriminatory and equal opportunity guidelines, and professed a commitment to promote individual cultures and black self-help groups. The Act also
created the Commission for Racial Equality to monitor British
race relations more effectively.

In between the resistance of black communities and the
activities of the state were the anti-racist activities of certain local
authorities.[6] Throughout the 1970s and early 1980s, radical
local authorities in Britain attempted to develop initiatives to
promote greater equality of opportunity for communities of
color. This was done largely in response to the urban unrest
mentioned above and increased mobilization of people of color
in the local system, and in the absence of new central government initiatives. Significant gains were made in the areas of
housing, employment, and education. For example, in the
sphere of education, local authorities in Dewsbury, Bradford
and Brent, among others, developed and implemented anti-
racist education programs in their schools. Yet these gains
proved vulnerable to sustained attacks from central government
and, more particularly, from the New Right.

Many of the reforms won by popular struggles for equality
and justice were secured during the period of economic expansion following the Second World War. The general strength
of the economy meant that people of color could advance
without necessarily challenging the economic well-being or
social status of whites. It also allowed governing elites to accommodate many of the more moderate demands of popular
movements since the state could afford to finance the institutionalization of a limited program of reform.

The New Right reaction, by contrast, was forged in a historical context marked by demobilization of popular struggle,
economic decline, conservative business mobilization, and the
breakdown of post-war political coalitions. Since New Right
racial ideology first emerged in response to popular resistance
and struggle in the 1960s and 1970s (that is, prior to the onset
of economic recession and its associated political dimensions),
these latter contextual factors cannot be held as causative
in the emergence (production) of New Right ideology. Yet
these factors did help facilitate its growth (transmission) and

popular appeal (reception). The context of reaction provided
a political space within which the New Right was better able to
manoeuvre in its struggle to retard the trajectory of racial
progress.

The New Right reaction was forged during the period of
economic contraction and conservative business mobilization
beginning in the mid-1970s. In the wake of the collapse of
fixed exchange rates and currency stability in 1971–2, and the
steep rise in oil prices at the end of 1973, both countries experienced recession and mounting economic difficulties. The
late 1970s witnessed rising unemployment, high inflation, declining productivity, decreased international competitiveness,
and under-investment.[7] In terms of the real value of people's
income, the ability to own a home, and living standards, the
majority of people were losing out.[8] While the characterization
of this situation as an economic 'crisis' seems misleading,
there is no question that both public and business confidence
in Keynesian economic strategies and prospects for economic
growth was severely damaged during this period of economic
contraction.

In both countries, declining economic confidence contributed to a marked rightward shift in the policy preferences
of significant sectors of the business community.[9] Broad-based
support for a more conservative domestic policy and a more
assertive foreign and military policy emerged within the business community, cutting across its conventional divisions.[10]
Liberal commitments shared by a majority of business groups
throughout the early post-war era now came increasingly
under challenge. The economic and political conditions that
previously had supported these commitments had changed,
with the effect that conservative and nationalist sentiments
within the business community began to soar.[11] The emergence of the New Right was to some extent consciously encouraged (not to mention actively funded) by conservative
business leaders, but at the same time it was to some extent an
independent development that nevertheless complemented
the aims of the newly-emerging elite industrial coalition.[12]

While the initial emergence of the New Right was very
much bolstered by the changing economic climate and the
rightward shift in the policy preferences of a segment of the
business community, its subsequent development and momen-

tum has been informed by a context of growing social inequality. British and US society has become more unequal in the past two decades, largely as a result of the fiscal policies and marketizing strategies of the Thatcher/Major and Reagan/Bush administrations. After documenting a range of economic indicators during the Thatcher years – wages, income, wealth – economist Will Hutton concludes, 'By any measure Britain is a substantially less equal society than it was.'[13] While some 55 per cent of the adult population held full-time, tenured jobs in 1975, the proportion fell to roughly 35 per cent in 1993.[14] According to estimates published by the Institute for Fiscal Studies, nearly 20 per cent of gross income is paid to indirect taxes by the poorest 10 per cent of the population, while the top 10 per cent pays roughly 8 per cent.[15] Commenting on wage inequality, Hutton writes, 'The wages of the top 10 per cent of male earners have risen from 1.67 times the median wage in 1979 to twice the median in 1993, while over the same period the wages of the poorest paid 10 per cent have fallen from 68.5 per cent to 58.2 per cent of the median. The gap between low and high wages is now the highest since records began'.[16]

Similarly, one of the most recent and comprehensive studies of the distribution of wealth in the United States concludes:

> After the stock market crash of 1929, there ensured a gradual if somewhat erratic reduction in wealth inequality, which seems to have lasted until the late 1970s. Since then, inequality of wealth holdings, like that of income, has risen sharply ... The rise in wealth inequality from 1983 to 1989 ... is particularly striking.[17]

In an appendix of his last major address as Labour Secretary, Robert Reich wrote, 'From the 1950s through most of the 1970s the income of the poorest fifth of Americans grew faster than the income of the top fifth. Between 1950 and 1978 the inflation-adjusted family income of the bottom quintile grew by 138 per cent, while the real income of the richest 20 per cent of families grew by 99 per cent.' By contrast, Reich noted that betweeen 1980 and 1995, the inflation-adjusted earnings of adults in the highest brackets increased by 10.7 per cent while the median worker's wages fell 3.6 per cent and those in the lowest brackets saw their wages decline by 9.6 per cent. Reich further elaborated, 'Wealth is even more unevenly distributed than income. Not only does the richest 20 per cent of the United States hold the bulk of the total wealth, but over the period from 1983 to 1992, this group received some 99 per cent of the total gain in wealth'.[18] The New Right has effectively tapped into the popular resentments and anger associated with declining economic standards and rising inequality. Moreover, the New Right's diagnoses of the current state of affairs has brought into question fundamental notions of the 'proper' role of the state, the ideological commitments of the major political parties, and the traditional loyalties of the electorate.[19]

The perceived and real failings of consensus politics has provided the symbolic space out of which the New Right has emerged to challenge the liberal vision of the role of state activity. The loss of economic confidence and the reality of decline has convinced conservatives of the limits of Keynesian economic theory and practice. New Right thinkers deem liberal policies, such as the 'War on Poverty' in the United States and the extensive welfare provisions in Britain, as the cause of contemporary economic problems. Interventionist policies are blamed for hindering the economy's 'natural' tendencies towards recovery. Welfare policies in particular are denounced for producing a 'dependency culture', stifling notions of individual responsibility, and destroying the fabric of the nuclear family. Liberal programs are seen by many as catering to (black) 'special interests', over and above the interests of the (white) majority. Such popular sentiment has facilitated a view of politics as a zero-sum game whereby gains for the poor and people of color are felt to be a loss for 'ordinary' citizens. The New Right has seized the political initiative and exploited this emerging popular anti-statist response with respect to both economic and social policy.

New Right discourse about race is situated within this context of a broad conservative re-interpretation of the liberal legacy. With the decline in popular mobilization in the mid-1970s, largely as a result of the institutionalization of a program of limited reform, combined with the material and political developments just outlined, a vacuum was created within which the dominant social bloc has mobilized to bring about a retreat. New Right symbolic conflict over racial meanings has been a central component of this elite project to reverse the broad trajectory of racial progress identified above. Given the racial and class unrest of the 1960s and 1970s, it should come as no surprise that the reaction to the liberal action has been at least to some extent racial.

The New Right has attempted to rearticulate the set of core assumptions that lay at the heart of racial progress in preceding decades: the definition of racism, the legitimate nature and scope of anti-racism, and the role of the state *vis-à-vis* the pursuit of racial equality. In the New Right worldview, racism is conceived as an irrational, prejudiced attitude certain individuals hold against other individuals because of their skin color. The term racism is entirely detached from the question of power so that anti-white prejudice is deemed just as reprehensible as anti-black prejudice. This assumption of fundamental symmetry and the associated neglect of the dimension of power has allowed the New Right to redefine racism as something people of color, in alliance with anti-racists, practice against white people as much as the reverse. In this way, classical anti-racist discourse is circumvented and used by the New Right in its struggle against what it understands as 'reverse racism'.

Since racism is redefined by the New Right in a radically individualistic manner, as a set of individual discriminatory attitudes and behaviors, it follows that the role of the state in responding to and managing problems concerning racism should be severely curtailed. In fact, the closest the New Right comes to a positive proposal for eradicating racism is its advocacy of the elimination of all anti-racist practices except those intended to counter overt, intentional discrimination. The increasingly interventionist role of the liberal state in racial matters, the New Right argues, has obstructed the opportunities of people of color themselves, discriminated against white people, harmed race relations, and disrupted the 'natural' functioning of society and the economy as a whole. New Right anti-anti-racism contributes to the conservative claim that state intervention in matters pertaining to race beyond securing the free competition of individuals and eliminating barriers created by racial discrimination harms rather than benefits society as a whole.

The question that remains to be answered is whether these New Right interventions in the arena of racial politics represents a new form of racism. The question, in actuality, breaks down into two: what is new about the racial discourse of the New Right, and is it in fact a species of racism?

NEW FORMS OF RACIAL DISCOURSE

There can be little serious doubt that there is much that is new in the politics of race and racism in the contemporary United States and Britain. More traditional notions of race and racism, dependent as they were on notions of biological hierarchies of inferiority and superiority, are today largely in disrepute. The explicit rejection of equal opportunity and civil rights for people of color is now virtually an absent political discourse except at the very fringes of national political debate. Even the militia movements in the United States and the likes of David Duke, former Grand Wizard of the KKK, avoid overt race-baiting in favor of a more sanitized and coded challenge to the role of government in mandating racial equality.

The fact that our understanding of race and racism is fluid and ever-changing should come as no surprise to those who have developed even the least bit of a sociological imagination. Shifts in language about race and racism reflect the deeper sociological truth that race is not an essence, not something fixed outside of history, but rather, in the words of Michael Omi and Howard Winant, 'an unstable and 'decentered' complex of social meanings constantly being transformed by political struggle.'[20] Throughout history, racial ideologies have gone through important transformations, both in terms of their internal form and content, and in terms of the role they play in the policy formation process. Racism is not a static package of irrational attitudes rooted in human nature, nor is it an inevitable part of civilization. Rather, it is a socio-historical construct that emerged and is still evolving in the context of unfolding social relations. Racism has assumed successive forms throughout history; in Britain for example, from the racism of slavery, to the racism of Empire, to anti-immigrant racism.[21] It is thus a complex system of symbols and meanings that modifies as a consequence of both structural changes and political struggles. As Stuart Hall has written,

> Racism is always historically specific. Though it may draw on the cultural traces deposited by previous historical phases, it always takes on specific forms. It arises out of the present – not past – conditions. Its effects are specific to the present organization of society, to the present unfolding of its dynamic political and cultural processes – not simply to its repressed past.[22]

The form that racism has taken in the present historical context has been labelled alternatively as the 'new racism' (Barker, 1981), 'cultural racism' (Seidel, 1986), 'differentialist racism' (Taguieff, 1990), 'neo-racism' or 'post-racism' (Balibar, 1991), 'symbolic racism' (Dovidio and Gaertner, 1986; Sears, 1988), 'modern racism' (McConahay, 1986), 'smiling racism' (Wilkins, 1984), and even 'anti-anti-racism' (Murray, 1986).[23] Before moving on to a discussion of what makes a discourse racist, we must first establish exactly what is new about New Right racial ideology, if anything, leaving aside for the moment the question of whether it does, in fact, constitute racism.

Three features of New Right racial ideology justify considering it a departure from right-wing racial ideologies of the past:

1. a sanitized, coded language about race that adheres to, more than it departs from, generally accepted liberal principles and values, mobilized for illiberal ends;
2. avid disavowals of racist intent and circumvention of classical anti-racist discourse; and
3. a shift from a focus on race and biological relations of inequality to a concern for cultural differentiation and national identity.

None of these features, of course, is entirely new. More traditional forms of racism involved coding, disavowals, and disclaimers that the intention of exclusion was in the best interest of all concerned, including people of color. However, these previously secondary features have come so much to the foreground of the New Right's ideology, while more traditional features related to overt racial prejudice and discrimination have receded to the background, that it is useful to place an analytic marker to signify a shift in both the form and content of racialized political language in the United States and Britain, and to examine both the reasons for the change as well as the political effects.

Racialized political language is today much more sanitized and indirect as compared to racial ideologies of the past, and New Right racial discourse very much reflects this trend. Racial discourse is, for the most part, no longer mean-spirited or derogatory in nature. In fact, the very category race is intentionally avoided by the New Right in an effort to distance itself from the racial extremism of the past.

Jeffrey Prager has developed the notion of a silence about race to capture this sanitary coding of the form and content of contemporary racial language.[24] He argues that, as a result of the symbolic and real gains of the civil rights movement, there is no longer an appropriate political language by which to challenge the goal of racial equality and that mainstream political discourse about race is characterized by public restraint. Prager rightly challenges the reader to see the positive aspects of the contemporary silence:

> Rather than seeing this period only as an era of political reaction, where earlier political struggles are being undermined by new coalitions and agendas, it is possible to see this time as one of rest; a period when there is occurring a solidification and crystallization of previous gains – like equal protection – accompanied by an unwillingness further to churn the waters. It is a period of silence, but also one of acquiescence to the achievements made from the turbulence of earlier decades. And, at the same time, the line is sharply drawn between the guarantee of civil rights and the extension of the meaning of social equality.[25]

Prager's muted optimism is consistent with the findings of recent studies on racial attitudes of the US public. For example, in *Racial Attitudes in America*, Schuman, Steeh and Bobo found that white racial attitudes remain contradictory – with much progress on the commitment to the abstract principle of racial equality coexisting with opposition to the implementation of these very same principles.[26]

This contradiction at the level of attitudes has caused contemporary racial projects to search for a new public language by which to exploit white racial anxieties while remaining discursively committed to the abstract liberal goals of equality and rights. This is precisely the point of those perspectives that advance the notion of codewords to understand the relative silence of race in people's thinking about the pressing problems to which the nation must respond. According to this popular view, perhaps best represented in the work of Michael Omi and Howard Winant, codewords revolving around ostensibly non-racial social categories such as welfare and crime have been mobilized to exploit the racial anxieties of white Americans without recourse to an explicitly racial discourse.[27] In this way, the racial dimension of a range of social issues is effectively conveyed in an implicit racial subtext, without attacking the racial gains of previous decades directly. Such a direct attack would actually limit the appeal of the New Right racial discourse, Omi and Winant argue, since it would challenge (explicitly) the widespread commitment to liberal attitudes of equality and fairness. New Right racial discourse has had to combine respect for the abstract liberal principles of equality and fairness with resistance to the demands of communities of color.

Although the sanitary coding of race and racism has received more attention in the US literature, this change in racialized political language has also been the subject of study in the British context. For example, Frank Reeves argues that while racism has not disappeared in Britain, references to biologically oriented racial themes have given way to more covert racist legitimations that more often than not work through social reformist, humanitarian and seemingly liberal discourse.[28] Indeed, it seems that one of the most fundamental changes marking the distinction between the old and the new racial language is that the latter operates by selectively drawing upon and reworking liberal and egalitarian principles for illiberal ends.[29] Omi and Winant essentially make this point in their use of the concept of rearticulation, or the process by which commonly accepted traditions and liberal principles such as equality and freedom are reinterpreted and given new meaning so that they are recognized in a new way.[30] In this way, apparently benign forms of political discourse are mobilized to argue for the New Right's racial project. As will be demonstrated below, democratic discourse and authoritarian effects are not mutually exclusive categories, the two can coexist symbiotically in racial discourse that denies that it is about race at all.

This insight leads to the second broad feature that marks New Right racial discourse as new: the avid disavowals of racist intent and the circumvention of classic anti-racist discourse for potentially exclusionary ends. New Rightists are keenly aware of the charges of racism commonly attributed to previous right-wing movements and consistently and proactively respond by insisting that their views do not represent racism but realism. The apparently benign nature and sanitary coding of their language superficially supports their claim of support for 'true' 'non-racism'. Racism is understood by New Rightists as an irrational attitude of racial prejudice held by the individual and, as such, condemned. Whether or not this condemnation is genuine is impossible to judge, and beside the point. The intentions of the speaker are less important to analyze than the effects of the speech; that is, the way in which the contradictory nature of the new forms of racialized political language on the one hand renders charges of racism difficult to sustain while on the other it provides ample scope for those supporters who wish to discover an implicit racist message.

Indeed, the apparently innocent language allows the New Right to provide a seemingly coherent interpretation for people's experiences without displaying itself as a coherent theory at all, but just common sense. The new racism works more via implication than explicit assertion. In fact, it is often expressed in the language of tolerance and in accordance with the tenets of egalitarian liberalism. As Stephen and Hillary Rose suggest, the ideas of freedom and equality that had been the subversive weapons of the struggle for racial equality and justice have become the legitimating ideology of those who wish to overturn the gains of that struggle.[31] Etienne Balibar argues that racial domination can be and today often is formulated in the language of universalism and, accordingly, insists on the importance of studying the discursive processes by which systems of racial domination are established and sustained within, and not outside, bourgeois ideology.[32] In fact, to understand racist ideologies as working on the basis of already-developed democratic doctrines helps make sense of their popular appeal, for it is the common-sense presentation and taken-for-granted quality that accounts for the ability of such ideologies to provide compelling interpretative repetoires to subscribers from a variety of class, regional, gender, and ethnic identities.

The new forms of racialized political discourse work by circumventing classical anti-racist discourse and appropriating it for the right. This circumvention allows the New Right to identify its vision of society, whether it be the color-blind vision of the New Right in the United States or the ethnic nationalism of the British New Right, as 'true' anti-racism or non-racism. It is a circumvention that rests on the New Right's assertion that anti-racist programs themselves are largely to blame for the continued oppression of people of color, as well as the persistence and even intensification of racial hostilities. In this sense, the new racism is in some ways more appropriately labelled 'anti-anti-racism'.[33]

New Right racial discourse is distinct from more traditional forms to the extent that it shifts hostility away from people of color to the state and, more specifically, to the activities of anti-racist bureaucrats. Instead of deriding people of color as lazy, stupid or dirty, derisions commonly associated with more traditional racist attitudes, New Right racial discourse is characterized more by an insistence on the priority of the rights of the citizen as against those of the state. For example, with respect to the affirmative action issue in the United States, the New Right holds that property-owners have the right over and above the government to dictate who they should employ in their factories, educate in their schools, or house in their neighborhoods. Or with respect to the immigration issue in Britain, the New Right holds that the 'home culture' has the right to be 'itself' and defend its 'way of life' against the 'invasion of outsiders'.

This shift in focus from the attributes of people of color themselves to the activities of anti-racist bureaucrats dovetails with the broader New Right theme of anti-statism and concern for the rise of the so-called 'new class'. Popularized by neo-conservatives in both countries throughout the 1980s, and one of the center-pieces of the Bush campaign during the

1988 elections, the 'new class' is an amorphous concept that generally refers to an alleged liberal elite of intellectuals, government bureaucrats, progressive activists and educators, and media personalities who are said to gain status and power through organizational position and fake compassion.[34] The concept has allowed the New Right to capitalize on the long-standing reservoir of populist resentment against non-producing elites, so that today the phrase 'special interests' calls to the popular mind liberal politicians and bureaucrats, rather than the business and financial elites to whom the phrase historically referred. In the most extreme use of the 'new class' concept, the notion of racism is dismissed as a mere fabrication on the part of anti-racist bureaucrats, who are said to exploit communities of color for their own opportunist and self-aggrandizing ends.

The 'new class' theme allows New Rightists to portray themselves as the true champions of the interests of people of color. Moreover, New Right disavowals of racist intent, and the shift in negative attention to the activities of the 'new class' of anti-racist bureaucrats, are bolstered as claims by the fact that the New Right in both the United States and Britain has increasingly reached out, and not entirely without success, to communities of color for support. The fact that people of color are supporters and even key activists within the movement is indeed a new phenomenon, even while it is used to legitimate the New Right's claim of advocating 'true' non-racism.[35] Perhaps more important than the actual participation of people of color in the movement is the symbolic effect of their rhetorical inclusion; for the New Right's benign inclusionary rhetoric is directed as much toward a white audience wishing to view themselves as tolerant as it is toward potential voters and recruits among people of color.[36]

The third feature that justifies the characterization of New Right racial discourse as new is the substitution of race with the ostensibly non-racial categories of culture and nation. Martin Barker, in a now seminal work entitled *The New Racism*, was the first to identify its key elements.[37] The new racism is not wholly new, Barker argues, but is nevertheless distinct from more traditional forms of racism primarily in that it works via notions of cultural difference rather than assertions of biological relations of inferiority/superiority. While notions of cultural difference do not represent the introduction of a new ideological element but rather the bringing to the fore of one that has long been present, and in fact integral, to more traditional forms of racism, and while biological notions have not completely disappeared, it is true to say that cultural themes have become more salient as biological ones have faded into the background, albeit still with telling effects. In analyzing what he calls the 'political re-emergence of ideologi- cally oriented racism in the Tory Party', Barker is especially concerned with the right's use of pseudo-scientific rationaliz- ation that he derides as signalling the re-emergence of Social Darwinist schools of human ethology and sociobiology. The main thrust of the book, however, is to expose the cultural bases of modern racism. Barker warns, 'Just as dangerous as prejudice about other people, if not more so, are theories that result in justification for keeping ourselves separate.'[38]

Many authors, particularly those writing in the European context, have since elaborated on this theme of the shift from an explicit focus on race and racial exclusion to concern over the ostensibly non-racial defense of cultural and national iden- tity. New forms of racialized political discourse are not so much *against* 'the other' or the values of 'alien cultures', as in previous discourses of empire and slavery, as it is *for* 'us' and the values of Western culture. In other words, exclusionary sentiment orchestrated through racial discourse no longer relies upon justifying the lack of civil and political rights of those excluded as it is about legitimating the 'natural' desire to remain 'oneself', to preserve the homogeneity of the nation's 'way of life', and to exclude those who purportedly undermine the shared sense of customs, history, language, and so on, that constitutes national identity. As Gill Seidel demonstrates in her discourse analysis of the British neo- conservative journal the *Salisbury Review*, right-wing racial dis- course is about what sort of people 'we' are.[39] In a similar vein, John Solomos argues that the portrayal of black people as a threat to social order and political stability in right-wing politi- cal discourse involves 'an interpellation of symbolic images of culture and nationhood with fear about the consequences of immigration and multiculturalism.'[40]

This culturalist theme also appears in studies of new racial discourses in, for example, the Netherlands (van Dijk, 1991),

France (Taguieff, 1990), and New Zealand (Wetherell and Potter, 1992).[41] Each broadly shares the view that the categories of nation and culture, rather than race, have taken over the ideological task of legitimating racism. For example, in their study of the racial discourse of Pakeha New Zealanders, Wetherell and Potter write,

> Culture discourse, therefore, takes over some of the same tasks as race. It becomes a naturally occurring difference, a simple fact of life, and a self-sufficient form of explanation. Culture also continues the doctrine of fatal impact and the white man's burden; but this time around the 'fatal flaws' in the Maori people do not lie in their genes but in their traditional practices, attitudes and values ... It [culture] covers over the messy business of domination and uneven development through advocacy of respect and tolerance for differences ... There is an inevitability and acceptability in the notion of 'culture contact' not found in the rhetoric of annexation, conquest and oppression.[42]

According to the above body of literature, there is a new form of racism that is not about erasing but rather multiplying difference. In reference to the new cultural racism in France, Pierre Taguieff develops the notion of a 'differentialist racism', in contrast to older versions of 'discriminatory racism', which rely on a defense of cultural identities and a praise of difference. Taguieff writes: 'If the central obsession of discriminatory racism is the loss of rank, and the debasement of superior peoples, the idee fixe of differentialist racism is the loss of what is characteristic, the erasure of the group's identity.'[43] In this way, new forms of racialized political language are articulated as 'the right to be different', 'legitimate defense of the nation', and 'the right to one's own cultural identity' – thus further bolstering New Right disavowals of racist intent and self-presentation as the champions of genuine anti-racism.

By celebrating difference in this way, the New Right circumvents the discourse of multiculturalism, and particularly its essentialist undercurrents against which Paul Gilroy and others have warned, and turns it against itself so that it is used for exclusionary rather than inclusionary ends.[44] Indeed, the significance of the shift from a discriminatory racism to a differentialist racism cannot be overestimated in terms of the implications for anti-racist politics. As Anna Marie Smith argues, definitions of racism that are linked to essentialist doctrines are incapable of challenging the new forms of racism championed by the New Right, since the New Right is explicitly anti-essentialist in its praise of difference (although I would add implicitly essentialist in its claim of entitlement to remain 'oneself'), while, ironically, many factions of anti-racists do operate on the basis of essentialist claims.[45] In this respect, analysis of the new forms of racialized political language demands that we rethink the very concept of racism, and do so with a keen awareness of the connection between the newness of the doctrines articulated by the New Right and the novelty of the political situations, material circumstances, and social transformations that have given them purchase.

A NEW RACISM?

Tackling the issue of racism head-on is crucial for a book of this kind, although much of the literature on the subject of race and the Right has managed to avoid doing so. Indeed, we have seen what is new about New Right racial discourse, but the question that remains is whether these new features of racialized political language in fact constitute racism? Have the forms of racial discourse been modified to such a degree that they no longer deserve the label racism? Is what we are seeing a new racism without race, or simply new forms of racialized political language that are not racist in form and content but nevertheless carry the potential of tapping into a latent popular and even state racism? In short, is racism internal or external to the silence on race about which Prager writes?

These questions are more complex than they first appear, and will surely be the subject of continuing debate – a useful debate, however, because the conventional definition of prejudice plus power equals racism is a product of the 1960s and now, I would argue, quite outdated. The goal of defining racism is riddled with difficulties but nevertheless provides an opportunity to think through all sorts of analytic difficulties: is

it possible to define a political project as racist when participants deny it and speak the language of anti-racism? Is it possible to define a political project as racist when the language is
in accord with mainstream liberal values of tolerance and
freedom? Is it possible to define a political project as racist
when the language praises difference and the political practice includes individuals from various communities of color?
In short, what does it mean to characterize a political project
or ideology as racist?

For reasons of space, I will attempt to simplify the matter by
drawing a distinction between a restrictive and an expansive
approach to the study of racism and the right. Supporters of a
restrictive conception of racism would take seriously New
Right disavowals of racism, and point out that race is not even
an explicit or primary concern for the New Right movement
as a whole.[46] New Rightists themselves would certainly challenge claims that their movement is racist, and would reserve
the term instead for those political projects (such as black nationalism) or policies (such as affirmative action) that employ
race either to discriminate against or give advantage to an individual on the basis of the color of his/her skin.

However, the main contention of this restrictive conception
is that racism must refer to a content with specific criteria so
as not to become so broadly applied that its critical edge
is blunted. This is the view of Omi and Winant in *Racial
Formation in the United States.* Having evaded the issue of racism
in the first edition, the authors attempt in the second to
explain what it means to characterize a political project as
racist. They begin by noting the overall crisis of the meaning
of the term racism today, and then move on to situate their argument between, on the one hand, those who define racism in
structural terms (which they warn, along with Robert Miles
and others, inflates the concept of racism to the point of
losing all precision), and on the other hand, neo-conservatives
who define racism so narrowly that it refers only to explicit attitudes of racial hatred and acts of discrimination with a clear
and identifiable intent to harm.[47] Insisting that racism changes
over time, Omi and Winant offer the following advise: 'A
racial project can be defined as racist if and only if it creates or
reproduces structures of domination based on essentialist
categories of race.'[48]

By this standard, the New Right's racial project is clearly not racist. Omi and Winant seem more comfortable in arguing that the hegemonic racial project at this time is about the retreat of social policy from any practical commitment to racial justice and the manipulation of white racial anxiety and resentment toward alleged 'special treatment' for people of color. While not racist because it does not rely on essentialist doctrines, this hegemonic racial project, they argue, nevertheless 'exhibits an unabashed structural racism all the more brazen because at the ideological or signification level, it adheres to a principle of 'treating everyone alike.'[49] Other works on race and the right influenced by the codeword approach, such as *Chain Reaction* by Thomas and Mary Edsall, also implicitly advocate a restrictive definition by avoiding use of the term racism and instead focusing on the manner in which right-wing conservative politicians have mobilized the racial anxieties of the public for partisan and electoral ends.[50] Writing in a comparative vein, Stephen Small argues that the Right's development of more sophisticated forms of racialized political language and activity certainly contributes to racialized hostility but is not best described as racism.[51] True, politicians fan the flames of popular racism that already exists independently 'out there', but this political use of racism is quite distinct from arguing that the race-neutral political discourse of the New Right is itself racist.

The restrictive conception of racism has merit in the sense that it is anti-expansionist. That is, by linking racism with a particular content, the term retains its critical edge and so avoids the levelling effects of those who, as a function of focusing on structural outcomes, either ignore the study of meaning and discourse altogether or conflate racism with mainstream meritocratic, liberal ideology. There can be no racism without race, according to the restrictive conception, for this would obscure the real qualitative differences between the racist discourses of the Right during the Jim Crow era in the United States, for example, or during the era of Empire in Britain, and the color-blind discourse of today's conservatives.

Those who advocate an expansive approach to the study of racism, as I will below, object to the restrictive conception's focus on the *content* of New Right discourse. Of course it is important to study the ways in which the content of racial discourse has changed over time, but such a task is of limited value if we recognize the degree to which the changed content nevertheless serves to justify the same old exclusionary practices, albeit in a new form. Today more than ever it is imperative to explore the connections between race-neutral discursive practices and the maintenance of institutional relations of racial domination. If the changed content of racialized political language and the New Right's avid disavowals of racist intent blind us to the dynamism of racism and the variety of discursive garbs in which it can appear, we will unwittingly abandon the study of the cultural and ideological (as opposed to the structural) dimensions of racism, except in their most exceptional forms, and so effectively absolve the New Right from blame for increasing racial inequality, prejudice, violence, and so on. As Wetherell and Potter write,

> Given this flexibility of the enemy, and the way the debates move on, it seems sensible not to commit oneself to one exclusive characterization of racist claims. There is a danger of being silenced when racist discourse continues to oppress but no longer meets the main characteristics of social scientific definitions of racism.'[52]

It is in the spirit of taking the warning of this danger seriously that I briefly outline below an alternative approach – what I label the 'dominance approach' – to the study of racism.

The dominance approach is grounded in a broader approach to the study of ideology that emphasizes not the false content of ideas, but rather the process by which meaning is mobilized in the service of power.[53] With this compass of power in hand, it is possible to define racism in a way that avoids the pitfalls of the restrictive approach. According to the dominance approach, a discourse is racist to the extent that it establishes, justifies and/or sustains practices that maintain systematically asymmetrical relations of racial domination. In this conception, there is no need to try to specify the propositional claims of ideology in advance. Most importantly, it allows for the operation of racist discourse without the category race.

The implications of the dominance approach for the study of racism are many. Most broadly, it avoids conceptions of race as something fixed and outside of history – what Paul Gilroy refers to as the 'coat of paint' theory of racism.[54] In this theory, racism is understood as somehow peripheral to the real substance of political life, thus leading to the conclusion that it can be eliminated without challenging the basic structures and relations of economy and society. The dominance approach to racism, by contrast, insists that racial ideology must be related to its material roots and symbolic functions in order to see how it is integrally bound up with the question of power. Understood in this way, the struggle against racism is at the same time a struggle over fundamental issues of social justice, democratic rights, and political and economic power.

The dominance approach also poses a challenge to those studies that implicitly or explicitly rely on an attitudinal conception of racism. Defining racism as a set of prejudiced attitudes on the psychological level was commonplace within the social scientific literature only a few decades ago, and continues to be the reigning assumption of those, including New Rightists, who deny the existence of a modern racism.[55] For those who adopt an attitudinal conception of racism, the 'American dilemma' continues to be one in which there is a conflict, located within the individual mind or value-system, between universal or inclusionary political values and anti-black sentiment.[56] To the extent that the codeword approach described above focuses on the tension between socially acceptable expressions of commitment to racial equality and more ill-spirited psychological drives, it remains implicitly locked into the prejudice model of racism.

Yet attitudes are merely the particular expression of a more general and pervasive worldview, and so constitute a relatively more superficial aspect of racial ideology. It is the worldview that New Rightists bring as ideological spectacles to a wide range of issues that generates their particular attitudes on issues involving race. Thus when inconsistencies are found, instead of positing the existence of codewords that steer between the contradictory attitudes, it is necessary to:

1. search for the underlying beliefs or assumptions that make these contradictory attitudes consistent in the minds of supporters; and

2. examine what social effects are secured by an ideology built on a unity of these particular opposites.

In this view, racism need not be regarded as a set of explicit attitudes about particular topics that many survey researchers attempt to study, but rather a complex assemblage of implicit, underlying assumptions inherent in ordinary ways of thinking and applicable to all domains. Defining racism thus does not presuppose a ready-made or static formalization of facts regarding race. Indeed, one of the functions of ideology, including racial ideology, is precisely to establish the 'facts' and interpret them in a way that legitimates certain courses of action over others. According to this view, the 'American dilemma' is located not within the mentalities of individuals but rather within the competing cultural frames and rhetorical resources available in a liberal society for articulating notions of the public good. As Wetherell and Potter write, 'There is no need to posit a set of prejudiced feelings that conflict with political values to explain modern racism. Egalitarianism does not seem to require an injection of anti-black effect to make it work for racism.'[57] Such an insight creates an analytic space to study the ways in which the rhetoric of color-blindness and equal opportunity, for example, lacking anti-black affect, nevertheless replaces the ideological function of old-fashioned racism – the organization and defense of white privilege.

The fact that the dominance approach highlights the function of racism to establish and sustain relations of domination is not to deny that it is expressive of the needs of supporters. It is expressive in the sense that New Right racial ideology speaks to real concerns and failures with respect to liberal anti-racist policies as implemented in practice. Many studies, such as the Edsalls' noted above, elaborate on the theme of the expressive role of racism in their examination of how conservative politicians have exploited what is considered to be the 'natural' responses of resentment and anger on the part of lower income whites toward liberal racial policies that transgress dominant meritocratic notions of justice. Though it is important to consider such populist sentiment, there is a danger of reifying white racial anxieties, thus neglecting the ways in which New Right discourse manipulates, even creates, the existence of mentalities for strategic and partisan advantage.

To do so would be to disregard what I contend to be most significant about New Right discourse on race; that is, the way in which it rearticulates underlying cultural beliefs and meaning frames shaping people's perception and interpretation of events so that they work for rather than against racism.

With these points in mind, it is possible to see the value of the dominance approach in overcoming what David Wellman has identified as a theoretical bifurcation in sociological studies of racism.[58] In the updated introduction to the second edition of *Portraits of White Racism*, Wellman usefully summarizes the current literature as falling roughly into two camps: the structuralist and the ideological. The structuralist camp explains the organization of racial privilege as a function of social location and economic organization, eschewing any concept of white racism. The ideological path corrects the structuralist's neglect of the centrality of race by focusing on processes of racial signification and processes of racialization, but to the deficit of an understanding of the structural organization of racial advantage. Neither approach, Wellman quite rightly points out, is up to the task of understanding the new forms in which racism now appears.

The symbolic conflict approach to New Right discourse about race, reliant as it is on a dominance approach to the study of racism, is offered in the next two chapters as an attempt to overcome this theoretical divide and, within one conceptual approach, understand the link between cultural codes, systems of meaning, processes of signification *and* the establishment and maintenance of existing structural relations of racial domination. It is with this object in mind that I now turn to a critical discourse analysis of the new racism of the New Right in the United States and Britain.

3 The New Right in the United States: Color-Blind Discourse and the Politics of Reverse Racism

The New Right emerged in the United States in the mid-1970s as both a legacy of a uniquely US history of right-wing reaction and as a novel political force in its own right. Throughout US history, hard times have facilitated the emergence of the hard Right. The disintegration of the Southern slave economy and the beginning of Reconstruction witnessed the emergence of the Klu Klux Klan (KKK) in the 1860s; the Great Depression fuelled the rise of populist demagogues such as Father Charles Coughlin and Huey Long in the 1930s; and the status insecurities of a burgeoning nouveau riche, combined with the apparent decline of US power on the world scene with the first shots of the Cold War, together provided the impetus in the 1950s for the anti-communist witch-hunts of Senator Joseph McCarthy.[1]

During such times of economic change and social strain, there emerges a period of symbolic conflict regarding the meaning of contemporary events and the recipe for future well-being. Such periods are characterized by the symbolic construction of political problems, leaders, enemies and solutions. The details of such symbolic construction change over time, yet continuities can and have been traced between different backlash movements and ideas. For example, whereas the identification of the enemy has shifted over time – between immigrants, Catholics, Jews, Communists and blacks – the process of enemy construction nevertheless has remained a constant feature of right-wing extremist movements in the United States.

By the late 1950s and throughout the 1960s, racism had replaced anti-communism as the central issue for the right wing. As resistance and struggle in the form of the civil rights

74

movement gained force, so too did the white backlash. This period witnessed the revival of the KKK, the birth of the John Birch Society, and the emergence of the Goldwater and Wallace Presidential campaigns in 1964 and 1968, respectively. Though the themes of previous right-wing movements – such as hostility to government power, anti-communism, adherence to traditional Christian values and belief in the absolute rights of individuals – remained present, it was arguably the significant racial subtext to this phase of right-wing response to socio-economic dislocation that most characterized such movements.

The form of expression of this racial subtext divided the Right by the mid-1960s into two wings – moderate and extremist. Conservatives from William F. Buckley (founding editor of the neo-liberal journal *National Review*) to members of the John Birch Society (an extremist, nativist, right-wing pressure group) had been more or less united behind the Goldwater presidential campaign of 1964. Yet, with Goldwater's defeat and utter failure to capture the support of working-class voters, significant differences re-emerged.

By 1968 a fissure on the Right was clearly evident. In the election of that year, George Wallace launched a third-party presidential campaign geared to exploit the growing white working-class backlash against 'big government'. More specifically, Wallace denounced liberal state accommodation to the demands of what he believed to be a Communist-inspired and Communist-led civil rights movement. Much of the Old Right (including Buckley and many former Goldwater supporters) was alienated from the pseudo-populist, semi-conspiratorial style of Wallace and voted instead for Nixon.

The emergence of the New Right in the mid-1970s served to decrease the distance between these two strands of the right wing, uniting the economic conservatism and anti-New Deal liberalism of the Old Right with the social traditionalism and pseudo-populism of the more extreme Right. While the Goldwater campaign had illustrated that old-style economic conservatism was not electorally viable, the Wallace candidacy showed just how limiting the charge of racism had become for the right-wing pursuit of electoral respectability. In attempting to fuse the two right-wing traditions in the United States, the New Right departed from both; eschewing the near-explicit

racism and downplaying the enthusiasm for discovering conspiracy of the more radical tradition while attempting to make
traditional economic conservatism appear more populist.

The particular historical debt the New Right owes to the
third-party campaign of George Wallace is especially noteworthy. The Wallace campaign anticipated many of the issues
the New Right would later champion. Specifically, Wallace employed coded racial appeals related to law and order and states'
rights to woo those who opposed the granting of concessions to
the civil rights movement without, importantly, engaging in
overt race-baiting. Wallace ran as a law and order candidate,
and voiced his opposition to the civil rights movement in an
apparently benign appeal to traditional values, states' rights,
patriotism and militarism. Wallace portrayed the civil rights
movement as the imposition of intrusive social engineering on
an unwilling public by a coercive federal government. In this
sense, like Enoch Powell in Britain, Wallace can rightly be considered the 'father' of the new racism in US politics.

Indeed, Wallace's success (he won the South and almost
14 per cent of the total vote) was to have a lasting impact on
the US political landscape.[2] For one, it caught the attention of
Republican Party strategists. In 1969, one such strategist and
Nixon-aide, Kevin Phillips, wrote a book entitled *The Emerging
Republican Majority*. Phillip's central argument was that thinly-
veiled anti-black campaign rhetoric could serve as a building
block for a conservative electoral realignment and eventual
majority.[3] Dubbed the 'Southern Strategy' and central to
Nixon's victory in 1972, the new racism thus moved one step
closer to the political center. It was out of this historical
context, one marked by the political exploitation of mounting
white opposition to civil rights gains and associated liberal
racial understandings, that the New Right emerged.

ORGANIZATIONS AND CURRENTS

The US New Right emerged in the mid-1970s as a small but
vocal political movement bent on moving conservatism 'out of
the closet and into the Oval Office'.[4] A new generation of conservative leadership appeared, one that rejected the anti-ism
of the post-war conservative movement and instead focused

energy on building a new populist style of non-party conservatism. Besides its populist style, the New Right coalition served to unite previously distinct strands of the right wing by promoting a common agenda of anti-communist militarism, moral orthodoxy, and free market capitalism – themes that would eventually deliver Reagan the White House. As self-avowed political mechanics, New Right strategists joined together in a common aim of developing their own constituency, their own institutions, their own agenda, and above all, their own leaders.

Richard Viguerie developed the direct-mail solicitation technique which allowed the new movement to, in his words, 'bypass the monopoly the left has in the media, and let us go directly to the people and tell them what the problem is and what to do about it.'[5] Howard Phillips likened the New Right's blueprint for reaching potential members to the principles of guerrilla warfare set forth by Mao Zedong, and under the auspices of the newly-founded Conservative Caucus, helped to build grassroots support for conservative candidates and to train workers at the precinct, district, and state levels.[6] Once dubbed the 'Robespierre of the Right', Paul Weyrich served as the ultimate networker and institution-builder for the New Right, founding such organizations as the Committee for the Survival of a Free Congress (now the Free Congress Foundation), The Heritage Foundation, Coalitions for America, and a range of single-issue groups that brought conservative secular and religious leaders together for the first time to plan collective action on issues of mutual concern.[7]

At the same time that these and other New Right leaders were busy building an infrastructure of new institutions to serve as a platform for their free market and counter-counter-culturalist agenda, they were also looking for a constituency. This they found in the form of what came to be known as the New Christian Right.[8] The New Christian Right, in concert with secular political leaders, succeeded in galvanizing at least a segment of the previously apolitical evangelical community into organized political action. In the words of TV preacher James Robison, 'I'm sick and tired of hearing about all the radicals and perverts and liberals and leftists and communists coming out of the closets. It's time for God's people to come out of the closets, out of the churches, and change America.'[9]

Among the organizations born of the budding relationship between conservative secular and religious leaders in the late 1970s were, most importantly, the Moral Majority (later the Liberty Federation), Christian Voice, and Religious Roundtable (now Roundtable). These newly-created organizations focused attention on a range of emotive social issues as part of their collective bid to mobilize millions of conservative Americans who had never before participated in politics. As Weyrich once said, 'We talk about issues that people care about, like gun control, abortion, taxes, and crime. Yes, they're emotional issues, but that's better than talking about capital formation.'[10]

After Reagan's election to office in 1980, the division between the secular and religious factions of the New Right began to blur. A new pro-family movement arose, less explicitly religious in focus and more grassroots in orientation. Especially important were the activities of pro-family coalition groups such as Beverly LaHaye's Concerned Women of America, James Dobson's Focus on the Family, and Phyllis Schlafly's Eagle Forum. The emergence of the traditional values movement in the mid-1980s was similarly indicative of the New Right's attempt to reach out beyond the hard core of committed conservatives and attract people still beyond the movement. Under the auspices of newly-founded organizations such as the Center for Cultural Conservatism and the American Coalition for Traditional Values, cultural conservatives such as William Lind advocated a program for the conservative renewal of US culture to complement legislative attempts to defeat the liberal agenda.[11]

Joining in a broad coalition with the New Right in the late 1970s and early 1980s were the neo-conservatives, a loose cluster of intellectuals who, despite the many differences that divided them, together contributed to the reshaping of the general climate of political opinion. Most neo-conservatives began their lives on the liberal/Left but, as a result of a process that began with the Nazi–Soviet pact of 1939 and which was strongly reinforced by the anti-Americanism and cultural disorder associated with the New Left and counter-culture, shared a common journey rightward, progressively abandoning their radical beliefs in favor of centrist, even conservative, ones. Others began their political lives as liberals and moved to the right as a result of being disillusioned by the apparent failure of the Great Society programs of the 1960s, programs that many of them had helped design. They are, as famously described by the 'Godfather' of neo-conservatism, Irving Kristol, 'liberals who have been mugged by reality'.[12] In this respect the prefix 'neo' refers to the shift in political beliefs of a particular group of mainly male, mainly Jewish, East coast intellectual refugees of the liberal Left.[13]

If the secular-political and religious factions of the New Right were engaged in a great war for the hearts and minds of people, then the neo-conservatives were the movements' organic intellectuals. Although neo-conservatives remained suspicious of the populist spirit and rabble-rousing style of New Right political operatives, their ideas dovetailed in important ways with the issues agenda of the broader movement. Neo-conservatism combined a guarded faith in the essential goodness of democratic capitalism and the American Creed of individual rights and equal opportunity with a positive valuation of the traditional moral values condemned by the counter-culture and new appreciation of the family, authority, traditional gender roles, and bonds of community. While neo-conservatism became distinctly less homogeneous throughout the early Reagan years, with many thinkers attempting to distance themselves from the label and others growing increasingly critical of the direction of Republican Party policy, the term remains useful as a shorthand identification of a particular fusion of liberal and conservative themes that helped provide intellectual ammunition for the New Right's assault upon the post-war liberal tradition.

During this early period, when the New Right was most clearly an insurgent social movement, racial issues were present but not predominant. Other issues related to the family, sexuality, and the economic realm appeared most salient, leading many commentators to conclude that racial issues were no longer useful as an organizational theme for the right wing. The relative silence around race during this period must be understood in the context of the enormous transformations regarding civil rights that had occurred less than a decade before, creating a deficit of political will to introduce race into the national debate and nervousness on the part of New Rightists eager to distance themselves from earlier conservative movements damaged by the charge of racism.

Yet, contrary to those who announced the dearth of right-wing racial appeals, issues of race continued to preoccupy the minds of many New Rightists, even during these early years. For example, the secular wing of the New Right demonstrated a sustained opposition to liberal racial remedies such as busing and all forms of so-called racial preferences, as evidenced in articles that appeared throughout the 1970s and 1980s in key New Right journals such as *Conservative Digest*.[14] Attention to ostensibly non-racial policy issues such as welfare and crime similarly provided a platform for New Rightists to spell out their views on the damaging implications of the liberal pursuit of racial equality.[15] New Rightists established networks with grassroots organizations such as the National Association for Neighborhood Schools (NANS), an anti-busing group, and local religious organizations supporting anti-integrationist Christian academies.[16] Indeed, the conflation of race with criticism of liberal social and economic policy was central to the New Right's construction of an organizational nexus capable of linking popular and elite opposition toward Great Society liberalism.

Racial issues also figured somewhat prominently in campaigns led by the Christian Right. For example, racial issues such as affirmative action quotas and school busing were regularly included on report cards, circulated by Christian Voice, rating Congressional and Presidential candidates on a scale of morality. One such moral report card opposed racial quotas on the basis that they 'have become a form of reverse discrimination which deny qualified individuals academic and occupational advancement opportunities'. Busing was opposed for being 'counter-productive in fostering improved racial relations' and for 'being wasteful of taxpayers' dollars'. The pro-family movements' belief in the utility of traditional values, too, became conflated with racial politics on several fronts: the growth of female-headed households, sexual licentiousness, 'subversive' and 'primitive' music, and multiculturalism. The Free Congress Foundations' Center for Cultural Conservatism disavowed any racial nationalist intent while attacking multiculturalism for legitimizing a diversity in value systems and lifestyles which directly contradicts the Biblical concept of moral absolutes.[17] The conflation of race and the values debate facilitated the New Right's argument that national decline can be reversed only if traditional values are restored, thus implying that the 'wrong' values or 'dysfunctional' culture is the underlying cause rather than an associated effect of economic problems in communities of color.

The only really principled assault on the axioms of a multi-racial society at the heart of intellectual debates over affirmative action and other race-conscious policies appeared in the writings of neo-conservatives. As early as the 1970s, intellectuals writing for the two most prominent neo-conservative journals, *Commentary* and *The Public Interest,* challenged the direction in which the executive and judicial branches of government were taking civil rights policy; in their eyes, away from the spirit of the 1964 Civil Rights Act.[18] In 1975, Nathan Glazer published *Affirmative Discrimination: Ethnic Inequality and Public Policy,* which introduced themes that would be reiterated through to today: most importantly, the idea that any public policy that goes beyond protecting the individual against intentional acts of discrimination is a transgression on the spirit of the 1964 Civil Rights Act and, in fact, constitutes a form of 'affirmative discrimination' against whites.[19] As the most consistent pundits on the subject, neo-conservatives continued to voice their opposition to race-conscious public policy throughout the 1980s, and many were appointed to positions of importance in the Reagan administration.[20] Neo-conservatives were joined during this period by a small group of prominent black scholars voicing similar concerns in the pages of black conservative journals such as *Lincoln Review.*[21]

New Right discourse on racial matters during this insurgent period of right-wing political activity is an example of the new racism in that it operated along the fault-line of support for the ending of formal segregation and opposition to further ameliorative measures to redress continuing and pervasive racial injustice. Explicit racism was rhetorically eschewed and, as early as 1984, efforts were launched to reach out to communities of color for support. True to the spirit of the new racism, the New Right's agenda to call a halt to programs that previous administrations had seen as a main vehicle for racial progress coexisted with the attempt to attract people of color to the movement and so avoid appearing as mean-spirited racists. The two most prominent journals of the secular wing of the New Right, *Conservative Digest* and *Policy Review,* published numerous articles that categorically rejected racism and in fact attempted to convince people of color that conservatives are their best allies.[22] For example, in a *Policy Review* article entitled 'Reaching Out to Black Americans', Adam Meyerson advises,

> Conservatives must speak out loud, long and clear with the message that we stand for opportunity for all Americans, and that we will toil ceaselessly until racial discrimination and prejudice have been banished from our land ... We must appoint blacks to positions of real power, influence and visibility.[23]

While it is not clear to what extent such outreach was actually aimed at wooing the vote of people of color to the Republican Party as opposed to reassuring white supporters that the movement was clean of racist sentiment, the outreach rhetoric nevertheless represented something new in right-wing political discourse.

Despite such discursive innovations, the new racism remained relatively dormant in terms of the political agenda of the New Right throughout the Reagan years. Even in the face of willingness on the part of senior Reagan administration officials, including Reagan himself, to take on the liberal 'truths' of the so-called civil rights establishment, political calculation dictated no action.[24] Instead, New Rightists engaged in a quite successful underground strategy on matters related to race, mobilizing codewords around issues such as welfare and crime to speak to white anxieties without directly challenging liberal racial understandings. It would not be until the 1990s that the unthinkable would become thinkable, and even politically possible, thanks in no small part to the discursive themes already established during this formative period of New Right activity.

The fact that the unthinkable became thinkable in the early 1990s owes less to a change of heart on the part of conservatives *vis-à-vis* race as it does to alterations in the broader political climate. Perhaps the most important factor of all was the collapse of the Soviet bloc. The end of the Cold War was significant for the racial project of the New Right on two counts. Firstly, it facilitated a shift from a focus on foreign to domestic enemies and issues. In the words of Grover Norquist, amicably known as the Grand Central Station of New Republicanism: 'Victory over the communist enemy meant that we could turn our attention on smashing the Left.'[25] Or as author Frederick Lynch explained, 'Until the fall of the Berlin Wall, it was markets and missiles and not much else.'[26] Since it was no longer relevant to taint the Democrats for being soft on communism, New Rightists constructed new moral and racialized boundaries between deserving and un-deserving citizen within the United States as a battering ram against the opposition.

Secondly, the end of the Cold War had the effect of disunit-ing conservatives, as anti-communism previously had served as a glue holding together diverse coalition tendencies. Fissures within the coalition were only aggravated as a result of the shift in political attention from foreign to domestic policy questions; for conservatives were notoriously more divided on the latter, with latent conflicts brewing under the surface over divisive social issues such as abortion, school prayer, and gay rights. Although divisions within the broad New Right coalition had existed from the very beginning, they were overshadowed throughout most of the 1980s by other pressures toward unity. Anti-communism in the midst of the Cold War was one such unifying force, as was the personal authority of Ronald Reagan. However, in the wake of the fall of the Berlin Wall and the de-parture of Reagan from office, a period of in-fighting began within the New Right wherein previously latent philosophical conflicts broke out into the open.[27] It is in this context of the post-Reagan era faction fights that race re-emerged as a salient theme in the national political conversation.

With the disappearance of the communist enemy, attention shifted increasingly to issues of national identity and culture, issues that were conflated to different degrees, depending on the particular right-wing tendency, with categories of race and ethnicity. Engagement in the so-called culture wars became the primary activity of the New Right during this period, a tempor-ary unifying strategy that leaders such as Paul Weyrich had been pushing as early as 1988, and which anticipated many of the themes and tactics that would come to characterize the new, more modern face of the Christian Right in the 1990s.[28] Racialized issues such as multiculturalism and 'political correctness' emerged as symbols around which a disunited New Right rallied in opposition, submerging their philosophical differences for a while in counter-counter-culturalist praxis.[29]

Almost as soon as the issue of race re-emerged in the political spotlight, however, divisions within the unsteady New Right coalition again manifested themselves. Disagreement over the question of the conflation of race and culture was one of the primary ingredients in the much publicized split between neo-conservatives and the self-proclaimed paleo-conservatives in the early 1990s, a division that remains salient in New Right circles to this day. While neo-conservatives continued to celebrate internationalism and the American Creed of individual rights and limited government, the rival paleo-conservatives distinguished themselves through their cultural/racial nationalist and isolationist agenda. Included in this agenda is opposition to US military intervention abroad and an expressed concern to uphold traditional morality and combat multiculturalism, affirmative action, and unrestricted black and Hispanic immigration at home. Paleo-conservative intellectuals such as Samuel Francis (editor of *Chronicles* magazine) and Patrick Buchanan (several-time Presidential candidate and nationally-syndicated columnist) spearheaded the drive to make cultural nationalism a centerpiece of public concern and public policy, repeatedly warning of the threat posed to white America by liberal racial policies and positively embracing the concepts of tribe and nation as constituent elements of a democratic polity.[30] In only a few short years, other paleo-conservative intellectuals such as Peter Brimelow (author of *Alien Nation*) and John O'Sullivan (former speech-writer for Margaret Thatcher and editor of *National Review*) would become almost household names. Although the division between paleo-conservatives and neo-conservatives seemed to repair itself temporarily in the run-up to the 1994 Republican landslide, politically and culturally this remains one of the biggest fissures within the increasingly fragmented New Right coalition.

Significantly, despite such rumblings of thunder on the horizon, the issue of race continued to be submerged beneath other less divisive issues throughout the early 1990s, an apparent victory for neo-conservatives keen to keep race off the national political agenda. Although the Bush administration's veto of the 1990 Civil Rights Act as a 'quota bill' indicated a growing willingness on the part of mainstream Republicans to make a frontal assault on liberal racial understandings, the Administration backed down and signed an almost identical bill in 1991 in the wake of the strong showing by David Duke in the 1990 Louisiana Congressional elections. The fact that the Administration's political will evaporated as soon as it became unclear that such a strategy would pay off at the electoral polls served only further to alienate New Rightists already disgruntled over the tenor of Republican Party policy in the post-Reagan era.

Only a few short months after the Los Angeles disturbances that had catapulted race to the center of US consciousness, speakers at the pre-election 1992 Republican Party Convention said almost nothing about race. Regarded as the most mean-spirited Republican Convention since 1964, when the Party nominated Barry Goldwater, race was conspicuously absent. Only Pat Buchanan dared break the taboo, albeit under the rhetorical cover of the culture war:

> Friends, this election is about more than who gets what. It is about who we are. It is about what we believe and what we stand for as Americans. There is a religious war going on in this country. It is a cultural war, as critical to the kind of nation we shall be as the Cold War itself, for this war is for the soul of America. And in this struggle for the soul of America, Clinton and Clinton are on the other side and George Bush is on our side ... Just as those boys took back the streets of Los Angeles, block by block, my friends, we must take back our cities and take back our culture and take back our country ... Just as we have led the crusade for democracy beyond our shores, we have a great task to do together in our own home.[31]

Instead, culture war themes related to family values were predominant, with speakers such as Pat Robertson and Dan Quayle lamenting the alleged liberal aim to destroy the traditional family. Delegates were quite explicit about the need to find new domestic enemies to replace anti-communism as a rallying cry against the Democrats, and these they found in the form of the unproductive, the un-Christian, and the un-straight.[32] In a prime-time address to the Convention, Pat Robertson tainted the Democratic Party with the image of being soft on a new menace, bureaucratic government:

> Seventy-five years ago a plague descended upon the world and covered the nations of Eastern Europe like a dark cloud. Slowly but surely this dreaded menace grew and spread until it threatened the freedom of the entire world. This menace was called Communism ... the Cold War is over and we won ... Ladies and gentlemen, a more benign but equally in-sidious plague has fastened itself upon the families of America. It is the belief that bureaucrats know more about managing people's affairs than the people do themselves. It is the belief that sweat and hard work and free enterprise are somehow suspect, a belief in higher taxes, crushing regu-lation, and centralized government. Ladies and gentlemen, the carrier of this plague is the Democratic Party.[33]

The bold public profile of the Christian Right at the 1992 Convention took many by surprise. Only a couple of years prior, pundits had announced the movement's political death, believing that it had been discredited beyond repair in the wake of such visible setbacks in the late 1980s as the scandals that had engulfed TV preachers Jim Bakker and Jimmy Swaggart, and Pat Robertson's relatively weak showing in the 1988 presidential primaries (even in the South where the most support was expected).[34] Moreover, by the late 1980s, many of the national headline organizations of the Christian Right had either disbanded or remained active in letter-head only.[35] While it was far from clear whether the moral posturing of the hard Right was a political asset rather than a liability *vis-à-vis* the electoral prospects of the GOP in 1992, it was at least certain that they now counted. As Sara Diamond writes,

> Gone were the days when born-again Christians shunned worldly affairs. Gone, too, were the days when Christian Right activists stood outside the halls of power, petitioning to get in. Now, at long last, they took their seats inside the Republicans' proverbial big tent. And they were there to stay.[36]

Indeed, by 1992 the Christian Right had emerged as the dominant faction within the New Right coalition in the United States. It was uniquely positioned to reap the benefits of two trends that characterized the post-Reagan/Cold War New Right: the shift to a focus on domestic issues such as abortion, gay rights, public art, and education ideology, and the philosophical infighting among the secular and intellectual wings of the New Right coalition.

Many had miscalculated the staying power of the Christian Right because its strategies had changed. During the 1990s, the Christian Right became more supple in tactics but still rigid in goals, as a new generation of leaders aimed to give the movement a softer, modern face. In 1990 *Policy Review* published an article by Thomas Atwood (a member of Pat Robertson's staff) entitled 'Through a Glass Darkly: Is the Christian Right Overconfident It Knows God's Will?', which warned against the authoritarian and intolerant streaks in Christian Right activity and argued that 'the best thing that could happen to the movement is for it to be less identifiable as a movement and have its people and its ideas percolate through the system'.[37] A few years later Ralph Reed of Pat Robertson's newly-formed Christian Coalition would reiterate similar themes in another article for *Policy Review* entitled 'Casting a Wider Net: Religious Conservatives Move Beyond Abortion and Homosexuality'. In this article, Reed urged leaders to broaden the issues agenda beyond policy-thin and value-laden moral issues so as to connect with average voter concerns in the areas of taxes, crime, government waste, health care, and financial security.[38] Moreover, the broadened issues agenda of the softer face of the Christian Right was augmented by a new quietist agenda which, while not really stealth, was orientated to grassroots local and state activity. Ralph Reed explains:

We believe that the Christian community in many ways missed the boat in the 1980s by focusing almost entirely on the White House and Congress when most of the issues that concern conservative Catholics and evangelicals are primarily determined in the city councils, school boards, and state legislatures.[39]

Throughout the early-to-mid 1990s, race did not appear to be a salient theme in right-wing politics. True, the issue was becoming increasingly salient in conservative intellectual circles with the publication of a range of biologically determinist tracts, the most notorious of which of course was *The Bell Curve* co-authored by Charles Murray, an established neo-conservative intellectual who had contributed to *Commentary* for decades.[40] But in terms of the agenda of the broader movement, now dominated by Christian Right groups such as the Christian Coalition and Focus on the Family, race was a secondary theme at best. Despite Reed's plea to 'cast a wider net', the most visible forms of Christian Right activity during the early-to-mid 1990s centered around the highly orchestrated pro-life demonstrations led by Operation Rescue and the controversial 'no special rights' anti-gay campaigns in Oregon and Colorado.[41] On race matters, the Christian Right engaged in selected activities, such as lobbying for the nomination of Judges Robert Bork and Clarence Thomas, both of whom are known public critics of affirmative action. Surprisingly, however, there was hardly a murmur around the controversial 1990/1991 Civil Rights Act (which eventually passed), perhaps because of the Right's general distrust and tepid support of the Bush administration.[42]

The most interesting development on the racial front involved a concerted attempt by Christian Right groups to link local and state campaigns in opposition to divisive social issues such as gay rights, abortion and welfare to a new effort to reach out to communities of color for support. In 1992, initiatives were launched in Oregon (Measure 9) and Colorado (Proposition 2) to overturn anti-bias laws to protect lesbians and gay men on the basis that they constituted undeserved 'special rights'. In both instances, a coalition of right-wing forces attempted to win the support of communities of color and the active participation of black and Hispanic church ministers by presenting themselves as the defenders of disadvantaged blacks and Hispanics against the encroachment of already privileged lesbians and gay men.[43] Then in the run-up to the 1993 school board elections in New York City, local Christian Right forces (the Christian Coalition, Concerned Parents for Educational Accountability, and the Family Defense Council) successfully mobilized an alliance of white middle-

class Catholics, evangelical Latinos and other socially conservative people of color against the Rainbow Curriculum, a
teacher's guide designed to help children understand the
diverse cultural, ethnic, family and religious backgrounds of
their fellow students.[44] Also unfolding during this period was a
series of racial reconciliation projects undertaken by various
conservative Christian churches and groups such as the
Promise Keepers.[45] Throughout these instances and others,
Ralph Reed of the Christian Coalition declared 'a genuinely
surprising level of support for the conservative, pro-family
agenda among Hispanics and African-Americans', pledged not
'to concede the minority community to the political left any
more', and professed his commitment to 'building a broad-
based, inclusive organization: Catholic, black, brown, yellow'.[46]
The Christian Coalition for one put its money where its mouth
was by appointing outreach people in California and Texas
to help court traditionally progressive black and Hispanic
voters and, arguably, to legitimize the coming attack on race
liberalism.

The attack did come, in the wake of the 1994 mid-term
election Republican landslide that secured Republican control
of both Houses of Congress for the first time in forty years.
As will be outlined below, the attack on so-called racial preferences came on practically all levels at once: legislative (the
Dole–Canady bill), grassroots (Proposition 187 and the
California Civil Rights Initiative), and intellectual (a range of
popular and academic books challenging the liberal pursuit
of racial equality). While many thought that race exploded on
to the national political landscape out of the blue, and while
New Rightists portrayed the backlash as a form of spontaneous
combustion of the 'natural' justice sentiments of 'angry white
males', the pre-history outlined above demonstrates that the
attack was long in coming. The sea-change in the national political mood, expressed most poignantly in the outcome of the
mid-term elections of 1994, signalled to the New Right that
the time was propitious to move race from an underground to
an above-ground issue. Moreover, conservative Republicans
now had the votes to do it.

Thus, the post-1994 attack on race liberalism is less an indication of a change in conservative strategy as it is the product
of a new political reality: the taboo subject of race is finally

being taken on by right-wing entrepreneurs of the white moral panic.[47] What was unthinkable in the 1980s became thinkable in the early 1990s, and politically realizable by the mid-1990s. The spell was broken by a combination of factors: most notably, the 1994 mid-term elections and the inauguration of the New Republicans, the success in 1994 of the anti-immigrant Proposition 187 in California and the introduction of the California Civil Rights Initiative in the run-up to the 1996 presidential elections, the explosion of black conservative publications and media personalities, and a range of new and revitalized counter-civil rights institutions willing and able to translate the new political mood into anti-anti-racist praxis.

No matter how you look at it, the outcome of the 1994 mid-term elections represents a big, big change in post-war US politics. Congress is now dominated by the most partisan and ideological Republican leaders in office at least since the Second World War. The Republican Party under the stewardship of Dick Armey (Majority leader) and Haley Barbour (Chairman of the Republican National Committee) is now more openly identified than at any time in recent memory with the kind of conservative ideas the New Right has been promoting for almost two decades. More than a mere public relations gimmick, the Contract With America has demonstrated that the issues agenda of the New Right is electorally viable. The upshot of all this has been to bring into being a new period of New Right politics more attuned to the difficulties of governing. Under the tutelage of seasoned New Rightists, conservative Republicans are returning to Politics 101. This has translated into a focus on institution-building and the revival of local Republican organizations as the Right has come to understand that there is more to winning than beating liberalism. Ironically, it is the New Republicanism that now embodies the insights of the symbolic conflict model by treating politics as symbolic warfare and arguing that the question of who gets what is less important than seizing the moral high ground in policy debates and engineering fundamental changes in the cultural sphere.[48]

A newly-configured coterie of Republican leaders has emerged to express the post-1994 conservative revolutionary mood.[49] Especially noteworthy is the coming-of-age of a second-generation neo-conservative phenomenon, or what some refer to as 'mini-cons', because several of the associated personalities are the sons of the first generation: William Kristol (son of Irving, former chief of staff to vice-president Dan Quayle and to William Bennett at the Department of Education, and now chairman of the Project for the Republican Future and editor at the *Weekly Standard*), John Podhoretz (son of Norman, former White House staff member under the Bush administration and now with the *Weekly Standard*), and Adam Bellow (son of Saul and editorial director at The Free Press). Dubbed the 'counter counterculture' by the *New York Times*, other important members include: David Frum (author of *Dead Right*), Danielle Crittenden (editor of the conservative *Women's Quarterly*), Lisa Schiffren (former speech writer for Quayle and architect of the Murphy Brown attack), James Golden (producer of the Rush Limbaugh television show), David Brock (with the *American Spectator*), Roger Kimball (cultural critic and editor for the *New Criterion*), and David Brooks (editor for the *Wall Street Journal* editorial page).[50] President Clinton has referred to William Kristol, undoubtedly a leading personality of the New Republicans, as the man who tells Republicans 'what to think up in Washington'.[51] As director of the Bradley Project in 1993, Kristol urged conservatives to embrace the concept of 'new citizenship' as a unifying principle for conservatives in the culture wars of the 1990s, and the concept indeed has been taken up by *Policy Review: The Journal of American Citizenship* as the centerpiece of their new format in 1996.[52] Besides Kristol's Project for the Republican Future, other newly-emergent organizations such as Empower America serve as strategic nerve centers for forging a coherent strategy for conservative reform.[53]

Yet, as the leadership battle for the 1996 presidential nomination demonstrated, no single charismatic articulator of the felt beliefs of the New Right has emerged to replace the breadth and vision of Ronald Reagan. Newt Gingrich, Speaker of the House, is perhaps the most notable exception, although he is clearly on the neo-liberal side of the divide. Gingrich refers to himself as a revolutionary and freely compares his mission to the way Vaclav Havel, Lech Walesa, and Boris Yeltsin brought down communism in their countries. His attacks on the Democratic Party are brutal and unrelenting. In the run-up to the 1994 elections, Gingrich called the Clintons the 'enemy of normal Americans' and 'countercultural McGovern-niks' and, with unblinking eyes, counselled voters that the way to prevent more Susan Smith killings (a young mother in South Carolina who murdered her two sons by drowning them in a car) was to vote Republican. In classical bullish Gingrich-style he said: 'We have to say to the counterculture: nice try, you failed, you're wrong. And we have to simply, calmly, methodically reassert American civilization.'[54]

In enacting their counter-counterculturalist agenda, New Rightists are demonstrating a fresh willingness to take on race as a new consensus issue. The fact that resentment of racial preferences and opposition to further (Hispanic) immigration was an apparently significant factor in leading a high proportion of white men to vote Republican in 1994 is a lesson not lost on New Republican leaders. The 'angry white male' factor (Republicans won 63 per cent of the white male vote in 1994), combined with an increasingly impatient Christian Right faction no longer willing to put its issues on the backburner and the new focus on domestic enemies in the post-Cold War era, is contributing to a new appreciation of the race issue as a battering ram against the Democrats.

Newly-emergent Republican strategists such as Grover Norquist (confidant of Gingrich, founder of Americans for Tax Reform, and leader of the 'Leave Us Alone' Coalition) viewed opposition to racial preferences as the definition of a perfect issue in the run-up to 1996: it united the Republican team, divided the Democrats, and it was worth winning.[55] According to Norquist, whereas conservatives have been on the defensive since the 1950s because of their lack of support for a color-blind society and as a result 'wet their pants whenever they thought about Selma and felt bad', it is now the Left that is on the defensive.[56] In his book on the 1994 elections titled *Rock the House*, Norquist argues that while Republicans favor treating everyone alike, it is the Democrats who now support government-funded bigotry:

Since the 1960s, the Democratic Party has become the party of racial quotas ... Americans have rightly rejected this racism by the Democrats as immoral, evil, and wrong. It is yet again another attempt by a faltering political Establishment to keep power by dividing Americans against each other.[57]

Norquist sees the issue of color-blind public policy (at the heart of the Dole–Canady bill introduced in the 1995 legislative session but put off until next year) as the Achilles heel of the Democratic Party, and calls for civil rights leaders willing to recover and uphold the original, color-blind principles of the civil rights movement.

Norquist's call to arms expresses a widespread sentiment in contemporary conservative circles that when it comes to the civil rights establishment, there is only one hand clapping.[58] While the New Right has built counter-establishments to fight the feminist and gay rights lobby, for example, virtually nothing exists on the civil rights front. Two important exceptions are the Institute for Justice and the National Center for Neighborhood Enterprise. Regarded as the ACLU of the Right, the Institute for Justice is a conservative public interest law firm founded in 1991 by Chip Mellor and Clint Bolick. As the Institute's vice-president and litigation director, Clint Bolick (former aide to Clarence Thomas at the Equal Employment Opportunity Commission [EEOC] and former director of the Landmark Center for Civil Rights) has fast become known as the conscience on civil rights in the conservative movement. During his tenure at the EEOC, Bolick opposed the use of quotas to resolve employment bias claims and represented Michigan teachers who charged they had been illegally laid off while minorities with less seniority kept their jobs, winning a 5–4 Supreme Court decision in 1986. More recently, Bolick has been recognized for his role in representing low-income parents in court defending the Milwaukee Parental Choice Program, and in leading the campaign to defeat the nomination of Lani Guinier for Assistant US Attorney General for Civil Rights by labelling her 'Clinton's Quota Queen'.[59]

Engaging in what he refers to as 'guerilla litigation', Bolick is leading a conservative legal counter-revolution by challenging regulatory barriers to entry-level entrepreneurial opportunities for people of color. Among his important victories are a lawsuit on behalf of a black entrepreneur – Ego Brown – in Washington DC, overturning a law that banned outdoor shoeshine stands, and another on behalf of a Muslim hairdresser – Taalib-Din Abdul Uqdah – challenging an ordinance that would have forced the hairdresser to close down his natural braiding business because his workers were not licensed cosmetologists. Framing his arguments for economic liberty by focusing on the little guy victimized by big government bureaucrats, Bolick has become increasingly effective in setting the terms of public debate. He has played a pivotal role in establishing the link between civil rights and empowerment that became a rhetorical staple of the Bush administration and now of the New Right Republicans. In 1991 he made the strategy crystal clear:

> if the GOP embraces empowerment in a big way, it could completely reverse the ordinary political equation. For once it will be Republicans who can go into the inner city offering tangibles – school choice, home ownership, jobs – while the Democrats argue about abstract intangibles … for once, the ball is in the Republicans' court on civil rights issues … the Republicans have the ideas and the momentum to shift the terms of the debate.[60]

In the wake of the 1994 elections, the Institute for Justice convened a briefing on Capitol Hill titled 'Looking Forward: A Strategy for Civil Rights and Empowerment' during which Bolick issued a call to end race and gender preferences in federal government policies and programs. Afterwards the Institute lauded the event as 'the first day of the new civil rights revolution' and, together with The Heritage Foundation, is co-sponsoring a working group to 'develop federal legislation and other approaches to curb government power to discriminate on the basis of race and gender'.[61]

The National Center for Neighborhood Enterprise, directed by Robert Woodson, has similarly attempted to forge coalitions with low-income people of color on a range of empowerment issues: among them, family preservation, economic development, alternative education, and crime prevention. Two of the Center's projects – the Neighborhood Leadership Institute and Americans For Self-Reliance – bring together successful grassroots leaders from across the country to share strategies for empowering low-income communities. Another Center project, the Neighborhood Capital Corporation, makes loans available to people of color who want to start a small business. It is interesting to note that in the wake of the failure on the part of the new Republican-controlled Congress force-fully to support school vouchers and the 1995 publication of *The End of Racism* by Dinesh D'Souza which he describes as 'Fuhrmanesque', Woodson appears to be distancing himself from the broader New Right movement.

> I feel they used me. The only time they [white conserva-tives] seem to show up was when there's a photo-op or a press conference ... I used to believe that a lot of my col-leagues were on the same page. I thought they believed that the purpose of political power was to empower the power-less to enrich the nation. But the moment [conservatives] got political power, they turned their back on some of us who were with them from the beginning. These are new revelations to me.[62]

Despite this apparent falling out, and probably in part a re-sponse to Gingrichs' remark that Farrakhan's 'Million Man March' represented a 'wake-up call to conservatives to reach out to the black community', Woodson has continued to meet with Republican lawmakers and strategists to discuss ways to disseminate and make more appealing the alternative GOP empowerment message.[63]

In 1995, there emerged for the first time a conservative think tank primarily concerned with issues related to race and public policy – the Center for Equal Opportunity (CEO) in Washington DC directed by Linda Chavez (former director of the US Commission on Civil Rights, former White House public liaison director, and author of *Out of the Barrios*), the CEO describes itself as 'the only think tank devoted exclusively to the promotion of colorblind equal opportunity and racial harmony ... and uniquely positioned to counter the divisive impact of race conscious public policies'.[64] The CEO has three focal points:

1. opposition to racial preferences in employment, edu-cation and voting;
2. promotion of immigration and assimilation policies that steer a middle ground between 'nativists who say that

today's immigrants cannot assimilate and multiculturalists who say that they should not'; and
3. opposition to multicultural and bilingual education policies that 'risk balkanizing our society'.

In its first year, the CEO sponsored debates and conferences on the California Civil Rights Initiative, bilingual education, and racial gerrymandering. Linda Chavez is emerging as a moderate voice of reason on civil rights among conservatives, and is highly regarded for her 1995 *Commentary* article on immigration policy, making the distinction between legal and illegal entries central and urging an assimilationist middle ground.[65] Less naïve than those who regard the attack on racial preferences as a simple consensus issue, Chavez recognizes the reluctance on the part of New Republican leaders to move beyond economic and family issues – in part because of the fear of being branded racist, but also because Republicans do not have clean hands on the issue – and is sure to be a key player when the issue resurfaces.[66]

If there are strategic divisions on the Right over the role of race in public policy, then why did the issue move to the above-ground post-1994 political landscape? The answer appears to turn on the white backlash that expressed itself in the form of the anti-immigration Proposition 187 on the 1994 California ballot and the California Civil Rights Initiative which fought its way on to the 1996 ticket in several states. Far from being an elite strategy to bring race above ground, the issue reared its head there from the bottom-up, and New Rightists decided to seize it. The success of Proposition 187 and the introduction of the California Civil Rights Initiative (CCRI) forced the few small right-wing think tanks concerned with race and public policy, for the most part lacking any appeal to broad-based organizations, to confront some difficult issues and at the same time choose sides. These issues are being argued out now, in the context of an apparent groundswell of public opposition to (Hispanic) immigration and so-called racial preferences.

In November 1994, California citizens voted overwhelmingly (a 59 per cent majority) for the 'Save Our State' initiative, or what came to be known as Proposition 187. The initiative supported a constitutional amendment to deny undocumented immigrants education, social services, and non-emergency health care, and represented one of the most mean-spirited public policy proposals this century. Under the Proposition's terms, educators, social workers, health professionals, and law enforcement agents would be required to report suspected illegal immigrants and their families to the appropriate governmental authorities. California Governor Pete Wilson made Proposition 187 a cornerstone of his successful re-election campaign, with many attributing his re-election to his backlash-pandering positions on immigration and affirmative action. Although it is certainly legitimate in a liberal society to entertain open debate about the merits and proper levels of immigration, the national conversation revolved around the illiberal premise that misguided welfare policies were serving as a magnet attracting a flood of unassimilable illegal immigrants from Mexico and elsewhere in Latin America and the Caribbean.[67] Despite contradictory evidence in the social science literature regarding the economic and social impact of immigration, supporters of Proposition 187 portrayed immigrants as 'welfare schemers', 'embezzlers of public funds', and as responsible for stealing jobs and worsening social problems such as crime, thus feeding into a long cycle of scapegoating immigrants during periods of economic strain. Although the amendment is now tied up in the judicial system due to concerns over its constitutionality, its successful passage led to vigorous debates within New Right circles, with neo-liberals writing for the *Wall Street Journal* favoring open borders, neoconservatives in the pages of *Commentary* supporting a policy of assimilation for legal entrants, and paleoconservatives such as Peter Brimelow advocating a fortress America against any further dilution of the nation's white racial stock.

Conveniently, in the midst of this ruckus, a lowest common denominator issue, one that had the potential to unite movement conservatives and the backlash sentiments of 'angry white males', manifest itself in the form of the California Civil Rights Initiative (CCRI). Two California-based academics – Tom Wood (adjunct philosopher and executive director of the California Association of Scholars) and Glynn Custred (tenured anthropologist at California State University at Hayward) – had long been trying to make opposition to racial preferences a matter of priority in public debate, with little success. Suddenly, in 1995, their Civil Rights Initiative became the center of gravity on civil rights, not only for conservatives but for the nation at large. Sometimes referred to as the 'son of 187', the CCRI reads as an almost exact quote from the 1964 Civil Rights Act, except for one small phrase about preferential treatment:

> Neither the State of California nor any of its political subdivisions or agents shall use race, sex, color, ethnicity or national origin as a criterion for either discriminating against, *or granting preferential treatment to,* any individual or group in the operation of the State's system of public employment, public education or public contracting.[68]

Should the initiative, which won voter approval, be declared constitutional by the courts where it is correctly being deliberated, it would essentially outlaw affirmative action in public university admissions, state employment, and minority set-aside contracts. Despite its constitutional air, Mr Wood has made it clear that the initiative is about backlash:

> Count me among those angry men. I know the sting of affirmative action. I was once passed over for a teaching job because, I was told privately, I was white and male. It didn't count that I was the most qualified. Well, we're going to put a stop to this. The worm has turned.[69]

Such sentiments were nothing new; indeed, only a few years before this academics such as Fred Lynch (professor of government at Claremont–McKenna College and author of *Invisible Victims: White Males and the Crisis of Affirmative Action*) articulated almost exact persuasions but were silenced by general ill-regard. Thus, the CCRI is significant not because it expresses something new but because sentiments that were previously regarded as marginal have become mainstream. This normalization of the white moral panic around 'reverse racism', long championed by the New Right, demonstrates the resonance of the new racism in contemporary US politics. Opponents of so-called preferential treatment have learned to soften their arguments by portraying such policies as unconstitutional and detrimental to the best interests of the nation, including people of color. Supported by prominent black spokesmen like Shelby Steele (author of *The Content of Our Character*) and Ward Connerly (a member of the University of California Board of Regents), the CCRI has served to unite otherwise fragmented New Rightists behind the lowest common denominator support for color-blind public policy.

In the meantime, the debate over what is to replace color-blindness once racial preferences are abolished is being argued out in New Right intellectual circles. Although neo-conservatism as an intellectual movement has long faded, a storm of conservative publications challenging liberal egalitarianism has appeared in the wake of the media attention granted to *The Bell Curve*. The first to appear on the racial front was *Alien Nation* by Peter Brimelow, who, in making his argument about the need to restrict black and Hispanic immigration, insists that there is nothing wrong with bringing racial consciousness into the public policy debate. This motif, and in particular the link between race and culture posited throughout the book, has fallen into general disfavor in wider New Right circles, indicating that 'the paleos are being outed'.[70]

Other books, such as *Naked Racial Preference* by Carl Cohen (philosopher at the University of Michigan) and *The End of Racism* by Dinesh D'Souza (senior fellow at the American Enterprise Institute (AEI) and author of *Illiberal Education: The Politics of Race and Sex on Campus*) make the more palatable argument that the meaning of justice is important for a democracy to work out and, accordingly, race should not be kept out of the arena of public policy debate. D'Souza argues that racism has been all but eradicated in US public life, save its appearance as an episodic, nuisance phenomenon.[71] In other words, according to D'Souza, justice has been served: the task now is to focus attention on what the civil rights movement neglected; that is, making people of color competitive in the professional and academic market. The dilemma for D'Souza is to establish a public framework of race neutrality combined with a campaign in the private sector (led primarily by people of color) to raise merit standards, a proposal that in practice would imply the gutting of Title VII of the Civil Rights Act.[72] The victim-blaming tone of D'Souza's book was so offensive to some in the conservative community that its publication led to the disaffiliation of prominent black conservatives Bob Woodson and Glenn Loury from the AEI, where D'Souza is a research fellow. Woodson denounced the author as 'the Mark Fuhrman of public policy' and called on conservatives to 'publicly disavow the racist ideology' his book espouses:

> This is a moment of truth for the conservative movement as to where they stand on the issue of race. The only time you hear from white conservatives is when there is a white fireman aggrieved over affirmative action. If they want to have any influence in this area, they have got to speak out when blacks and Hispanics are aggrieved. This is one such occasion.[73]

The argument that merit and not racism is now primarily responsible for race inequality is a popular theme in the explosion of recent publications by black conservatives. Although black conservatives received media attention throughout the 1980s for their criticism of the alleged destructive cycle of dependency fostered by liberal social programs, they only became a phenomenon in the wake of the attack on the nomination of Supreme Court Justice Clarence Thomas.[74] In 1995 and 1996 alone, nearly a dozen books were published by well-known black conservatives, united by their conviction that racism, if not quite a thing of the past, is at least not responsible for black failure.[75] The major obstacle to further racial progress is not white racism and the unjust economic arrangements that feed it, black conservatives argue, but rather the lack of self-development within the black community. Glenn Loury (an economist at Boston University) writes,

> What is important to the alleviation of black poverty and racism is not the economic structure of the United States, nor the racist behavior of whites, but African Americans' behavior. Further progress toward the attainment of equality depends most crucially at this juncture on the acknowledgment of the dysfunctional behaviors which plague black communities and so offend others.[76]

Affirmative action programs are criticized for having caused people of color to focus more on government handouts than

on their own self-development, and that the resulting dependency culture has further hindered their prospects for upward
mobility. This perspective has offered a clear meeting point
for New Rightists interested in recruiting prominent people
of color to lead their cause, a sound objective according to the
likes of Walter Williams (black neo-conservative and Hoover
Institute scholar) who writes, 'I have no doubt that blacks are
about to become the staunchest conservative group in
America, and the why is that liberalism has done to blacks
what slavery, Jim Crowism and the rankest racism combined
could never have done.'[77]

Although black conservatism is primarily an intellectual
phenomenon, new dimensions have emerged amid growing
signs of diversity amongst black voters and disenchantment
with the liberal agenda. Deborah Toler has documented the
involvement of black conservatives in the Reagan and Bush
administrations, the emergence of a few prominent black conservative women, and even a faction of black conservatism
closely associated with the religious-orientated traditional
values movement.[78] More recently, a group calling itself
Project 21 emerged in the wake of the 1992 Los Angeles disturbances to give black conservatives a national voice, and to
counter what is regarded as increasingly out of touch black
leaders.[79] In 1995 the group issued a call for a Contract With
Black America which, among other things, urged Congress to
hold hearings in inner-city communities in search of long-
term solutions to the problems that disproportionately affect
black Americans. Speaking in defense of the idea, Stephen
Craft (a member of Project 21) says, 'The word conservative in
black people's minds raises up a red flag of kooks and the Ku
Klux Klan. The white conservative movement has a responsibility to correct some of these images. Stop putting us in the
corner, in the dark. We're ready to go on the front lines.'[80]
The Center for New Black Leadership is the newest organization to emerge (founded in 1995), and is similarly orientated
to advocating alternatives to those traditionally favored by the
so-called civil rights establishment, such as school vouchers
and enterprise zones. An advertisement for the Center appearing in *Issues and Views* states: 'Our goal is to develop and
strengthen sound ideas and institutions consistent with our
community's long-held commitments to individual initiative

and personal responsibility'. New Republican black politicians such as J. C. Watts (Oklahoma) and Gary Franks (Connecticut) are bringing this alternative voice into the Halls of Congress, helping to legitimate the retreat from racial equality in key legislative areas.

Finally, a range of new black conservative publications has joined the more established *Lincoln Review* and *Issues and Views*. Perhaps the most important is *National Minority Politics* (*NMP*), a monthly publication that features black and Hispanic conservative columnists. Founded in 1994 by the Houston-based couple, Willie and Gwen Richardson, *NMP* presents itself as a clearing-house for moderate black and Hispanic conservatives concerned to reverse what is regarded as the social pathology so prevalent in most black and Hispanic inner-city neighborhoods. In 1995, the Richardsons founded what aims to be a broad-based conservative organization called Minority Mainstream. With a self-stated objective of giving the mostly white conservative wing of the new GOP majority a black and Hispanic presence, Minority Mainstream has already begun mobilizing in favor of color-blind public policy, welfare reform, and economic opportunity issues. For example, although generally supportive of the New Republicans, Minority Mainstream has publicly criticized the Contract With America for not going far enough to remove long-time welfare recipients from the public payroll, and has countered with a proposal to phase out the current welfare system over five years.[81] Add to these media outfits the popularity of black conservative radio and television personalities such as Armstrong Williams, a nationally-syndicated talk show host, public relations executive, and regular contributor to the *Washington Times*. Regarded as a mega-multi-media wonderkid, Williams hosts a nightly radio show 'The Right Side', during which he rehearses now familiar claims: that blacks are duped by power hungry civil rights leaders who create the politics of grievance rather than manage the politics of solution, that welfare operates as a new plantation system, and that the answer to current problems in the black community is to celebrate the value of personal responsibility.[82] Clearly the latest media phenomenon on the right after Rush Limbaugh, Weyrich's National Empowerment Television – dubbed 'C-Span with an attitude' – recently has signed Williams to host 'The Armstrong Williams Show'.

In summary, the divisions that had traditionally marked the right wing in the United States receded in the mid-to-late 1970s and early 1980s, as a whole constellation of secular-political, religious, and intellectual conservatives came together under the umbrella of the New Right. Although meaningful differences re-emerged during Reagan's first term and upon his exit from office, these forces arguably continue to act as a hegemonic coalition today, helping to reshape the general climate of opinion in favor of conservative policy solutions. Armed with a new-found if tenuous conservative unity, the New Right has set out to stem the tide of what it sees as the political and cultural dislocation caused by liberal New Deal and Great Society programs and, in the process, to consolidate a new conservative majority. Thus, while attention to the stylistic and other significant differences that distinguish each strand of the New Right from one another and across time is in all respects valid, it need not obscure the wider networks of meaning that they together share and reinforce.

THE NEW RACISM: KEY CATEGORIES OF MEANING

On race matters, the New Right has brought to the center of national debate a set of shared assumptions and beliefs that has affected both popular attitudes and the direction of government policy formation. Again, meaningful differences exist, on this as on other controversial issues. While the secular-political wing of the New Right employs codewords to exploit growing white racial anxieties for electoral gain, neo-conservative intellectuals, by contrast, are engaged in serious intellectual debate with regard to the meaning of equal protection of the law in a multiracial society. Such divisions have been augmented in the 1990s by strategic fissures among New Rightists united in their opposition to liberal preferentialism, but confused about the proper nature and limits of color-blindness. While anti-discrimination has provided a useful rhetorical tool in building opposition to race-conscious policies such as affirmative action, the current brawl over the question of immigration indicates that there is no clear consensus regarding what is to replace them. Nevertheless, despite such fault lines, the New Right coalition is united in the attempt to link race with national decline, cultural disarray, and the apparent failure, even destructiveness, of liberal social policy – all the while eschewing explicit racism and reaching out to communities of color for support.

The conflation of race with criticism of liberal social policy remains a crucial element in the New Right's struggle to mobilize cross-class support for their conservative agenda. In doing so, the New Right has put into circulation a range of meanings and interpretations described here as a form of the new racism. Race has not therefore 'declined in significance' in US society, as suggested by William Julius Wilson's now well-known thesis. Rather, racism has changed along with trans-forming social relations. It is less explicit today than it was in the past, and is submerged beneath a broader range of issues. Most importantly, racism today has less to do with the articula-tion of a set of prejudiced attitudes, coded or not, than with the rearticulation of very general philosophical tenets long es-tablished within the liberal tradition. The key categories of meaning emphasized in New Right discourse in the United States are identified and discussed below.

Color-blindness

Color-blindness, a key category of meaning emphasized in New Right racial discourse, implies the belief that government should disregard race as a factor when determining policy. As Charles Murray writes:

> My proposal for dealing with the racial issue ... is to repeal every bit of legislation and reverse every court decision that in any way requires, recommends, or awards differential treatment according to race ... We may argue about the ap-propriate limits of government intervention in trying to enforce the ideal, but at least it should be possible to iden-tify the ideal: Race is not a morally admissible reason for treating one person differently from another. Period.[83]

Responding to the 1991 Civil Rights Act, Paul Weyrich comments,

> The time is right to seize the initiative and chart a new course for the future. That course should be a bold policy

agenda of opportunity based on a foundation of non-discrimination. America must say no once and for all to the notion that race is a legitimate basis for decisions in employment, government benefits, housing, education and the like. Discrimination on the basis of race is immoral, and if it is morally wrong, it cannot be politically right.[84]

Rush Limbaugh advises that race should 'no longer be a criterion either for discriminating against or giving preferential treatment to anybody'.[85] Similarly lauding the CCRI, Edward Erler (political scientist and senior fellow at the Claremont Institute) comments,

> A racial classification that is designed to benefit rather than disadvantage a member of a 'discrete and insular' minority is no less offensive to constitutional principles. There can never be a racial preference without a corresponding racial injury. Equal protection of the laws, properly understood, does not allow for the consideration of racial classes. The rule of law demands race neutrality.[86]

The color-blind approach rests on the argument that in order for racial discrimination and inequality to be eliminated, it is necessary that government policy treat individuals qua individuals – that is, on the 'content of their character', not the color of their skin. This means that, in formulating policy, rewards must be based upon personal merit – and penalties according to the lack of it – irrespective of the individual's race.

The color-conscious approach, by contrast, shares the vision of the good society wherein racial differences will be of no consequence, at least from the perspective of government policy formation, but differs over the question of the means to achieve such a laudable end. For the advocate of color-conscious policies, it is necessary to pay attention to race as a means to eradicate it as a differentiating factor. That is to say, only when policies are pursued that positively aid subordinated racial groups in achieving parity with their white counterparts will the material basis for the perception of racial difference – a perception which itself helps to maintain the system of racial inequality – be eliminated. Examples of color-conscious policies in the United States include: affirmative

action, Headstart, the Comprehensive Employment and
Training Act (CETA), minority set-aside business contracts,
and procedures to ensure that federally-funded entities (such
as schools or private employees) are obliged to make race-
conscious enrolment or employment decisions. Thus, rather
than being based upon the absence of the ability to see color,
the color-conscious approach emphasizes presence – that is,
the ability to view an individual as part of a racial group. Only
with such an ability, argues the advocate of color-conscious
remedies, is it possible to address compelling social needs
(that is, the elimination of racial inequality).

It is interesting to note the historical trajectory within which
these two approaches are situated. The color-blind approach
was once the exclusive position of liberals and anti-racists in
the United States. In the decades preceding the Civil Rights
Act of 1964, liberals argued for individuals to be treated
without regard to their race in their drive to abolish the system
of Jim Crow. Paradoxically, in recent years, it is conservatives
who have been the main purveyors of this former liberal ideology. According to Chester Finn, an Assistant Secretary of
Education in the Reagan administration and Professor of
Education and Public Policy at Vanderbilt University, the
color-blind vision is:

> rooted in the Enlightenment ideas that undergird American
> democracy; in the thirteenth, fourteenth, fifteenth and
> nineteenth Amendments to the Constitution; in the civil
> rights legislation of the 1860s and 1870s; in a series of
> Supreme Court decisions beginning with Brown *v.* Board of
> Education; and, especially, in the Civil Rights Act of 1964,
> that great congressional mandate for equal individual
> opportunity within a color-blind society.[87]

In the present historical context, however, the rhetoric of
color-blindness assumes a whole new meaning. As previously
discussed, the civil rights movement, especially in its later and
more radical phase, succeeded in winning a government commitment not only to the formal right of individual equality of
opportunity, but also a commitment to notions of group rights
and equal outcome. (Interestingly, it was the Commerce

Clause, not the Reconstruction Amendments or the 1964 Civil Rights Act, which provided the legal basis for such a commitment.) More than a decade of struggle had thus rendered the concept of color-consciousness a progressive symbol. Against such a historical backdrop, the New Right's advocation of a color-blind vision, via recourse to a literal translation of the Reconstruction Amendments and the 1964 Civil Rights Act, transforms what was previously a progressive vision into a reactionary one. It is reactionary since, in the present historical context, the concept of color-blindness seeks to call a halt to gains won during the past and continuing struggle for racial equality and bring about a retreat.

The appropriation of color-blind discourse by conservatives is ironic, indeed. Whereas in the decades prior to the civil rights era the undeniable intention of the color-blind discourse demands that individuals be treated irrespective of their race was to eliminate the institutional and legal barriers to racial inclusion and progress, its function in recent decades has been to put at least some of those obstacles back in place. This is the import of the New Right insistence that the government's commitment to pursue equality for subordinate racial groups has gone too far in making real this commitment via the pursuit of a version of positive action orientated to the goal of equal results or statistical parity.

Yet, color-conscious policies such as affirmative action have been developed not as a function of discriminatory intent, but rather in the face of the almost complete failure of the abstract guarantee of individual equality of opportunity to deliver any positive results. In the context of institutional relations of inequality and cultural disadvantage, policies of positive action seem the only (temporary) means to achieve any results at all. As Supreme Court Justice Blackmun wrote in his dissenting opinion in the Bakke 'reverse discrimination' case:

> I suspect that it would be impossible to arrange an affirmative action program in a racially neutral way and have it be successful. To ask that this be so is to demand the impossible. In order to get beyond racism, we must first take account of race. There is no other way. And in order to treat some persons equally, we must treat them differently.[88]

Importantly, such sentiments are sometimes echoed in the writing of black neo-conservatives, indicating the fragile nature of the New Right coalition. For example, Glenn Loury is now voicing criticism of race neutrality as a public ideal,

> The principle of public action can hardly claim general validity if, by adhering to it, it becomes impossible to correct the consequences of its violation ... the principle of race neutrality is generally inconsistent in just this way. Historical departure from equal opportunity in economic transactions, together with ongoing social segmentation along racial lines, generally means that in the absence of further departures from race neutrality, the implication of the initial violation will be permanent inequality between racial groups.[89]

Loury concludes, 'To be blind to color, given our history and our social structure, may well mean that one must be blind to justice as well.'

Despite such emerging fissures, the abstract liberal principle of color-blindness continues to unite most factions of the New Right coalition, although divisions over its precise meaning are sure to come to the surface if and when legislation such as the California Civil Rights Initiative (Proposition 196) emerges successfully from the court battles where they are currently embroiled. True to the spirit of the new racism, the rhetorical tool of anti-discrimination, absent anti-black sentiment or prejudice, allows New Rightists to oppose key items on the black agenda while adhering to dominant constitutional principles and cultural codes.

Equality

Closely linked to the key category of color-blindness is that of equality, and New Rightists make what they consider to be a crucial distinction between contending interpretations of it. The need for government to equalize individual opportunities for all (that is, irrespective of the individual's race) is affirmed, yet 'preferential treatment' for people of color is opposed. A distinction is thus drawn between *equal treatment* defined in terms of individual opportunity, and *equal outcome* defined in terms of group rights for people of color.

This distinction forms the basis of the position elaborated by the Heritage Foundation in *Mandate For Leadership,* which argues that it is correct for government to seek civil rights protections as legislated in Title VII of the 1964 Civil Rights Act, yet misguided for it to strive for racial parity through the redistribution of economic, political and/or educational resources as mandated by the 1965 Executive Order 11246.[90] New Rightists insist that the duty of government is to remove the barriers obstructing the road to racial equality, not guarantee that racial equality be achieved in fact. As Charles Murray quips, 'Billions for equal opportunity, not one cent for equal outcome.'[91]

New Rightists believe in a society in which individuals rise and fall in the social hierarchy on the basis of individual merit. Indeed, the acceptance of inequality as a social inevitability, even a social good, is a definitive hallmark of the right wing. Irving Kristol warns: 'The kind of liberal egalitarianism so casually popular today will, if it is permitted to gather momentum, surely destroy the liberal society.'[92] In *The Bell Curve,* Herrnstein and Murray write, 'Affirmative action, in education and the workplace alike, is leaking poison into the American soul ... It is time for America once again to try living with inequality, as life is lived ...'[93] And in his book *In Defense of Elitism,* William Henry argues that it is wrong to cling to what he refers to as the 'myth of egalitarianism', and, in a chapter titled 'Affirmative Confusion', sets out to debunk the liberal assumptions that everyone is or should be alike, and that all cultures and races are equal.[94]

It is from this wider perspective that the New Right opposes affirmative action guidelines that impose quotas, goals or timetables, and which thereby deem underutilization or underrepresentation as sufficient proof of discrimination. The point of such guidelines is to ensure effort on the part of employers, but New Rightists charge that such guidelines run counter to the ideal of equal protection. According to Tom Wood, head of the California Association of Scholars and co-architect of the California Civil Rights Initiative, 'Affirmative action fundamentally violates the principle that everyone deserves equal protection under the law without regard to membership in any group.'[95] Andrew Sullivan, former editor of *The New Republic*, writes,

> Liberalism was once the creed that said you were equal before the law. Parentage, gender, race, religion: none of that mattered. The individual citizen was what counted. Now, in extending the power of government further and further, in regulating the precise percentages of racial and other minorities in a whole range of activities and places, liberalism has become the very force it was born to oppose.[96]

The 1964 Civil Rights Act is drawn upon to support the New Right's argument that government need only ensure equal opportunity, not guarantee equal results. Title VII (Section 703 (i)) of the 1964 Civil Rights Act states:

> Nothing contained in this title shall be interpreted to require any employer ... to grant preferential treatment to any individual or to any group because of the race, color, religion, sex, or national origin of such individual or group on account of an imbalance which may exist with respect to the total number or percentage of persons of any race, color, religion, sex or national origin employed by any employer.

The statutory language lends legitimacy to the New Right's conviction that it is only moral and just to legislate against discrimination defined as wilful action.

The corollary is that the goal of statistical parity (that is, quotas, goals, timetables) is unconstitutional. New Rightists argue that government should forbid all deliberate racial discrimination, including forms of positive action for people of color, save only in cases where such attention to race is necessary to give redress to those individuals who themselves have been the victims of discrimination. In an article for *Commentary*, Carl Cohen states boldly, 'One purpose only may justify numerical schemes using racial categories: the making whole of those to whom redress for racial injury is specifically owed, by those who owe it'.[97] Thus, the New Right adheres to a highly individualistic conception of compensation for racial injustice.

New Rightists draw a firm distinction between permissible remedy for past discrimination (to the individual) and impermissible racial preference (for people of color as a group). In an essay entitled 'Fair Shakers and Social Engineers', Morris Abram decries the shift in the early 1970s from the 'fair-shake' principle of equal opportunity to the 'social engineer's' concept of proportional representation of ethnic groups as the institutionalization of a 'crude spoils system' and 'color-coded group rights' inconsistent with the US civil rights tradition of color-blindness.[98] Edward Erler argues, 'the notion of individual rights cannot coexist with the notion of equal results. An injustice is certainly perpetrated when those who are equal are treated unequally, but this is no less true when those who are unequal are treated as if they were equal.'[99]

By arguing that a meritocratic system is the only basis of legitimate governmental authority, the New Right arguably masks the politics of tokenism as the pursuit of equality. Adherence to the principle of equal opportunity is used to justify inequality in the United States by reaffirming the belief that anyone can 'make it' as long as they try hard enough. The achievements of the growing black middle class are emphasized and the opportunity structure is itself deemed open and fair. The disproportionate failure of people of color to achieve social mobility speaks nothing of the justice of present social arrangements, according to the New Right worldview, but rather reflects the lack of merit or ability of people of color themselves. In this way, attention is deflected away from the reality of institutional racism and towards, for example, the 'culture of poverty', the 'drug culture', or the lack of black self-development.

While there is some degree of merit to conservative arguments, in the sense that individual ambition and ability are of course an important ingredient for achievement and success (however defined), the New Right attempts to delegitimate government efforts to eliminate racial inequality, suggesting that all that is required is that we change the attitudes and habits of the disadvantaged, and failing that, institute a policy of 'benign neglect'.[100] Since inequality is merely an inevitable consequence of differences in individuals' *natural* or inherited abilities, according to New Rightists, it is impossible to eradicate it below its *natural* level, and wrong for government to attempt to do so. Thus, by relocating the cause of inequality from the social structure to individual ability, the New Right arguably naturalizes racial inequality. In this way, the New Right transforms the ideology of egalitarianism from a weapon critical of the (inegalitarian) status quo to an ideological crutch in support of it.

In the last few years, the attempt to circumvent the meaning of egalitarianism has given way to a frontal assault on the very notion that equality should be an aim of public policy, thus exposing the morbid underside of the New Right's defense of equal opportunity. The publication of *The Bell Curve* by Richard Herrnstein and Charles Murray is only the most extreme example of the argument that intellectuals and policymakers have overlooked the role intelligence plays in determining wealth, poverty and social status.[101] Murray and Herrnstein argue that the United States is becoming dangerously polarized between a smart, rich and educated 'cognitive elite' and an unintelligent, poor and uneducated 'underclass'. As regards race matters, the authors argue that the disproportionately black and Hispanic underclass suffers from an intelligence deficit, with little for government to do in terms of creating equality between groups distinguished by race and/or class. Armed with what Murray jokingly calls 'the 800-pound gorilla in the corner', the authors present evidence to prove that blacks and Hispanics as a group are intellectually inferior to whites and, on this basis, call for the outright abolition of the welfare system and for limitations to be placed on affirmative action. Although the authors feign uncertainty as to whether this intelligence deficit is due to genetic or environmental factors, they speculate that 'the evidence eventually may become equivocal that genes are also part of the story'.[102]

Publication of *The Bell Curve* represents a new face, if a controversial one, of the New Right assault on liberal egalitarianism in the 1990s. The arguments presented in the book signal a shift from a focus on the 'dysfunctional' behaviors of the poor that riveted the attention of most underclass warriors in the 1980s (including Murray), to low IQ as the explanatory variable for many important negative social and economic indicators in the black and Hispanic community. While the so-called dependency culture previously served as the ideological articulator of the conservative assault on the welfare state and its associated democratic values, now it is the alleged genetically-constituted intelligence deficit of the black and Hispanic underclass that is justifying more aggressive policies of benign neglect. Evoking what he calls a 'wise ethnocentrism', Murray cheerily imagines 'a world in which the glorious hodgepodge of inequalities of ethnic groups ... can be not only accepted but celebrated.'[103] Dubbed an 'intellectual snake charmer', Murray plays into widespread public anxieties over crime, illegitimacy and racial friction, all the while vehemently denying that he is a racist. The effect of Herrnstein and Murray's foray into the terrain of racial determinism has been to make conservative arguments about the government's role *vis-à-vis* the pursuit of race and class equality, regarded as extremist less than a decade ago, appear mainstream.

Individualism

While conservatives like Ronald Reagan and Barry Goldwater opposed the 1964 Civil Rights Act on the ground that it trammeled individual rights, today's New Right opposes liberal race equality policies with the same argument. The New Right interprets civil rights legislation as granting rights to individuals and not social categories. Indeed, within the individualistic logic of the US Constitution, such an interpretation makes perfect sense. The corollary to the New Right insistence that individual citizens (not groups) possess rights is that individuals should be judged on the basis of merit and not group membership. From this logic, the concept of group entitlement upon which anti-racist policies such as affirmative action or school busing are based is rendered illegitimate. Thus do legislative and sometimes constitutional principles provide a basis upon which New Right symbolic conflict over the meaning of racial progress is waged.

The conviction that rights are possessed by individuals and not groups derives from the supreme if not uniquely American belief in the primacy of the individual. Accordingly, in no instance should one individual's rights be greater or lesser than anothers' because of race, gender, national origin or any other inherited characteristic. It follows from such an individualistic conceptualization that the notion of group entitlements has no place in US political culture. Society, according to the US Constitution, is an aggregate of individuals. The role of law is to ensure the protection of the natural rights of individuals. As the Supreme Court wrote in Shelly *v.* Kraemer 334 US 1, 22 (1948): 'The rights created by the first section of the Fourteenth Amendment are, by its terms, guaranteed to the individual. The rights established are personal rights'. Carl Cohen puts it thus:

> The appealing argument by which so many are persuaded makes the faulty supposition that, if X has gained fortuitously but undeservedly from some unidentifiable Y, we are morally justified in taking from him and giving to a wholly different Z who suffered no loss to X's benefit, but who happens to be of the same race as that injured but unidentifiable Y. Buried in this reasoning process is the mistaken premise that the distribution of goods and opportunities is rightly made by racial categories. Z, the person now given preference over X because of race, has a right to get from him (this premise presupposes) because Z is black, and blacks have been so long oppressed. *But rights do not and cannot inhere in skin-color groups. Individuals have rights, not races.* It is true, of course, that many persons have been cruelly deprived of rights simply because of their blackness. Whatever the remedy all such persons deserve, it is deserved by those injured and because of their injury; nothing is deserved because of the color of one's skin.[104]

Similarly, Linda Chavez offers the following response to a dilemma posed by William Raspberry in the *Washington Post* about how to fix the score of a basketball game where referees cheat during the first half of the game, 'My response is simple: Award points to players who were robbed of baskets in the first half. In other words, compensate the victims of discrimination. Award specific remedies to specific individuals who suffered from specific acts.'[105]

In a political culture that adheres to the belief that individuals may swing their arms however they please as long as they do not hit the nose of another, there exists scant room for the competing conception of society as an aggregate of competing and compelling social needs, or for a more positive conception of freedom. It follows from the individualistic logic described above that, according to the New Right, color-conscious remedies are counter to individual equality of opportunity as guaranteed by Title VII of the Civil Rights Act. Moreover, the embrace of the concept of individual rights allows New Rightists to distance themselves from the blatant racism of those on the Far Right who resist integration as a public good. For example, Adam Meyerson writes, 'Conservative Republicans are opposed to quotas precisely because we're against people like David Duke. We are explicitly for integration and civil rights for everyone – but civil rights based on individual characteristics, not genetic code.'[106]

The New Right understands color-conscious remedies as a denial of the promise of equal rights for all individuals, and that they in effect make the rights of people of color *more equal* than those of white people. In explaining the differences between what he describes as the competing philosophies of 'tribalism' and 'personalism', Russell Nieli (part-time lecturer in the Department of Politics at Princeton University and editor of an Ethics and Public Policy volume on the affirmative action debate entitled *Racial Preference and Racial Justice*), writes:

> The personalistic perspective ... is incompatible with any kind of group-think that attempts to wrench the center of Meaning and Mystery out of individual persons, and transfer it to a nation, a tribe, a class, or any other collective entity conceived as a mysterious Super-Person.[107]

Or as William Bradford Reynolds, a leading ultra-conservative on racial matters and head of the Justice Department's Civil Rights Division under Reagan, states: 'We are all – each of us – a minority in this country: a minority of one.'[108]

In his book *Ethnic Dilemmas*, neo-conservative author Nathan Glazer similarly supports individual over group conscious policies, thus mandating that public policy be 'group-blind' as well as color-blind. 'I would place individual rights at the center, and groups would then exist only as the result of the free choice of individuals, and the existence of a group would derive no advantage in public law for its members.'[109] Glazer continues and asks:

Is it possible for all groups to take the route of individual rights, trusting to the opportunities offered by a free and open and tolerant society? Or are we doomed, now that we have abandoned the state exercise of discrimination, to keep groups down, to the state exercise of discrimination to prop them up?[110]

In a *Commentary* article titled 'Individualism Before Multiculturalism', Glenn Loury asks, 'Why should we care about group inequality per se? Why not focus on inequality among individual persons, and leave it at that?'.[111]

Ironically, it is the New Right that has succeeded in presenting itself as heir to Martin Luther King's call that society judge an individual by the content of his character, not the color of his/her skin. Quota-critic Frederick Lynch, a self-described flaming moderate, writes:

The academic and intellectual communities which once embraced Martin Luther King's call to judge an individual by the content of his character, not the color of his skin, now do precisely the opposite. They bow reverentially to the gods of tribalism.[112]

This is the central thesis of the national best-seller written by Shelby Steele entitled *The Content of Our Character*. Steele, a black neo-conservative, writes, 'race must not be a source of advantage or disadvantage for anyone'.[113] What is needed, according to Steele, is not new programs of entitlement, but a new spirit of pragmatism in racial matters whereupon black Americans are judged on the basis of hard work, education, individual initiative, stable family life, property ownership – in short, on their character, just as other ethnic groups were judged in previous decades. Therefore, in addition to the New Right's insistence that individuals and not groups possess constitutional rights is the assumption that the individual is a product not of social conditions but of the sum of his or her choices and behavior (that is, methodological individualism), and that the success or failure of ethnic groups can be explained by recourse to their values and culture. As Lawrence Mead (neo-conservative author of *Beyond Entitlement*) writes in an article for *The Public Interest*:

American thinking assumes that individuals are self-reliant and responsible for their own actions ... for the disadvantaged, however, whether individuals can be held accountable for their actions is precisely the issue. The very assumptions about social discrimination and acute need that surround the idea of disadvantage militate against assigning responsibility.[114]

The key category of individualism facilitates two repetitive motifs throughout New Right racial discourse: the strategy of victim-dividing and the strategy of victim-blaming. The New Right sets up an opposition between the 'good' and the 'bad' black; and between the 'deserving' and the 'undeserving' poor. For example, Pat Buchanan creates a division between the black criminal and the innocent, hard-working black when he writes:

[T]he ugliest expression of racism in America – the kind that manifests itself in interracial muggings, murders and rapes – is, like sickle cell anemia, a ghetto sickness, a malady afflicting the black underclass, not a suburban phenomenon ... If liberals were truly Lancelots of America's poor, they would be the most implacable enemies of those assaulting the poor – black criminals ... Is some white male who tells a dumb racist joke a worse enemy of the black man than the black thugs molesting his daughter in junior high school?[115]

Buchanan concludes with a call for conservatives 'to liberate Black America from a worse enemy than the Klan ever was, the black criminal'.

New Rightists urge that we stop looking to white racism as an explanation for black poverty, and instead focus on the behavior and attitudes of black people themselves. Walter E. Williams, a black neo-conservative and Hoover Institution scholar, writes, 'Somebody should tell the emperor that he has no clothes on. For years now, black "leaders" have been pretending that all the problems of black people can be attributed to white racism.'[116] Glenn Loury echoes this sentiment when he argues:

Today we are faced with a new American dilemma ... the bottom stratum of the community has compelling problems which can no longer be blamed solely on white racism, and which force us to confront fundamental failures in black society ... Though most are too polite to say so, they see the poverty of these communities as substantially due to the behavior of the people living there. They are unconvinced by the tortured rationalizations offered by black and (some) liberal white spokesmen. They do not think of themselves or their country as responsible for these dreadful conditions.[117]

Paleo-conservative Peter Brimelow writes,

Grant that blacks suffer occasional slight, crude name-calling, and some discrimination. But how damaging are these compared to the self-inflicted wounds of black America? And what prompts this white behavior? Is endemic white racism any more reasonable an explanation for the situation than endemic black criminality and the defensive nervous hostility it produces among whites?[118]

In *The End of Racism*, Dinesh D'Souza goes one step further by arguing that black deviancy perpetuates what he regards as a *rational* form of white racism.

Nothing strengthens racism in this country more than the behavior of the African-American underclass which flagrantly violates and scandalizes basic codes of responsibility and civility ... if blacks as a group can show that they are capable of performing competitively in schools and the workforce, and exercising both the rights and responsibilities of American citizenship, then racism will be deprived of its foundation in experience.

In the context of the failure of black self-development, D'Souza argues, 'the prejudice is warranted ... a bigot is simply a sociologist without credentials'.[119]

While it is in all ways valid (and certainly not racist) to call attention to manifest patterns emerging in poor communities of color, such as low educational achievement or rising crime rates, New Rightists of all stripes do so without relating such patterns to material circumstances, the objective opportunity structure, or the continued reality of institutional racism.

Emphasizing the achievements of the growing black middle class in the United States, New Rightists deny that race is still a significant variable that accounts for socio-economic location. High rates of black unemployment (twice the rate of whites), black poverty (nearly a third of all blacks live below the official poverty line), and prison incarceration (blacks, 12 per cent of the US population, constitute nearly half of the nation's prison population) are understood instead as manifestations of personal failure and/or a poverty of values.[120]

Responsibility for socioeconomic location, as well as the burden of change, is thus (dis)placed wholly upon the shoulders of marginalized populations themselves. Lawrence Mead writes, 'It is difficult to see how the disadvantaged can become mainstream Americans, in either their own eyes or the eyes of others, without a greater commitment to the mainstream economy; this is where further integration must take place.'[121] It follows that the solution to patterns of inequality, for the New Right, is to orientate policies to the changing of the individual behavior of the disadvantaged rather than toward institutional reform or collective self-emancipation. Mead continues:

> It has become clear that merely opening doors for the lower class and raising its income does not assure it the skills and attitudes necessary to participate more fully in American life. Indeed, the social capacities of the group seem actually to have declined as its income and prospects have risen ... More than any further economic resource, the disadvantaged now need a more secure sense of order in themselves and the neighborhoods around them. They need to be able to trust themselves and others. Their problem is now more a *moral* one than an economic one, and so is the challenge facing the welfare state.[122]

In this way, through the symbolic construction of individual blame and responsibility, the key category of individualism enables the New Right to oppose affirmative action and other items on the black political agenda without appearing as mean-spirited racists. Relations of class and racial inequality are thereby legitimated, at the same time that the pursuit of larger, more structural political solutions is foreclosed. In all of this the New Right affirms its conviction that color-conscious anti-racist initiatives run counter to individual freedom, and thus, counter to the 'American way of life'.

Enemies of the 'American Way of Life'

Individualism coexists in New Right ideology with the apparently contradictory category of the 'American way of life'. Indeed, the key categories of meaning within New Right ideology do not form a unified and coherent whole, but mix contradictory themes together in a way that is compelling for groups with diverse life situations and experiences. Thus, not only does the New Right portray society as an aggregate of isolated individuals (as in the neo-liberal category of individualism), but also as a social whole that requires public order, authority, and the viability of traditional units such as the family, neighborhood organizations and ethnic communities. Such concerns form the heart of the category of the 'American way of life' – one that I will argue carries implications for the politics of racial inclusion/exclusion.

The category of the nation's 'way of life' differs in significant ways from the same found in the case of Britain. For the British New Right, the main threat to the homogeneity of the nation's 'way of life' was and remains the black immigrant and/or 'bogus' asylum-seeker. In the United States, rhetoric around the threat to the nation's 'way of life' in the past has revolved less around the issue of cultural exclusivity than debate about the appropriate means of constitutional inclusion of people of color into the mainstream of nation's economy and society.

Throughout the 1970s and 1980s, political exploitation of the issue of immigration was more characteristic of the Far Right in the United States; individuals and groups such as the Liberty Lobby, David Duke, the Federation for American Immigration Reform (FAIR), English First, and the English Only Campaign. Even here, concern for levels of immigration tends to be expressed in terms of a more pragmatic opposition to immigration in keeping with the principles of liberal individualism (that is, the 'illegal alien' as taking jobs, lowering wages, and straining the nation's limited resources and already overburdened welfare system). Attention is called to the influx of 'illegal aliens' from Cuba, Haiti, Mexico, Cambodia (and other countries), and the burden this influx places upon social services at a time when these programs are being cut back for disadvantaged Americans. Already existing patterns of prejudice and xenophobia are exploited by focusing attention on allegations of stereotypical behavior on the part of immigrants: drug use, terrorism, welfare fraud, and the spreading of communicable diseases such as AIDS.

Such concerns were not significantly evident in the publications and direct-mail materials of New Right organizations during this period. Importantly, much of the New Right, and especially the intellectual wing (that is, the neo-conservatives), expressed support for liberal immigration policies. The expression of nativist sentiments in the United States is limited by a political culture that continues to pay homage to an image of America as a nation of immigrants. US political culture is characterized by what Nathan Glazer refers to as the 'voluntary character of ethnicity', meaning that 'one is required neither to put on ethnicity nor to take it off.'[123] In *Commentary*, Ben Wattenberg and Karl Zinsmeister express the tenets of the 'American way of life' thus:

> When it comes, finally, to a sense of shared national values, in the United States this has almost never been based on common blood but rather on specific traits and attitudes, both real and idealized. And the simple fact is that those traits and attitudes – self-reliance, a disciplined work ethic, strong family attachments, religiosity, an inclination toward entrepreneurship, a stress on education, independence of mind, an appreciation of individual liberty – are often notably prominent among immigrants to this country ... We have long since passed the point when we could hope to be a nation in the tribal sense. We are ethnically, religiously, and racially diverse. This does not always make for easy relations, but there is no changing it.[124]

Indeed, the 'American way of life' has long been conceived as being about regard for universal values such as equality, individual rights and achievement. Such universal values, by the New Right's own admission, prove to be assimilable by immigrants. Thus, the 'American way of life', at least in principle, is inclusive. Considering the national pride in the United States as a 'nation of immigrants', and the continued salience of the cultural ethos of the 'melting pot', it is not surprising that the issue of immigration has been a limiting one for the New Right in the United States, especially given the attempt to distance itself from the explicit racism of the Far Right. However, as we shall see below, conservatives have become increasingly divided over the issue, with some paleoconservatives willing to take on the issue as part of a newly-emergent racial nationalist project.

In the recent past, New Right discourse regarding the 'American way of life' has tended to focus less on the invasion of outsiders and more on the 'enemy within'. In the first defensive stage of the New Right's symbolic construction of the 'enemy within' in the late 1970s and throughout most of the 1980s, the enemy was the so-called education establishment and secular humanism. The campaign was dominated by the pro-family and religious factions of the New Right. Mounting federal interference in education (especially as it concerned desegregation, school busing and affirmative action guidelines) and the teaching of secular humanism in the schools (in the guise of teaching racial and gender equality) were regarded by the New Right as a threat to the 'American way of life'.[125] In an article entitled 'Egalitarian education brings us all down', Pat Buchanan writes,

> What happened to American education is that somewhere, about a quarter century ago, the idea of excellence was displaced by the egalitarian ethic. Equality of funding for schools and the racial composition of the classroom became more vital considerations than whether learning was taking place ... The egalitarian ideology maintains its iron control over public education because it has seized the commanding heights in an institution to which government has granted and guaranteed a monopoly. America's public school children are economic and political captives of the Education Establishment.[126]

Importantly, New Right opposition to anti-racist initiatives in the sphere of education was expressed positively, focusing on the right of parental control and the importance of neighborhood schooling, as well as the demand that traditional, Christian values be represented in school textbooks, serving, in their view, as a legitimate defense against the imposition of secular humanism.

In the late 1980s and early 1990s, the New Right campaign against the 'enemy within', especially as it concerns the sphere of education, shifted to a more formative assault on a new enemy – 'political correctness', or 'PC'. The phrase was first coined among the Left in the United States as a joke on those who seemingly took the progressive commitment too far. For example, to be 'politically correct' was to refer to 'people-holes' instead of 'man-holes'. Although the phrase was certainly mocking in tone, the intention was good.[127] The New Right appropriated the term for partisan advantage; an appropriation formative in representing an ideological assault upon the very principles (not simply a defensive campaign against the practices) of multicultural/anti-racist programs in higher education.

The anti-PC campaign first emerged in embryo in 1987 with the publication of Allan Bloom's best-seller *The Closing of the American Mind*.[128] In this book Bloom (a University of Chicago Professor, now dead) blamed the radical movements of the 1960s for undermining the quality of university education. In an interview with *Conservative Digest*, Bloom introduced the subject thus:

[T]here has arisen a conspiracy of sorts in the liberal arts to take much of that [quality education] away in the name of freeing us from the dominance of the 'white Western male'. This movement claims not only that the great books are no longer sources of liberation, but that they are sources of enslavement. This is happening all across America, but people are hardly aware of it because such thinking has taken the high moral ground in the universities under the guise of equality for women and blacks. This particular ideology, the principal advocate of which is a small force of radical extremists, nonetheless has enormous influence and protection within our universities.[129]

The anti-PC campaign ascended in the furor in 1989 over Stanford's revision of its core curriculum to include at least one course in the work of non-Western authors. It gained further momentum in 1991 with the publication of *Illiberal Education* by Dinesh D'Souza, in which the author links multiculturalism to affirmative action and study programs developed for women and people of color during the 1970s, and denounces them together as part of the 'Victim's Revolution'.[130] In 1990 and 1991, media publications such as *Newsweek*, *Time*, the *New York Review of Books*, and *The New Republic* ran a series of articles on 'political correctness', with titles such as 'The Thought Police', 'The PC Front', 'The Victim's Revolution', and 'The Storm Over the University'. The New Right campaign against PC also gained force at the local level as the National Association of Scholars succeeded in organizing right-wing academics in universities across the nation.

According to anti-PC ideologues, universities have been overrun by 'PC thought police'. Progressive students and professors are charged with conducting a McCarthy-style witchhunt against conservative students and professors. In the National Association of Scholars' journal *Academic Questions*, member John Roche writes, 'in percentage terms there are more "terrified" faculty today than there ever were in the era of H.U.A.C. and Joe McCarthy, but they are afraid of the lynching bees of a minority of organized students, and not of official inquisition.'[131] Various university speech codes, implemented in the wake of a rash of racist incidents on campuses across the nation, are denounced by the New Right as a form of 'thought control' and as 'suppression of incorrect ideas'.[132]

Indeed, according to anti-PC ideologues, it is not racism (or sexism) which is the real threat to tolerance and freedom on campus, but rather the creed of political correctness itself. On the one hand, political correctness is presented as being totalitarian in character. In an article denouncing multicultural education as a form of political correctness, neoconservative author Irving Kristol asserts that 'multiculturalism is as much a "war against the West" as Nazism and Stalinism ever were'.[133] On the other hand, 'political correctness' is presented as being a tool of the revolutionary Left. NAS member Walter Lammi writes,

According to the theorists of curriculum change, the real purpose of education for difference is not academic success but 'empowerment'. Empowerment means learning how to struggle relentlessly against the oppression of the 'dominant culture', in other words, Western civilization, capitalism, and almost every aspect of mainstream American culture and politics.[134]

Lammi concludes with a plea of tolerance for the people of the West (that is, white people), reminding his readers that tolerance means accepting people of *all* cultures. Armed with this double move, the symbolic construction of the PC enemy has allowed New Rightists to erode progressive anti-racist gains in the sphere of higher education while speaking in the name of tolerance and free speech.

Interjecting itself into the middle of the culture wars in the mid-1990s is what could be regarded as a shift from the project of eroding liberal policies such as multiculturalism in the name of constitutional principles of fairness to a more bold defense of the dominant (white) culture against challenge. Signalling a convergence of sorts with British New Right discourse about the 'alien wedge', New Rightists in the United States are beginning to address the conflation of race and nation head on, even to celebrate it. In the policy area of multiculturalism, New Rightists no longer simply attack liberal educators as enemies of tolerance, but rather assail the very assumption that all cultures are equal, all the while holding up the ideal of white culture as the standard by which all others are judged. For example, in *The End of Racism*, D'Souza writes 'the pathologies of black culture suggest that the racists were right all along ... What blacks need to do is to act white ... to abandon idiotic back-to-Africa schemes and embrace mainstream cultural norms so that they can effectively compete with other groups ...'[135] Indeed, the New Right is engaged in an attempt to reconstruct white as a non-racist cultural identity, or what Robert Blauner calls 'a dominant white racial identity'.[136]

A constituent element of this new narrative of whiteness is a fresh boldness on the part of a certain faction of the New Right coalition to take on the issue of immigration. The paleoconservative faction of the New Right coalition in particular is demonstrating a new willingness to introduce the question of the racial and ethnic composition of the United States into the public debate. The interjection of race into the culture wars under the auspices of the immigration debate has been bolstered in the wider culture by a series of media stories reinforcing the idea that immigrants – both legal and illegal – constitute a threat to the 'American way of life'. Implying that the ethos of America as a melting pot may be reaching the point of a boiling cauldron, the mainstream media was blitzed in the run-up to the 1994 vote on Proposition 187 with images of the Statue of Liberty in distress. For example, a July 1993 *Newsweek* article illustrated what it called the 'immigration backlash' with a cover depicting the Statue of Liberty up to her nose in a rising tide of boat people. *Chronicles* magazine ran a headline story 'Bosnia USA', accompanied by a picture of a throng of pointy-eared, fiendish creatures scrambling up a crying Mother Liberty. The metaphor of floods, waves and a nation drowning are reminiscent of Powells' 'rivers of blood' speech (discussed in the next chapter) that caused such a political storm in Britain more than two decades ago.[137]

The neo-liberal and neo-conservative wings of the New Right, for the most part, continue to avoid the issue of the racial/ethnic origin of recent immigrants and focus instead on the question of their values and whether they are in the USA legally or not. Keenly aware of the fact that many anti-immigrant campaigns in past US history were driven by racism and xenophobia, these factions of the conservative coalition persist in adhering to the idea that US national identity is about a set of liberal ideals rather than the Burkean concepts of tribe and kin. For example, writing about a Firing Line debate held at Bard College in June 1995, Arianna Huffington comments,

> Instead of being an opportunity society where hard work, enterprise and commitment are rewarded with success, or at least a decent living, America has become an entitlement society, fostering a culture of rights, subsidies and dependence that has infected millions of new immigrants as it has trapped millions of native-born Americans in an ever-growing underclass ... The problem is not immigration in and of itself, but rather the combustible combination of high levels of immigration and the bankrupt social policies of the last 30 years.[138]

For conservatives like Huffington, the questions of how many or what color are less important than the issue of the potential for recent immigrants to assimilate into the mainstream economy and society, as did previous waves of immigrants. To the degree that new factors such as the growth in the size of the welfare state and the practice of multiculturalism have served as a disincentive for immigrants to enter the mainstream economy and society, pro-immigration New Rightists argue that welfare and other liberal policies – not immigrants themselves, many of whom are esteemed as among the country's most productive citizens – are the real culprits in destroying the 'American way of life'.[139] Ron Unz (chief executive officer of Wall Street Analytics, Inc.) writes, 'Even the most stubborn liberal Democrats must realize that extending America's generous welfare benefits to all Third World inhabitants who cross our borders would quickly bankrupt any economy, and cause the collapse of the modern welfare state.'[140]

A number of paleo-conservative intellectuals – most notably, John O'Sullivan (editor of *National Review* and an emigrant from Britain) and Peter Brimelow (senior editor of *Forbes* and also an emigrant from Britain) have begun to lay the bases for a new ideological war that transcends conservative policy proposals to combat illegal immigration and instead challenges the heart of the national creed of America as a nation of immigrants. Sounding suspiciously similar to right-wing populists in Europe, such paleo-conservatives warn that, in the context of Census Bureau projections that the majority of the US population will become 'non-white' by the year 2050, current high levels of black and Hispanic immigration will drastically alter the US national identity, and in fact lead the US down the road to national suicide. Peter Brimelow opens his book *Alien Nation: Commonsense About America's Immigration Disaster* with the words, 'There is a sense in which current immigration policy is Adolf Hitler's posthumous revenge on America.'[141]

In warning against this 'alien nation', Brimelow and others advocate a new willingness to embrace an identity defined in explicitly racial and ethnic terms. In other words, the quality as much as the quantity of recent immigrants is a subject of concern. The 1965 Immigration Act is lambasted for dropping the principle of preference for immigrants from Northern and Western Europe in favor of the principle of family unification. Not only has this shift in priority rendered the judgement of productive skills less relevant, according to anti-immigration campaigners, it has also wielded significant implications for the racial composition of the United States, and in fact set in motion a process which if left to its own dynamic will eventually end by reducing US whites to minority status. Referring to the liberal assumption that a common ethos will bind the nation together whatever its ethnic composition (in 1994 80 per cent of immigrants were from either Latin America or Asia) as 'an extraordinary experiment' and analogous to 'replacing all the blood in a patient's body', Brimelow argues, 'Americans have a legitimate interest in their country's racial balance ... [and] a right to insist that their government stop shifting it.'[142]

Translated into the political sphere, paleo-conservatives such as Patrick Buchanan are manipulating the issue of immigration as part of an aggressive bid for power. In a 1996 'Buchanan For President' direct-mail appeal, Buchanan opines,

Working together, you and I can take back America for the values that were instilled in us as children ... Today, illegal immigration is helping fuel the cultural breakdown of our nation. That cultural breakdown, which you and I have recognized and sworn to fight, is the single most important factor which has impelled me to run for President.[143]

Illustrated with a picture of Buchanan holding a copy of *Alien Nation*, the appeal concludes with a call for a five year moratorium on legal immigration. In a *Washington Times* article entitled 'Populist Revolution', Buchanan argues,

It is quite simple: California is being invaded, and the federal government is obligated to defend California's border, and expel the invaders. What is so difficult about that? Any nation incapable of defending its borders in this age of mass migration is on its way to extinction.[144]

Elsewhere Buchanan asks: 'Who speaks for the real Americans, who found the U.S.A. ... is it not time to take America back?'[145]

Although the immigration debate is much broader than its racial infusion, Buchanan has made it clear that his concern is more than economic in nature. In an article titled 'Immigration: Reform or Racial Purity?', Buchanan writes,

> The burning issue here has almost nothing to do with economics, almost everything to do with race and ethnicity. If British subjects, fleeing a depression were pouring into this country through Canada, there would be few alarms. The central objection to the present flood of illegals is they are not English-speaking white people from Western Europe, they are Spanish-speaking brown and black people from Mexico, Latin America and the Caribbean.[146]

In another article, this time on the subject of Proposition 187, Buchanan explains,

> California's Proposition 187 ... is about more than just money. Indeed, the roots of this dispute ... are grounded in the warring ideas that we Americans hold about the deepest, most divisive, issues of our time: ethnicity, nation, culture ... ethnic militancy and solidarity are on the rise in the United States; the old institutions of assimilation are not doing their work as they once did; the Melting Pot is in need of repair ... If America is to survive as 'one nation, one people', we need to call a 'time-out' on immigration.[147]

In this way, Buchanan explicitly links the issue of immigration with multiculturalism, warning of the mortal threat to US civilization posed by their combined force. Several other paleo-conservatives are joining the likes of Brimelow and Buchanan and together serving as a bridge between a Far Right that has long exploited the racial referents of the immigration debate and the wider New Right movement concerned more about economic and citizenship issues.[148]

Despite this attempt on the part of paleo-conservatives to bridge the New/Far Right divide, support for anti-immigrant initiatives such as Proposition 187 remains a minority perspective within the New Right coalition as a whole. Organizers such as Ralph Reed are worried that such initiatives will alienate new immigrant voters from Latin America and the Pacific

Rim, many of whom he insists are conservative, pro-family, and devoutly religious. Jack Kemp and William Bennett, co-founders of Empower America, were perhaps the leading opponents of the emerging anti-immigrant sentiment within the GOP, at least until Kemp's nomination as Dole's running mate in the 1996 presidential election season and his about-turn on the issue. For example, in an article entitled 'The Fortress Party?', Kemp and Bennett express their concern that 'the legitimate concerns about illegal immigrants are broadening into an ugly antipathy toward all immigrants' and that such Big Brother-type policies will be 'a mandate for ethnic discrimination'.[149] Others such as Linda Chavez argue that immigrants provide a net positive gain for America and advise that any type of anti-immigration plank will be a loser for the GOP in the long term.[150] Demonstrating the continuing tension between those New Rightists concerned with liberal free market policies and limited government and those who advocate cultural conservatism and a racial-nationalist agenda, deep internal divisions within the New Right coalition over the issue of immigration signal a likely strategy of evasion in the near future. This means that the enemies of the 'American way of life' will probably continue to be 'illegals' who break the law and the impersonal liberal social policies such as welfare that destroy the fabric of society, while the racially coded symbol of the black and/or Hispanic immigrant will remain subtextual, there for those who wish to discover it.

'Reverse Racism'

The final and perhaps overarching key category of meaning (in the sense that it links up with each of the four above) is what is variously identified as 'affirmative discrimination' (Glazer), 'affirmative racism' (Murray), the 'new racism' (Allen), and 'naked racial preference' (Cohen).[151] The argument that anti-racist initiatives constitute a new form of racism – against white people – is especially prevalent within neo-conservative discourse on the subject of affirmative action.

In making the argument that anti-racist policies discriminate against white people, neo-conservatives play on the

central contradiction that while such policies are social in conception (in that they are geared to address a compelling social
need), they are necessarily individual at the point of implementation. This is a real contradiction that deserves serious
attention. The neo-conservative critique of affirmative action
(and other policies) cannot therefore be convincingly written-
off as simply a codeword or semantic strategy to hide alleged
racist intent. Neo-conservative opposition to affirmative action
as a form of 'reverse racism' is in fact a logical culmination of
the set of key categories of meaning (that is, the worldview)
outlined above.

Positive action for people of color beyond the guarantee of
individual equality of opportunity, according to New Rightists:

1. discriminates against the (white) majority and so con-
    stitutes 'reverse racism';
2. creates a special class of people protected by the law and
    so makes people of color more equal than others;
3. harms the very groups that it sets out to help;
4. causes and perpetuates, rather than resolves or rectifies,
    racial conflict and polarization; and
5. fuels the tyranny of the 'new class' of government bureau-
    crats.

Below each of these assertions is explored in turn.

First, beginning from the assumption that color-blindness is
the proper goal of government policy, neoconservatives
charge that color-conscious policies (geared to aid the upward
mobility of people of color and redress past discrimination)
create new forms of discrimination which, intentionally or
not, replace the old. The editors of the leading black conservative journal *Lincoln Review* write, 'current affirmative action
programs represent a new racism which we should oppose as
contrary to our goal of a color-blind society ... It violates our
very basic principles of individual freedom and our hope for
continuing progress.'[152] Neo-conservative thinker Carl Cohen
denounces such policies as:

> deliberately visiting the sins of the fathers upon their inno-
> cent sons and grandsons, to the special advantage of
> persons not connected with the original sinning ... To

suppose that both the beneficiaries of redress and those who are made to carry its burden are properly identified by race is, to be plain, racism.[153]

During a 1985 speech at Stanford University, Clarence Pendleton (former chairman of the US Commission on Civil Rights) similarly referred to proponents of affirmative action as the 'new racists':

To prefer one group over another is discriminatory. The faster we can rid ourselves of special protection the faster we can move to a race-blind society. The new racism is like the old racism: they want to treat blacks and other minorities differently because of race. This is as bad as the old racists. They really are saying that blacks and whites should not compete as equal – and that the blacks should expect guarantees.[154]

In breaking with the principle of color-blindness, so the argument goes, color-conscious policies create in their wake new victims of racial injustice. According to New Right ideologues, 'affirmative discrimination' is tantamount to saying 'no whites or males need apply'. Fred Lynch writes:

[A]ffirmative action must necessarily operate in a zero-sum context: when one person was hired because of race, ethnicity, or gender, others were thereby excluded on the same discriminatory grounds. Yet to recognize that affirmative action could not help without hurting ran up against an absolute dictum of the Marxist/feminist orthodoxy which had crept into the everyday academic world view of the 1970s and 1980s: the idea that only certified minorities – especially blacks and women – could be victims. To suggest that white males were being injured by affirmative action invited righteous scorn and contempt – even among white males themselves.[155]

In making such an argument, quota critics such as Lynch are exploiting very powerful sentiments. A 1990 Times Mirror survey showed that 81 per cent of white males oppose preferential treatment for people of color. Moreover, a recent study by Sniderman and Piazza demonstrates that such negative attitudes affect how whites perceive people of color on other issues as well.[156] Indeed, evidence suggests that there is a growing sentiment on the part of relevant social groups that the white male is being treated unfairly at the hands of women and people of color – that is, that they are in fact the new victims of racial discrimination. Lynch quotes a respondent who, when asked 'Who do you think gets a raw deal?', answered: 'The middle class white guy. Cause women get advantages, the Hispanics get advantages, Orientals get advantages. Everybody but the white male race gets advantages now.'[157] In another article, this time with regard to school busing, Philip Perlmutter quotes one white anti-busing demonstrator in Boston as saying: 'We are the new minority. We are discriminated against because of our ancestry and skin color ... We have been scared, threatened, beaten, arrested, prosecuted, and persecuted. We have suffered enough. We intend to get our fair share.'[158] Such symbolic construction of victimhood on the part of white males and the blatant hypocrisy it evokes was captured in an editorial cartoon published in June 1995 following a series of Supreme Court decisions limiting affirmative action. The cartoon showed a white man bounding down the steps of the Supreme Court shouting 'Free at last. Free at last. Thank God almighty, free at last.'[159]

In advancing the claim that white males are the new victims of 'reverse racism', the New Right is not simply disguising racist attitudes now in disrepute, but rather addressing the important question of the meaning of equal protection of the law in a multi-racial society. New Rightists answer this question in a way which makes symmetrical and ahistorical that which is profoundly asymmetrical and historical – relations of racial dominance – so that the politics of anti-racism is equated with the politics of the old racism (that is, against people of color). For example, in an article appearing in *Conservative Digest* entitled 'The New Racism is the Old Power Grab', William Allen equates the racism of Jim Crow with that of affirmative action and concludes, 'The racism of racial preference remains the same old racism, whether it places American whites at the top of the scale, or at the bottom.'[160]

Indeed, anti-racism is presented in New Right discourse as a new form of racism just as sinister as the white racism of the fascist right. 'Racism is racism whether it is anti-white or anti-black.'[161] The use of race (and gender) as a source of entitlement in policies to eradicate relations of domination are thereby equated with their use in upholding it. Black conservative author Shelby Steele writes:

> It is certainly true that white maleness has long been an unfair source of power. But the sin of white male power is precisely its use of race and gender as a source of entitlement. When minorities and women use their race, ethnicity, and gender in the same way, they not only commit the same sin but also, indirectly, sanction the very form of power that oppressed them in the first place.[162]

The existence of institutionalized racism against people of color (acknowledgment of which led to the passage of color-conscious measures in the first place) is thereby overlooked, while the purported existence of institutionalized discrimination against white people in the form of 'positive discrimination' or 'reverse racism' is emphasized.

From such symbolic (mis)description, it is one short step for New Rightists to hold anti-racism itself accountable for increasing racial tension and hostility. Since (a) anti-racism creates a special class of people protected by the law, and (b) such protection makes people of color more equal than others, then (according to the New Right), it follows that (c) white animosity toward people of color is naturally and understandably aroused. The granting of 'special privileges' only serves to ignite white animosity, argues anti-PC ideologue van den Haag (distinguished scholar at the Heritage Foundation and John M. Olin Professor of Law at Fordham University), who assures his readers that '[t]he minority is disliked not qua minority but qua preferred and privileged'.[163]

At issue is the question of the legitimate means to redress racial inequality. Armed with the set of assumptions previously discussed, New Rightists deem racial discrimination (defined in an individualistic rather than institutional manner) as a thing of the past – that is, as eradicated by the Civil Rights Act of 1964. It follows from this assumption that the only legitimate means for the redress of inequality in a liberal society is to ensure the individual right to compete in a fair system. The demand for more than this in the form of positive action is understood by New Rightists as being not about the elimination of institutional racism but about power – about the power of minority special interests as against those of whites or universal interests. To identify a proposed solution (that is, affirmative action) for a problem (that is, institutional racism) as its cause is to make a 'category mistake' of the most severe kind.[164] In this way, the New Right presents its opposition to key demands on the political agenda as true 'non-racism'.

Third, New Rightists claim that liberal anti-racism harms the very groups it purportedly sets out to help. Throughout the 1980s a variety of neoconservative intellectuals joined the New Right in documenting the alleged harm done to the integrity, initiative and self-development of communities of color in the name of progress. The central claim uniting otherwise diverse authors is that affirmative action (and other anti-racist initiatives) stigmatize their supposed beneficiaries. In *Naked Racial Preference*, Carl Cohen writes, 'Racial classifications, whether intended to benefit some or to burden others, stigmatize those groups singled out for differential treatment. They undermine our national commitment to evaluate individuals on their individual merit.'[165] In the chapter entitled 'The Road to Hell is Paved With Good Intentions', Cohen insists, 'Underlying all racial preference is the notion that members of certain minorities, needing favor, are inherently less able to compete on their own.'[166] Brownfield and Parker, the editors of the *Lincoln Review*, write: 'Affirmative action programs based on race are ... demeaning to the very groups they are meant to serve, implying that members of these groups cannot compete successfully in the open market place. This is the new racism of paternalistic liberalism.'[167] In a similar vein, Clarence Pendleton Jr. (now deceased former chairman of the Civil Rights Commission under the Reagan administration) asks:

> How long can blacks and other minorities let themselves be used? How long will they continue to be saddled with the public perception and private self-doubt that they wouldn't and couldn't make it without help and special treatment. There's no emancipation here. Minorities are being kept in

bondage because they are robbed of being judged on their own as individuals.[168]

Thus, New Rightists argue not only that are anti-racist initiatives unproductive and unnecessary, since people of color have made considerable progress without them, but that they have had precisely the opposite effect from that intended. They have served to heighten rather than undermine racist stereotypes, and in so doing, have made the hard-won achievements of certain upwardly-mobile people of color appear as mere conferred benefits.

More than this, by discriminating on the basis of race (albeit in favor rather than against people of color) 'preferential treatment' is said to heighten rather than reduce racial discord, thus twice negating its self-stated goals. Nathan Glazer writes, 'New lines of conflict are created, by government action. New resentments are created, new turfs to be protected; new angers arise.'[169] Carl Cohen writes:

> Ironically, the drive to achieve racial 'balance' has consequences the very reverse of those hoped for. Wanting racial justice, the advocates of group proportionality do racial injustice; seeking to eliminate discrimination by race, they encourage and even employ it. The racial bitterness it has taken our country decades to reduce is now recreated and exacerbated by delicate racial favoritism.[170]

Linda Chavez counsels, 'Affirmative action advocates can't have it both ways. A system that depends on holding minorities to different – and lower – standards than whites invites prejudice and bolsters bigotry.'[171] Thus, rather than focus on the continued reality of racial prejudice and discrimination in US society, New Rightists insist instead that the cause of racial inequality and subordination is the implementation of misguided anti-racist policies themselves. While open debate regarding the effectiveness of such policies must of course be safeguarded, such a focus – serving to deflect attention from the material circumstances and institutional inequalities that keep the majority of people of color in a condition of subordination – must be contested as a category mistake of the first rank.

Finally, over and above such pragmatic criticism of the effectiveness of anti-racist policy is the claim that government has overextended its legitimate role in promoting policies of positive action. Such policies are understood as fuelling what New Rightists refer to as the tyranny of the 'new class' of government bureaucrats. For example, New Right Senator Orrin Hatch contends that the Civil Rights Act of 1984 (designed to overturn the Supreme Court decision Grove City v. Bellin in which the Court interpreted Title IX in a relatively narrow manner) would be better described as the 'Civil Privileges Act of 1984' since it is, in his words, 'a bill in which legitimate state and local prerogatives, as well as private interests, are run over roughshod so that our social engineers in Washington can better structure society to their own liking.'[172] In *Masters of the Dream*, black neo-conservative and one-time 1996 presidential contender Alan Keyes writes,

> They [black leaders] achieve personal power by inducing people in the community to rely on them for access to government patronage and benefits. Therefore, these leaders don't represent the strength of the black community; they represent its weakness, dependency, and continued political subjugation.[173]

Thus, true to the tenets of the new racism, the New Right's animosity is directed not so much toward people of color themselves as toward the government agencies and bureaucrats responsible for administering civil rights policy.

Advocates of affirmative action and other anti-racist initiatives are construed as 'an administrative empire serving itself in the name of the disadvantaged'.[174] A 1992 direct mail letter distributed by the Lincoln Institute stated: 'The radical self-appointed "Civil Rights" establishment led by Jesse Jackson and the NAACP is trying to turn America into a land of quotas and special privileges – for blacks and other minorities.'[175] In a similar vein, Patrick McGuigan, senior editor at the Free Congress Center for Law and Democracy wrote an article for *Conservative Digest* entitled 'The Racism Scam: How liberal black leaders perpetuate dependence', in which he charges 'a clique of black neoracists' and their 'paternalistic white allies' with perpetuating dependence in order to 'counter anyone

and anything which threatens the machine-like domination
they exercise over the voting choices of millions of black
Americans'.[176]

In pursuing its aims, the 'new class' is presumed to run
against the grain of common sense of even those in whose
name it presumes to speak. In a *Conservative Digest* article opposing the 'new class' policy of school busing, Thomas Sowell
explains, 'Black children were forced to run a gauntlet of violence and insults for the greater glory of institutional grand
designs.'[177] Charges of institutional racism are reduced to fab-
rications by the 'new class' and said to be devised in the
absence of clear evidence. Such an argument provides the
basis for New Right opposition to the concept of statistical
parity, without which anti-racist procedures have no enforcement bite. Sowell continues:

> Today's grand fallacy about race and ethnicity is that statisti-
> cal 'representation' of a group – in jobs, schools, etc. –
> shows and measures discrimination. This notion is at the
> center of such controversial policies as affirmative action
> hiring, preferential admissions to college and public-school
> busing.[178]

New Rightists point instead to other factors as alternative explanations for racial disparities: in employment, factors such
as age, number of years in the country, number of children in
the family, and educational attainment; and in the area of education, factors such as residential concentration, a preference
for neighborhood schools, the interests of teachers and ad-
ministrators, and the legitimate educational decisions of educators. While each of these are surely relevant variables, New
Rightists examine them in place of rather than as integrally
related to factors more directly related to race.

Indeed, government bureaucrats are understood to be the
central purveyors of what New Rightists identify as the 'new
racism'. In an article entitled 'Affirmative Racism: how preferential treatment works against blacks', Charles Murray
writes:

> The new racism that is potentially most damaging is located
> among the white elites – educated, affluent, and occupying

the positions in education, business, and government from which this country is ruled ... The new racists do not think blacks are inferior. They are typically longtime supporters of civil rights. But they exhibit the classic behavioral symptom of racism: they treat blacks differently from whites, because of their race. The results can be as concretely bad and unjust as any that the old racism produces ... Always, blacks are denied the right to compete as equals.[179]

Walter Williams equates civil rights organizations with white racist groups when he writes,

[civil rights] organizations once part of a proud struggle have now squandered their moral authority. They are little more than race hustlers championing a racial spoils system. They no longer seek fair play and a color-blind society; their agenda is one of group rights where quota is king and color-blindness is viewed with contempt. Today's civil rights organizations differ only in degree, but not in kind, from white racist organizations past and present.[180]

The New Right's brand of anti-anti-racism has allowed conservatives to claim moral authority on the subject of civil rights, and to bash the Democrats as racist because they are race-conscious. For example, Rush Limbaugh taints the Democrats as bigots for opposing the CCRI:

This is such a great thing because it points out the truth here about who's racist and who's not, who's bigoted and who's not. And guess who it is that's sweating this out, guess who it is that's biting their nails? ... It's Democrat ... What are we going to call them? Bigots. They will be bigots. The people who oppose ending discrimination.[181]

Today the argument that anti-racism harms the very groups that it sets out to help is voiced in softer terms. As compared with the 1980s, New Rightists are now more prone to acknowledge some of the positive effects of affirmative action, especially its role in the growth of the much celebrated black middle class. Increasingly pervasive is an argument centering around the theme that 'racial preferences' have outlived their usefulness and now represent the politics of diminishing returns. For example, in a *Policy Review* article entitled 'Nixon's Ghost', Adam Meyerson (editor of *Policy Review*) writes,

> Even if racial preferences have been justified on a tem-
> porary basis, they surely cannot be justified for more than a
> generation ... Government-imposed racial preferences
> played an important part [in] ... smashing through the in-
> stitutional barriers to black advancement that were the
> legacy of centuries of discrimination. But reverse discrim-
> ination was always a questionable remedy to earlier preju-
> dice. By failing now to offer opportunity to poor black
> males, racial preferences have outlived whatever usefulness
> they may have had. It is time for them to go.[182]

In a *New York Times* op-ed piece entitled 'Let Affirmative Action Die', Andrew Sullivan writes,

> As an ideology, affirmative action in 1995 is beginning to re-
> semble Soviet Communism in 1989. Outside the sheltered
> elites, the majority of people loathe it. The circumstances
> in which it was dreamed up no longer exist. It is clearly
> teetering, its legitimacy under mortal threat. The decision
> by the University California Board of Regents to abolish
> preferences in admissions and hiring policies is the un-
> mistakable sound of a wall coming down.[183]

The argument that 'racial preferences' now offer diminishing returns is not matched by any new ideas regarding alternative government ameliorative programs to address continuing rela-tions of racial inequality. Instead, New Rightists have become even more bold in asserting that there is nothing for govern-ment to do. In the thirtieth anniversary issue of *Commentary*, Nathan Glazer criticizes his book *Affirmative Discrimination* for being too complacent about the racial divisions that continue to mark the US landscape. Rather than revise his assumptions regarding the role of government *vis-à-vis* the pursuit of racial equality, Glazer concludes, 'Government action can never match, in scale and impact, the effects of individual, voluntary decision. This is what has raised group after group, this is what has broken down the boundaries of ethnicity and race in the past ... .' The struggle for racial equality, Glazer continues, has to be 'one by one, individual by individual, family by family, neighborhood by neighborhood. Slowly as these work, there is really no alternative.'[184]

Another increasingly salient argument about affirmative action, one focused less on mending it than ending it, to echo President Clinton's well-known bumper sticker phrase, is that a class or income-based system may serve as a better alternative to race-based programs. In making this argument, New Rightists are circumventing a long-held criticism within progressive circles that affirmative action is not radical enough in that it primarily benefits middle-class and upper-class blacks, rather than the 'truly disadvantaged'.[185] For example, at the 1995 National Leadership Conference hosted by National Minority Politics titled 'Conservative Politics in the 21st Century: Plotting a Course for the Nation's Future', Gwen Richardson argued forcefully for race criteria to be replaced by income/economic criteria in the government's formulation of affirmative action, and that race specific government remedies be replaced with targeted programs for the poor of all colors that emphasize hard work, merit, and free enterprise.[186] In *Illiberal Education*, Dinesh D'Souza concludes that universities should retain their policies of preferential treatment, but alter their criteria from race to socio-economic disadvantage.

In conclusion, the symbolic construction of the key category of meaning of 'reverse racism' allows New Rightists in the United States to deny the systemic and continued reality of racism in US society by directing attention to both the (alleged) new victims of 'reverse racism' (that is, white males, as individuals but also as a group) and the new enemies of racial equality (that is, the anti-racist 'new class'). In so doing, New Rightists present themselves as the true champions of equality and individual liberty, and the set of policy proposals which they advocate as true 'non-racism'.

4 The British New Right: A Discourse of Culture, Nation, and Race

The New Right emerged in Britain in the 1970s as an heir to a long history of right-wing politics and as a distinctive political development in its own right. The aim of this chapter is to explore whether and to what degree a racial subtext exists beneath New Right discourse on a range of themes – especially those related to culture and nation. While particularistic racist attitudes and overt racism have been conspicuously absent, it is nevertheless compelling to address the question of the importance of symbolic conflict over race as one component of the British New Right's project to establish social conservatism as politically dominant.

In the years prior to 1945, right-wing racism focused less on the presence of black people in Britain (as that presence was still very small) than on Jews and the Irish. Racism against black people was expressed in this era of Empire more in the form of the 'white man's burden', which constructed the colonized peoples of Africa, Asia and the Caribbean as primitive and uncivilized; thereby serving as an ideological justification for colonization.

Racism's material basis changed as former colonies became independent following the Second World War. Many citizens of what came to be known as the 'New Commonwealth' (India, Pakistan and the Caribbean islands of Jamaica, Trinidad and Barbados) took advantage of the rights conferred by the 1948 British Nationality Act, passed at a time of labor shortage, to come to work and settle in Britain. The very presence of New Commonwealth migrant laborers became the primary focus of British racism in the post-war era.

Their presence was not considered to be a serious political problem in the first half of the 1950s. However, as the housing shortage in urban centers (especially London) worsened, as social and educational services remained sub-standard, and as unemployment rose with the easing of the labor shortage, symbolic conflict over the meaning of their presence and the significance of their race became more heated.

Conservative politicians such as Cyril Osborne and Norman Pannell emerged in to the national spotlight as ideological warriors in the battle to define the presence of the 'colored immigrant' as a socio-political problem of considerable proportions. This was the beginning of the right-wing call for controls to be placed upon the numbers of New Commonwealth citizens allowed entry. It was also the renaissance of the symbolic construction of Britain as a 'white man's country', and of the 'colored immigrant' as possessing 'altogether a different standard of civilization'.[1] Yet such racist sentiments were operating at this time very much on the fringe of British politics. More importantly, restriction of the right of entry for New Commonwealth migrant workers was still outside the parameters of government policy formation.

By the early 1960s symbolic conflict over race had replaced alternative political and ideological reactions to the presence of New Commonwealth migrant labor. The racism of Empire (which previously had justified colonization) was thereby replaced with anti-immigrant racism (which justified the exclusion of New Commonwealth migrants from entry into the political and economic mainstream of British society). With the right-wing interpretation of contemporary social problems as having essentially to do with race increasingly validated by politicians and the media – and its proposed solution of immigration control largely endorsed by government in the form of legislation (the 1962 Commonwealth Immigrants Act) – the anti-immigrant lobby stepped up its campaign for ever more stringent immigration controls, as well as the repeal of what little race relations legislation existed.

The campaign became salient in the late 1960s with the emergence of Powellism.[2] No longer on the fringe of British politics, certain sections of the Right found a key spokesman in Enoch Powell, a senior MP at that time. Indeed, Powell gave a series of now notorious speeches in 1968 that struck certain themes the New Right would later champion. Powell did not so much create these themes as package very old ideas in a new way. In this respect, Powell, like George Wallace in the

United States, can rightly be considered the progenitor of the new racism in British politics.

Powell vehemently denied racist intent. Consistent with the tenets of the new racism, he portrayed black people not as inferior, only different. It was a difference expressed in terms of culture rather than biology. Black people were said to possess a different 'way of life'. It was a difference, moreover, which was deemed incompatible with the 'British way of life', and indeed destructive. Black people were constructed as others; as in but not of the nation. They could never truly belong, even those black people born in Britain, since Britishness, for Powell, had less to do with geography than a set of unspoken inherited cultural characteristics that could not simply be adopted:

> The West Indian or Asian does not, by being born in England, become an Englishman. In law he becomes a United Kingdom citizen by birth; in fact he is a West Asian or Indian still ... With the lapse of a generation or so we shall at least have succeeded – to the benefit of nobody – in reproducing in 'England's green and pleasant land' the haunting tragedy of the United States.[3]

In this way, the idea of race was conveyed by Powell in the language of Britishness; of nation and culture. It was expressed in terms of legitimate self-defence on the part of the indigenous British (that is, white) majority who simply wanted to remain themselves. In the words of Powell: 'We have an identity of our own, as we have a territory of our own and the instinct to preserve that identity is one of the deepest and strongest implanted in mankind.'[4]

In the aftermath of his now notorious 'rivers of blood' speech in which he warned of impending racial civil war, Powell was dismissed from the Tory shadow cabinet. Yet his message arguably remained popular, leading many to conclude that although Powell had lost the political battle, he had won the ideological war. This view seems to have been partially vindicated by the subsequent institutionalization of tighter immigration controls by the Heath administration (that is, the 1971 Immigration Act, although this Act fell far short of Powell's call for repatriation) and, more importantly, the right turn of the Conservative Party itself. The transformation of the Conservative Party culminated with the election of Margaret Thatcher to the Party leadership in 1976.

THE BRITISH NEW RIGHT ORGANIZATIONAL NEXUS

Central to the story of the emergence of Thatcherism is the renewed salience and co-ordinated activity of a network of right-wing pressure groups, think tanks, media commentators and intellectuals denoted here by usage of the term New Right. The British New Right is a loose network of individuals and organizations on the right of the political spectrum that emerged in the mid-1970s in an effort to displace the apparently moribund social democratic consensus and replace it with a conservative one.

The New Right is closely connected with both the Conservative Party and more extreme right-wing groups (the British National Party, Right Now!, Revolutionary Conservative Caucus, and the National Front), and so serves as a kind of bridge between the two. New Right organizations include right-wing political pressure groups such as the Monday Club and The Freedom Association; pro-Thatcherite foundations such as Conservative 2000 and Conservative Way Forward; think tanks such as the Social Affairs Unit and the Centre for Policy Studies; a group of conservative-minded intellectuals known collectively as the Salisbury Group and another called The Group; and a whole range of right-wing media commentators writing for a variety of newspapers, quality and tabloid.

The Monday Club is an important social authoritarian pressure group in Britain today, although relatively small and increasingly peripheral to mainstream Tory Party activities. The Club was founded in 1961 in the wake of Macmillan's 'winds of change' speech in South Africa, which was given on a Monday. After the collapse of the fascists as an electoral force in 1979, the Monday Club helped to fill the vacuum for many of their activists and sympathizers looking for a way to influence the mainstream political culture. The Club's self-stated aim is to promote 'true' conservative values at the local and national level, and to give support to those

Members of Parliament who share its vision. It holds meetings, often in the House of Commons or Lords, arranges dinners and receptions, presents speakers at the annual Conservative Party Conference, and publishes a regular newsletter and *Journal* (formerly *Monday News*). Officially outside the Conservative Party, it has always been very close to it. The Club's current Chairman is Lord Sudeley, its Vice-Chairman is Andrew Hunter MP, and membership includes Members of both Houses of Parliament, as well as active Conservative Party supporters throughout the country.[5] The Club's membership secretary, W. Denis Walker, emphasizes that it is a private organization, and so does not reveal any actual membership figures or names, both of which he insists are confidential.

The Monday Club is paradigmatic of the social authoritarian strand of the New Right in its belief that a purely economic focus to contemporary social problems is too narrow, and its corresponding campaign to broaden its aims to the social and moral realm. John Biggs-Davison (now dead former MP, Monday Club member, and council member of The Freedom Association) warned: 'There has to be a balance between freedom and order, because it is clear that where there is no order there is no freedom.'[6]

Included in the Club's 1995 publication of its 'Aims and Objectives' is a call to rally in opposition to the 'Race Relations Industry', the new face of its long-standing drive to repeal most existing race relations legislation and abolition of institutions such as the Commission for Racial Equality, alleging that they serve to maintain the black community and its 'special needs' as separate from the English. The Club also opposes what it calls 'excessive and indiscriminate immigration', again a continuation of long-standing efforts to strengthen the Party's anti-immigration policies. In the 1970s, the Club organized a 'Halt Immigration Now Campaign' and, in Thatcher's first term, Harvey Proctor MP (chair of the Club's Immigration and Race Relations Committee) produced a series of reports advocating a program of 'constructive repatriation'. Included was a proposal to rename and reorder the Ministry for Overseas Aid as a Ministry for Overseas Resettlement.[7] Today this objective is expressed in terms of support for 'a properly funded scheme for voluntary repatriation' and an appeal that 'new immigrants should not be allowed to take unfair advantage of our Welfare System'.[8] In the late 1980s, the Monday Club was active in protests around the country over the Hong Kong Bill and the so-called Rushdie Affair, the controversies surrounding Salman Rushdie's publication of the allegedly blasphemous book *The Satanic Verses*. Monday Club leaflets were distributed in Bradford, for example, entitled 'Civil War in Bradford?' and 'End Immigration or it will be God help Bradford'.

The Thatcher administration restored and nurtured better relations with the Monday Club, an important development considering that branches had been closed down under the Heath administration due to infiltration by the National Front.[9] However, by the end of the Thatcher administration's tenure the Monday Club was once again very much on the periphery, as illustrated by its exclusion from the program of fringe events at the 1989 Conservative Party Conference in Blackpool. In the wake of the right-wing take-over of the Monday Club by racist and fascist groups in early 1991, the Club has been even further alienated from the Conservative Party. During this period, the Club's executive council included former members of the British National Party and fostered close ties with an organization that calls itself Western Goals, itself closely linked with the Front National in France, the racist party led by Jean-Marie Le Pen, and with the Republikaner Partie in Germany.[10] There also has been much cross-fertilization between the Monday Club and extremist fringe organizations such as the Revolutionary Conservative Caucus, Fair Play, and *Right Now!* Of particular importance is Right Now!, a quarterly magazine rapidly replacing the Monday Club as the organ of the Tory Party right, and increasingly looking to New Rightists such as Newt Gingrich and Charles Murray in the United States to justify their policies.[11]

Reflecting this shift to the more extreme right in the early 1990s, the Club's policy on matters of race and immigration became more radical in outlook, as summed up by the following statement by Gregory Lauder-Frost, the Club's then new political secretary: 'There are a great many people who are economic immigrants who certainly didn't come here because they liked King Arthur. They're not interested in being British, they're interested in wearing saris and so on.' Lauder-Frost continued to urge that even second generation immigrants be 'voluntarily' repatriated. 'I don't believe these people are British. Just because they were born here is of no consequence.'[12] This more extremist face of the Monday Club, one which clearly resonated with the current 'Rights for Whites' message of the British National Party, proved highly embarrassing to the Conservative Party, keen to deny the extent of racism in its ranks, especially as the take-over occurred in the wake of the internal Party row over the selection of a black parliamentary candidate in Cheltenham, John Taylor (a black barrister and former adviser on race relations in the Home Office). Several MPs – including George Gardiner and Julian Amery – resigned from the Club in protest, and Club officials admit that few MPs remain. Lauder-Frost himself has since resigned from the Monday Club in the wake of a fraud conviction. Lord Sudeley told the author that Saatchi and Saatchi has been employed to polish up the Club's image, indicative perhaps of a forthcoming effort by the Monday Club to eschew the more explicit expressions of racism and extremism in its ranks.

Although many consider the Monday Club to be a dying organization, it continues to hold fringe meetings at the annual Tory Party Conference, some fairly well-attended (40 plus). Three such meetings were held at the 1995 Conference in Blackpool, on the subjects of 'immigration', 'law and order', and 'a German Europe'. On immigration, Mrs Joy Page (Chairman of the Immigration Control Association) complained of immigrants having too many babies and taking away 'our' womenfolk. She told stories of black landlords forcing out their white tenants by hanging shrunken heads in the hallway, and warned of the takeover of 'our' inner cities by the Japanese Ninja. She went on to explain, 'There are 300 mysterious men in Europe manipulating immigration policy across the continent in order irrevocably to alter the blood of this country. And those anti-racist marchers you see in our cities, they are paid to do it by these men'.[13]

During the meeting on 'law and order', the speaker, Mrs Peacock MP, expressed her belief in the need for tougher sentencing, and above all public humiliation, as effective deterrents for criminals. Drawing repeatedly on lessons from the US experience, she put forward policy recommendations that included capital and corporal punishment, bringing back the stocks, and the introduction of chain gangs. Although the speaker spoke in a tone appropriate for a current MP, several members of the audience took her call for public humiliation to its logical if absurd (by the Monday Club's own admission) conclusion, with one suggesting flogging of criminals on the childrens' television show *Blue Peter*, and another urging Mrs Peacock to consider introducing crucifixion as a suitable form of punishment. Such meetings, and the apparent extremists they continue to attract, no doubt cast doubt on the ability of even the best advertising firm to polish up the Club's image.

Another important New Right pressure group, and much more representative of the Tory right-wing, is the National Association of Freedom (NAFF), founded in 1975 but later renamed The Freedom Association (TFA) in order to avoid confusion with the National Front (NF). Formed directly in opposition to the Heath administration's supposed embrace of collectivism, supporters are united by their belief in the need for defense of the free enterprise culture and middle-class Toryism outside the Conservative Party. The Association's chairman is Norris McWhirter (of the *Guiness Book of World Records*), its general director and editor of its journal *Freedom Today* (formerly *Free Nation*) is Philip Vander Elst, and the director is Gerald Hartup.

By contrast to the Monday Club, The Freedom Association is often considered to be part of the libertarian strand of the New Right, and its early 'Charter of Rights and Liberties' clearly reveals a concern with economic freedom over and above issues of social order. The Charter enshrines a very negative conception of freedom; one that is limited to the 'freedom to engage in private enterprise', 'the right to private ownership', and 'freedom to belong or not to belong to a trade union'. Chief among the concerns voiced in *Freedom Today* are opposition to closed shops and other alleged trade union abuses, collectivism in general, so-called 'new class' privileges, and support for denationalization as well as education and health vouchers. TFA activities in past years have included court action against the Union of Post Office Workers for boycotting mail to South Africa, backing management in the Grunwick dispute, and taking the case of three British Rail employees who were sacked for refusing to join the Transport

Salaried Staffs Association under a closed shop agreement to the European Court of Human Rights.

While TFA is still chiefly concerned with economic freedom, its editorials and policy statements make it very explicit that 'freedom cannot be defended as a value outside the moral order'.[14] Moreover, a shift in focus from primarily economic concerns to moral and social issues, especially so-called family and other cultural conservative issues, can be detected around the beginning of Thatcher's second term. This shift is to a large extent a result of the former being realized under the Thatcher administration. Victories for specific proposals such as denationalization of British Telecom and the privatization of large sections of local government have been secured, while trade union power has been significantly curtailed. These victories, combined with genuine conservative principles that recognize the danger of the pursuit of liberty for its own sake, have allowed TFA to concentrate more on social matters. One member urges: 'We have shown how economic attitudes can be changed, now let's set to work on the social front.'[15]

Symbolic conflict around racial issues has been part of this project. TFA has warned repeatedly, especially in its early years, of a 'native fear that the British national and cultural identity is being eroded' by black immigration. It also has gone on the public record as actively opposed to multicultural education programs on the basis that they discriminate against the (white) majority and deride the Western cultural heritage. More recently, a top TFA priority on the racial front involves vilification of the doctrine of 'political correctness' and the associated alleged abuses of the 'race relations industry'. TFA personalities were active in supporting the Ethnic Harmony Campaign, an initiative that emerged in July 1990 but then faded away, the stated purpose of which was to:

1. end state intervention in the arena of race relations (including the 1976 Race Relations Act) which it describes as 'notoriously discriminatory and inflammatory';
2. repeal Section 11 of the 1966 Local Government Act (under which central government provides funds to meet the 'special needs' of black communities) which it refers to as a form of apartheid; and

3. abolish the Commission for Racial Equality (CRE) which
    it portrays as a 'force for divisiveness and inter-racial
    conflict'.[16]

For the most part, however, leading members are astute
enough to realize that too much public attention to such
matters runs the risk of stigmatizing TFA as being obsessed
with race and thus intolerant. Perhaps as a result, most recent
articles on 'political correctness' and race that appear in
Freedom Today are actually reprints of *Conservative Chronicle* articles written by US black neo-conservatives such as Thomas
Sowell and Walter Williams.

However in practice, and often behind the scenes, TFA has
been at the forefront of efforts to challenge what it refers to as
the misuses of the 1976 Race Relations Act, compelling employers such as the Probation Service, Citizens Advice Bureau,
local authorities, and the BBC to drop recruitment 'colour
bars'. In 1995, one such controversy arose when TFA took on
the BBC over its recruitment advertisement seeking ethnic minority applicants for traineeships at the senior producer level.
Despite the fact that such a form of positive discrimination in
employment and training schemes is legal in cases of professional under-representation under Sections 37 and 38 of the
1976 Act, the BBC quietly backed down under fire from the
Association.[17] The Association similarly voiced its objections to
the CRE over a number of adverts specifying a desire for
ethnic minority candidates, under the rubric of Section
5(2)(d) of the Race Relations Act, such as the one aimed at
applicants for a Professional Qualifying Programme in
Community and Youth Work Studies at the University of
Durham, and another seeking a Lecturer in Youth and
Community Work at Leeds Polytechnic.[18] In all of this, The
Freedom Association plays on ambiguities within the 1976
Race Relations Act, positioning itself as the fair defender of
non-racial competition.

TFA director Gerald Hartup in particular has been at the
forefront of efforts – both discursive and legal – to expose what
he refers to as the misrepresentations and injustices wrought by
institutional anti-racism. For example, in a pamphlet entitled
Misreporting Racial Attacks written for the Hampden Trust (the
charitable arm of The Freedom Association), Hartup objects to

the principle, and the statistics based on it, that only whites can be guilty of racial attacks, insisting that such anti-racist dogma serves only to exacerbate rather than ameliorate racial conflict.[19] Parading as a sort of watchdog of watchdog organizations, Hartup has similarly challenged the use of statistics by the CRE, in one recent instance forcing the Commission to withdraw a *Fact Sheet on Employment and Unemployment* because of its allegation that only one per cent of solicitors in England are from ethnic minority communities, when in fact the correct statistic is 3.4 per cent.[20] Hartup has also been active in pressurizing the CRE to respond to racially exclusive meetings and organizations, such as a GCSE Homework Club for black children in Lambeth or a Brixton Town Hall meeting called for black people to discuss the aftermath of the 1992 Los Angeles disturbances.[21] Although such racially exclusive meetings and organizations are permissible under Section 35 of the Race Relations Act, if designed to meet the special needs of that group in relation to education, training or welfare, the phrase 'special needs' is ambiguous enough for New Rightists such as Hartup to sink their teeth into and claim that they are in fact discriminatory against whites and thus racially inflammatory.

While anti-anti-racism therefore has remained a consistent focus of TFA, the leading priority of the Association now appears to be opposition to European Unification. TFA presents itself as the leader of the 'stormtroopers of the new orthodoxy': Euroscepticism. TFA campaigned hard against the Maastricht Treaty, and has continued to fight it under the auspices of the Campaign Against a Federal Europe which it founded in 1991, and the European Anti-Maastricht Alliance which it cofounded in 1992. In 1993 TFA chairman Norris McWhirter alleged treason against the Foreign Secretary and other government ministers for signing the Treaty which he regards, among other things, as undermining the Sovereign Queen and Parliament, and today advocates the repatriation of powers from Brussels back to Britain. Although the issue of Europe is an extremely complex one, involving as it does the contradiction between the protection of free trade capitalism and the nation state within Tory Party ideology, race serves in the debate as an important secondary bond. Eurosceptic concern to retain national sovereignty and preserve cultural freedom in the face of challenge from the European 'superstate' has clear racial overtones, even if not stated explicitly, as does the more direct warning that Britain could lose control over internal borders if she were to relinquish to Brussels the capacity for independent decision-making.

Now twenty years old, The Freedom Association is still active, and enjoys a membership of roughly 5000. It continues to be at the forefront of battles against censorship imposed by purported 'politically correct' thinking and against the threat of foreign rule through Maastrict. The Association hosted three prominent fringe meetings at the 1995 Tory Party Conference in Blackpool, all relating in one way or another to opposition to the European Union. Interestingly, one un-advertised fringe meeting was held, hosted by Gerald Hartup and formally under the auspices of the Hampden Trust. During the meeting, entitled 'Towards Responsibility in Race Relations', Hartup rehearsed his now familiar themes: that equal opportunity policies are unequal, that political correct-ness inhibits relevant policy formation, and that the operation of the Race Relations Act unwittingly damages prospects for ethnic minorities.

While the Monday Club and The Freedom Association are formally outside the Conservative Party, there also exist right-wing foundations within the Tory Party that can rightfully be considered as part of the New Right. The two most notable in-ternal pressure groups to appear in the last few years are Conservative Way Forward and Conservative 2000. Conservative Way Forward (CWF) was founded 'to defend and build upon Thatcher's vision of individual ownership and freedom of choice within the Conservative Party'. CWF publishes policy papers and a magazine called *Forward*, and hosts seminars and receptions to put forward its views. Its Council is constituted by Lady Thatcher (president), Lord Tebbit (vice-president), Lord Parkinson (chair), and Sir George Gardiner (editor).

The CWF emphasizes the moral need to foster individual re-sponsibility (minimize the welfare state and public spending), and advocates a conservative approach to economic policy (tax cuts and enterprise culture), education (vouchers and grant-maintained schools), law and order, and is most actively opposed to European Union and 'political correctness'. The Foundation enlists the active support of New Right politicians, popularly known as Thatcher's children, such as Michael

Portillo (Secretary of Defence), Peter Lilley (Social Security Secretary), and John Redwood (MP and former Secretary of Wales). In the wake of Conservative Party losses in 1994's by-elections, local elections and then Euro-elections, and as a response to the apparent popularity of the new Labour leader, Tony Blair, CWF published a compendium of speeches by Michael Portillo MP that lays out a conservative strategy for how to establish 'clear blue water' between themselves and the Labour opposition.

One essential part of this strategy appears to be the symbolic construction of 'political correctness', as always accompanied by subtle and not-so-subtle racial overtones. For example, in the Autumn 1995 issue of *Forward*, John Bercow (member of the CWF Council) writes,

> Haringey spent £77 000 on a lesbian and gay centre for black people, Camden frittered nearly £12 000 on its 'nuclear free zone', Birmingham coughed up £2.5 million teaching some forty women to be carpenters or electricians – unsuccessfully – while Nottingham banned social workers from asking for black or white coffee because of 'racist overtones'. This poison of political correctness is fast becoming the norm wherever Labour rules.[22]

In this way, the 'clear blue water' strategy invoked repeatedly during the course of the 1995 Party Conference in Blackpool operates, at least in part, by stigmatizing the opposition for swimming in water contaminated by 'loony lefties' and black 'special interests'.

The Conservative 2000 Foundation is the newest of right-wing organizations within the Tory Party. Founded by John Redwood MP in the wake of his failed leadership challenge in June/July 1995, and infused with strong financial backing from the business community, the Foundation aims to promote Redwoods' views (most notably his Euroscepticism) and influence the Party's intellectual climate more generally in a conservative, pro-Thatcherite direction. Similar in style to the early days of the Centre for Policy Studies (see below) and to US think tanks such as the Heritage Foundation, Conservative 2000 is likely to be an important organization on the Right in coming years.

The two most prominent New Right think tanks are the Centre for Policy Studies and the Social Affairs Unit. The Centre for Policy Studies (CPS) was set up in 1974 by Sir Keith Joseph MP (now dead), with Margaret Thatcher as president, as an alternative to the Tory Party's own Research Department. Generally regarded as part of the neo-liberal arm of the New Right, the self-stated aim of the CPS was originally to turn the Tory Party away from the pragmatism and interventionism of the Heath years and to change the way in which the Conservative Party regarded the task of government. Upon taking leave as director of CPS in 1984, Alfred Sherman summed up its function thus:

> Although the Centre is frequently referred to as a Tory think tank, we assigned ourselves a more active role, to undertake the reshaping of the climate of opinion nationally, in order to widen the range of options open to a Conservative government which dared to take them ... unless the new ideas are fed in somehow or other, the public never will be ready, and the post-war settlement will go rolling on by its own momentum until it crushes us all.[23]

In fulfilling this function, the CPS has helped provide an intellectual foundation for a Thatcher-style brand of conservatism.

Although the Centre's current chair, Brian Griffiths, admits to a period of retrenchment in the early 1990s, the Centre is in the process of expanding its activities. According to the remarks in the *1995 Annual Review* offered by Gerald Frost, Centre director until 1995, it appears that this expansion involves a shift in focus away from the economic and industrial issues that dominated its agenda in the past, and toward identity and other cultural and social issues. At the top of the Centre's priorities are: education, social policy, trade/privatization, reducing the interventionist state (in Westminster and Brussels), promoting the liberty of citizens and institutions of civil society, and fostering law and order. A newly created CPS Policy Forum brings together government ministers (including Lilley, Portillo and Redwood), chief executives of major companies, and policy experts (including US neo-conservative Irving Kristol and John O'Sullivan, former leader writer for the *Daily Telegraph* and currently editor of *National Review*) for open discussions on a wide range of topics.

Although very little has been published by the CPS that is directly concerned with race, the way in which the Centre approaches a variety of other social issues divulges an affinity with other New Right groups in Britain. For example, the Centre has advocated more parental choice in education in order to counter the trend of British schools becoming 'instruments of revolution' (*Choice in Rotten Apples*, by Mervyn Hiskett); opposed anti-racist education with the charge that it teaches children that British society is rotten with institutional racism (*Trials by Honeyford*, by Andrew Brown); warned of the dangers of egalitarianism (*The Egalitarian Conceit: true and false equalities*, by Kenneth Minogue and *The Politics of Manners: the uses of inequality*, by Peregrine Worsthorne); and denounced multicultural education for denigrating British culture as only one culture amongst others that are equally valid (*Education, Race and Revolution*, by Antony Flew).

Moreover, statements in the past by persons closely associated with the Centre reveal an ideological affinity with groups espousing more explicit views on race and immigration. For example, in an article for the *Daily Telegraph*, former CPS director Alfred Sherman described 'the imposition of mass immigration from backward alien cultures' as 'just one symptom of this self-destructive urge reflected in the assault on … all that is English and wholesome.'[24] Sherman also came under attack in the autumn of 1987 for inviting Jean-Marie Le Pen, the leader of the Front-National in France, to address a fringe meeting at the 1987 Conservative Party Conference.[25] However, there is no doubt that the CPS has become more moderate over the years, and this trend away from ideological fervor will likely be accelerated by the replacement in 1995 of Gerald Frost with Tessa Keswick, considered more government-friendly, as Centre director.

The Social Affairs Unit (SAU) was established in 1980 as an offshoot of the Institute of Economic Affairs, one of the earliest post-war libertarian think tanks. The SAU is a research and educational trust which focuses on social affairs and controversies in contemporary culture. Its self-declared aim is to analyze 'the factors which make for a free and orderly society in which enterprise can flourish', by influencing government policy in areas such as education, health, social welfare, and discrimination. The director is Digby Anderson (previously Research Fellow at the University of Nottingham and author of numerous books and articles on social policy), assisted by David Marsland (senior lecturer in the Sociology Department at Brunel University). Other important advisory council members include: Nathan Glazer, Kenneth Minogue, Dennis O'Keeffe, Geoffrey Partington, David Regan, and Julius Gould. Most recently, the SAU has been concerned with moral issues, as evidenced by a 1992 publication edited by Anderson entitled *Of Virtue: Moral Confusion and Social Disorder in Britain and America.*

Included in the Unit's conservative response to social issues are:

1. denial of the validity of minority groups collectively organizing for their rights in favor of a highly individualistic analysis (*Reversing Racism* (1984), by Holland and Parkins);
2. criticism of a 'new class' of homosexual, female and black activists who allegedly hurt the very groups they claim to represent (*The Kindness that Kills* (1984), by Anderson); and
3. denunciation of multicultural education (*Schooling for British Muslims* (1989), by Hiskett) and the liberalization of education more generally (*The Wayward Curriculum* (1985), by O'Keeffe).

The Unit is particularly vocal in its denunciation of the 'new class', and its discourse on race-related issues reflects this concern. For example, SAU director Digby Anderson wrote an article for *The Times* entitled 'With friends like these ...' in which he insists that:

The interest, and indeed right, of all these 'Blacks' is to be treated according to their individual and varied behaviour and those of the group they themselves choose to belong to; not to be dragooned into an artificial culturally and morally neutered class of 'Blacks' because it suits the political purposes of some activist, desperate to invent a new lower class to replace the unfaithful 'White' one.[26]

In 1992, the SAU published a report by Professor Antony Flew (Emeritus Professor of Philosophy at the University of Reading, founding member of the Education Group of the CPS and of the Council of the Freedom Association) entitled *A Future for Anti-Racism?*, in which the author argues for the need to review the 1976 Race Relations Act (RRA) and the whole set of doctrines and institutions associated with anti-racism. Similar in tone to the ideas behind the California Civil Rights Initiative in the United States, Flew positions himself against individual discrimination while at the same time being critical of the many ways in which anti-racism has developed since 1976. In particular, Flew draws a distinction between the type of racist behavior at which the RRA was originally targeted, and the racist thoughts against which the 'politically correct' thought police allegedly patrol. True to the new racism, Flew protects his own non-racist self-image by arguing that the lumping together of different races and cultures into the category black is itself racist, while simultaneously questioning the claim that all cultures are in fact equal.

The most representative of groups on the British intellectual right is the Salisbury Group (sometimes known as the 'Peterhouse Group' because of its close ties with Peterhouse, Cambridge). The Salisbury Group takes its name from Lord Salisbury, Conservative Prime Minister (1885–92 and 1895–1902), who, incidentally, resigned from the government in 1867 when the franchise was given to certain male, property-holding members of the working class. Formed in 1977 as a forum of discussion, with no official ties to the Conservative Party, the Salisbury Group brings together academics, journalists writing for the quality press, and high-ranking politicians to discuss issues of the day.[27] Participants have included: Roger Scruton (Professor of Aesthetics at Birkbeck College, London, and editor of the *Salisbury Review*), Charles Moore (former editor of the *Sunday Telegraph* and newly-appointed as editor of the *Daily Telegraph*), John Casey (Fellow of Caius College, Cambridge), Maurice Cowling (recently retired as director of history at Peterhouse, Cambridge), Peregrine Worsthorne (columnist and former editor of the *Sunday Telegraph*), Edward Norman (formerly Dean of Peterhouse, Cambridge), Michael Portillo MP (former Peterhouse student and currently

Secretary of Defence), John Vincent (Professor of History at Bristol University and columnist in the *Sun*), and even Enoch Powell and Margaret Thatcher herself. Theirs is a more subtle and sophisticated variety of conservative discourse as compared to the other factions of the New Right described above.

The Salisbury Group first published a collection of papers edited by Maurice Cowling in 1978 entitled *Conservative Essays*.[28] It became much more active in the wake of the 1981 Brixton riots, however, and in early 1982 published a pamphlet by Charles Moore entitled 'The Old People of Lambeth' which claimed that the inhabitants of Lambeth felt that 'white English life' was being disrupted by the presence of West Indian life lacking in 'a richness of civilization'.[29] Later that same year the Salisbury Group launched their own journal, the *Salisbury Review*, as part of their bid to make conservative notions of hierarchy, order and discipline intellectually dominant.

Theirs is a rhetoric of order defined by disregard for liberal principles such as individualism, equality and freedom, and a corresponding concern for the existence of a ruling class and a powerful state. In *Conservative Essays*, Maurice Cowling writes: 'It is not freedom that conservatives want: what they want is the sort of freedom that will maintain existing inequalities and restore lost ones.'[30] In the same volume Peregrine Worsthorne writes:

> The urgent need today is for the State to regain control over 'the people', to re-exert its authority, and it is useless to imagine that this will be helped by some libertarian mishmash drawn from the writings of Adam Smith, J.S. Mill and the warmed-up milk of 19th century liberalism.[31]

By contrast to the neo-liberal arm of the British New Right, these thinkers generally favor the free market not as a good in itself, but as a convenient instrument of discipline and authority.

The Salisbury Group is paradigmatic of the social authoritarian strand of the New Right in its belief that there is more to conservative politics than *laissez-faire* economics. Roger Scruton puts the point thus: 'I think there has been a mistaken emphasis on the free market as the basic Conservative principle in recent years. And this shows the harmful influence of Socialism which seems always to put economics first and politics second.'[32] Thus, while generally supportive of the Thatcher and Major governments, this section of the New Right is critical of its economic liberalism and its 'obsession with business efficiency and its managerial approach'.[33] Its brand of conservatism is expressed less in terms of freedom and individual rights as in the language of state and nation, culture and shared community values.

If culture and nation are at the root of their brand of conservatism, then, arguably, symbolic conflict around racial issues is also at play. The Salisbury Group's self-stated aim is to give voice to conservative instincts. According to articles regularly featured in The *Salisbury Review*, conservative instincts appear to be concerned with 'multi-ethnic intolerance' (Summer 1983), 'our loss of sovereignty' (Autumn 1982), 'one nation: the politics of race' (Autumn 1982), 'the race relations industry' (Winter 1984), 'law and order' (Summer 1986), 'education and race' (Spring 1987), 'Maas treachery' (September 1993), 'on being an immigrant' (December 1991), 'racial bullying in the schools' (December 1992), and 'race and political correctness' (September 1993). In the first issue of the *Salisbury Review*, Cambridge don John Casey describes how the 'great English cities are now becoming alienated from national life and that the Victorian achievement of civilizing them and rescuing them from the old city mob shows signs of breaking down.' Casey's suggested solution is 'retrospectively to alter the legal status of the coloured immigrant community, so that its members become guest workers ... who would eventually return to their countries of origin'.[34]

Although the Salisbury Group continues to devote attention to the issue of immigration, the racial dimension that was so self-evident in its early years has been recoded. This recoding no doubt owes in part to an attempt to deter the frequent charges of racism leveled against it, but also has to do with the fact that most immigration today comes not from Commonwealth countries but from the European Community (EC) and the newly-'liberated' countries of East/Central Europe. With this reference point in the immigration debate changed, the Salisbury Group has increasingly voiced its nationalist concern in terms of sovereignty and ethnicity, not race. Although the face of the 'alien wedge' is increasingly a white face, Salisbury intellectuals continue to play the numbers game, warning for example that the rise of neo-Nazism across Europe signals the failure of multi-ethnic state experiments and accordingly reaffirms the need for strict immigration controls in order to maintain good race relations. Besides immigration, the twin issues of 'political correctness' and the follies of the 'race relations industry' continue to capture the imagination of Salisbury intellectuals. Numerous *Review* editorials and articles focus attention on the 'disease of political correctness', exposing its 'Leninist roots', portraying it as 'new face of Soviet practices ... hostile to Western culture and civilization', and challenging the 'manifest falsehoods' of anti-racism that are thereby propagated.

A new generation of populist right-wing intellectuals, mostly historians, writing for the conservative quality press has emerged in the past few years, many of whom attest their loyalty to Maurice Cowling as a kind of intellectual mentor. Known blandly as 'The Group' but referred to by one commentator as the 'dial-a-don phenomenon', its most notable members are: Andrew Roberts (former stockbroker and author), John Charmley (Lecturer at the University of East Anglia and author of *The End of Glory*), Professor Norman Stone (leading light in the UK Independence Party), and Niall Ferguson (Fellow at Jesus College, Oxford).[35] 'The Group's coherence owes to its Euroscepticism, hostility to the Major government (it backed Redwood in the leadership contest), an activist political role as so-called public intellectuals, and a distinctly elitist approach to modern history. During the 1995 leadership contest, members of The Group publicly suggested that the time may have come to launch a National Party as a spin-off of what they regard as a Tory Party captured by an Establishment conspiracy.

Overlapping with the above intellectual circles but also an independent force in their own right are many right-wing commentators and journalists in the British media. Right-wing British journalists not mentioned above who frequently have written on racial issues include: Paul Johnson of the *Daily Mail* and the *Sun;* Andrew Alexander in the *Daily Mail*; Ray Mills in the *Daily Star*; Ronald Butt, until 1991 associate editor and leader writer of *The Times*; George Gale (now dead) formerly of the *Daily Express*; former assistant editor of the *Daily*

Telegraph; T.E. Utley (now dead), a former member of the *Salisbury Review*'s editorial board). Regular features by such right-wing media personalities focus on issues such as 'the loony left', law and order, indoctrination in schools, restriction of immigration, and the injustices wrought by anti-racism.

While many of the New Right groups described above are uncompromisingly intellectual in approach and so have had apparently limited impact on the Tory rank and file, the British press, more than most other sections of the British New Right, has been crucial in shaping the popular political imagination. Writing in a style that is partisan and often self-righteous, this section of the right wing has become increasingly institutionalized within the media world, as evidenced by the Autumn 1995 editorial reshuffles that left the three leading Conservative papers – the *Daily Telegraph*, the *Sunday Telegraph* and the *Daily Mail* – edited by right-wing Major sceptics. Particularly significant was the selection of Charles Moore (Salisbury member and author of T*he Old People of Lambeth* mentioned above) as editor of the *Daily Telegraph*, thereby ending the internal warfare between Max Hastings (the previous editor and supporter of one nation conservatism) and a hard-right clique represented by Mr Moore.[36]

Similarly indicative of the extent to which the right turn in policy formation has been matched by an associated but independent right turn from below is the explosion of a plethora of small business organizations and middle-class groups (the National Federation of Self-Employed, the Middle Class Association, and the National Association of Rate-Payers' Action Groups) as well as the emergence of a range of grass-roots moral and religious groups (Mary Whitehouse's National Viewers' and Listeners' Association (NVALA) and Festival of Light; Victoria Gillick's campaign against giving contraception to girls under the age of sixteen and her association with the Responsible Society, an anti-sex education group; the Society for the Protection of Unborn Children (SPUC); and various education campaigns arising out of the Black Paper critique of progressive schooling).[37] However, while there is no doubt an important and growing moral, even Christian, dimension to New Right beliefs, there is no equivalent in Britain today of the Christian Coalition in the United States, and the failed 'Back to Basics' campaign launched by the Major administration signals the limitations of using religion as a mobilizing force in British politics.

Nor has there been a comparable development in Britain of the increasing involvement within the New Right movement in the United States of black conservative scholars and activists. There have been a few inroads in this area, arguably, as is evidenced by the formation of a new journal named *Ethnic Enterprise News* (which brings together British New Rightists and US black neo-conservative scholars), the inclusion of a number of black people on the committee of the Ethnic Harmony Campaign that has sought to appear multi-racial, and rising black media personalities such as Donu Kogbara (a journalist writing for the *Sunday Times*). More notable perhaps are the efforts of the Department of Community Affairs in the Conservative Central Office to encourage black people to join the party in greater numbers through the Anglo-Asian and Anglo-West Indian Conservative Associations and the One Nation Forum, with some result. Although there are now a number of prominent black members of the Conservative Party, most appear to play a peripheral role in the party as a whole. It is this sense of alienation that led Joyce Sampson (a member of the party for twelve years and a leading light of the Tories' One Nation Forum) to resign on the eve of the party's 1994 annual conference, complaining about the lack of opportunities for black and female party activists. A number of prominent Asian members of the Small Heath Conservative Association in Birmingham – all elected officials – also resigned on the eve of the conference amid allegations of racism and right-wing plots, claiming disillusionment with what they referred to as disrespect for them on the part of fellow Tories.[38]

The British New Right, therefore, in reality is not one movement but many. Certain strands of the New Right advocate limited government and free market solutions to contemporary social problems, including racial inequality, while others advocate increased positive duties of the state to defend British cultural heritage and to control those who threaten to undermine it. The social authoritarian and religious/moral right are united in their opposition to prioritizing the rights of individuals, while the neoliberal arm of the New Right holds these rights in the highest regard. All strands respect the free market, but the social conservatives depart from their libertarian counterparts by arguing that the free market requires a strong state in order for the market to remain free. Social conservatives thus distrust the purely economic theories of the neo-liberals and remain sceptical of government's ability to manage society's problems. The long-standing conflict between the radically libertarian Federation of Conservative Students and traditional conservatives in the Party during much of the 1980s, resulting in the expulsion of the former from Central Offices in 1987, as well as the current conflict within the Party over Europe and especially the divisive issue of identity cards, highlights the degree to which the tension between freedom and order remains salient within the New Right movement as a whole.[39]

In some ways the New Right is more united on what it opposes than on what it proposes. This is especially true with concern to racial issues. Whether the New Right's anti-antiracism is expressed in the form of the neo-liberal attack on the 'new class' of anti-racists, or the social authoritarian charge that the presence of colored immigrants is threatening the survival of the distinctive British cultural heritage, the New Right arguably shares a common project of mobilizing popular and elite opinion in opposition to social democratic values associated with the pursuit of racial equality.

In fact, emphasis on the differences that distinguish New Right organizations from one another would obscure precisely that which is most distinctive about the new racism of the New Right; that is, the degree to which it combines the neo-liberal concern with freedom from unwarranted state regulations and the social conservative concern with defending established cultural mores and maintaining social cohesion. Thus, while differences between the various British New Right groupings described above are important to acknowledge, this study will emphasize the wider constellation of ideas on race that they share.

THE NEW RACISM: KEY CATEGORIES OF MEANING

The new racism of the British New Right is not set out coherently or systematically in any one place. Rather, it is scattered throughout journals and newspapers, speeches and books, often authored by individuals whose views differ in many important respects. As Gordon and Klug note, it is precisely because the new racism is not associated with a coherent theory but rather hidden inside more seemingly respectable and common sense assumptions that it is all the more pervasive and dangerous.[40] The key categories of meaning that underlay the new racism of the British New Right are identified below.

Human Nature

New Right racial ideology is deeply imbued with a particular view of human nature as immutable and hostile to those who are different. It is natural, according to New Rightists, that whites should want to be with other whites, just as Asians presumably want to be with other Asians, Jews with Jews, and so on. For example, former Bradford Headmaster and critic of multiculturalism Ray Honeyford refers to 'the tendency we all have, whatever our colour, to adopt a narrow and rejecting view of others'.[41] In *The Meaning of Conservatism*, Roger Scruton of the Salisbury Group claims that 'illiberal sentiments ... are sentiments which seem to arise *inevitably* from social consciousness; they involve *natural* prejudice, and a desire for the company of one's own kind.'[42] Echoing the key tenets of the new racism, right-wing journalist Robin Page writes, 'It is from a recognition of racial differences that a desire develops in most groups to be among their own kind; and this leads to distrust and hostility when newcomers come in ... the whole question of race is not a matter of being inferior, dirty or clean, but of being different.[43]

Such a view is then employed by the New Right in its construction of nationhood and national identity as natural rather than socio-political. For example, Mary Kenny writes in a *Daily Mail* leader, 'if there are English who like to be with other English people in their own country – what's so strange about that? This is the way human beings are: they feel more at home with the familiar.'[44] In the *Salisbury Review*, New Rightist Sally Shreir (a free-lance writer on political matters) writes, 'National identity is founded on natural emotions and natural allegiances.'[45] Again in the *Salisbury Review*, Clive Ashworth (lecturer in the Sociology Department at the University of Leicester) writes:

> Nationalism is ... a ubiquitous attitude stamped on the human species by nature ... we may say that the nation is ubiquitous, and that human being live in nations with the same certainty as certain species of fish live in shoals, and certain species of dogs live in packs. We may also say that because of their ultimate nature, nations require of their members a transcendent loyalty which knows nothing higher.[46]

What is missing is the racial basis of the 'familiar'; for when New Rightists write of the English it is clearly a racially-specific, or white England to which they refer. Though a politics of difference need not be racist if difference is related to the historical and structural context in which it originated and evolved, it is important to explore the degree to which the New Right refers the alleged different culture of immigrants back to skin color. In this way the racial subtext beneath the politics of cultural difference can be divulged.

By arguing that it is only natural to feel solidarity with 'one's own kind' and animosity towards those with a different culture, such an immutable conception of human nature allows New Rightists paradoxically to deny that their views are racist by recourse to a language of culture, not skin color, and at the same time legitimate exclusive views on race by recourse to the assumption that it is natural to prefer and defend one's own race. Ivor Stanbrook MP argues:

> Let there be no beating about the bush. The average coloured immigrant has a different culture, a different religion and different language. This is what creates the problem. It is not just because of race. The people in our cities feel strongly about immigrants. I believe that a preference for one's own race is as natural as a preference for one's own family. Therefore, it is not racialism ... it is simply human nature.[47]

Once natural instincts are conceived as being the basis of genuine fears, it follows that such natural instincts, when unheeded or frustrated, lead to 'natural' hostility towards the 'other'. Sir Alfred Sherman writes, 'National consciousness like any other major drive – all of which are bound up with the instinct for self-perpetuation – is a major constructive force provided legitimate channels; thwarted and frustrated, it becomes explosive.'[48] At the most extreme, human nature is used to justify repatriation. Not only is it natural to form a bounded community, separate from others, but this community is not open to new people who want to integrate; for it is a community defined by culture, naturally constituted, not by geographical location. Foreigners, too, have their 'natural' home. 'Your natural home is really the only place for you to be; for that is something rooted in your nature, via your culture.'[49]

While such views continue to resonate in the 1990s, the naturalization of exclusionary racial sentiments and policies by such circumvention of the politics of difference has become more complex and subtle as the issue of European integration, rather than immigration, has become the focal point of the New Right's nationalistic and sometimes xenophobic rhetoric. Michael Portillo's notorious speech at the 1995 Tory Party Conference, during which he lambasted the European Union as the alien enemy, is evidence of the promotion of ever-more subtle brands of racism within the right wing of the Tory Party that deny the possibility of integration of different peoples without having directly to invoke the category of race.

The implications of such naturalization of exclusive views on race are important to contest. The contention that the desire to be with one's 'own kind' is just 'the way people are' renders the political struggle against racism irrelevant. An editorial in *Free Nation* states:

The main task ahead is the absorption of coloured immigrants already resident in this country into the body social, not an easy operation since racial prejudice is *innate in human nature,* which no amount of liberal social engineering can eliminate.[50]

By naturalizing racial prejudice and discrimination in this way via recourse to such a static view of human nature, the New Right arguably depoliticizes the question of racism and thereby helps to justify the official retreat from racial equality in thought and policy.

The 'British Way of Life'

The notion of the 'British way of life' is perhaps the most over-arching key category of meaning associated with New Right racial ideology. The construction of who 'we' are, a construction that at the same time demands a corollary notion of the 'other', as I will argue below, pervades New Right discourse about race.

In the New Right worldview, the concept of culture conveys a particular sense of nationhood, one identified with a particular (that is, white) ethnic group. Moreover, its culture embodies Victorian values such as work, respectability, the need for social discipline, and respect for the law. An imagined past, characterized by supposed homogeneity of British culture and continuity of national stock, is understood to have been diluted by 'alien strains', a process that is believed to coincide with national decline. In short, the rearticulation of the thematic structure of Englishness has been integral to the working of New Right racial discourse. New Rightists have attempted to redefine who 'we' are as part of their hegemonic project to construct an authoritarian national identity.

Homogeneity of culture is what constitutes the nation for the New Right. Enoch Powell states: 'Every society, every nation, is unique: it has its own past, its own story, its own memories, its own ways, its own language or way of speaking, its own – dare I use the word – culture.'[51] What binds the nation together is a shared 'way of life', one that cannot be adopted but must be inbred. As Cambridge don John Casey wrote in the first edition of the *Salisbury Review*, nationalism is 'inseparably bound up with shared history, law, custom and kinship'.[52] National consciousness, not class, is the agent of history in the New Right's view, so if this consciousness is diluted or challenged in any way, the unity and stability of the nation is endangered. In the words of Enoch Powell: 'The disruption of the homogeneous we, which forms the essential basis of our party democracy and, thus, of our liberties, is now approaching the point at which the political mechanism of a "divided community" take charge and begin to operate autonomously.'[53]

The notion that a homogeneous 'British way of life' is the basis of nationhood is at the root of New Right discourse on immigration. Racist intent is denied, but the survival of the nation is considered to be of the highest order of moral ideals. The mere presence of black people in Britain is considered to be a threat to that survival. A territorial imperative is evident in the presentation of this threat, as is illustrated by the circulation of a Monday Club anti-immigration leaflet entitled 'Is this the end of the English?'. The leaflet shows a picture of Asian and Afro-Caribbean people pouring out of a dustbin on to a map of Britain.[54]

Linked to the idea of the invasion of British territory is the theme of the threat that black immigrants allegedly pose to the 'British way of life' and the need to allay the genuine fears thereby created. Columnist Paul Johnson warns of this alleged imminent threat when he opines, 'When different races live together all kinds of dilemmas arise.'[55] Genuine fears are then organized accordingly. Neighborhoods surely have changed in recent decades, crime rates have soared, and family structures have changed, so that popular fears are not delusional, they have a real material basis. However, to jump from the claim that popular fears are genuine to the claim that the location of the particular source of those fears (that is, black immigration) is correct must be problematized.

It is precisely the struggle to link genuine fears with a particular phenomenon such as black immigration – as opposed to, for example, complex sources of structural change, lack of community resources, or inadequate job training programs – which constitutes the New Right's ideological work. For example, in *The Old People of Lambeth* published by the Salisbury Group in the wake of the Brixton disturbances in 1981, Charles Moore chronicles conversations he had with old people in Lambeth. He emphasizes the fact that these people have nothing against blacks as such, but that they believe, quite rightly (in his view), that foreigners should adapt their ways to fit the English. For example, one woman exclaimed: 'Foreigners should live like us if they come here. ... Of course, there are problems with their habits ... they should go round and look for work, not riot.'[56] Instead of highlighting the social causes of unemployment and rioting, for example, Moore legitimates and reinforces the hostility that the popula-

tion of Lambeth feels toward West Indian immigrants by concluding that 'white English life has a richness of civilization
which West Indian life lacks ... the old people of Lambeth can
see with their own eyes that they are surrounded by people
more primitive than they.'[57] In this way, the ideological and arguably racist distinction between 'us' and 'them' is both
evoked and upheld.

Although discourse around the threat of immigration has
receded in recent years, in large part because policies pursued
in the very first years by the Thatcher administration virtually
stopped all further black immigration, its symbolic resonance
has been taken up by discourse around alleged 'Euro-
scroungers', 'bogus asylum-seekers', and 'illegal immigrants'.
For example, in April 1995, Winston Churchill (MP for
Davyhulme in Manchester, and the grandson of the former
Prime Minister) warned on a BBC local radio station that
'more and more hungry mouths and hungry bellies' are
seeking to emigrate to Britain. 'It is no wonder, when they see
on their television screen the life that exists in Europe and the
USA, that if they can get on a banana boat or a 747, they will
come by any way – legally or illegally'.[58] Mr Churchill's comments were a re-run of his speech just a year before when he
claimed that the 'British way of life' was under threat from a
relentless flow of people from the Indian sub-continent.[59]
Similarly, a concerted campaign against so-called bogus
asylum-seekers has been waged in the right-wing press in the
1990s, with lurid accounts of the criminal activities and fraudulent claims of economic migrants masquerading as political
refugees, and doomsday scenarios of the potential divisive
socio-cultural consequences of Labour's supposed open-door
policy.[60]

Besides immigration, education has become a central arena
of New Right symbolic conflict to define who 'we' are, and
arguably to suppress difference. Multicultural teaching is conceived as a subversive assault on British culture; one that encourages anti-British prejudice. Former Bradford Headmaster
Ray Honeyford writes that multi-ethnic education will undermine 'any sense of there being a distinctive British cultural
heritage'.[61]

The conclusions of the Swann Report, commissioned to
inquire into the education of children from ethnic minority

groups, are denounced out of the same concern to protect the proper teaching of the 'British way of life' in schools. The Report's view of multiculturalism, by no means radical, is attacked for trying to remould British culture. 'The ethnic minorities cannot be asked to fit into the mould of British society but the indigenous population may be required to accept major changes in its own way of life.'[62] Alfred Sherman, former director of the Centre for Policy Studies, warns:

> Extending the right to state-financed schools would remove pretexts for creating a procrustean pidgin culture to be imposed on majority and minorities alike, as proposed by the Swann report ... Swann's interim draft in effect out-lawed the concept of the English nation. Instead there would be a 'white community' existing alongside other – more deserving – communities.[63]

Sherman concludes this article by advocating separate schools. Yet the same themes are expressed by others, such as Simon Pearce (Deputy Chairman of the Monday Club's Immigration and Race Relations Committee and author of its paper 'Education and the Multi-Racial Society') who similarly criti-cizes the Swann Report but advocates assimilation instead of separate schools. Pearce warns:

> To impose the anti-racist/pluralist ideology on our schools ... will serve only to undermine our way of life and unleash destructive forces. ... Pluralism involves an erosion of the right of white English parents to see their heritage taught in schools. ... British citizenship involves a commitment to certain aspects of British life.[64]

Similar sentiments were expressed in the 1987 debate over the Government's General Certificate of Secondary Education (GCSE) proposals, about which Joanna North warns, 'the sen-sitive appreciation of British culture and British ways of life is precisely what is likely to disappear from education if the philosophy of the GCSE is successfully implemented.'[65]

More recently, right-wing educators in Britain have bor-rowed from the New Right in the United States the symbol of 'political correctness' as the new guise under which the threat

to the national 'way of life' appears in stealth. 'Political correctness', or 'PC', has been constructed on both sides of the
Atlantic as a totalitarian left-wing ideology alleged to have
politicized thought and language, inside and outside institutions of higher learning, to such a degree that it has foreclosed opportunities for free, open exchange of ideas. The
term is racialized to the extent that much of the PC animosity
has been directed at multicultural/anti-racism in particular, although concern over homosexuality and feminism has also
been particularly salient in anti-PC diatribes. For example, a
1993 editorial in the *Salisbury Review* applauds Enoch Powell
for his courage to speak up against black immigration against
the current PC climate that flings the racist charge at anyone
who dares to speak the 'truth' about their dislike of 'the
foreign one'.

The anti-PC campaign has been galvanized of late in the
wake of an announcement in the autumn of 1995 by
Dr Nicholas Tate (chief executive of the School Curriculum
and Assessment Authority) that the schools must teach children a strong sense of British culture, no matter what their
racial or ethnic background. The next week's *Sunday Telegraph*
carried an article by Digby Anderson critical of Tate's decision
(a surprising stance considering Anderson's usual derision of
multiculturalism), until the reader discovers the reason for
Anderson's objection – students should be taught English, and
not British, culture:

> [Tate] is undoubtedly right in worrying that the children
> may be learning a wishy-washy multiculturalism, a sort of
> cocktail identity. But he is wrong in suggesting Britishness
> classes. For the true identity of most of our children is not
> Britishness at all. It is Englishness. Indeed, Britishness is
> almost as artificial and newfangled an imposition as multi-
> culturalism.[66]

Anderson goes on to define Englishness as 'the only way any
decent chap would behave' and concludes by urging that
Mr Major consider requiring old-fashioned English cricket in
the Government's initiative to restore sports to schools. A
similar rejoinder to Tate's announcement was offered by the
Salisbury Group's John Casey:

We are all born into a culture, whether we will or no. Education consists of bringing out the possibilities of our own culture, rather than in preparing us for the exciting prospect of deciding for ourselves, by a process of trial and error, whether the Tale of Genji will mean more to us than the Odyssey, or a Balinese gamelin orchestra than Mozart.[67]

Casey concludes with the statement, 'Eurocentrism is a necessary condition of our being citizens of the world.' Although the two authors disagree over the question of whether Englishness or Eurocentrism should form the basis of belonging, both share the project of discrediting multiculturalism in the schools as a threat to national and cultural identity.

All symbolic constructions of the nation and national identity depend upon some kind of boundary, either implicit or explicit, between insiders and outsiders. The British New Right's invocation of the 'homogenous we' represents a particularly exclusionary and even authoritarian definition of the nation as it defines all those not born on British territory, and even those born in Britain and a citizen by virtue of the historical legacy of the Commonwealth, as an alien wedge. The fact that the New Right's imagined community of homogenous British stock is operationalized in the context of debate over policy areas such as black immigration and multiculturalism reveals that the boundary between insider and outsider is also a racialized one. The recourse to a notion of a homogenous 'way of life' weakened by those who are different – by virtue of citizenship, culture or race – serves to unify the targeted conservative constituency across class against the racialized other. At the ideological level, it functions to justify the exclusion – both physically in the case of immigration and asylum policies and culturally in the case of multiculturalism – of those who are defined as inherently outside the boundaries of the nation. It is here that we see the link between the New Right's conception of the 'British way of life' and the symbolic construction of racialized enemies to which I now turn.

The Enemy Within

A corollary to the construction of a homogeneous 'we' is the presentation of black people as the 'other'. There is a clear slippage from the discourse on the 'British way of life' to a focus on the forces that are undermining it. Ray Honeyford writes:

> The familiarity of the Trojan horse should not blind us to the essential truth it conveys – that an unwary nation can collapse through the efforts of forces generated from within; that its institutions, moral capital, and sense of uniqueness can all fall prey to internal forces. The enemy does not always need to seek entry – he is, as it were, often part of the family. This thought is raised in my mind by the way this country has responded to its transformation into a multi-cultural society over the past 30 years or so.[68]

New Right journalist Peregrine Worsthorne writes, 'Although Britain is a multi-racial society, it is still very far from being a multi-cultural nation. Its heart does not beat as one. ... Birds who are not of the same feather do not flock together at all easily.'[69] Thus, according to the New Right, the presence of people with an alleged cultural difference poses a problem for the health and viability of the British nation.

Discourse around the theme of the enemy within reveals that, for the New Right, national identity depends upon race – not geography. The New Right's conception of national identity turns on their particular definition of citizenship. Citizenship allows the right of abode in a nation but does not and cannot make a person automatically of the nation. Alfred Sherman of the CPS argues, 'Nationhood ... includes national character reflected in the way of life ... a passport or residence permit does not automatically implant national values or patriotism.'[70]

National character turns, in the New Right view, not on principles of law but chance of birth. This is the essence of Alfred Sherman's remark that Parliament could 'no more turn a Chinese into an Englishman than it can turn a man into a woman'.[71] Differences between cultures, here conflated with the social construction of differences between races, appear in New Right discourse to be inevitable and irreconcilable. In an article on proposed changes in immigration rules, Sherman maintains that 'the relationship between indigenous Britons and this country is inherently different from that of Asians and most other migrant stock'.[72] Thus, in the minds of certain New Rightists, legal citizenship does not change the fact that immigrants owe their national loyalties elsewhere, and thus feel no responsibility nor ties to Britain, but regard it as 'simply a haven of convenience where they acquire rights without national obligation'.[73]

Enoch Powell is the most notorious for using the theme of the alien wedge in his warning in 1968 that 'rivers of blood would flow' if immigration was not curbed. In 1976 he reiterated the same theme:

> The nation has been and is still being eroded and hollowed out from within by implantation of unassimilated and un-assimilable populations ... alien wedges in the heartland of the state. ... It is ... truly when he looks into the eyes of Asia that the Englishman comes face to face with those who would dispute with him the possession of his native land.[74]

Thus, blacks cannot form part of the British nation not just because they are foreign – but because their differences are allegedly of an alien and hostile nature. Worsthorne warns:

> The presence in Britain's capital and other major cities of such a large proportion of citizens whose allegiances may lie with the enemies of the West could be a real and growing danger ... our new ethnic minorities do not sound as if they were at all proud and grateful to have become British. Indeed, their community leaders give the impression that they hate Britain for her past imperial sins.[75]

In the 1990s, discourse around the alien wedge is being operationalized in a very different historical context than only a decade ago. Following the disintegration of the former Soviet bloc and the increasing integration of Europe, new enemies have been discovered in the form of the so-called Euroscrounger and the illegal immigrant. The nature of the threat posed by the enemy within has changed accordingly, in that it revolves less around the allegation of foreign loyalties and otherness than on alleged criminal behavior and economic leeching. The symbolic construction of the Euroscrounger has contributed to a new form of popular racism that is serving to legitimate increasingly mean-spirited policies toward political refugees, black people, and the poor.

The new xenophobic archetype of the 'Euroscrounger', like the black immigrant and Powell's alien wedge before it, is being constructed by the New Right to justify new definitions of the boundary between deserving and undeserving citizens. Importantly, the new discourse about the enemy within relies less on notions of the threat to cultural survival as on the economic imperatives involved in rooting out illegal immigrants, 'bogus' asylum-seekers, and welfare cheats. For example, the *Daily Star* recently warned of a 'new breed of beggar roaming the streets of Britain, "Yugo-leeches" who come from the wreckage of Yugoslavia' and are 'leeching on you and me'. According to the *Star*, Britain provides a safe haven for 'every bug-ridden waif and hate-filled political stray'. Once they come, they immediately get a council house, nice flat and state benefits 'so that they can sit around and have their teeth fixed and new glasses and the occasional baby on you and me'.[76]

The shift from a focus on black immigrants as an alien wedge to the Euroscrounger is integrally related to a context of profound social and economic transformation taking place across Europe. Less noted is the relationship between the symbol of the Euroscrounger and a right-wing agenda that has shifted its attention in the late 1980s from immigration policy, on which so much was already achieved during the early Thatcher era, to reducing the costs associated with the welfare state. The symbolic image of the undeserving and often criminal Euroscrounger makes more palatable New Right criticism of the welfare state and the culture of entitlement that it purportedly promotes.

The New Class Enemy

It is not only the presence of blacks in Britain that constitutes a threat to the nation, but also so-called new class bureaucrats who allegedly manipulate black people and their communities for their own purposes. This oscillation between blacks as a problem (the enemy within) and blacks as victim (of the new class) is an important characteristic of the new racism.

The new class theme was first taken up in Britain by Enoch Powell in the late 1960s. Powell argued then and continues to argue now that the real enemy is not simply the presence of black people in Britain or lax immigration laws, but the new class that exaggerates, even creates, racism in order to secure more power for itself. He argues that race itself is not the issue. Race, he claims, is used by liberals inside government and the media to achieve unstated and often illicit ends. Powell warns:

> We are seeing the growth of positive forces acting against integration, of vested interests in the preservation and sharpening of racial and religious differences, with a view to the exercise of actual domination, first over fellow-immigrants and then over the rest of the population ... for these dangerous and divisive elements the legislation proposed in the Race Relations Bill is the very pabulum they need to flourish.[77]

With regard to multi-cultural education, Ray Honeyford defines the new class thus:

> The multiculturalists are a curious mixture: well meaning liberals and clergymen suffering from a rapidly dating post-Imperial guilt; teachers building a career by jumping on the latest educational bandwagon; a small but increasing group of 'professional' Asian and West Indian intellectuals; and a hard-core of left-wing political extremists, often with a background of polytechnic sociology. They are united by two false and subversive notions: that we all ought to sentimentalize and patronize ethnic minorities, and that society has a duty to impose racial tolerance by government dictat. They are supported by an irrelevant if not positively malign quango (the Commission for Racial Equality), by a huge ragbag of dubious voluntary organizations, and by a growing army of so-called 'advisers' hired by misguided authorities in order to prove their progressive intentions.[78]

An alliance is posited to exist between the new class and the dispossessed in the former's bid to remould British society; a bid that is conceived as being at the expense of the wishes of the majority of 'ordinary citizens'. An opposition of interests is thus created between the new class and the silent majority of conservative citizens who purportedly have to pay a heavy price for new class projects. For example, Alfred Sherman of the

Centre for Policy Studies, writing about the question of whether to allow Asian fiances into the country, described the issue as 'the tip of a submerged but inescapable problem: the conflict between the instincts of the people and the intellectual fashions of the establishment where British nationhood is concerned'.[79] George Gale of the *Daily Express* once argued that the 'society which was Britain never wanted to become multi-racial, and it does not want to now', and that 'race relations' legislation was designed to 'frustrate the determination of the British people to retain their own identity'.[80] In this way, New Rightists present anti-racism as a zero-sum game; attempts to protect black people are presented as an attack on the majority population, British institutions and national identity.

Sometimes New Rightists take this zero-sum argument one step further to allege that anti-racist initiatives themselves are to blame for the existence or at least exacerbation of racial animosity. Harvey Proctor writes in a Monday Club policy paper:

> The liberal establishment has connived to make allowances and concessions to the immigrant communities at the expense, both financial and social, of the indigenous population. In the same way that the CRE, through its harassment of employers, landlords, clubs and other individuals, has stoked up increasing resentment against the protective cocoon woven around the ethnic minorities, so the surreptitious attempts by Government to give unfair opportunities to immigrants in our society will exacerbate that existent resentment, increase racial tension and ultimately risk a backlash by the indigenous population.[81]

In this way, white racism is offered as a justification for the retreat from the pursuit of racial justice, a retreat made more palatable by reference to the subversive intentions of the so-called race relations industry.

The 'race relations industry' is understood as pretending to help blacks in their struggle for equality and justice when in fact it is merely using them to further their own political agenda. It is said to operate 'behind the lines of public life, using every device available'; to 'undermine the stability of the state'; and 'to destabilise the masses, break their instinctive loyalty to, and affection for, the old country'.[82] Donu Kogbara, a rising black journalist writing for the *Sunday Times*, writes:

'The CRE promotes dependency, encourages sloth, creates a victim mentality and only truly benefits those who are steering the race industry gravy train.'[83] Ray Honeyford argues in *Integration or Disintegration* that anti-racist rhetoric is not concerned with the elimination of racism as claimed, but revolution by Marxists in the name of black people.[84] An editorial in *Ethnic Enterprise News* claims that organizations such as the Commission for Racial Equality are 'not about creating racial harmony, eliminating discrimination and creating equal opportunities. It is just one means of effecting social change in British society to meet their ideological revolutionary goals.'[85] References to the alleged revolutionary goals of the 'race relations industry' and the Leninist roots of anti-racism have, in the wake of the collapse of the Soviet Union, given way more recently to diatribes against 'liberal social engineering' and the pursuit of 'illiberal notions of equality' as the new face of the threat to freedom.

The work of anti-racist organizations such as the Commission for Racial Equality, the Runnymede Trust, and the Institute of Race Relations is deemed harmful, or at best useless, since it allows the black community to blame their failure on the British system instead of themselves, and so serves to prevent further assimilation. Russell Lewis, editor of a book entitled *Anti-Racism: A Mania Exposed*, goes further and equates the anti-racist movement with Nazism and pronounces the policy of positive action to be destructive of the goal of tolerance.[86] Roger Scruton does the same in an article for *The Times* entitled 'The paths blocked by anti-racists' in which he compares the methods and goals of the anti-racist movement with those of the Nazi movement.[87] In another column entitled 'Who are the real racists?', Scruton identifies anti-racists as the 'real racists' and accuses them of 'terrorising the white population'.[88]

Thus, racism is not the problem in need of addressing, according to the New Right, but the activities of the 'race relations industry' are. CPS scholar Antony Flew claims, 'The incidence of alleged racism in a given society will vary in direct proportion to the number of people generously paid and prominently positioned to find it', and concludes with a reminder to his readers, 'Never ask the barber whether you need a hair cut.'[89] In a similar vein, New Right commentator Peregrine Worsthorne argues:

Much more effective than the National Front in stirring up racial hatred today are those ostensibly dedicated to anti-racism ... the formenting of bad race relations ... is increasingly what the anti-racist lobby now sets out to do ... a society without racial tension would remove their power base; their political raison d'etre.[90]

An editorial in *Ethnic Enterprise News* announces:

Every year over one hundred million pounds of tax payers' money is spent by the government creating racial conflict in Britain. That is the annual sum spent by the government on the race relations industry. We believe that as racial conflict is caused by subsidising preferential treatment for any racial group in the community it is money ill-spent.[91]

Acknowledging that anti-racist organizations and the individuals associated with them are sometimes self-serving is altogether different from claiming that anti-racists are actually the cause of racism, and by implication that without them racism would disappear.

New Right discourse about the so-called new class and the race relations industry is heir to a long tradition of conspiracy theorization that a secret plan, a hidden agenda, is identified as lurking behind benign liberal opinion. The New Right's preoccupation with identifying the forces allegedly undermining the British way of life helps make sense of its simultaneous concern with blacks as a *threat* to the British nation and as *victims* of the new class conspirators. An aim of all conspiracy theorists (and the main reason for their appeal to the lower middle-class) is to achieve just this double objective: to justify their own exploitative relations to the classes below them, and at the same time to justify resentment of those classes above them. David Edgar, playwright and social critic, notes, 'The new class concept is precisely such a conspiracy theory, creating a common enemy that at one and the same time consists of "affluent liberals" and the black ... "parasites" on welfare.'[92] Moreover, such a conspiracy theory is consonant with the wider Conservative Party objective of rolling back the welfare state; for the new class is presented as living off the welfare machine and promoting racism and other social problems in order to preserve their power base.

The right-wing media has popularized the new class theme in the form of the 'loony left' signifier. The loony left is portrayed as enforcing silly notions of anti-racism, such as reprimanding those who ask for black coffee instead of coffee without milk. Discourse on the loony left is often conflated with the anti-racist activities of local authorities. The argument often offered alleges a conflict of interest for anti-racist organizations – that if they were actually to eliminate racism, they would have worked themselves out of a job. New Rightists argue that, by stressing racial failure and the existence of institutional racism, such organizations actually create the very culture of resentment against which they are ostensibly fighting, thus unwittingly playing into the hands of the BNP. The ready conclusion is to withdraw all public funding from the whole arena of race relations with the justification that if there were no race relations lobby, there would be no racism.

The symbolic construction of the new class enemy has allowed New Rightists to challenge many anti-racist programs previously regarded as legitimate while portraying themselves as the true defenders of tolerance, freedom, and even the nation. Moreover, by focusing so much attention on the alleged manipulations of the new class, the legitimate grievances of the black community are rendered illegitimate, while the real concerns of anti-racists are both trivialized and obscured.

Anti-Anti-Racism

British New Rightists vehemently deny that they are racist. They do this by defining racism in a particularistic manner (that is, as an attitude of racial superiority), and then declaring their rejection of it. In this the New Right is clearly borrowing from Enoch Powell who said in a 1969 interview:

If by being a racialist, you mean a man who despises a human being because he belongs to another race, or a man who believes that one race is inherently superior to another in civilization or capability of civilization, then the answer is emphatically no.[93]

In a similar vein, Charles Moore writes:

> A racist, surely, is someone who subscribes to a theory about
> races. That is to say, he believes that races are the main ex-
> planation of people's character and the determinant of
> culture and civil society. He probably also believes that some
> races are morally and intellectually superior to others, and
> perhaps that some races have a high destiny which involves
> the defeat or destruction of the inferior ... (i.e. Hitler). If
> you are not racist in this sense, you are not a racist at all.[94]

Rather than conceive racism as a product of unjust social
arrangements and the ideology that springs from them,
racism is wholly detached from the social arena and personalized so that it becomes a mere matter of individual choice.
An editorial in *Ethnic Enterprise News* states: 'People who practice racial discrimination, whether they are black or white,
merely exercise personal choice based on ignorance. They
harm themselves as much as anyone else. No amount of legislation in the world will eliminate it.'[95] In *A Future for Anti-
Racism?*, Antony Flew writes, 'to speak where intention is
absent of either institutionalized racism or institutionalized
violence is a perversion ... racism is a characteristic of individuals, not social institutions.'[96]

Similar to the notion of reverse discrimination in the US
context, such symbolic conflict over the definition of racism is
the first twist in the New Right's ideological struggle to identify anti-racism as the new racism – racism against English
(white) people. By detaching the study of racism from relations of a more institutional nature (that is, power relations),
it is made so elastic that blacks are portrayed as being racist
against whites as much as, even more than, the reverse. Frank
Palmer (former teacher and editor of a volume entitled *Anti-
Racism: An Assault Upon Education and Value*) declares, 'I refuse
to support definitions of "racism" which effectively imply that
racism can only be committed by white society.'[97] In a SAU
book entitled *The Wayward Curriculum*, Geoffrey Partington
(senior lecturer in the Education Department at the Flinders
University of South Australia) writes, 'A new racism emerged
in Britain in the early 1980s. ... The main tenets of the creed
are that Britain is suffused with the "central and pervasive

influence of racism" and that all children must be initiated into "black perspectives"'.[98]

Systemic sources of discrimination – in education, employment, housing and the legal system – are usually not recognized, and when they are, they are understood as a function of lack of personal merit. For example, a press release put out by the Social Affairs Unit states:

> Britain's West Indians and Asians are not all members of a single oppressed underclass. Many are doing well in jobs, education and housing. Those who are not, do not owe their problems uniquely or even largely to 'racism'. Government intervention to rig employment or educational opportunities in their favour would be self-defeating and itself racist.[99]

The social structure is deemed open and fair, equal opportunity is purported to exist, and so it is declared to be up to each individual whether or not to 'choose' to take advantage of available opportunities. When undeniable proof of discrimination is provided, in employment for example, it is attributed to 'personal unsuitability' or 'lack of the right qualifications', the sort of discrimination based on free competition and meritocracy that is 'perfectly right and proper'.[100]

New Rightists emphasize isolated individual black success stories in order to make the point that society is not to blame for the relative lack of black upward mobility, while anti-racists are criticized for treating people in terms of a category – black – instead of as a function of individual merit. A color-blind approach to race relations is advocated, one based on free competition and meritocracy. The color-conscious approach, by contrast, is derided as unjust and harmful. In *Free Nation*, multicultural education critic Antony Flew claims, 'The injustice consists – not in treating people in different ways, and hence unequally; but in treating differently, and hence unequally, people who are themselves, in all relevant respects, the same.'[101]

Since New Rightists regard each individual as a master of his or her own fate, whether he or she is black or white, the very possibility that their views are racist is denied. Rather, they argue, the real racists are the collectivists, Marxists and

anti-racists who view blacks as the product of structures.
Director of the Social Affairs Unit Digby Anderson asks:

> How long before the many hard-working, decent Caribbean
> people start objecting to the activists' persistent failure to
> give their hard work and decency its due, by submerging
> them in the all-embracing category of 'Blacks' The activists
> – indifferent, even hostile to their achievements – treat
> them as a chunk of social structure ... The interest, and
> indeed right, of all these 'Blacks' is to be treated according
> to their individual and varied behaviour and those of the
> groups they themselves choose to belong to; not to be dra-
> gooned into an artificial, culturally and morally neutered
> class of 'Blacks' because it suits the political purposes of
> some activist, desperate to invent a new lower class to
> replace the unfaithful 'white one'.[102]

In this way, the very category black is made to appear illegitimate in New Right discourse – as is the category women and
homosexual – a rhetorical eradication that is profoundly political since it precludes the possibility of any collective political
emancipatory project.

Moreover, color-conscious policies such as positive action or
minority recruitment initiatives are held to harm more than
help their supposed beneficiaries. Frank Parkins of the Social
Affairs Unit claims just this when he writes, 'Positive discrimination promotes racial discrimination, racial disharmony, race
and color consciousness, undesirable group images, inferior
self-images among minority groups and welfare dependency.'[103] Color-consciousness is redefined as being itself
harmful; a redefinition that can only occur once racism is so
radically separated from the social arena and individualized as
an attitude existing in this or that head, not in institutions. An
editorial in *Ethnic Enterprise News* states:

> Not only does discrimination, which is essentially a matter of
> personal choice and therefore a matter of some complexity,
> not lend itself to legal regulation: the pursuit of eliminating
> discrimination by legal, and thus by heavy-handed methods,
> may in fact deter and damage good relations between
> members of different racial groups.[104]

Similarly, critic of multiculturalism Ray Honeyford asks, 'If the schools help deprive the majority of any sense of attachment to their indigenous roots and identity, whilst emphasizing the importance of minority cultures, is this not likely to create feelings of deprivation and resentment?'[105]

Anti-racist organizations such as the CRE are criticized for perpetuating and further aggravating the very racial divisiveness against which it is meant to work. For example, Antony Flew writes,

> It is, it seems, impossible to persuade the CRE that this [Section 11] funding of racially discriminatory privilege is incompatible with the first of its own stated aims: 'the elimination of discrimination and promoting equality of opportunity' ... Are we not to expect such practices to generate resentments among the racially excluded, and others who may choose to share their not unreasonable resentment?[106]

Similarly, in a 1992 book entitled *Race and Free Speech: Violating the Taboo*, Ray Honeyford compares the ambitions of the CRE with those of the Spanish inquisition and draws an analogy between the current taboo against addressing race relations issues with what he terms the Galileo syndrome of the Middle Ages. After blaming what he terms the race relations industry and its alleged institutionalized pessimism for encouraging anti-social behavior and producing bad race relations, Honeyford concludes by advocating that the 'publicly-funded race relations lobby must be abolished, together with its patronizing paraphernalia of social and racial engineering ...'[107] Glory Osaji-Umeaku, the Nigerian-born editor of *Ethnic Enterprise News*, recently published a pamphlet entitled *British Race Relations Legislation: How Democratic?*, in which he argues that racial equality laws hurt poor whites, Asians and blacks alike because they restrict their freedom to operate in the marketplace.[108] All these authors agree that, far from eradicating discrimination, anti-racist organizations and racial equality legislation have actually validated and institutionalized racism.

The English are consistently portrayed in New Right discourse as victimized by anti-racist initiatives. For example, a group that called itself 'Majority Rights' was formed in March, 1988 (although it disbanded soon thereafter) in order to 'speak out for the indigenous population' and to combat race relations legislation and multicultural education programs that it deemed 'almost entirely anti-English in effect'.[109] Ray Honeyford became notorious for his campaign against multi-ethnic education on the basis that it discriminated against white schoolchildren by denigrating the British Empire, by 'forcing them to read "Inglan is a Bitch" alongside Wordsworth and Shakespeare', and by undermining 'any sense of there being a distinctive British cultural heritage'.[110] Campaigns against racism (as well as those against sexism and homophobia) are thus, in one stroke, delegitimized for causing, rather than responding to, conflicts of a social and/or material kind.

Another organization aimed at combating the so-called race relations industry emerged in the 1990s, calling itself Fair Play. Organized by Ralph Michael Harrison, first editor of *Right Now!*, the group postures as a defender of the white community against discrimination and calls for the repeal of all those provisions of the Race Relations Act 1976 that promote black people. Harrison is particularly vocal in his criticism of the Major administration over its lack of attention to the issue of affirmative action, and even goes so far as to attribute responsibility for the BNP victory in the Millwall 1993 council by-election to the conservatives' silence. In a recent issue of *Right Now!*, Harrison charges that 'the greatest engine for "politically correct" fascism is now the "conservative" government. Like two giant maggots, the Commission for Equal Opportunity and Race Relations are eating away at our freedom to choose how we wish to live and undermining our traditional standards and values.'[111]

The onus of responsibility for bettering race relations and redressing patterns of racial inequality is laid on the black and migrant communities themselves. Monday Club ideologue Derek Laud writes, 'Only when immigrants are encouraged to owe their loyalties to "Britain" in an integrated society, only when they are discouraged from creating their own foreign "nations" within the U.K. will there be any real hope of long term racial harmony in this country.'[112] The onus of responsibility for rising levels of racist violence, too, is placed upon the victims rather than the perpetrators. A leader in the *Daily Mail* warns:

Either they forgo the anarchic luxury of these orgies of arson, looting and murderous assaults against the men and women whose task it is to uphold the laws of this land or they will provoke a paramilitary reaction unknown to mainland Britain. ... Either they obey the laws of this land where they have taken up residence and accepted both the full rights and responsibilities of citizenship, or they must expect the fascist street agitators to call ever more boldly and with ever louder approval for them to 'go back from whence they came!'[113]

Such sentiments became even more salient in 1989 in the midst of what came to be known as the 'Rushdie Affair', the controversy surrounding the international Muslim response to the publication of *The Satanic Verses*. The New Right reaction to the Affair reinforced in the minds of many the proposition that black people (and in this case Muslims in particular) do not share the dominant political values of British society. For example, an editorial that appeared in the *Daily Telegraph* concluded: 'In the wake of *The Satanic Verses*, there must be increased pessimism about how far different communities in our nation can ever be integrated, or want to be.'[114] An article entitled 'In bed with bigotry' in the *Daily Mail* stated:

Where it [the melting pot] emphatically doesn't work is when we find ourselves acting host to those who impose their culture on English neighbourhoods in much the same manner as we used to plant our red telephone boxes and gentlemen's clubs in the far-flung corners of the Empire. This isolationism, or Little Islamism as we may call it in the case of the Moslems, arises directly out of our race relations policy as it was formulated in the transition to the multiethnic society we find ourselves living in today. The emphasis was not on assimilation, not on the newcomers adapting themselves to our little ways, but on our adapting ourselves to theirs.[115]

In this way, the Rushdie Affair added impetus to the New Right argument that the development of ethnic pluralism via anti-racist initiatives could have potentially dangerous consequences for the social stability and cohesion of the nation.

Throughout the 1990s, the New Right's anti-anti-racism has relied increasingly on the symbolic construction of cultural and even moral distinctions between the majority population and communities of color. In so doing, New Rightists have helped justify the new spirit of social meanness *vis-à-vis* the pursuit of racial equality, especially as it relates to the welfare reform debate and the alleged drain on national resources represented by 'bogus' asylum seekers and 'illegal' immigrants. As British New Rightists have looked to the other side of the Atlantic for right-wing role models, what they have found and in fact borrowed is a moralistic rhetoric about the deserving and the undeserving poor (that is, the underclass), as well as other symptoms of alleged dysfunctional values.

For example, right-wing Tory politicians and think tanks have attacked the rise of lone-parent families, believing that the ideal of the traditional family must be resurrected if society is to turn itself around. Dr David Green, director of the Institute of Economic Affair's health and welfare unit, caused a political storm in 1993 when, referring to the need for a return to Victorian values such as self-sacrifice, suggested that if unmarried mothers were to qualify for housing benefits, they should live in hostels. According to Green, such a move would prevent single mothers from having babies in order to move ahead in the housing queue, discourage them from having 'a string of boyfriends', and offer the advantage of a 'restrictive life-style' and 'guidance on how to bring up a child'.[116] Mimicking George Gilder (the US neo-conservative author of *Wealth and Poverty*), Green also suggested that young fathers should be forced to pay child support in order to provide sanction for more responsible behavior. While the call for a return to Victorian values is not inherently racist, the implicit moral distinction evoked between deserving and undeserving citizen operates on a terrain that is already heavily racially coded – both ideologically and materially. Racism is an important secondary bond in the values debate, there for those who wish to discover it.

Much of the intellectual ammunition for the British New Right campaign against single mothers and 'deadbeat dads', both of which became centerpieces of the failed Major initiated 'Back to Basics' movement in 1993, was provided by

Charles Murray, US neoconservative author of *Losing Ground* and, most recently, coauthor of the highly controversial *The Bell Curve.*[117] Invited by the Institute of Economic Affairs on several occasions in the late 1980s and early 1990s, Murray published an IEA pamphlet on what he termed the emerging British underclass and wrote a piece for the *Sunday Times* that rehearsed his now notorious belief that lax welfare spending is responsible for creating a permanent underclass, defined by its behavior of unemployability, crime and, most importantly, illegitimacy.[118] Murray's call for punitive measures to deter such 'dysfunctional' behavior of the poor is controversial enough in the United States where, because the nation's civil religion is defined by individualism, explanations for social phenomena often turn on individual rather than social factors. However, in Britain, where social democratic values remain deeply rooted, the introduction of the underclass debate, alleging that poverty is caused by lone parenthood and other behavioral attributes of the poor rather than the other way around, represents a bold and frontal assault on the political culture's way of thinking.

While the concept of the underclass does have a certain usefulness if it refers to structural features of the economy, as distinct from the alleged behavioral features of its members, the New Right's use of the concept resonates not because it offers sophisticated social analysis, but because the term reintroduces morality and emotion into the national conversation about rising crime, increasing social inequality, and family break-down. In doing so, New Rightists blame already victimized groups of people such as poor people of color, who are disproportionately represented in the underclass, all in the name of battling the so-called dependency culture and defending the common virtues they regard as indispensable to liberty.

In this reversal of cause and effect, victim and perpetrator, New Right anti-anti-racism constitutes a category mistake of the most severe kind by identifying anti-racism as the cause of racial animosity and resentment. New Right anti-anti-racism kills two birds with one stone: it unites those whom the New Right opposes in spheres as various as education, left-wing local government and immigration into one single new class of anti-racists, and second, it deflects responsibility for social problems from state institutions onto those who are most victimized by these problems – the black and the poor.

In conclusion, British New Right discourse circulates a set of meanings concerning race that serves to establish and sustain relations of racial domination. White majority fears of being swamped by alien cultures are naturalized via recourse to a static and immutable view of human nature. British culture is construed as being static and homogeneous, and inevitably weakened by alien strains, thus unifying 'the people' across classes against the racialized other. Political enemies are constructed both in the form of the enemy within and the new class, thus serving to deflect attention from complex structural sources of change. Finally, existing social relations of racial domination are legitimated by denying the existence of institutional racism and by employing the discursive strategy of victim-blaming. As a totality, the ideological mechanisms of naturalization, unification, construction of political enemies, and legitimation together constitute the new racism of the British New Right.

5 The New Racism and the Racial State

The weapons used in symbolic conflict are ideas, but the outcome can be measured only in terms of the impact of those ideas on government policy formation and the construction of popular opinion. The categories of meaning employed by government in defining an event or issue do not passively reflect an objective reality, but rather actively construct which social problems are significant and which insignificant, and accordingly, which political solutions are judged beneficial and which misguided. Thus, since every policy issue is contested in a symbolic arena, an analysis of the new racism of the New Right would be incomplete without an examination of the symbiotic relationship between it and the policy formation process in the era of Reaganism and Thatcherism and beyond.

The elections of Ronald Reagan and Margaret Thatcher to office represented a break from the prevailing post-war political settlement in each country (that is, New Deal/Great Society liberalism in the United States and social democracy in Britain). Both their projects signified a radical departure from this settlement in the sense that they challenged in principle many of the core assumptions that had governed the politics and ideology of both countries for the past half century. These assumptions include, most importantly, government commitment to full employment, welfare state support, equality of opportunity (particularly for women and people of color), and neo-Keynesian economic management. In their place a new philosophy of social conservatism was articulated at the very (right of) center of political debate.

In the process, prevailing assumptions about the role of the state in ensuring the socio-economic well-being of its citizenry, and the appropriate scope and means of social policy to achieve that goal, were fundamentally reworked. Both administrations argued that, as to the problem of social

191

inequality, government was part of the problem rather than the solution. Together they urged that responsibility be shifted from central government to the individual, family, church, and other voluntary associations at the local level. In their aftermath, subsequent administrations – conservative and liberal – have continued down the path set by Reaganism and Thatcherism, reaffirming in the process the ideological terrain set by the New Right. While the degree to which a new conservative consensus can be said to have been forged is ambiguous in many ways, with progress both sketchy and contradictory, it is clear that a change has occurred and that many core liberal and social democratic assumptions have been challenged.

One important aspect of the right turn in US and British and politics is the challenge to former liberal assumptions specifically relating to race. Race has been a key factor in the unraveling of post-war liberal/left coalitions in both countries and in provoking a realignment of social, political and individual identities towards the right. Government policies on matters pertaining to racial inclusion, as well as the ideological perspectives that in the past have informed them, have been dramatically transformed.

Over the course of the past two decades, government policy formation in the arena of race relations increasingly has dovetailed in important ways with the key categories of meaning produced and circulated by the New Right. While the erosion of many of the gains of previous struggles for racial equality and justice may not have been the primary motivation behind the right turn, and while racism defined in the particularistic sense has been conspicuously absent, the new racism nevertheless has served as an important secondary bond. Symbolic conflict about race has been used especially by the right wing of the Republican and Tory parties in the internal debate and struggle within the dominant social bloc around which political strategies to adopt in pursuit of their sometimes contradictory economic interests, to erode those aspects of progress that have been perceived to interfere with the forward march of the neo-liberal economic agenda, and has also provided a powerful emotional source of popular mobilization behind the wider conservative agenda.

THE NEW RACISM AND THE POLITICS OF REAGANISM

Although not able to reverse the march of history, Ronald
Reagan did succeed in slowing the tempo by creating a
climate in which the fact and appearance of retrenchment
was possible ... Although the Reagan presidency has shown
that full retreat may not be possible, it has shown that
advance can be arrested.[1]

The election of Ronald Reagan to office signalled a
significant departure from the post-war political settlement.
More specifically, Reagan broke with the general trajectory of
racial progress that marked the post-war period. Although
Reagan's electoral victories, like Thatcher's, should not be
read simply as a popular mandate for his racial politics, it is
clear that a profound shift was under way in the assumptions
that underlay government policy formation on matters pertaining to race.

The significance of Reagan's retreat from the federal commitment to redress the effects of past and present racial discrimination can best be appreciated against the backdrop of
his predecessors. President Truman was the first to initiate
meaningful civil rights enforcement efforts at the federal level,
his Administration's most significant act being the desegregation of the armed forces. Although Eisenhower the man expressed much reluctance to use federal authority to advance
civil rights, the force of historical and popular pressure led
him to sign into law the country's first civil rights bill (1957)
and to enforce federal desegregation efforts (at Little Rock,
Arkansas, for example).

With Kennedy in the White House, and with the gathering
momentum of the civil rights movement, the enforcement
of civil rights became a highly visible national priority. Yet it
was Johnson, under the heat of enormous popular pressure,
who actually carried through much of Kennedy's mandate, securing passage of the most far-reaching civil rights legislation
yet: the Civil Rights Act of 1964, the Voting Rights Act of 1965,
the Age Discrimination in Employment Act of 1967, and the
Fair Housing Act of 1968. Moreover, Johnson launched the
War on Poverty that extended the struggle for civil rights into

the economic arena. His Administration also took steps to ensure effective enforcement of such legislation as was passed. These steps included affirmative action programs mandated by Executive Order 11246, as well as the creation of bureaucratic entities such as the Equal Employment Opportunity Commission (EEOC) and the Office for Federal Contract Compliance Programs (OFCCP).

The Administrations of Nixon, Ford and Carter oversaw a period of spectacular decline in popular mobilization and the economic recession of 1973–75. With respect to civil rights, this was a mixed period of advance in some areas (appointments of black leaders under Carter, for example), consolidation in others (with greater powers of enforcement granted to the EEOC and OFCCP under Nixon), and selective retreat (for instance, rejection of school busing by Nixon and Carter).

It was not until Reagan's election to office, however, that a principled assault upon many of the key gains of the popular struggles of the 1960s was waged at the heart of government, and particularly against the gains of popular struggles for racial justice and equality. In this respect, the politics of Reaganism can rightly be considered a radical departure from the previous broad trajectory of racial progress. Reagan succeeded in rolling back many of the key gains of the civil rights movement without, significantly, appearing as a mean-spirited racist. His Administration did not rely on particularist racist attitudes, but rather on more widespread and general assumptions relating to the appropriate means by which to redress past discrimination, the proper scope of state activity, and the responsibility of individual citizens for their own social location.

In so doing, the Reagan administration acknowledged and validated many of the key categories of meaning produced and circulated by the New Right. Professing deference to the federal commitment to oppose racial discrimination and defend equality of opportunity, the Reagan administration set out to undermine racial progress as part of its broader aim of making social conservatism politically dominant. While the Reagan administration ultimately failed to secure a complete reversal on policy matters pertaining to race, as we shall see below, it did succeed in critically slowing the momentum of racial progress and radically changing the terms of the debate by:

1. denouncing affirmative action as a form of government-mandated 'reverse discrimination';
2. critically undermining federal enforcement efforts;
3. drastically slowing the pace of school desegregation; and
4. eliminating many of the social welfare programs upon which people of color disproportionately rely.

The new racism of the New Right helped to provide the Reagan administration the required ideological formulations with which to rationalize such an unprecedented reversal of federal commitment. As we shall see below, these formulations continued to shape and justify government policy formation under the Administrations of George Bush and Bill Clinton.

Affirmative Action

The Reagan administration's rhetoric on affirmative action resonated with each of the New Right key categories of meaning outlined above. During the 1980 presidential campaign and throughout his tenure in the White House, Reagan advocated a color-blind approach to civil rights policy. A commitment to equal rights for all individuals was professed, and racism was denounced as in all cases abhorrent. In making such a commitment, however, the Administration was clear to draw the distinction between support for equality of opportunity for the individual, which it supported, and equality of results for the group, which it opposed. The 1980 GOP Platform stated:

> The truths we hold and the values we share affirm that no individual should be victimized by unfair discrimination because of race, sex, advanced age, physical handicap, difference of national origin or religion, or economic circumstance. However, equal opportunity should not be jeopardized by bureaucratic regulations and decisions which rely on quotas, ratios, and numerical requirements to exclude some individuals in favor of others, thereby rendering such regulations and decisions inherently discriminatory.

Thus, true to the New Right's own position, the Administration took a strong and principled stand against all forms of quotas as constituting 'reverse discrimination'. The New Right vision of a society wherein an individual may be judged on his or her own individual merit, and one in which individuals rather than groups are in possession of Constitutional rights, was thereby affirmed by civil rights policy under the Reagan administration.

Within weeks of being elected to office, Secretary of Labor Raymond Donovan issued new regulations for the Office of Federal Contract Compliance Programs that substantially undermined affirmative action requirements attached to federal contracts. These guidelines relaxed standards for minority representation, exempted government contractors from filing affirmative action plans, ruled that compensation should be made only to identifiable victims of discrimination, and that back pay as a class remedy should be awarded only in the most extreme situations. The new proposals reduced the number of businesses required to establish affirmative action goals and timetables, the number of forms to be completed, and the frequency with which affirmative action plans were to be updated.

Despite such action, tensions emerged almost immediately between the New Right and the Reagan administration. New Rightists objected to the fact that reforms were being justified in terms of the 'excessive paperwork' involved in administering affirmative action programs rather than as principled opposition to the concept itself.[2] New Rightists urged principled opposition to 'all color-conscious public policies, especially those which permit quotas, timetables, goals, ratios, or numerical objectives on the basis of race, color, sex or national origin' as a form of 'reverse racism'.[3]

New Right complaints of betrayal were compounded further when Reagan-appointee Attorney General William French Smith announced that the new Administration would abide by the Professional and Administrative Career Examination (PACE) consent decree (negotiated under the Carter administration) with only minor modifications. This decree stated that PACE would be phased out on the grounds that, since minorities disproportionately had failed the exam, it was discriminatory *in effect*. Certain New Rightists took the decision as a retreat from Reagan's earlier principled rejection of the concept of group rights.[4]

Increasingly, a new combination of categories of meaning and assumptions – what will be referred to here as a paradigm – emerged in the government's justification of its retreat from the concept and practice of affirmative action. One of the first signs of the emergence of this 'reverse racism' paradigm was the historical reversal of sides by the Justice Department in cases of racial discrimination. Previously the Department brought suits against those who failed to adhere to affirmative action guidelines. Under Reagan, the Department brought suits that opposed those same guidelines on the basis that they instituted a new form of racism. William Bradford Reynolds, Assistant Attorney General for Civil Rights in the Justice Department under Reagan, said before a Congressional subcommittee:

> We no longer will insist upon or in any respect support the use of quotas or any other numerical or statistical formulae designed to provide to non-victims of discrimination preferential treatment based on race, sex, national origin, or religion. To pursue any other course is, in our view, unsound as a matter of law and unwise as a matter of policy ... By elevating the rights of groups over the rights of individuals, racial preferences ... are at war with the American ideal of equal opportunity for each person to achieve whatever his or her industry and talents warrant ... Nor is there any moral justification for such an approach. Special treatment of people in the field of employment, based on nothing more than personal characteristics of race or gender, is as offensive to standards of human decency today as it was some 84 years ago when countenanced under *Plessy v. Ferguson*.[5]

Reynolds continued to speak out against quotas as 'morally repugnant' and likened them to 'prescribing alcohol to get beyond alcoholism'.[6] Attorney General Smith under Reagan supported his colleague when he told the American Law Institute: 'While well intended, quotas invariably have the practical effect of placing inflexible restraints on the opportunities afforded one race in an effort to remedy past discrimination against another. They stigmatize the beneficiaries.'[7] At issue was whether the government commitment to guarantee equality of opportunity required it to take remedial action only in cases of proven *intent* to discriminate, or in cases of discriminatory *effect* as well. The Justice Department under Reagan consistently affirmed that it would embrace only the former.

Such a (re)interpretation had a wide-ranging impact. The Justice Department dropped desegregation cases in cities such as Houston and Kansas City, and integration efforts were slowed in cities such as Chicago, Phoenix and Rochester. In 1983 the Department declared 'illegal and unconstitutional' the Detroit Police Plan that called for the promotion of white and black officers in equal numbers until such time that racial balance was achieved in fact. In 1985, the Justice Department opposed efforts in the city of Indianapolis to use hiring quotas in local government, and urged cities across the nation to 'voluntarily' (under threat of court action) remove numerical goals and quotas from affirmative action plans.[8] These actions and others, justified on the basis of lack of proof of *intent* to discriminate, signalled a clear policy reversal since all previous Administrations with the mandate to enforce affirmative action had required only demonstration that a practice was discriminatory *in effect*.

The question of whether discriminatory intent or discriminatory effect was the legitimate basis for the imposition of government sanction came to a head in 1981–2 over the Congressional extension of the 1965 Voting Rights Act. In early 1981, prompted by a case in Mobile, Alabama, Congress proposed an extension of the Voting Rights Act to bar electoral arrangements that had the practical effect of diluting the black vote in a particular community. The proposed extension was meant only to make the proof of discrimination easier, and expressly forbade the use of quotas. Yet, throughout the spring and summer of 1981, Reagan roadblocked the extension on the principle that there was no proof of intent, and so to support the extension would violate the Administration's opposition to group rights and color-conscious policy. Reagan stated that the Act would lead 'to where all of society had to have an actual quota system'.[9] In making such a statement, Reagan endorsed New Right Senator Orrin Hatchs' insistence that all the law could do was to 'ensure equal access by minorities to the registration process and the ballot box' not, he insisted, 'to ensure equal results and equal outcome' for such groups.[10]

Despite his initial opposition, Reagan eventually backed down and supported the extension of the Voting Rights Act. This reversal came in the wake of the eruption of the controversy over Reagan's support for tax exemptions for segregated private schools (see below). Together the two issues lent credence to the opposition's charge that Reagan was hostile to civil rights and the goal of racial equality. In order to salvage the Administration's self-cultivated image as a friend of civil rights, Reagan capitulated. Once again the New Right was up in arms, feeling that the conservative movement had been further betrayed by the Administration. New Rightists charged that the Administration had abandoned its principled opposition to color-conscious policies and, by signing the Act, had indeed condoned them.

New Right ideologues continued to criticize the Administration's handling of the affirmative action issue. Chester Finn described Reagan's handling of the quota issue as:

> a fitful and uneven process, in which the nation's long slide into color-coded policies and group entitlements was somewhat slowed but hardly stopped by an administration that seemed uncertain whether it really wanted to apply the brakes and not altogether sure where to find them.[11]

Attention to the significant conflict between the New Right and the Reagan Administration over such matters, particularly marked during these early years, should not, however, obscure the degree to which affirmative action under the Administration was severely undermined. The emphasis placed upon proof of discriminatory intent, albeit blocked at many points by Congress, did serve to reduce the initiation of anti-discrimination litigation by the executive branch of government since it is much harder to prove intent than to demonstrate the effects of discriminatory practices.

Thus, while it is true that the Reagan administration was forced to sacrifice some principle for the pragmatism of politics once in office, government policy initiatives, and the rhetoric used to justify them, served to reinforce the New Right theme that affirmative action was indeed a new form of racism. Limited in what and how fast it could dismantle affirmative action programs without jeopardizing its self-avowed commitment of support for racial equality, the Administration began to aim at the bureaucracies responsible for administering and enforcing the programs (rather than at the legitimacy of the concept itself). Indeed, as discussed in the following section, the cause of racial justice was weakened most severely by the Reagan administration's stacking of civil right organizations with conservatives and by undermining their power of enforcement.

The Assault upon the Civil Rights Establishment

Federal enforcement of civil rights and equal opportunity legislation was relaxed under the Reagan administration as part of the wider conservative project to limit the role of federal intervention and regulation. Indications of this reduction can be seen in the decline of real budgetary outlays for civil rights enforcement agencies, staff reductions, and the corresponding decline of the pursuit of anti-discriminatory activities by organizations such as the Equal Employment Opportunities Commission (EEOC), the Office for Federal Contract Compliance Programs (OFCCP), and the Civil Rights Division of the Justice Department.

John Palmer and Isabel Sawhill, two analysts of the Reagan record, found that total real outlays for all civil rights and equal opportunity enforcement throughout the federal government declined by 9 per cent from 1981 to 1983.[12] Adjusting for inflation, the budget for the EEOC was reduced by 10 per cent while that of the OFCCP was reduced by 24 per cent during this same period. These cuts resulted in staff reductions of 12 per cent and 34 per cent, respectively. While the budget of the Civil Rights Division of the Justice Department remained about the same, its staff was reduced by 13 per cent. These trends were rationalized with the view that most civil rights goals had been accomplished by the equal opportunity legislation of the 1960s, and that the activities of the civil rights establishment were therefore no longer needed – a rationalization that clearly echoed the New Right's own position.

One of the first signs of the emerging hegemony of the 'reverse racism' paradigm in the justification of government policy was Reagan's appointment of Clarence Thomas to the chairmanship of the EEOC. The appointment of a long-time and principled opponent of affirmative action to one of the key government agencies responsible for the enforcement of affirmative action guidelines served for awhile to reassure New Rightists of the Administration's commitment to the principle of color-blindness.

By the time of the appointment, Clarence Thomas had made his reputation as a leading black neo-conservative who championed the view that affirmative action programs stigmatize their beneficiaries and that it is wrong to infer discrimination from the number of minority group members employed in a particular enterprise. In an article for the black neo-conservative journal *Lincoln Review*, Thomas stated:

> I am unalterably opposed to programs that force or even cajole people to hire a certain percentage of minorities. I watched the operation of such affirmative action policies when I was in college and I watched the destruction of many kids as a result. It was wrong for those kids, and it was wrong to give that kind of false hope.[13]

In the same article, Thomas asks, 'Would you go to a black lawyer if you felt he was there just because he was black?' In the face of the Bush administration's race-conscious appointment of Thomas to the Supreme Court, such a rhetorical question is ironic indeed!

The political posture of the EEOC shifted under the chairmanship of Clarence Thomas – with telling effects. The Commission condoned the Labor Department's reduction of the number of federal contractors required to fill affirmative action guidelines. The cases of employment discrimination brought by the EEOC declined by half in the first three years, while the number of complaints brought by individuals increased over that same period by 50 per cent.[14] Cases in which the 'no cause' finding was recorded increased by over a third. The emphasis was changed from class-action lawsuits to individual ones, while the burden of proof (as with cases of sexual discrimination) was shifted from the employer to the plaintiff.

The above patterns also hold true for the OFCCP. The number of administrative complaints filed by the OFCCP against government contractors dropped from fifty-three in 1980 to five in 1982 and eighteen in 1983.[15] The amount of financial compensation awarded fell from $9m in 1980 to less than $4m in 1983, in the context of a 50 per cent increase in the number of complaints investigated.[16] Such a decline can be attributed in large part to the government's endorsement of the New Right theme that only identifiable victims of discrimination have the right to compensation.

Ironically, in order to *reduce* the federal role in the enforcement of civil rights, the Reagan administration had actively to *intervene* in the affairs of already-existing enforcement agencies. The most dramatic example of this was its virtual coup against the Civil Rights Commission (CRC) in 1983. The CRC was founded as an independent, non-partisan watchdog organization responsible for monitoring the activities of the civil rights enforcement agencies of the federal government. Its independence was diminished gradually during the first years of the Reagan administration, as the Commission's support for affirmative action was clearly at odds with the Administration's own position.

It was not until 1983–84, however, that the battle over the CRC came to a head. Frustrated by the Senate's refusal to allow him to appoint new Commissioners more in keeping with his views, Reagan fired the three Democrat-appointees (out of six, the other three being Republican) who had been the most critical of his civil rights policies. This was an unprecedented action as the CRC was supposed to be independent of the executive in performing its mandate from Congress. Yet Reagan claimed on his side the Constitutional power of appointment. The action was overruled later by a district court and the reinstatement of the three ordered. The court order became moot, however, in the wake of the fashioning of a new compromise between the Administration and Congress. It was agreed that the number of Commissioners would be increased from six to eight: four of whom would be appointed by the president; two by the majority and minority leaders of the Senate (one each); and two by the majority and minority leaders of the House (one each).[17]

When the newly-constituted CRC met for the first time in early 1984, it became clear that the compromise was to work very much in the Administration's favor. With a majority of

Commissioners sympathetic to the Reagan administration's own positions, statements were issued that reversed previous CRC positions favoring affirmative action, racial quotas, court-ordered busing and bilingual education. The additional appointment of Linda Chavez as staff director, an outspoken critic of quotas as discriminatory against white males, served to tilt the CRC even more in the Administration's favor. In the words of Mary Frances Berry (one of the three Commissioners originally fired in 1983): 'The Commission on Civil Rights has become a parody of its former self, a politicized institution for the first time in its history.'[18]

Symbolic conflict over the issue of affirmative action and methods for its enforcement remained underground yet vital throughout the 1980s and into the 1990s. During the tenure of the Bush administration, one of the most significant instances involved the controversy surrounding the 1990 Civil Rights Bill. The Bill attempted to expand employment discrimination protection for people of color and women, as well as overturn a series of 1989 Supreme Court decisions limiting the scope of employment discrimination law. In particular, it aimed to overturn a ruling (Wards Cove Packing Company *v.* Antonio) that allowed companies to use ability tests and other hiring criteria that adversely affect blacks and Hispanics if such criteria met the standard of 'business justification'. In effect, the Wards Cove ruling partially reversed an earlier Supreme Court ruling (Griggs *v.* Duke Power Company) which held that if hiring or promotion procedures are found to have 'adverse impact' on people of color – that is, if disproportionately more people of color than whites are rejected – employers must demonstrate that such tests are essential for business operation and meet a stringent 'business necessity' standard. The Wards Cove ruling explicitly declared that 'there is not requirement that the challenged practice be "essential" or "indispensable" to the employer's business.'[19] The 1990 civil rights bill would have added such a requirement, returning to the clause 'business necessity' as originally contained in the Griggs case. As Thomas and Mary Edsall note, drawing upon two studies by the National Research Council documenting the importance of restricted ability testing for the employment prospects of blacks and Hispanics, the Bill's more stringent requirements would have carried significant positive consequences *vis-à-vis* the hiring of people of color.[20]

The Bush administration vetoed the Bill, labelling it a 'quota bill'. The Administration insisted that the Bill would provide a strong incentive for employers to avoid costly litigation by adopting de facto, although not official, quota systems. Although commentators charged that the quota issue was strategically used by the Republican Party for electoral gain, and specifically to woo white voters away from the Democratic Party, it is important to note that the legitimate question of the proper interpretation of Title VII of the 1964 Civil Rights Act was once again at stake. At issue were the familiar questions raised by the New Right: does proof of discrimination require demonstration of discriminatory intent or only disparate outcomes? Do civil rights belong to individuals or groups? Is it proper for the state to impose costly constraints on business productivity and efficiency in the name of pursuing racial equality?

Professing his commitment to the belief that not all differences in group outcomes are attributable to discrimination, President Bush declared in his Rose Garden civil rights speech in the summer of 1990 that empowerment, rather than quotas, should form the cornerstone of future civil rights policies. Empowerment initiatives include parental choice in education, enterprise zones, tenant ownership of public housing, and anti-crime legislation. After Congress failed to override Bush's veto (it was sustained in the Senate by one vote), the Administration introduced a 'civil rights and individual opportunities' legislative package on 27 February 1991, which linked civil rights and empowerment measures, a linkage that the New Right had been urging for over a year. An article in a Heritage Foundation Backgrounder applauded the package:

> The Administration's proposals are a first step in shifting the terms of the debate over civil rights issues, away from divisive and counterproductive social engineering schemes and toward efforts to eliminate barriers to opportunity. They reflect the first attempt by a Republican administration to do something more in the civil rights area than merely to oppose or imitate liberal civil rights proposals.[21]

Yet certain New Rightists remained skeptical of the Bush administration's commitment to truly break with the liberal civil rights agenda. For example, in an article for *Policy Review* entitled 'George Bush's Quota Bill', Terry Eastland (author, most recently, of *Colorblind Justice: The Case Against Affirmative Action*) criticized the Bush administration's alternative to the bill, revolving as it did around a dispute over the meaning of 'business necessity', for assuming the validity of disparate impact theory.

> Both bills support the dreaded 'Q' word: both, to one degree or another, support quotas. Both the president and congressional Democrats would require employers to justify any hiring or promotion standards that result in less-than-proportionate employment of minorities and women ... If the Bush administration survives the current effort to codify disparate impact theory, it should rethink its civil rights strategy. It may have committed a serious strategic mistake by failing to make a public case for the superiority of the original understanding of Title VII.[22]

In a similar vein, a Heritage Foundation *Backgrounder* criticized the Bush administration's handling of the controversy, charging that its failure to effectively link civil rights with empowerment strategies had allowed Congressional Democrats to dictate the terms of the debate.[23] Indeed, New Rightists had a point; for the differences between the Democratic and Republican plan were minuscule: both would have shifted the burden of proof of discrimination to employers. The only difference between the two plans, and the crux of the whole quotas argument, reduced down to a difference between the Democrats' wording that emphasized the need to demonstrate that ability tests had a 'significant and manifest relationship to job performance' and the Republicans focus on whether or not hiring criteria 'serves in a significant way ... legitimate employment goals'. Yet, on the symbolic level, Bush managed to paint this as the difference between fair and effective civil rights legislation and immoral quotas.

New Right critics were vindicated when, the next year, Bush backed down and signed an almost identical bill. Although a myriad of factors contributed to the Administration's change of heart, one contextual factor was particularly salient: David Duke's (former Grand Wizard of the KKK) success at the polls that year as a candidate for the Louisiana Senate. Duke's strong showing took many pundits by surprise, and embarrassed the Republican Party since Duke's platform on matters such as welfare and affirmative action was strikingly similar to their own, leading then Vice-President Dan Quayle to lambaste the messenger while affirming the message. Despite such maneuvering, the Bush administration began a public relations campaign aimed at distancing itself from such extremism, and one result was a lack of willingness to take the issue of affirmative action head-on. It would not be until the mid-1990s that the Republicans would have the votes to do it.

It was in the wake of the 1994 so-called 'Republican Revolution' that affirmative action entered center stage of the US political scene; all of the sudden, resentment of state-order 'preferences' became politically smart. Then Senate Majority leader Bob Dole, Kansas Republican, a one-time supporter of affirmative action, began to criticize the policy as ineffectual and unfair. In early 1996, two other important Presidential hopefuls besides Dole – Phil Gramm of Texas and California Governor Pete Wilson – promised to abolish racial 'preferences' if elected. President Clinton eventually came round to give his tepid support for affirmative action, but only after commissioning a five month Labor Department internal review process to study its effects. Although in the wake of this review Clinton eventually concluded 'mend it, don't end it', the way in which he carefully distinguished his supporting views of the policy from those that would condone the use of quotas or any form of 'reverse discrimination', sent a signal of less than total commitment. Moreover, the manner in which the Administration groped for middle ground by backing the principles behind affirmative action while simultaneously criticizing particular programs reaffirmed the New Right's concern for fairness rather than the alternative script focusing on power, advantage and control. The Clinton administration thereby responded in an indirect way to, and thus reinforced, the New Right's solicitation of empathy for white male victims of 'affirmative discrimination'.

Reform of affirmative action, both in the run up to the 1996 presidential election and afterwards, has been spearheaded by a number of different players: state lawmakers bolstered by anti-affirmative action local campaigns; a new Republican Congressional majority taking aim at the Democrats' civil rights record and proposing color-blind legislative initiatives; and the Courts where cases are being decided that challenge race-based affirmative action in student admissions, federal contract assignments, and employment.

It was the California Civil Rights Initiative (CCRI), or Proposition 209 as it appeared on the 1996 November ballot in California, that first broke the mould. If voter approval of Proposition 209 is subsequently upheld by the courts where the battle is now being waged, the California constitution will be amended to prohibit programs that work to open up opportunities for people of color and women in public employment, education, and contracting. Outreach and recruiting programs designed to encourage people of color and women to apply for jobs and contracts will be outlawed, as will goals and timetables for hiring qualified people of color and women for jobs where they have traditionally been excluded. Similar initiatives are being circulated in at least six other states. True to the tenets of the new racism, the way in which the initiative is worded has confused even strong supporters of affirmative action into believing that it advances civil rights, prompting a legal battle over whether the words affirmative action must be included in the title to make clear what the initiative is actually about. The deceptive nature of contemporary backlash sentiments is precisely why public opinion polls are so ineffectual in evaluating support for the new racism. For instance, when first reading the CCRI text, 78 per cent of California voters supported it, with only 17 per cent in opposition. But when it was explained to voters that the CCRI would actually eliminate affirmative action programs, support collapsed to 31 per cent while opposition rose to 55 per cent.[24]

Despite Patrick Buchanan's remark that the CCRI 'will make the battle over Proposition 187 look like a pillow fight in a sorority house', the battle in fact has centered around the apolitics of administrative and regulatory fiat.[25] In June, 1995, California Governor Pete Wilson issued an executive order dismantling some twenty-one of California's affirmative action programs. A month later, the University of California Board of Regents voted to eliminate so-called racial preferences in admissions and hiring. Since then, many other governing boards of public university systems (most notably, Colorado and Texas) have met to curtail or end affirmative action in determining college admission and financial aid. Many useful affirmative action programs have been eliminated as a result, programs like a scholarship financed by Hispanic alumni of the University of Colorado and available only to Hispanic students. And in meetings in state legislatures and governor's offices in Pennsylvania, Arizona, South Carolina, Colorado, Michigan and elsewhere, various proposals to end affirmative action are receiving a serious hearing.[26]

The New Republicans in Congress have sought to jump on the bandwagon, thereby maximizing electoral benefit from such local and state legislative and bureaucratic activity and the popular sentiments they purportedly reflect. Although earlier Congressional initiatives had taken aim at affirmative action, such as the amendment to the 1991 Civil Rights Act proposed by Jesse Helms that would have barred employers from granting any kind of 'preferential treatment' and abolished all race-based government 'preference' programs, it was not until the 1995 legislative session that it appeared that the Party was willing to tackle the issue of affirmative action head-on. For an answer to the question 'why now?', one is ill-advised to look for any significant change in public opinion; rather, the reasons can be found in two simple facts: first, Republican victories in 1994 meant that critics of affirmative action now controlled key Congressional committees and, second, the 1996 presidential campaign season was around the corner.

Representative Charles Canady (Florida Republican) was particularly active in organizing strategy meetings and oversight hearings aimed at demonstrating that the Clinton administration's civil rights policies exceeded or otherwise transgressed the original intent of Congress. Then, in the spring of 1995, Senate Majority Leader Bob Dole and Representative Charles Cannady introduced identical pieces of legislation – one to the Senate, the other to the House – entitled The Equal Opportunity Act (EOA), informally referred to as the Dole–Canady Bill. Although the Bills never came up for a vote in either chamber before the 1996 summer break, if adopted in a future legislative session, they

would bar the federal government from giving any preference by race or gender or obliging others to do so. Essentially
a federal version of Proposition 209, the Bills go so far as to
actually block federal efforts to provide remedies for proven
racial and gender discrimination, as well as severely restrict
civil rights enforcement through the courts. The Bills virtually eliminate the Executive Order 11246 'goals and timetables' program, used as a measure to cure discrimination since
the Nixon Administration, which bars discrimination by government contractors. Similar statutes are in the works in a
variety of state legislative chambers. In South Carolina and
Michigan, efforts are also underway to enact constitutional
amendments forbidding preferences. In introducing the
EOA, Dole said: 'For too many of our citizens, our country is
no longer the land of opportunity but a pie chart, where jobs
and other benefits are often awarded not because of hard
work or merit, but because of someone's biology', and concluded by insisting that his bill 'would get the federal government out of the business of dividing Americans.'[27] On
another occasion, and clearly echoing the New Right's own
position, Dole was reported as saying, 'We have lost sight of
the simple truth that you don't cure discrimination with
more discrimination.'[28]

At one point in 1995, the explosion of the affirmative action
issue onto the national political landscape seemed imminent,
and those making a case against the case against affirmative
action within the Republican Party (including, at this time,
Jack Kemp) were on the outs. Newt Gingrich in particular
used his new-found power as Speaker of the House to
lampoon liberalism on the issue: 'The founders guaranteed
the pursuit of happiness, not happiness quotients, happiness
set-asides, the Federal Department of Happiness.'[29] In his
book, *To Renew America*, Newt Gingrich wrote,

> We're not backing off on affirmative action ... Affirmative
> action, a bureaucratic approach to assisting minorities and
> women, stems from the same misguided impulse that
> created our nightmarish welfare state. Just as we ask what
> will replace the welfare state, we can also ask what will
> replace affirmative action. The answer is the same – an
> opportunity society.[30]

And then, suddenly, the Republicans backed off and began to debate what the answer, in fact, should be. Opposition to affirmative action, the much celebrated battering ram against the Democrats, began to inflict ugly splits within the Republican Party itself at a time, in the run-up to the 1996 general election, when Party unity was essential. Congresspersons who conceived of anti-affirmative action posturing as an effective tool against the Democrats or were ideologically tied to the New Right advocated a full-steam-ahead approach, while those concerned about the potentially destructive impact of the issue on the Republican's own team and/or prospects for outreach to communities of color encouraged a go-slow approach; a tension that led to a series of disagreements and prevarications on Capitol Hill. In the summer of 1995, Representative Gary Franks, a black Republican from Connecticut, got caught in the cross-fire when Newt Gingrich blocked an amendment he had drafted to halt federal set-asides. In the face of an explanation from Gingrich's spokesperson that the House leadership's withdrawal of support had more to do with the crush of legislative business than any backsliding on the issue of affirmative action, Franks retorted that he did not believe the speaker had 'the stomach' for dealing with the issue.[31]

In an about-face, Newt Gingrich began to argue for the go-slow approach, and even to suggest that it might be better to reform affirmative action, rather than simply abolish it, by targeting socio-economic as opposed to racial disadvantage. With the November 1996 election on the horizon, the speaker urged Republicans not to use affirmative action as a wedge issue but focus instead on how to design a helping hand. Gingrich argued that it was politically irresponsible to consider comprehensive repeal of affirmative action until the Party developed a better policy alternative to replace it. The Republican case against affirmative action thus began to take second seat behind the project to keep up inclusive appearances.

Just when it appeared that affirmative active was last year's issue, an important Supreme Court ruling in March 1996 – Cheryl Hopwood *v.* the State of Texas – brought it back to political life. The Hopwood case involved a two-track admissions system at the University of Texas Law School put in place for the purpose of eliminating the vestiges of past discriminatory policies at the University and increasing diversity in the student body. The Court's decision, referred to by many as Bakke II, essentially proscribed the use of race-based prefer-ence devices in institutions of higher learning unless they can be shown to serve a compelling government interest and are narrowly tailored to satisfy that interest. The Court concluded, '[T]he law school has failed to show a compelling state inter-est in remedying the present effect of past discrimination sufficient to maintain the use of race in its admissions system.'[32] To strive for the goal of racial diversity in an enter-ing class, said the court, 'is no more rational on its own terms than would be choices based upon the physical size or blood type of applicants'.[33] Referring to the decision as 'a stunning blow to affirmative action', the *Chronicle of Higher Education* concluded that Hopwood would have a huge impact upon the laws governing race-based programs in higher education and, at least in the short term, inevitably result in decreased minor-ity enrollment.

In supporting the four white students who brought the case against the University of Texas Law School, complaining that they had been denied entry while less-qualified minority can-didates were admitted, the Supreme Court explicitly rejected the use of past societal discrimination to justify race-based re-medial programs. This rejection was a severe one considering the background of the University of Texas policy. Until 1950, the University excluded blacks entirely. In response to a judg-ment in 1965 by the US Department of Health, Education and Welfare that the University had failed to eliminate rem-nants of past discrimination, a new admissions policy was adopted: black or Hispanic applicants would now be consid-ered by a separate committee and admitted under lower standards than those required of whites. With this perspective in mind, the Court's declaration that such a two-track system represents an unconstitutional denial of equal protection de-livers a severe blow to any activity – goals, timetables, out-reach, quotas – that is geared to address compelling social needs related to the elimination of racial inequality as opposed to the competing New Right script focusing on pro-tection of individual rights. The Hopwood decision is a victory for New Rightists who have long argued that rewards and punishments should be meted out only in cases of direct and intentional discrimination, and that justifications related to past or societal discrimination are too amorphous to determine either effect of antidote.

The Hopwood case is the cap of a series of decisions, taken by an increasingly conservative Supreme Court, that have chipped away at the legal foundation and narrowed the scope of affirmative action. For example, in 1989, the Supreme Court struck down a program in Richmond, Virginia – Richmond *v.* the State of Virginia – that set aside 30 per cent of municipal contracts for people of color, declaring that any government program favoring one race over another (through minority set-asides) is 'highly suspect'. Also in 1989, the case Wards Cove *v.* Antonio held that employees must prove there was no legitimate business reason for a firm's alleged discriminatory acts. Five other close Supreme Court decisions that year contributed to limit remedies for job discrimination, an accumulated effect that prompted legislation (the 1990/1991 Civil Right Act) to overturn them. In 1992, school desegregation requirements were relaxed (Freeman *v.* Pitts) and the requirement for Justice Department preclearance of changes in local election districts was removed (Presley *v.* Etowah County Commission).[34] In 1993, a divided Supreme Court made it more difficult for employees to prove they had suffered discrimination on the job by shifting the burden of proof from the employer to the employee, arguing that it was not enough to prove the employer had lied, proof of actual discrimination must be demonstrated. In his opinion, Justice Scalia wrote that 'we have no authority to impose liability upon an employer in the absence of proof of discrimination.'[35]

Such an opinion, and the fundamentally hostile posture of the Supreme Court *vis-à-vis* so-called racial preferences, racial gerrymandering, and other results-oriented forms of affirmative action that it portends, is a significant lease-on-life for the new racism, not to mention a vindication of the meanings and policy proposals circulated by the New Right for the past twenty plus years. It is precisely because the new racism is characterized by public disavowals of racist prejudice and avoidance of overt discriminatory practices that outcomes-orientated public policies such as affirmative action are so needed in the post-civil rights era.[36] If political and judicial leaders are serious about the pursuit of racial equality, then it is more essential than ever to address practices that are fair in form but discriminatory in operation. If public ire, government policy and judicial action are targeted exclusively on combatting more traditional forms of racism and discriminatory exclusion, as the above paragraphs suggest is the case, then the silence that speaks so loud in the face of the new forms of racism and indirect exclusion will facilitate a deterioration into an increasingly undemocratic public arena more interested in protecting the non-racist self-image of the dominant society than in building a truly equal, opportunity-driven and open society.

The fact that such a society does not exist is born out be a myriad of reliable indicators that expose the hypocrisy of New Right cries of 'reverse racism' and the collusion of those who participate in the silence. Far from painting a picture of people of color robbing white men of opportunities in any systematic way, recent studies indicate that although white men have lost ground since the mid-1970s, they have not lost power or advantage.

In the sphere of employment, although blacks represent 12.4 per cent of the US population, they account for only 4.2 per cent of doctors; 5 per cent of college professors; 3.7 per cent of engineers; 3.3 per cent of lawyers; 1.4 per cent of architects; and 6.5 per cent of construction trades.[37] Employment data for Hispanics is not much different. Blacks with college degrees are twice as likely as white graduates to be unemployed.[38] According to a 1993 analysis by the Equal Employment Opportunity Commission, blacks were the only group to suffer a net loss of jobs in the 1990–1 recession; whites gained 71 144 jobs among firms reporting to the EEOC while blacks lost 59 479.[39] According to the 1995 Glass Ceiling Report, commissioned by the Bush administration to examine whether or not such a ceiling persists in the nation's largest companies, just over 0.6 per cent of senior managers are blacks, 0.4 per cent are Latinos, and 0.3 per cent are Asian Americans.[40] White men, while constituting about 43 per cent of the workforce, hold about 95 of every 100 senior management positions, defined as vice-president and above.[41] The report cites various studies suggesting that 'the glass ceiling exists because of the perception of many white males that as a group they are losing – losing the corporate game, losing control and losing opportunity'.[42] The report concludes,

'Despite three decades of affirmative action, glass ceilings and concrete walls still block women and minority groups from the top management ranks of American industry.'[43] Such findings, and the new, modern cultural forms of discrimination to which they direct attention, are consistent with other studies that have argued that there is no idea of merit that is innocent of prejudice.[44] Managers base their decisions on considerations that include the extent to which they feel comfortable with a given candidate and a vague sense of how the candidate will 'fit' into the workplace. Although such criteria do not fall in line with conventional notions of prejudice or bigotry, they do allow for the operation of prior assumptions and generalizations about a given job candidate that often work to the negative advantage of black candidates and to the positive advantage of whites.

A comparison of black and white income similarly demonstrates persisting white advantage. Two reports issued by the Census Bureau in 1995 show that, despite public policies geared to addressing the racial dimensions of economic inequality, little progress in narrowing the income gap between blacks and whites has been achieved. The reports demonstrate that in 1993 the median income for black men employed full time was $23 020, about three quarters of the $31 090 for white men, a proportionate disparity reduced only slightly since 1979.[45] The income gap between black and white women, historically narrower than that between men, has widened slightly between 1979 and 1993, with black women earning $19 820 compared to $22 020 for white women.[46] In 1992, the median income for white women was $21 659; for black women it was $19 819; and Latina women earned $17 138.[47] The real, inflation-adjusted median income of black families in 1993 was 3.1 per cent lower than it was in 1973, whereas the median white family income had grown by 1.8 per cent in the interim; the ratio of black to white median family income fell from 57.7 per cent to 54.8 per cent in the same period.[48] A 1989 National Academy of Sciences report on the status of black Americans demonstrates that although the earning power of both white and black males with a high school degree deteriorated between 1969 and 1989, the white male's lowest earnings was higher than the black male's top earnings.[49] In another study on the income gap, a Princeton political scientist concludes, 'Even after controlling for a wide range of non-race-related differences, black men's wages remain about ten to twenty percent below white men's wages. The monetary return for an additional year of education or labor market experience remains noticeably lower for blacks than whites ...'[50]

Moreover, a 1995 study on black and white wealth by two sociologists, Melvin Oliver and Thomas Shapiro, demonstrates that the discrepancy between wealth in black and white communities is even greater than the income gap.[51] Comparing middle-class whites and blacks earning $25 000–50 000, the authors found that the net worth (the values of all assets less debts) of white Americans in this income was $44 069, while the net worth of blacks in this same category was almost three times less at $15 250.[52]

While some claim that such indicators are the consequence of the operation of a color-blind market economy and disparate human capital, other studies document the continued existence of systematic discrimination against people of color. A report published by the Chicago Federal Reserve Bank shows that black applicants for home loans are more than twice as likely to be denied credit as whites with the same qualification, while Hispanic applicants are more than one and a half times as likely to be denied.[53] Similarly, a study of discrimination in mortgage lending carried out by the Federal Reserve Bank of Boston in the early 1990s concluded that racial discrimination was widespread in the banking industry.[54] A University of Colorado study of bank lending in Denver in 1994 and 1995 found a 51 per cent denial rate for black businesses versus a 15 per cent rate for whites; for the largest and best-established enterprises, the rejection rate for blacks was over 50 per cent, for whites it was 4 per cent.[55] An Urban Institute report entitled *Opportunities Denied, Opportunities Diminished: Discrimination in Hiring* demonstrates that, even when white and black qualifications are identical, differential and unequal treatment of black jobseekers is entrenched and widespread. When equally qualified jobseekers applied for entry-level jobs, blacks were unable to advance as far in the hiring process as often as whites 20 per cent of the time, and were denied jobs offered to equally qualified whites 15 per cent of the time.[56] Still other studies have pointed to discrimination in the housing market and the associated feedback effects furthering black impoverishment and segregation. For example, in their study of *American Apartheid*, authors Douglas Massey and Nancy Denton state that 'race remains the dominant organizing principle of the US urban housing markets. When it comes to determining where, and with whom, Americans live, race overwhelms all other considerations.'[57]

Against the background of these indicators, precious little evidence exists to bolster the New Right's charge that white men are being victimized by 'reverse racism'. A National Opinion Research Center Survey in 1990 found that while more than 70 per cent of white Americans asserted that whites were being hurt by affirmative action for blacks, only 7 per cent claimed to have experienced any harm themselves, and only 16 per cent knew of someone close who had. Fewer than one in four could even claim that it was something they had witnessed or heard about at their workplace. The vast majority claimed to have heard about the problem either through the press, politicians, or some other second-hand source.[58] In 1994, the federal government received more than 90 000 complaints of employment discrimination – less than 3 per cent of which were for 'reverse discrimination'.[59] A report commissioned by the Labor Department and written by a Rutgers University law professor, Alfred Blumrosen, found that, of more than 3000 reported federal district and appellate court decisions in discrimination cases between 1990 and the middle of 1994, fewer than 100 opinions involved claims of 'reverse discrimination'. Not only were the majority of cases found to be without merit, several were brought by whites or men who were less qualified than the persons of color or women who were hired or promoted. There were only six cases in which white or male employees were successful in individual claims that they were discriminated against in favor of people of color or women.[60]

With these statistics in mind, it is hard to reconcile New Right claims that affirmative action is one big hand-out when the purported 'spoils of victimhood' do not appear to be landing in the hands of most people of color. As one author concludes, 'White men remain on top, dismantling affirmative action would ensure keeping them there.'[61] Whether the strategy for dismantling affirmative action is one of cutting the budgets and staff of civil rights enforcement agencies, as under the Reagan administration, or the more formative attempt to legislate color-blind federal policy, as under the Bush administration and the New Republicans, it is clear that affirmative action has been delivered a severe blow in the past two decades, albeit in the spirit of advancing civil rights and in accordance with the principle of non-racialism. Despite continuing divisions within and between the Republican Party and the New Democrats about how far and how fast to dismantle the policy, there can be little doubt that a new consensus is emerging, with the New Right as its political midwife, in favor of abstract notions such as color-blindness and equal treatment. Such notions have been hijacked from the civil rights movement and detached from their critical content, this time to serve an agenda in favor of rather than as a challenge to systematically asymmetrical relations of racial advantage.

Education

In keeping with the broader philosophy of social conservatism that guided civil rights policy as a whole, the pace of school desegregation was slowed under the Reagan administration. The duty to monitor and enforce compliance with federally-mandated desegregation plans rests primarily with the Office of Civil Rights (OCR) in the Education Department. Under Reagan, the OCR staff was reduced substantially. The number of investigations per employee dropped from just over ten in the last year of the Carter administration to just over four in 1981.[62] The overall number of complaint investigations and compliance reviews of school districts decreased. In the few cases referred to the Justice Department before 1984, no action was taken. As noted above, the Justice Department was most active in opposing desegregation efforts in many cities. In rationalizing this trend toward non-enforcement of federal non-discrimination laws, officials in the Reagan administration acknowledged the New Right argument that remedial action should be taken only in those schools where racial imbalance is the product of the known discriminatory practices of school officials.

In addition to this narrowing of the range of practices considered discriminatory was a principled assault upon specific methods previously used to redress the effects of past discrimination. For example, the Reagan administration deregulated federal bilingual education programs ostensibly to give local school districts more flexibility in choosing teaching methods. The Administration also opposed the practice of Court-ordered school busing. Soon after his appointment as Assistant Attorney General for Civil Rights in the Justice Department, William Bradford Reynolds made Reagan's intentions clear: 'We [the Justice Department] are not going to compel children who don't chose to have an integrated education to have one.'[63] Echoing the New Right's own position, the Administration argued that 'involuntary' busing should be abandoned since it encouraged white flight, inhibited parental choice, and destroyed neighborhood schools.

The combination of the Administration's relentless assault upon school busing and its lack of enforcement of alternative means to descgregate the nation's schools cast doubt in the minds of many of Reagan's commitment to a truly color-blind society. This doubt was reinforced in 1982 in a controversy involving the granting of tax-exempt status to private Christian schools. In the past, Internal Revenue Service (IRS) regulations had been applied against private schools (such as Bob Jones University and Goldsboro Christian) that were found to discriminate on racial grounds. Such regulations mandated that any such private school would lose its tax exempt status. This meant that the school would not be allowed an income tax deduction for contributions made to it. This procedure is an essential part of the federal effort to enforce its policy of nondiscrimination since many of these private schools had been set up for the express purpose of evading public school desegregation.[64] By Reagan's first year in office, more than a hundred such discriminatory private schools had been denied their tax-exempt status.

In 1982 the Reagan administration announced that it would oppose the IRS policy. Reagan argued that 'the procedure had no basis in law' and that it was harmful to private schools.[65] In doing so, the Reagan administration adopted a position contrary to the expressed intent of the regulations and at odds with the position taken by previous administrations. Although the IRS position was upheld later by a federal appeals court, the Administration persevered in its advocacy of the policy of non-enforcement and countered with the argument that the IRS had no authority to enforce its rulings. Faced with defeat by the judicial branch of government, and deeply wounded by a public relations furor, the Administration finally reversed its position. The Administration's willingness to tolerate, and even aid, institutions that were overtly discriminatory arguably had jeopardized the Administration's portrayal of itself as a 'friend' of civil rights.

In higher education, too, the Reagan administration moved to weaken the enforcement of federal non-discrimination policies as consistent with its broader conservative philosophy. Under the leadership of Secretary of Education Terrel Bell, non-discrimination regulations on federal funding of colleges and universities were relaxed. Bell urged that federal aid to college students did not constitute aid to the institutions they attended. Such a reinterpretation of federal guidelines would have spared about one thousand institutions of higher learning from compliance with civil rights legislation tied to federal aid.[66]

The Administration's rationalization for such a move borrowed from New Right themes that penalties should be administered only to those schools that intentionally discriminate and remedies should be awarded only to those individuals who are themselves the victims of segregated schooling. The new regulations, informally known as Grove City (after a Supreme Court ruling that held that anti-discrimination provisions on the use of Federal aid apply only to specific programs, not to an entire institution, and that, in effect, discrimination in a Grove City College sports program did not justify the denial of Federal aid outside that program), were overturned in 1988 by Congress – a significant defeat for the Administration.

The Bush administration turned to a more direct assault upon the very principles behind anti-racism in higher education. Bush exploited the issue of 'political correctness', or 'PC', which the New Right had succeeded in making such a key symbol in the politics of education in the early 1990s. In a 1992 address to graduating students at the University of Michigan, former President Bush stated: '[Political] extremists roam the land, abusing the privilege of free speech, setting citizens against one another on the basis of their class or race. ... The notion of "political correctness" has ignited controversy across the land. Although the movement arises from the laudable desire to sweep away racism and sexism and hatred, it replaced old prejudices with new ones. It declares certain topics off-limits, certain expressions off-limits, even certain gestures off-limits.'[67] In this and many other instances, the Bush administration echoed the New Right view of anti-racist educators as the 'new McCarthyites'. The New Right's anti-PC campaign provided the Bush administration with a set of meanings with which it attempted to rationalize the government's lack of action regarding the promotion of racial diversity within institutions of higher learning. Bush promoted the New Right idea that the educational establishment had become captive to black (as well as homosexual and radical feminist) 'special interests'.

Yet a brief glance at the empirical evidence reveals that such an assertion is unfounded. Partly as a result of the more negative climate for affirmative action and financial aid programs in recent years, the hiring of black and Hispanic faculty has slowed and the enrollment of people of color in national terms has dropped. In 1985 university faculties were ninety percent white.[68] Just over 2 per cent of full professors nationwide are black, and the number of enrolled black doctoral students in 1991 remained significantly below the 1982 level.[69] According to a Carnegie Commission report, when educational attainment and scholarly productivity is equal, blacks still receive tenure and promotion at a lower rate than whites; this despite the New Right charge that less-qualified blacks are displacing more-qualified whites in the university.[70] Whites hold 78 per cent of PhDs but occupy 87 per cent of tenure-track faculty positions.[71] In 1975, 32 per cent of black high school graduates enrolled in institutions of higher learning; by 1988 the figure had dropped to just over 28 per cent.[72] While anti-PC ideologues working under the auspices of the National Association of Scholars charge that affirmative action discriminates against white students in favor of less-qualified blacks, in reality the proportion of blacks enrolled in college dropped more rapidly than the proportion of whites between 1976 and 1986.[73] A report published by the American Council on Education showed that of all 18 to 24-year-old high school graduates, 42 per cent of whites were enrolled in college in 1993 but only 33 per cent of blacks and 36 per cent of Hispanics. And while blacks and Hispanics constitute about

26 per cent of the college-age population, they account for less than 17 per cent of the enrollment at institutions of higher education.[74] Federal funding for disadvantaged students has been drastically cut while tuition fees have continued to skyrocket.[75]

These trends will not be offset by any new programs of federal assistance. On the contrary, they will be reinforced by the ruling in December 1991 by the Department of Education that race-based scholarships run counter to the color-blind stipulations of the 1964 Civil Rights Act. Although the decision was later partially retracted, permitting money for race-based scholarships from private donations earmarked for such purposes but not from a university's general operating fund, it nevertheless reinforced the New Right's color-blind interpretation of civil rights law. Bush's condoning of the New Right anti-PC campaign arguably represented an attempt to rationalize these negative trends and to forge a new conservative consensus on matters pertaining to race and education that the Reagan administration had failed to secure previously.

Welfare

It is important to understand the erosion of the federal commitment to racial equality within the broader context of a concerted governmental assault upon so-called welfare state liberalism. Upon election to office, Reagan broke with the general pattern of governmental welfare provision in place (more or less) since the Great Depression. Analysts Palmer and Sawhill write: 'Not since 1932 has there been such a redirection of public purposes.'[76]

The social effects of this redirection of public purposes were real enough. Under Reagan, the nation witnessed an unprecedented rise in social inequality. Big business and the wealthy were the primary winners of the Reagan era. Upon taking office in 1981, Reagan announced plans for major tax cuts for corporations. As a consequence of the combined effects of the 1981 Economic Recovery Tax Act and the 1982 Tax Equity and Fiscal Responsibility Act, business tax rates decreased from 33 to 16 per cent.[77] The tax rate on income from capital fell by 14 per cent overall.[78] Tax rates on new investment in plant and equipment fell by 52 per cent.[79] The 1986 Tax Reform Act cut tax rates for the richest individuals from

70 per cent in 1981 to 28 per cent in 1988 – the lowest rate for some six decades.[80] As Republican political analyst Kevin Phillips sums up these trends in *The Politics of Rich and Poor*:

> By the middle of Reagan's second term, official data had begun to show that America's broadly defined 'rich' – the top half of one percent of the U.S. population – had never been richer. Federal policy favored the accumulation of wealth and rewarded financial assets, and the concentration of income that began in the mid-1970s was accelerating ... No parallel upsurge of riches had been seen since the late 19th century.[81]

These trends continued in the post-Reagan era so that, in 1991, the top one per cent of the US population in 1991 was reported as having a greater total wealth than the bottom 90 per cent.[82]

The primary losers of the Reagan era, on the other hand, were the working poor and unemployed. By 1983 more than 15 per cent of the population was living below the official poverty level, an increase from 11 per cent in 1973.[83] The percentage of families living in poverty increased during Reagan's two terms in office, so that by 1987 more than one-third of all single-parent families lived below the poverty line. While the wealthy enjoyed tax breaks, those earning under $10 000 per annum saw their taxes rise by 22 per cent. The minimum wage remained at three dollars and thirty-five cents throughout Reagan's tenure, a drop in real income of 36 per cent.

While Reaganite 'trickle-down' economic policies, in combination with a declining economy, affected the whole of the working class, they disproportionately affected black people. Despite the fact that a small but growing black middle class has emerged in recent decades (in large part as a consequence of the gains of the civil rights movement, such as affirmative action), the gap between blacks and whites increased overall in the 1980s. Before Reagan took office, the average annual income of blacks was 63 per cent of that of whites. By the time he left, the figure had fallen to 56 per cent – the same as before the Great Society programs of the 1960s. And while long-term unemployment among whites increased by roughly 2 per cent during Reagan's first term, it increased 72 per cent among blacks.

By the end of Reagan's first term, the Center on Budget and Policy Priorities reported that 'the average black family in every income strata – from the poor to the affluent – suffered a decline in its disposable income and standard of living since 1980'.[84] Black families in which one parent worked and the other took care of the children were hit hardest, losing an average of more than $2000 in disposable income from 1980 to 1984. The poverty rate among blacks reached almost 36 per cent, the highest since 1968.

By the time Reagan left office, blacks were more than twice as likely as whites to be jobless; the median black family income was 56 per cent of a white family's; and a newborn black baby was twice as likely as a white baby to die before its first birthday.[85] Nearly a third of all blacks, and two thirds of all black families headed by women, lived below the poverty line – as compared to 10 per cent of whites. Blacks (12 per cent of the national population) constituted nearly half of the nation's prison population, and a black man was six times as likely as a white man to be murdered, homicide being the leading cause of death for black youth. Such statistics are offered not by way of suggesting that Reagan created such disparities, only that his Administration's policies served to exacerbate and obscure those institutional relations of racial inequality already in place.

Significantly, the trend toward greater social inequality was met with less rather than more federal assistance. Reagan proposed a change in the scope of social programs, their goals, and the means used to achieve those goals. In order to limit their scope, Reagan requested a cut of $140 billion from social programs over the years 1982–4 (more than half of it from income-maintenance programs for the poor); a request granted by Congress in the 1981 Omnibus Reconciliation Act.[86] If Reagan had not subsequently been thwarted by Congress in his request for additional cuts, the net effect of his proposed reductions would have been to reduce annual spending for social programs by over $75 billion by the fiscal year 1985, or more than one-sixth below prior policy levels.[87] Overall, social spending went down from 28 per cent of the federal budget in 1980 to 22 per cent in 1987.[88]

As spending for social programs declined, the interpretations of their goals were narrowed. The duration of unemployment benefits decreased from a maximum of fifty-two weeks to twenty-six weeks, so that by 1990 only one in three of the unemployed were entitled to collect benefits (compared to two in three in 1981).[89] Federal outlays for employment and training programs fell from eleven to five billion dollars between 1981 and 1986.[90] Direct federal aid to cities fell by more than sixty percent (adjusting for inflation).[91] Moreover, many of the rules governing welfare were changed so as to make benefits harder to get. For example, in Wisconsin, new legislation mandated that Aid to Families with Dependent Children (AFDC) benefits be frozen if the recipient gives birth to more than two children and/or if her child misses more than a few days of school each year (the latter has since been ruled unconstitutional).

In attempting to rationalize this reversal of federal commitment *vis-à-vis* social inequality, the Reagan administration drew upon many of the critiques raised by New Right thinkers with regard to the progressive expansion of state activity. Books such as *Losing Ground* by Charles Murray, *Beyond Entitlement* by Lawrence Mead, and *Wealth and Poverty* by George Gilder provided the Administration with the ideological reference points it needed to justify the reduction in federal outlays for social programs.[92] By arguing that welfare and other federal income-transfer programs had failed to ameliorate problems related to social inequality, and had in fact made matters worse by creating a 'culture of dependency' and facilitating the breakdown of the nuclear family structure, such books helped legitimate the Administration's efforts to shift responsibility for such problems away from the federal government and toward the individual, family, church, and other voluntary associations at the local and state levels. Moreover, negative evaluations of the social effects of welfare programs helped absolve governing elites of culpability for the patterns of social inequality their economic policies in large part had exacerbated.

The response by Bush administration officials in the immediate aftermath of the 1992 Los Angeles rebellions illustrates the degree to which this line of reasoning remains compelling in the post-Reagan era. White House Spokesperson Marlin Fitzwater said that the social welfare programs of the 1960s and 1970s were responsible for the 'riots', and specifically, their effect of making poor people feel they had no responsibility for their own 'deviant behavior'.[93] Vice-President Dan Quayle added fuel to the conservative fire by launching an attack on Murphy Brown, a popular television show, for legitimating single-motherhood as 'just another life-style', and for thus contributing in its own way to the outbreak of violence in Los Angeles.

It is important to note the significant racial subtext beneath the Reagan-Bush challenge to 'welfare state liberalism'. Both Administrations attempted to appeal, without saying so directly, to voters who feel that Democratic welfare programs are tilted towards 'special interests', and towards blacks and Hispanics in particular. In fact, there is a great deal of evidence to venture further and suggest that conservative policy-makers have deliberately fed such a misperception. Cutbacks in social spending have been justified consistently with racialized stereotypes about welfare, drugs and crime. For example, Reagan repeatedly spoke of 'welfare cheats' picking up their checks in cadillacs and 'welfare queens' having more and more babies in order to get increased benefits.[94] Such welfare abusers are almost always depicted as black; this despite the fact that roughly two-thirds of welfare recipients are white.[95]

Racial subtext or not, it became clear that by the late 1980s a new consensus on welfare was emerging within Congress and the political culture more generally. The 1988 Family Support Act (requiring benefit recipients to participate in work-fare related education, training and placement programs, among other things) punctuated the end of a long process whereby a new 'dependency' paradigm was replacing the poverty paradigm that had reigned from the New Deal and Great Society eras and beyond, with an attendant shift in focus on the part of policy-makers from structural sources of inequality to the behavioral habits of the poor. This new paradigm was captured by Senator Daniel Patrick Moynihan (author of the controversial 'Moynihan Report') when he said, 'Just as unemployment was the defining issue of industrialism, dependency is becoming the defining issue of post-industrial society.'[96] The dependency paradigm reflects and evokes a revival of nineteenth-century fears of the low morality and anti-social behavior of the poor, or what is referred to today as the 'underclass', as well as distinctions between the so-called deserving and undeserving poor. The policy upshot of this paradigm shift has been a change in focus from a war on poverty to a war on the poor.

It was not until after the 1994 mid-term elections, however, that truly radical conservative welfare reform became politically possible. It is interesting to note that although Democrats had led efforts related to welfare reform during most of the post-war period up to the present, it is now the New Republicans, with New Democrat collusion, calling the shots and redefining the nature of the social contract between the government and the poor. One of the ten planks in the New Republican's 'Contract with America' was welfare reform, thus turning to Republican advantage Clinton's 1992 pledge to 'end welfare as we know it'. Nine of the ten planks outlined in what critics became fond of referring to as the 'Contract *on* America', were successfully turned into bills during the first ninety-three days of the 104th Congress, including welfare (only term limits went down to defeat). Newt Gingrich justified the new welfare legislation with a rhetoric of compassion for poor people that has become the most recent side-kick of the new racism: 'By creating a culture of poverty, we have destroyed the very people we are claiming to help. Caring for people is not synonymous with care-taking for people', Gingrich opined.[97] Armed with this new tough-love approach, New Republicans have transmuted the Reagan era argument that poor people are abusing welfare programs to one that avows that the programs are abusing poor people.[98] When a journalist highlighted this rhetorical twist, Gingrich reportedly smiled and said, 'You cracked the code'.[99]

The specific proposals related to welfare reform in the Contract were set out in a draft Bill called the Personal Responsibility Act (PRA). The PRA proposed massive cutbacks in a host of programs designed to alleviate poverty – Aid to Families with Dependent Children (AFDC), food stamps, school lunches, Supplemental Security Income (SSI), Women, Infants, Children (WIC), and all the major low-income housing programs. If passed into law, the PRA would have sliced $12 billion from welfare over seven years and nearly $90 billion from other anti-poverty programs.[100] It was estimated that cuts in the nutrition programs alone would have amounted to eighteen billion dollars in one four-year period.[101] Among the most controversial items in the PRA were proposed AFDC provisions that included: denial of benefits for a child whose paternity is not established, a requirement that minors with dependent children live with their parents or other adult, denial of aid for the needs of a child born out of wedlock before her mother's eighteenth birthday (with an option for state's to raise the age to twenty-one), denial of aid to children born to current or recent recipients of aid, federal funding for orphanages or other alternative care, and denial of aid to resident non-citizens regardless of their length of residence or circumstances.[102]

Regardless of whether Republicans argue that the poor are abusing welfare programs such as AFDC or the reverse, the fact is that such welfare reform is occurring at a time when benefit levels have reached their lowest point in over twenty years. According to a report published by the Center on Social Welfare Policy and Law, the current level of benefits leave families well below the poverty line in all fifty states and the District of Columbia; in forty-two states, AFDC benefits plus food stamps come to less than 75 per cent of the poverty line.[103] Current benefits are worth a mere 63 per cent of their 1975 levels (roughly $366 per month for a family of three). Since 1988 alone, there has been a loss of purchasing power of 10 per cent or more in forty-five states. And as the report shows, at the same time that benefit levels have reached an historic low, the need for AFDC has increased to the highest point ever.

Despite this contradiction between the symbolic dimensions of welfare policy reform and the material dimensions of poverty, the basic architecture of the 1994 PRA became law in the form of the 1996 Personal Responsibility and Work Opportunity Act (PRWOA). True, the addition of the WO to the acronym softens the blow rhetorically and adds a touch of structure to a debate that otherwise has focused, on both sides of the Congressional aisle, on the culture of the poor. Yet, notwithstanding this seemingly compassionate wink, the Act effectively abolishes the whole system of welfare policies and their associated assumptions about responsibility, work, race and human nature in place for the past half century. In announcing the bill, President Clinton said, 'Today we are taking a historic chance to make welfare what it was meant to be: a second chance, not a way of life.'[104]

Under the plan, no US citizen can collect welfare benefits for more than a cumulated total of five years in a lifetime, no matter what the circumstances. The head of most families on welfare would have to find work within two years or face the loss of benefits. After two years, able-bodied adults unable to find private-sector work might be offered community service jobs, if states and localities are willing and able to pay for them. Single mothers on welfare who refuse to co-operate in identifying the fathers of their children could lose at least 25 per cent of their benefits. Unmarried teenage mothers are eligible for benefits only if they stay at home and in school. States that fail to move 20 per cent of their caseloads from welfare to work by the end of 1997 – 50 per cent by 2002 – would face cutbacks in their block grants. Existing cuts amount to some $56 billion dollars over six years, coming mostly through reductions in food-stamp programs and restricted eligibility for legal immigrants.[105]

The Welfare Bill was not signed without protest, with some criticism coming from unlikely sources. An Urban Institute study predicts that the legislation will cause a 12 per cent increase in child poverty.[106] Others fear that states will lower the level of benefits in order to encourage poor people to move elsewhere. Even Senator Daniel Patrick Moynihan, regarded as a conservative on welfare matters, albeit in new post-industrial garb, criticized the legislation as an 'obscene act of social regression', complaining that 'the premise of this legislation is that the behavior of certain adults can be changed by making the lives of their children as wretched as possible.'[107] Many Republicans in state locales are upset too, for it is they who will be required to foot the bill as the federal government pulls out. For example, in California, officials released a report estimating that their state will lose more than $1 billion a year in aid from the federal government because of the Bill, mostly from cuts in benefits to legal immigrants. Even the likes of conservative Governor Tommy Thompson of Wisconsin, usually held up as a Republican model for welfare reform because his state cut its caseload by 44 per cent since 1987, criticized the Bill by arguing that the secret is to spend more, not less, on the poor by investing millions of dollars into job training, health benefits, child care and other support. 'You can't just pass a Bill and assume you'll save money the next day', Thompson says. 'How can you ask a welfare mom to get a job if she has to give up the medical insurance she gets on welfare, if she has no training or bus ticket to get there, if she can't find a safe place to leave her children? But I don't think anybody's listening.'[108]

Clinton certainly is not listening, although judging from his 1992 campaign, he used to believe in those very same words. By signing the Bill, Clinton has ensconced himself fully within the dependency paradigm of the New Right's making. In announcing his decision to sign the Bill, after having vetoed two earlier welfare-overhaul measures on the basis that they undermined efforts to bring people out of poverty and conveyed misplaced priorities, Clinton invoked a so-called culture of poverty constituted by single-parent, non-working households as the culprit behind negative social and economic indicators in poor communities, thereby refuting his earlier focus on the need for jobs and training. The adoption and use of the conservative-laden culture of poverty thesis by New Democrats already has served to foreclose policy discussion around contextual considerations such as economic dislocation, the deterioration of inner-city neighborhoods, and changing family patterns.

The fact that these contextual considerations are relevant has been born out recently by various studies showing that welfare recipients outnumber the jobs they might fill.[109] Economists concede that in many cities, such as New York and Los Angeles, the economy is growing much too slowly to absorb the number of unskilled and inexperienced people, and in such a short period of time, that will be forced on to the job market as a result of the Welfare Bill. The chasm between fact and fiction is even deeper if one considers the element of mismatch between those sectors of the economy that are experiencing growth – business services, media, computer and data services, the securities industry – and the skills of most welfare recipients. Moreover, the crowding that will inevitably result in those sectors of the economy that demand relatively little experience or skill will inevitably produce downward pressure on wages, only further reinforcing the very structural binds in which poor people now find themselves.

While some berate Clinton for selling out the poor, it is important to recognize that the Democrats lost the debate on welfare long ago. They lost the debate not because of the wishy-washy character of party leaders nor opportunistic or misplaced electoral ambitions, but rather because the New Right won the debate on values. In other words, the Democrats lost the debate on welfare because they lost the broader debate on what the debate was about; by acquiescing to the New Right's construction of the 'problem' of poverty as one of values and culture, the Democrats ceded control of the assumptions and symbols that drive the struggle for legitimacy in the policy-making arena, and so surrendered their ability to defend the poor. In this sense, the Clinton administration is complicitous with the New Right in constructing welfare recipients as scape-goats for a whole myriad of negative social and negative ind-icators: family breakdown, economic downturn, joblessness, crime and violence, a sense of pervasive normlessness, and so on. Such a simplistic explanation for today's troubles, suggest-ing that if only the poor could be rehabilitated through government coercion or benign neglect, then the nation's past glory can be reclaimed – represents a cynical and profoundly unsociological narrative, one more concerned with the con-struction of meanings and assumptions about US society and how it works than with concrete policy effects. Having won the debate on values, it has been difficult to dissuade those who agree with the New Right in advancing the idea that the way to eradicate poverty is to spend less on the poor.[110]

The newly-ascendant dependency paradigm in the arena of welfare policy, and the attendant focus on values and culture, is far from color-blind in its operation. Indeed, color has been infused into what has come to be known as the 'culture wars', reviving past images of black 'welfare queens' and reincarnat-ing them into a new folk devil – the Hispanic immigrant. Although there is a long tradition of anti-immigrant sentiment in US history, today this sentiment has become increasingly conflated with the debate on welfare reform. Proposition 187 which won voter approval in California in 1994 proposed to deny social services, education, and non-emergency health care to undocumented immigrants. As a spin-off of the 'Contract with America', Congressional legislation was drafted in late 1994 that would have barred most legal immigrants from sixty federal programs, prohibiting them from receiving free childhood immunizations, housing assistance, Medicaid, subsidized school lunches and many other federal benefits. The 'Contract' itself included proposals to significantly increase efforts to limit illegal entry into the country and to make illegal migrants ineligible for almost all federal, state and local welfare benefits, with the exception of emergency medical services and nutrition programs. The 'Contract' also allowed for the deportation of legal immigrants who receive more than twelve months of public assistance during their first five years resident in the United States. Bill Clinton once again responded in a manner that reaffirmed the discursive links being forged by the New Right – in this case, between welfare dependence and (Hispanic) immigration – by issuing a directive that called for a crackdown on employers of illegal aliens, and more money (an extra $1 billion in the fiscal year 1996) to thwart illegal entry into the United States. The Welfare Bill that he signed in August 1996 follows through on most of the stipulations outlined above and also places a ban on most forms of public assistance and social services for legal immigrants who have not become citizens.

Once again, a brief glance at the empirical evidence reveals that the symbolic construction and uses of the Hispanic immigrant as a new folk devil reveals more about the insecurities and scripts of the dominant (white) society than the purported 'problems' related to immigrants and immigration to which welfare reform is ostensibly targeted. According to the Immigration and Naturalization Service (INS), the number of legal immigrants entering the country has fallen by more than 20 per cent during the last two years (the largest two-year drop in legal immigration since the 1930s and part of an overall trend in immigration during the last four years), prompting the Senate Judiciary Committee to approve legislation that would slightly increase the number of foreign-born relatives who can be brought into the country by American citizens and legal residents.[111] Other studies indicate the net positive economic gain resulting from legal immigration, and divulge the mythic element of New Right charges that immigrants are more likely than the native-born to be on welfare. A recent study published by The Urban Institute shows that working-age immigrants have substantially lower welfare rates than natives – 2 per cent for those who have come since 1980, compared with nearly 4 per cent of natives. The only two groups of foreign-born persons that have higher than average rates of 'dependence' are refugees and the elderly.[112] Moreover,

already existing laws prohibit illegal immigrants from eligibil-
ity for publicly funded welfare assistance or food stamps, and
allow for those who produce or obtain fraudulent work
permits to be criminally prosecuted.

Viewed in this context, racialization of the welfare debate
via the construction of the Hispanic immigrant – whether
legal or illegal – as the new folk devil responsible for America's
moral and economic decay represents a dangerous turn
toward a more mean-spirited and direct form of exclusionary
politics. Once again, the symbolic dimensions of policy formation are being orchestrated at the expense of substantive
benefits and are serving to foreclose discussion of policies orientated toward other, more structural interpretations of the
sources of America's troubles. Not only has this symbolic form
of politics shaped and reinforced public animosity toward immigrant groups, as illustrated by the videotaped beating of two
Mexicans by police officers in California in the spring of 1996
or the citizen groups patrolling airports to root out illegal immigrants, it has also offered a convenient way to deny the
need for policymakers to confront the difficult economic realities that are emerging and to justify the retreat from the idea
that the government has an obligation to ensure a decent
social wage.

THE NEW RACISM AND THE POLITICS OF THATCHERISM

The election of Margaret Thatcher to power, like that of
Ronald Reagan's in the United States, signalled that a profound shift in the assumptions underlying government policy
formation on matters pertaining to race was under way. This is
not to say that Thatcher's electoral victories should be read as
a popular mandate on race, but rather that a significant shift
in the ideological paradigms that in the past informed racial
policy formation within the state had occurred.

The Thatcher administration challenged assumptions regarding the viability of a multi-racial nation and the appropriate means by which government should protect the rights of
black people. In doing so, the Administration retarded what
little racial progress had been achieved in previous decades by:

1. instituting the strictest controls on the immigration of New Commonwealth citizens since the right to immigrate was granted;
2. imposing social discipline on those migrants and their dependents already here;
3. limiting the scope of race relations legislation already in existence and reducing the effectiveness of its enforcement, and
4. undermining anti-racist/multicultural programs in the nation's schools.

As demonstrated below, in each of these policy areas the Thatcher administration drew upon critiques raised by the right-wing of the Conservative Party, or the New Right. And as we shall also see, this new ideological climate on racial matters dictated by the New Right continues to pervade the racial politics of the post-Thatcher era.

Immigration

Under the leadership of Margaret Thatcher, the Tory government contributed to the entrenchment of the view that the immigration of people from the Commonwealth (that is, West Indians and Asians), and indeed their continued presence in Britain, constituted a problem at the very center of national political debate. This was not a wholly new development, since controls had been instituted from 1962 (and after) by both Tory and Labour governments.[113] What was new was the combination of categories of meaning and assumptions with which the Thatcher administration justified the placement of ever-more stringent controls upon Commonwealth immigration.

The institutionalization of immigration controls in preceding decades had been justified within the ideological paradigm of 'integration'. Implicit in the goal of integration was the idea that it is necessary in a society with scarce resources to restrict the numbers of 'coloured' immigrants allowed entry in order for peaceful race relations to be maintained. This paradigm was captured by then Labour MP Roy Hattersley with the slogan: 'Without integration, limitation is inexcusable; without limitation, integration is impossible.'[114]

With the emergence of Thatcherism, there occurred a paradigm shift in the justification of immigration controls. While the integration paradigm was still present, it was supplemented by an argument that government had a duty to respond to popular fears that the 'British way of life' was being changed as a result of Commonwealth immigration. In 1978 Thatcher was quoted in an ITV interview as saying:

> If we went on as we are, then by the end of the century there would be four million people of the New Commonwealth or Pakistan here. Now that is an awful lot and I think it means that people are really rather afraid that this country might be swamped by people with a different culture. And, you know, the British character has done so much for democracy, for law, and done so much throughout the world, that if there is a fear that it might be swamped, people are going to react and be rather hostile to those coming in.[115]

Echoing the New Right assertion that the desire to be with one's 'own kind' is natural, and the fear of the dilution of the 'British way of life' by alien strains legitimate, Thatcher made a campaign promise to end immigration, a promise that proved to be electorally popular. In 1978 Thatcher made a speech that made her intentions *vis-à-vis* immigration policy clear:

> I shall not make it [immigration policy] a major election issue but I think there is a feeling that the big political parties have not been talking about this and sometimes you know, we are falsely accused of racial prejudice ... that means we do not talk about it perhaps as much as we should. In my view, that is one thing that is driving some people to the National Front. They do not agree with the objectives of the National Front, but they say that at least they are talking about some of the problems ... If we do not want people to go to extremes we ourselves must talk about this problem and we must show that we are prepared to deal with it. We are a British nation with British characteristics. Every country can take some small minorities and in many ways they add to the richness and variety of this country. The moment the minority threatens to become a big one,

people get frightened ... We are not in politics to ignore people's worries: we are in politics to deal with them.[116]

As others have pointed out, the concept of 'genuine fears' here serves as an ideological bridge between an apparently factual description of reality (that is, that people have fears and attribute them to the presence of black immigrants) and a theory of race (that is, that the fears are legitimate and control of immigration is needed in order to preserve the 'British way of life'). Moreover, the appeal to the sentiments of 'the people' obscures the complex ideological process by which particular political problems (such as 'coloured' immigration) are constructed from above to the exclusion of others (such as the reality of unemployment or housing shortages).

Within a year of being elected, the Thatcher administration introduced new restrictive immigration rules. Strict limitations were imposed upon the entry of parents, grandparents and children over the age of eighteen, and the right of women to bring in foreign-born husbands/fiancés was removed. In 1981 the British Nationality Act was passed into law, abolishing the automatic conferral of British citizenship to those born in Britain. Tory MPs justified such measures with language appropriated from the New Right. For example, Tony Marlow MP defended the measures thus: 'People have criticised these measures because they say they are racialist, as if racialist is a word of abuse. What does racialist mean? It means tribal. After all, man is a tribal animal. We have a feeling of kith and kin for people like ourselves, with our own background and culture.'[117]

In addition to its symbolic implications, the Act has had real consequences for people of the Commonwealth (and others) seeking to migrate to Britain, and for those already settled in Britain. From 1981 on, asylum-seekers were the only significant group of immigrants allowed access to Britain, and then only temporarily. The number of people accepted for settlement or arrival in Britain fell in 1982 to 54 000, the lowest level since immigration controls were instituted first in 1962.[118] Following a dramatic increase in the number of raids on Asian businesses, the number of 'illegals' detected and removed without the right of appeal rose to its highest level ever during Thatcher's first term. The number of deportations also increased; from 792 in 1979, to 969 in 1980, and 946 in 1981.[119]

The issue of immigration continued to be constructed as a major political problem throughout Thatcher's tenure, as illustrated by the attention granted it in each of the three Conservative electoral manifestos. This at a time when net emigration was higher than net immigration, and when over 40 per cent of those identified as 'immigrants' were British born.[120] As the party in government, the Tories remained largely faithful to their promise to restrict immigration. In 1981 more than 60 per cent of asylum-seekers who managed to enter Britain were eventually granted refugee status, but by 1988 the figures had dropped to only 25 per cent.[121] Between 1984 and 1986, only 240 asylum-seekers for every one million of Britain's inhabitants were accepted for settlement (i.e., a proportion of 0.024 per cent), thereby establishing Britain as the holder of one of the worst records in Europe for its treatment of asylum seekers.[122]

The 1987 Carriers' Liability Act has served to exclude would-be asylum-seekers at the supply side, preventing them from ever leaving their country of origin. The Act introduced stiff fines (the amount doubled in 1991) against airlines and shipping companies that carry passengers without proper documentation or visas.[123] It is thought to have led to a number of human rights infractions, including incidents in which shiphands, afraid that the fines might come out of their own pockets, throw stowaways overboard to their death.[124]

Rather than placate the New Right, the speedy implementation of nearly all the Manifesto commitments on immigration granted right-wingers increased confidence to press for even stricter controls. Indeed, as early as 1980, New Rightist Ronald Butt complained of the government's broken promises, 'It has done nothing of importance to redeem its pledge to stop further immigration.'[125] The New Right saw as further betrayal the relaxation of government restrictions, under pressure from the European Commission on Human Rights, on the entry of foreign-born husbands and fiancés. On these and other occasions, the New Right criticized the government for granting concessions to politics over principle, and even charged that the government's commitment to end immigration was more vote-catching rhetoric than reality. Such tensions revealed the deep and continuing divisions between an Administration committed to immigration controls and certain sections of the New Right committed to the policy of repatriation. This conflict, however, should not obscure the fact that the Tory government under Thatcher moved closer to the New Right definition and interpretation of the 'problem' of black immigration. Indeed, having ceded the ideological ground to the New Right up to the point of repatriation, it became difficult for government to dissuade those who looked to repatriation as the logical conclusion of its own policies and rhetoric.

The immigration issue decreased in salience in the late 1980s; in part because so much action in the realm of government policy already was taken successfully, and also because other race-related issues such as the urban riots of the mid-1980s and the attack on local authority anti-racism in the late-1980s, as we shall see below, took over much of the ideological work that the immigration issue had provided in the run-up to Thatcher's election. Yet, in the post-Thatcher era, marked by a Conservative Party deeply divided over a number of issues (most importantly Europe) and eager to establish 'clear blue water' between itself and New Labour, the issue of immigration has once again come to the foreground.

Racist anti-immigrant sentiment has been recoded in the post-Thatcher era, focusing less on the threat posed by Commonwealth immigrants to the 'homogenous we' and instead on two folk devils: the 'bogus' asylum-seeker and the 'illegal' immigrant. The presence of these racialized folk devils, not so much new as infused with fresh resonance in the context of the debates over European Unification, is presented as a problem of the highest order. In particular, their alleged milking of the benefit system and other varieties of criminal activity attributed to them have been offered as justifications for strict legislative controls. However, perhaps due to internal divisions within the Conservative Party, there is no singular ideological paradigm used to justify the policy response. Instead, a range of justifications for the crackdown are offered: as necessary in order for the healthy integration of previously resident Afro-Caribbean and Asian communities to proceed and to stem the rise of neo-Nazism in Europe, to deter economic migrants from taking part in 'benefits tourism' or 'Euro-scrounging', and to stop illegal immigrants and other 'welfare cheats' from robbing taxpayers of their hard-earned money.

One of the earliest and most significant measures on immigration to be taken by the Major administration was the 1993 Asylum and Immigration Appeals Act. The Bill was first introduced in 1991, but was a casualty of the run-up to the 1992 general election, indicating that perhaps immigration as an issue had lost some of its electoral capital as compared to the late seventies. The Bill proposed that the right of appeal for short-term visitors be removed, and that appeal procedures for asylum-seekers be tightened. Kenneth Clarke (then Home Secretary) introduced the legislation at the 1991 Conservative Party conference, warning of the dangers of Labour's 'open door policy' and saying that the number of asylum-seekers necessitated legislation to ensure that 'the bogus were quickly weeded out' and reiterating the numbers game theme that good race relations were heavily dependent on strict immigration controls.[126] The measures were portrayed as a reasonable policy response to the recent increase in the number of black asylum-seekers, an increase that government ministers warned could reawaken the immigration debate and fuel the kind of racist sentiment that the British National Party and other neo-fascist parties across Europe were keen to exploit. In this way, the rise of racist violence in Britain and elsewhere was used as a justification for the further institutionalization of racist immigration policies. True to the New Right's own logic, the very presence of black refugees was constructed as a political problem in need of addressing, and assaults on their democratic rights were justified via the deployment of anti-anti-racist/Nazi language.

Under the provisions of the Act that eventually came into law in 1993, those potential asylum-seekers who stop in a third country on their way to Britain are deported within days of arrival and without having had their asylum application reviewed. This so-called 'third country' rule is based on the assumption that any 'genuine' refugee would have declared it so in the first 'safe' country entered, and has led to a situation wherein many potential refugees are bounced between various West European states or, worse still, sent back to their unsafe country of origin.[127] Of those refugees who do have the good fortune to have their asylum applications reviewed, increasing numbers are being held in prison-like immigration detention centers, such as the newly-built Campsfield site near Oxford custom-designed for exactly this purpose. In 1993 the detention of asylum seekers more than doubled to reach 10 530, and a recent wave of hunger strikes by detainees indicate that conditions are far from ideal.[128] By December 1994, 75 per cent of asylum seekers were being refused entry to Britain, up 16 per cent from only fifteen months before.[129] In the wake of the 1993 Act, levels of violence by police and immigration officers – both state and private – have climbed to an unprecedented level.[130] That such forcible deportations occur with unnecessary degrees of violence and cruelty is perhaps best illustrated by the ordeal of Joy Gardner (a Jamaican immigrant denied the right to settle in the Britain) at the hands of three police officers (later acquitted) who, while attempting to enforce the deportation orders served her, wrapped thirteen feet of sticky tape around her mouth and head, causing her death.

Despite such measures, relying as they do on the more moderate neo-liberal themes for justification, right-wing ideologues have continued to warn of the danger immigration poses to English traditions and national identity. For example, in 1993 Winston Churchill MP said that the British risked suffering the type of violence seen recently in Germany unless the Government takes a firmer grip on immigration. Speaking to Bolton Conservatives, Churchill challenged the Major administration thus:

> Mr. Major promised us that fifty years from now, spinsters will still be cycling to communion on Sunday mornings – more like the Muezzin will be calling Allah's faithful to the High Street Mosque ... We must call a halt to the relentless flow of immigrants to this country, especially from the Indian Sub-continent.[131]

Although Major rebuked Churchill and professed his commitment to remove any barrier built on race, the remarks nevertheless embarrassed the Administration at a time when it was attempting to reach out to Afro-Caribbean and Asian communities for support.[132] Churchill's remarks indicate that the issues of race and culture continue to be significant in the Right's perception of British identity. The political reaction to his remarks reflects the uneasy alliance and ambiguities that continue to exist among Tories on policy questions pertaining to race.

In 1996, it appears that the sentiments of the Churchills are winning the day. Tory MPs have tried recently to whip up hysteria over so-called 'illegal' immigrants living in Britain following the resignation of Home Office minister Charles Wardle in early 1995. Wardle resigned amidst claims that Britain's immigration controls were at risk from the EU, insisting that 'the British people have never been asked if they want to leave the back door open to uncontrolled numbers of immigrants', and warning that these immigrants would have a 'severe and damaging impact on the generally harmonious balance in race relations' and on social services.[133] With the support of Michael Howard, the Home Secretary, as well as other members of the Cabinet, a new crackdown on illegal immigrants was announced, and a White List of countries from which asylum claims will no longer be entertained was drawn up. With the flow of refugees already rigidly restricted as a result of previous legislative initiatives, and the number of successful applicants for British citizenship at its lowest for ten years, it is hard to imagine that ulterior motives (electoral or internal party political) were not at play.[134]

A new Asylum Bill was introduced in the November 1995 Queen's Speech, glimpses of which were offered by Michael Howard in his speech at the Conservative Party conference in Blackpool earlier that year. Introduced only two years after the Asylum and Immigration Appeals Act came into force, the Bill represented an unnecessary and cynical piece of legislation geared less to addressing the ostensible 'problem' than to construct a compelling Rorschach-type scapegoat on to which a whole range of popular anxieties can be projected in the run-up to the May 1997 general election. Strikingly similar in style to Proposition 187 in California, which ministers apparently studied closely, the new proposals effectively prevent refugee status applicants from claiming social security, housing benefits, free national health treatment, and student loans. Accordingly, public officials – including local authority housing and education officers, teachers, doctors – will be given new powers to identify illegal immigrants and stop them claiming benefits and other services. Under the new rules, at-port applicants (around a third of asylum-seekers) will still qualify for social security, but in-country applicants (the rest on tourist, student or business visas), supposed to be less 'genuine', will not. Representing an extension of the principle of the Carriers' Liability Act, employers who hire 'foreign cheats' will be fined.

The Home Secretary introduced the new proposals with the justification that ineligible foreigners defrauded Britain's welfare state to the tune of some £100m in 1994, although he later admitted that he had no exact figure to back up such a claim, nor even an exact figure for the number of people in Britain without fully accredited residential status.[135] Moreover, such a claim flies in the face of evidence that, according to a report by the Institute of Public Policy Research entitled 'Strangers and Citizens', immigrants often contribute more to the economy than they take from it. A report released in 1995 by the Home Office itself demonstrates that recent asylum-seekers to Britain are among the most highly qualified and valuable additions to British society, thereby contradicting the popular belief reinforced by New Rightists that refugees and immigrants represent a drain on national resources and a threat to the social status of whites.[136] Moreover, claims of fraud and scrounging must be understood in the context of the fact that checking immigration status has become completely institutionalized in the Department of Social Security (DSS) since 1988, when new income support regulations made it directly relevant to benefits. In 1991, the Home Office and the DSS further bolstered such preventative measures against fraud by introducing stringent identity procedures (including fingerprinting) for new claimants.[136]

A leaked Cabinet memo in the wake of Howard's announcement indicates that the new proposals may prove to have been one step too far in the direction of the New Right. In the memo, Gillian Shephard (Secretary of State for Education and Employment) expressed her concern that '[t]here is a danger that employers will concentrate checks on prospective employees whom they a see as a risk, if not simply exclude them from consideration for the job. Either way there could be racial discrimination.'[138] Implying that the sanctions may be out of all proportion to the actual scale of illegal immigrants working in Britain, Shephard also demanded to know whether Howard had 'any indication of the scale of the problem of employers taking on illegal workers'.[139] The leaked memo was an embarrassment to Howard, who was only just recovering from a public relations brawl over statements that conflated blacks with muggers, and from opposition politicians who were criticizing Howard for playing the race card in the run-up to the general election.

Despite its half-hearted criticisms, New Labour has failed to adequately respond to the Conservative Party's racist strategy of linking immigration issues to the social security budget as a whole. Instead, mimicking the equation of asylum-seekers with cheats and scroungers, Roy Hattersley assured the Commons that, if and when re-elected, Labour would weed out the 'undeserving': 'Let us make clear – beyond doubt I hope – that bogus asylum-seekers must be prevented from entering the country. This is an honourable and sensible objective and our amendment reflects our determination to ensure that bogus asylum-seekers are identified and denied entry.'[140] Jack Straw, Labours' shadow Home Secretary, told the *New Statesman* that 'you couldn't get a cigarette paper between Labour and the Tories over the question of immigration.'[141] Although New Labour under Tony Blair has promised to repeal the new 1995 measures if re-elected, the categories of assumptions and ideological paradigms employed in making that promise have served to reinforce those of the New Right.

As the millennium approaches, it is likely that the issue of immigration will be treated increasingly within a pan-European context. As the EU debates the merits of the free movement of people within Europe's internal borders, British spokespersons – both Conservative and Labour – have emerged as leading the campaign to guarantee that Europe's external borders be tightened up. Institute of Race Relations director Sivanandan has written of the dangers of a 'fortress Europe', stating that '[t]he problem of an open Europe is how to close it – against immigrants from the Third World.'[142] In documenting the emergence of a new pan-European racism that 'defines all Third World people as immigrants, refugees, terrorists and drug-runners', Sivanandan notes, 'We are moving from an ethnocentric racism to a Eurocentric racism;

from the different racisms of the different member states to a common market racism.'[143] Although it appears increasingly unlikely that internal borders will be removed in the near future (especially now that France has re-staffed hers in the wake of a spate of terrorist attacks in the summer of 1995), public opinion nevertheless is being softened up to the Euro-sceptic cause through the racist construction of the 'Euro-scrounger' as the new face of the enemy within. While the battle within the Tory Party over the question of Europe reveals the continuing rift between neo-liberals committed to free market capitalism that respects no borders and social au-thoritarians deeply wedded to the nation state, both strands are unified in whipping up racism against immigrants in order to justify the record number of asylum seekers Britain now turns away, their denial of citizenship rights and basic social services, and the criminalization of the black population already resident in Britain. It is to the link between illegal im-migration and crime and crime with race that the next section is devoted.

Law and Order

> And where the shift to authoritarianism first manifests itself is in the distinction the police makes between its publics, as to whom it shall serve by consent and whom control by force – and, in the forcing, remove them from the public domain, 'de-citizenise' them.
>
> (Institute of Race Relations)[144]

The symbolic construction of the 'problem' of Commonwealth immigration and its institutionalization in state policy merged in the 1970s with the symbolic construction of the law and order crisis. With primary (black) immigration halted and the entry of dependents severely curtailed, the New Right and the Thatcher administration together turned their attention toward the black population already resident in Britain.

In a book entitled *Policing the Crisis*, Stuart Hall and his col-leagues at the Centre for Contemporary Cultural Studies demonstrated that a series of moral panics were cultivated as government responded to the new crime identified as 'mugging', and then, I would add, to the subsequent urban disturbances of 1981, 1985 and the early 1990s.[145] The political reaction to these events, not the events themselves, reinforced the New Right belief that black people, whether British-born or not, are incapable of sharing a civilized social life in common with the (white) indigenous majority. In this way, law and order, like immigration, became a condensation symbol for the racial and status anxieties of part of the public.

Again several ideological paradigms can be identified in the justification of the institutionalization of law and order campaigns. The symbolic construction of the moral panic over mugging in the early 1970s first indicated a paradigm change. The emerging paradigm focused less on competition for limited resources as an explanation for urban disturbances (as in the wake of the 1958 disturbances in Notting Hill and Nottingham), than on the construction of black people as, by nature or culture, hostile to authority and British customs.

From the mid-1970s, the New Right became the key purveyor of this paradigm; the Thatcher administration institutionalized it in state policy. Not only were complex social processes such as urban decay, unemployment and increasing violence on the streets thematized as predominantly racial in essence but, as will be demonstrated below, the nature/culture of the 'black criminal' was identified as their cause. Such a category mistake fit nicely with the New Right view that the 'British way of life' was being disrupted by alien strains. Complex changes in post-war Britain were contrasted with a nostalgic portrait of Britain before the arrival of black immigrants as a safe and peaceful haven; the New Right pointed to the black criminal as the cause of the changes.

Symbolic conflict over the interpretation of an issue is so important, let us remember, because it goes a long way in determining the sort of solution pursued. Under the Thatcher administration, the political solution to the realities of urban decay and violence was geared more and more to policing the urban ghettos and the black poor. The justification offered for the pursuit of this more authoritarian response, as opposed to others orientated to addressing the social causes of the disturbances, borrowed from the New Right paradigm of assumptions described at length above. Commitment to this particular solution (policing the black and poor communities) followed from the New Right's particular identification of the problem (the black criminal). In the process, the role of government urban policy, white racism, and police behavior in contributing to the urban disturbances of the 1980s was obscured.

The Thatcher administration identified the urban disturbances of 1981 in Liverpool, London and Bristol as almost exclusively a law and order issue. The social causes of the disturbances, including the fact that the Administration had cut funds for the Urban Program by £7m in 1979, were ignored. The role of white racism, police harassment, and material deprivation pointed to by the Scarman Report (set up by the Administration to investigate the disturbances) were rejected. No charges against the police were ever brought. Seeing only the law and order dimension of the issue, the logical focus of state policy was to grant expanded powers to the police. In July of 1981 Thatcher told Parliament, 'Until law and order and public confidence have been restored, we cannot set about improving the economic or social conditions of this country.'[146]

The Thatcher administration thus condoned the view of the social authoritarian strand of the New Right that the pendulum of freedom had swung too far, and that social discipline had to be restored. For its part, the New Right used the incident to assert more boldly its belief that government activity in the economic sphere had to be matched by the necessary social means to police the social order. One New Right ideologue put it thus: 'Such pathetic non-preparedness is a disgrace to a Tory Administration which seems to confuse Adam Smith's invisible hand with the smack of firm government ... better heads cracked by a policeman's truncheon than souls swamped by society's pity.'[147] Thatcher herself later echoed such sentiment when she said, with reference to the 1981 disturbances:

We are reaping what was sown in the '60s. The fashionable theories and permissive claptrap set the scene for a society in which the old virtues of discipline and self-restraint were denigrated. Parents, teachers and other adults need to set clear consistent limits to the behaviour of children and young people. Children need, respond to, and too often lack clear rules. Only in this way will they grow up in a framework of certainty and learn the self-control necessary to cope with the problems of life.[148]

The 1983 Conservative Manifesto backed up such an interpretation with increased support for the police and a government mandate for the imposition of social discipline more
generally.

Similarly, in the aftermath of the Handsworth disturbances
in 1985, Thatcher dismissed suggestions that the 'riots' might
have had something to do with social and economic conditions. Again the disturbances were identified as 'race riots'
and interpreted as an outbreak of anti-social behavior.
Although the 1985 disturbances erupted only a year after the
increased law and order powers granted by the Police and
Criminal Evidence Act, they convinced government (consistent with its own logic) of the need for ever more powers to the
police. These were granted in the Public Order Act of 1986.
Thatcher defended the trend toward more authoritarian measures in the wake of 1985 disturbances by saying:

> We are right to provide the police and courts with whatever
> means are necessary to defend and protect us all against
> those who would undermine our society – the traffickers in
> drugs who seek to spread their poison, the international
> terrorists who do not hesitate to kill and maim; those who
> forment racial tensions in our cities; and those who exploit
> real or imagined grievances and turn them into violence.[149]

In responding to the urban disturbances of 1981 and 1985,
the Administration was motivated less by an assessment of
various instrumental solutions to the problems of urban decay
and violence than by an ideological reaction to them. This
ideological reaction borrowed from broader New Right
themes of morality, the nation's traditional 'way of life', the
need for authority and social discipline, and the new racism. It
took the form of locating the complex structural problems
magnified by the disturbances (lack of adequate housing and
welfare services, unemployment, police harassment, urban
decay, and so on) in the embodied symbol of the black criminal. Public attention was thereby deflected from the deleterious social and economic impact of government monetarist
and·'public order' policies, with blame shifted onto those arguably most affected by such policies – the black poor. Thus,
instrumentalist policies geared to redress the social and econ-

omic problems of the communities in distress were displaced by ever more authoritarian measures to 'police the crisis'.

It is important to note, however, that the theme of law and order is not as racialized as it is in the United States. Except for the issues of drugs and mugging, the call for the restoration of law and order in recent years has been directed at the increase in hooliganism, arson, looting and joyriding, crimes that are principally perpetrated by white youth. Then Home Secretary Kenneth Baker emphasized the Party's determination to crack down on lawlessness at the 1991 Conservative Party Conference, dismissing the argument that deprivation may have been partly behind the urban disturbances of 1991:

> There are some who would have us believe that all these outbreaks of hooliganism were due to the perpetrators feeling 'deprived'. But, I'll tell you who the really deprived people are. They are elderly people deprived of their day centres, children deprived of their schools, families deprived of their homes, and shopkeepers deprived of their livelihoods.[150].

Thus, while race may no longer be as important to the symbolic construction of the law and order problem as it was a decade ago, the government's reaction to it continues to borrow from New Right themes that emphasize individual over social responsibility.

Such New Right themes were also evident in the Major administration's call for the nation get 'Back to Basics'. In a speech in October of 1993, Major said: 'It is time to return to the old core values. Time to get back to basics. To self-discipline and respect for the law. To consideration for others. To accepting responsibility for yourself and your family – and not shuffling it off on the state ... It is time to return to our roots.'[151] The recent discursive attacks on single mothers and the introduction of legislation (the 1993 Child Support Act) to track down absentee husbands, or 'deadbeat dads', who have failed to pay child support, are similarly indicative of the increasing use of moral discourse by the Conservative Party on matters related to discipline and social order.

In the pre-election climate of the mid-1990s, race is again becoming conflated with law and order themes in a way that dovetails with arguments put forth by the New Right. In the wake of a series of confrontations between the police and predominantly Asian young people in Bradford, Luton, Nuneaton, Liverpool and Leeds in June/July 1995, the Home Office issued a statement that predicted that the riots are symptomatic of a likely new upsurge in criminality among young Pakistanis and Bangladeshis. Senior police officials offered explanations based on an alleged generational and cultural gap of the so-called perpetrators. For example, the chief constable of West Yorkshire said, 'What we are dealing with here is young men, Bradford-born, brought up and educated. They have lost in some way their ties with their old religion and their country, yet they feel alienated within Western culture.'[152] In this way, attention was shifted from the reality of racial disadvantage and insensitive policing methods to the failure of Asian parents properly to socialize their children and/or the failure of Asian youth to embrace Western culture.

It is against this backdrop that the Commissioner of the Metropolitan Police, Sir Paul Condon, issued a contentious study that purported to show that 80 per cent of muggings in London are committed by young black men. In a letter to the black community announcing the launch of 'Eagle Eye', an anti-mugging campaign, Condon wrote that 'very many of the perpetrators of mugging are very young black people'. This attempt to link black youngsters to London's crime levels invited condemnation from the United Nations Human Rights Commission.[153] Responding to the controversy, Professor Jock Young of Middlesex University offered the following analysis:

> Street robbery is the most amateurish crime and therefore generally committed by the poorest people. While they are likely to be black in inner London, they will almost certainly be white in Newcastle or Glasgow. Sir Paul is confusing poverty and inner city dwelling with race. If all else were standardized – education, employment, housing, life chances – race on its own would have virtually no significance.[154]

Acting together as mutually-reinforcing processes, the criminalization of the black community and the racialization of the law and order crisis helps absolve the police force of racism and the wider society of inequality of social conditions and life chances. Forty-two per cent of those stopped and searched by the police in London in 1994 were black people, a figure that is more than double their distribution in the London population.[155] According to an investigation carried out by researchers at Middlesex University, black people in London are four times more likely than whites to be stopped and searched by the police. Although black people account for only 18 per cent of the local population, their stop rate was 78 per 100 residents, while the overall rate was 39 per 100 residents.[156] Such police racism will only be reinforced as a consequence of the passage of the 1994 Criminal Justice Act, which grants the police extended stop and search powers reminiscent of the old 'sus' law of the 1970s.[157] Importantly, none of these measures have been matched by concerted efforts on the part of government policy-makers to address the causes of public disorder highlighted in the Scarman report following the Brixton riots in the early 1980s, most of which still exist today. Tony Speed (liaison officer for the Scarman report) said, 'Scarman referred to a balance between urban deprivation and fair, but firm policing ... It is to the national shame that we read the 1994 urban trends report where ... the conditions that prevailed in the early 1980s, which are generally blamed for the widespread urban disorder, remain.'[158]

Race Relations

Preoccupied as it was with the issues of immigration and law and order, the Thatcher administration proposed relatively little in the 1979 Conservative Manifesto on race relations. What action the Administration did take in the first term was largely negative. The Central Office's Department of Community Affairs was closed down. The budget for the Commission for Racial Equality, created by the 1976 Race Relations Act, was cut by £1m, or 16 per cent.[159] A request for more staff was refused, and in 1980 the appointments of five commissioners (four of them black) were not renewed. Moreover, the scope of the Commission's activities was challenged in 1980 when the Home Office attempted to prevent an investigation into the government's administration of immigration control.

In explicitly rejecting all but two of the fifty-seven recommendations put forward by the parliamentary Home Affairs Committee on racial disadvantage, the Thatcher administration borrowed from New Right ideas on the destructiveness of positive action policies. Then Home Secretary, Douglas Hurd, condemned positive action by stating, 'Positive discrimination is patronising and merely replaces one form of discrimination with another.'[160] Further legislative attempts to enforce racial harmony were ruled out on the grounds of maintaining good race relations. Hurd berated the excesses of the 'race relations industry' and denounced the idea that white racism was the main obstacle to racial harmony as a 'flawed and partial analysis'.[161]

In the wake of the 1981 and 1985 urban disturbances, the government did make room for a few members of the black elite in the existing structures of government, but such a symbolic concession fell far short of an endorsement of positive action. Interestingly, the only piece of legislation passed by the Thatcher administration mandating the use of positive action was the 1989 Fair Employment Act directed toward the treatment of Roman Catholics in Northern Ireland. The thrust of all other measures was clearly in opposition to all forms of positive action and contract compliance, as being both unfair and unnecessary.

Rationalizations for the government's retreat from the commitment to promote racial equality borrowed from the New Right assertion that racism had been eliminated by the equal opportunity legislation of the 1970s. Yet institutional relations of racial inequality were maintained throughout Thatcher's administration and in some spheres grew even worse. Despite the growth of a small (particularly Asian) black middle class, British blacks generally failed to match the mobility of the white population during the 1980s. According to the 1985 Labour Force Survey (LFS), the unemployment rate for West Indian men was twice that of white men; Pakistani and Bangladeshi men were over two-and-a-half times more likely to be unemployed than white men; and only Indian men, with an unemployment rate of 18 per cent, came at all close to the 11 per cent rate for whites.[162] The positions and patterns of disadvantage that faced black people when they entered

Britain a generation ago as migrants have, in the absence of any form of positive action, simply reproduced themselves. The third PSI survey concluded thus:

> Britain's well-established black population is still occupying the precarious and unattractive position of the earlier immigrants. We have moved, over a period of 18 years, from studying the circumstances of immigrants to studying the black populations of Britain only to find that we are still looking at the same thing.[163]

While it would be wrong to suggest that all group differences are a product of racial discrimination, still other studies have demonstrated that such disparities primarily have to do with white racism at both the individual and institutional levels. For example, in the area of employment, a 1984 report by the Policy Studies Institute found that roughly one-third of British employers discriminated against blacks.[164] A 1988 study by Ohri and Faruqui found an unequal process to operate at all levels of employment, promotion, redundancy, and the treatment of black employees.[165] It is in this context of continuing institutional disadvantage for the British black population that the assault upon anti-racism must be understood.

Despite the Administration's crackdown on the institutional sources of anti-racist activity, tensions with the New Right reemerged when the Administration balked at removing the right of councils to promote race relations through works and business contracts. In 1987 Nick Budgen (MP for Wolverhampton) led a right-wing Tory revolt over proposals to preserve the councils' duty to enforce and promote racial equality under the Local Government Bill. One of the ten Tories in the revolt said:

> The positions of the minority has not been made better by the Race Relations Act. It has made the presence of that minority more resented than it would otherwise have been. Many people believe that this Act confers special rights and privileges upon a minority identified by the colour of their skin. We are not attacking the whole of the race relations nonsense, but we are just taking a useful bite at it.[166]

Although the revolt failed completely when the issue came to a vote, much ideological ground was ceded as New Right arguments about the ostensibly harmful effects of anti-racism became accepted tools of debate at the very center of British politics.

The impact of the New Right's new racism paradigm became apparent again near the end of Thatcher's third term with regard to the Rushdie Affair in 1989 and the debate on the Hong Kong Bill in 1990. In the aftermath of the death threat issued by the Iranian government against Salman Rushdie, author of the allegedly blasphemous book *The Satanic Verses*, certain right-wing politicians came forward to denounce the presence of 'alien cultures' and their incompatibility with the 'British way of life'. Rather than relax popular racial tensions by appealing for calm and an end to racist attacks, the response by government, focusing as it did on the impossibility of 'dual loyalties', helped to fuel them. For example, John Patten, then Minister of State at the Home Office, wrote a letter to the Home Office advisory council on race relations that concluded: 'Being British means exactly what it says. One cannot be British on one's own exclusive terms or on a selective basis. Nor is there room for dual loyalties where these loyalties openly contradict one another.'[167]

Although the issue is far from simple, such a response arguably reinforced the popular interpretation of the problem as one of 'them' versus 'us'. Such statements, mimicking as they did the New Right theme of mutual opposition between being black and being British, provoked more extreme calls by government officials and New Right ideologues alike for Muslims to share common respect for the rule of law and assimilate into 'our way of life'. Conservative MP Mr. John Townend stated the ultimatum as follows:

When Muslims say they cannot live in a country when Salmon Rushdie is free to express his views, they should be told they have the answer in their own hand – go back from whence you came ... England must be reconquered for the English ... Have we become so debilitated that the English have lost their voice and no longer think of themselves as the sole possessors of England? Every year that goes by the

English are battered into submission their own country, and more strident are the demands of ethnic nationalism.[168]

The ideas behind the New Right policy of repatriation were thereby being tacitly endorsed.

The endorsement went a step further in debates surrounding the Hong Kong Bill. Former chairman of the Conservative Party Norman Tebbit had called for a referendum on the Bill, warning that the immigration of Hong Kong Chinese would lead to civil strife and ethnic tensions. Tebbit and other right-wing conservatives accused the government of breaking its election promise to put an end to immigration. The day before the debate on the Hong Kong Bill, Tebbit proposed, in an interview with the *Los Angeles Times*, a 'cricket test' of loyalty for ethnic minorities living in Britain. 'Which side do they cheer for?', he asked. 'It's an interesting test. Are you still harking back to where you come from or where you are. I think we've got real problems in that regard.' Tebbit continued, 'Well you can't have two homes. Where you have a clash of history, a clash of religion, a clash of race, then it's all too easy for there to be an actual clash of violence.'[169]

It soon became apparent, however, that this one step closer to the New Right solution was one step too close. The controversy that emerged as a result of the comments created a barrage of negative press coverage and ruined Tebbit's already minimal chances of leadership of the Conservative Party. Although Thatcher disassociated herself from Tebbit's comments, government rhetoric and policy on racial matters under her Administration had in large part condoned such views. While the styles of the Townends and the Tebbits differed from that of Margaret Thatcher, the messages were arguably much the same – Britain may be a multicultural society, but it is not and will not become a multiracial nation.

Attacks on institutional forms of anti-racism have continued during the Major administration, albeit in a kinder, gentler manner. Although Major and other members of his administration have expressed commitment to the goal of a multiracial society wherein color is of no consequence, tacticians at Conservative Central Office have revived the 'loony Left' signifier. For example, Gloucester City Council came under scrutiny in 1995 over its funding of ethnic minority schemes; including a Jamaican sports and social club, a luncheon club for black elderly people, and a Pakistani centre.[170] Such attacks have caused even some Tories to criticize the Major administration for talking about race only in a negative context. Defeated black conservative election candidate John Taylor said,

> I feel I cannot let my Party off the hook and must speak out about the vacuum that exists in our race relations policy. The party must learn that holding three or four receptions for Asian millionaires every year does not amount to a race relations policy. Whenever I go to Central Office the only other black face is the security guard on the door.[171]

The lack of positive governmental effort must be understood in the context of evidence that reveals blacks are continuing to do badly as compared to their white counterparts. In 1995, two new major sets of statistics were published charting social trends in modern Britain. *Social Trends*, the Government's annual source book of social statistics, demonstrates the degree to which black people in Britain have been disproportionately affected by the growing inequalities between rich and poor. For example, in 1994, the unemployment rate for Afro-Caribbean and Asian people was 27 per cent and 28 per cent, respectively, compared to a 10 per cent rate for whites.[172] A report by the Joseph Rowntree Foundation on income and wealth distribution finds that inequalities have grown wider in Britain than in any other industrialized country apart from New Zealand. It documents that, while inequalities decreased during the 1970s, they have increased dramatically since 1979, the year that Margaret Thatcher was elected Prime Minister. It shows quite clearly that black people are far more likely than white people to be found in the poorest fifth of the population, and far less likely than white people to be in the richest fifth.[173] Research recently released by the Equal Opportunities Commission has found that black women earn on average forty percent less than men, compared with twenty percent for white women.[174]

　　Such statistical evidence makes suspect the portrayal of the pursuit of equal opportunity gone mad, and directly contradicts the argument that anti-racism poses a threat to the majority white society. Indeed, as the chair of the CRE, Herman Ousley, points out, if there is a trend it is a powerful and dangerous movement of opinion in favor of the status quo – with all its inequality, bigotry and discrimination – masquerading as a consensus of common sense and freedom and in which sensible action for racial equality is under attack for being politically correct.[175]

Education

Under the Thatcher administration, the major tendencies dominating post-war education policy were challenged in both practice and principle. With the election slogan 'Educashun isn't working', Conservatives moved to restructure education by:

1. increasing the central authority of the state over the determination of curriculum content;
2. empowering parent groups to take advantage of opportunities for local autonomy;
3. drastically reducing the rights and influence of the National Union of Teachers;
4. reshaping the organization and financing of schools in order to give greater weight to market forces as against those of Labour-controlled local authorities, and
5. narrowing the range of ideas and teaching methods regarded as educationally permissible.[176]

One often neglected aspect of this attempt to restructure education was the very successful campaign mounted by the Thatcher administration against anti-racist/multicultural education in particular.

Very little innovation in the realm of education policy occurred during Thatcher's first two terms. This was a period of largely symbolic gestures toward the New Right and their ideas on how to reform education. For example, in 1983 then Education Secretary Keith Joseph gave a speech that derided the teaching of history from a multicultural perspective as counter to the goal of assimilation of racial and ethnic minorities into the 'British way of life'. In 1985, leading New Right authorities on education such as Ray Honeyford and Caroline Cox were invited to Downing Street for a meeting, during which Thatcher herself denounced the politicization of the curriculum (and the trend toward multiculturalism in particular) as an assault upon education and value. That same year, Thatcher expressed a variation on the same theme at the Conservative Party Conference at Blackpool when she stated: 'Some teachers and parents are speaking out. Those who believe – as we do – that the schools of this country are for teaching and learning, not for political indoctrination.'[177]

It was not until the beginning of Thatcher's third term, however, when education became a key arena of political and symbolic contest, that any comprehensive policy initiatives were put forward. Kenneth Baker had replaced Keith Joseph as Secretary for Education, and although many considered him to be more of a moderate, Baker proved to be the overseer of the most radical restructuring of British education in the past half century. The 1988 Education Reform Act (ERA) instituted a truly radical reform package that challenged the entire conception of public, non-market orientated education.

The ERA combined a powerful shift toward centralization with a radical move toward greater autonomy for individual schools and the process of selection. True to the goals of the Campaign for Real Education that worked hard for its passage, the ERA granted the right of schools to opt-out of local authority control, promoted new methods of allocating and controlling school finances (making them more open to market forces), and established a universal system of testing for ages seven, eleven and fourteen with prescribed and detailed levels of attainment. This emphasis on testing, along with plans to introduce a national curriculum, served to curtail the autonomy of local authorities and individual teachers to develop multicultural/anti-racist teaching methods.

The ERA carried within it ramifications for the viability of multicultural and anti-racist education programs in particular; ramifications, it should be emphasized, more to do with the conservatives' broader social agenda than with hidden racist intent. The transfer of power to determine policy from local educational authorities to school governors inevitably meant a weakening in the power of those authorities (the leading force behind the development of anti-racism in the schools in the

early 1980s) to promote anti-racism. Indeed, the ERA included no requirement that school governors take steps to
safeguard the rights of black students, nor that they continue
to pursue those anti-racist programs already in place. On the
contrary, scant room was provided for anti-racist perspectives
in the new national curriculum, with its emphasis on the
testing of core subjects. Educator and poet Chris Searle writes:

> Baker's acts envisioned one, unitary post-imperial culture
> across British schools, a notion of 'British glory' rooted in
> the 'Victorian values' of an ideology nostalgic and assertive
> of imperial centrality. There was no place in this recon-
> structed culture for the distinctive experiences, struggles
> and perspectives of Britain's black people: their languages
> were discounted from the new curriculum, their history
> written out of it, school assemblies were to have a 'Christian'
> character and all testing (from the age of seven) was to be
> conducted in Standard English, no matter the first language
> of the child.[178]

The language of social conservatism – of parental choice,
quality education and local control – while not inherently
racist, in fact has obscured the extent to which Thatcher's
reforms, intentionally or not, have made very real the
prospect of school resegregation along both race and class
lines. This is especially true today now that the opt-out regulations are in force, allowing whites in effect to set up white-
only schools. Indeed, ever since the Dewsbury case in 1987
(when a number of white children were removed from schools
where a majority of students were of Asian origin) the court's
protection of the right of parents to withdraw their children
from school has been a major tactic of protest against multi-
racial education and a symbolic coup against the principles of
non-discrimination enshrined in the Race Relations Act.[179]
Moreover, schools themselves have begun to impose unofficial
quotas of black pupils so as to avoid such disputes in the
future, and even to exclude black children deliberately either
at the point of admission or through racist suspension and expulsion policies.[180] Baroness Hooper, Under-secretary of State
at the Department of Education and Science (DES), said
this about the prospect of resegregation: 'If we are offering

freedom of choice to parents, we must allow that choice to operate. If it ends up with a segregated system, then so be it.'[181] Asked to repudiate Hooper's statement, Thatcher declined and stated instead that she was merely interested in parents getting the best education possible for their children.

Although there have been many White Papers on education published under the Major administration, repeating the emphasis on the goals of excellence for all students and greater autonomy for schools, one of the most significant developments for the present analysis is the cut in Section 11 funding. Section 11 funding was set up in 1966 under the Local Government Act to help local councils promote racial equality. The funding mainly gives salaries for teachers, bilingual assistants and school liaison workers. After a wide-ranging review of Section 11 was conducted in 1991–2, the Major administration announced major cuts. These cuts mean, in effect, that funds to local councils for services targeted at black people have suffered a 40 per cent reduction, including the loss of 4000 jobs in 1994 alone.[182]

Although the curriculum now in place is not due to be revised until the year 2000, debate over future initiatives already has begun. As regards race matters, Dr Nicholas Tate (the chief executive of the School Curriculum and Assessment Authority) provided a sense of things to come in the summer of 1995 when he said that 'the multicultural approach to education should be swept away and replaced by a national sense of identity and purpose' and that children should be taught what it means to be British, no matter what their ethnic background.[183] Arguing against the view that no culture or one set of values is superior to another, Tate told a gathering of head teachers that 'there is a mistaken notion that the way to respond to cultural diversity is to try to bring everything together into some kind of watered-down multiculturalism' and continued by insisting that the best guarantee of strong minority cultures is the 'existence of a majority culture which is sure of itself, which signals that customs and traditional are things to be valued and which respects other cultures.'[184] Responding to Tate's concern that there is a danger of an underclass forming with no felt connection with the rest of society, Police Commissioner Paul Condon advised that citizenship classes be set up in primary schools to teach children right from wrong.[185]

The move toward greater centralization and reduced commitment to equal educational opportunity for students from all backgrounds thus has found a new and compelling ideological justification in the symbol of race. The set of ideological formulations used to rationalize and build popular support for such conservative education reform has resonated in important ways with the key categories of racial meaning produced and circulated by the New Right. Echoing the New Right's denunciation of the new racism of anti-racist educators, the rhetoric of government policy-makers has portrayed anti-racism programs in the schools as pandering to the 'special interests' of black students and as interfering with the educational opportunities and rights of the (white) majority. While many New Right policy proposals in the area of education were never instituted under Thatcher or Major, such as the introduction of education vouchers, New Right symbolic conflict over race has provided right-wing Tories with the set of meanings and reference points they have needed to buttress support for the reversal of liberal education reform.

THE CENTER MOVES RIGHT

The paradigms of assumptions and beliefs employed by government policy-makers in both the United States and Britain reveal that the new racism of the New Right did in fact have a significant impact upon government rhetoric and policy formation. In major policy areas, the key tenets of the new racism were adopted and espoused. Many were institutionalized in state policy.

The New Right provided government policy-makers with a set of meanings – race being only one important component – with which they were able to justify or rationalize the right turn in policy formation. The new racism was an essential ingredient in breaking with New Deal/social democratic assumptions, as well as central to the forging of a new consensus based around conservative principles. In addition, the key tenets of the new racism served the more immediate political goal of rationalizing the government's deradicalization of anti-racism.

Yet, as demonstrated above, the relationship between the New Right and government policy-makers was a strained one. New Rightists frequently felt betrayed by the very governments they credit themselves with bringing to power. Many of their policies were disregarded, while others that were instituted have since been reversed. Moreover, while it seems beyond debate that the old consensus has been fractured, it is far from clear that a critical realignment toward the right has been secured. Both the Republican and Tory Parties are fractured with deep ideological divisions. Surveys of public opinion continue to reveal significant commitment among the US and British publics to liberal/social democratic policies, leading some analysts to conclude that the right turn in public policy has not been matched by a right turn in public opinion.

While such a thesis is an important and convincing challenge to those who argue that a new conservative era has been heralded, its narrow focus on public attitudes, immediate political advantage, and electoral arithmetic neglects the broader ideological consequences of the right turn from above. These broader consequences are harder to measure but have to do with the construction of a rightward shift in the popular political imagination (that is, the construction of worldview among relevant groups, of interpretative schemes, national identities, and 'common sense' assumptions about what government can and should do). Only with such a broadened focus does it become possible to argue that even if no lasting electoral alignment toward the right has been achieved, the New Right nevertheless has succeeded in fracturing the liberal/Left opposition and winning the political initiative.

To argue that the New Right has won the political initiative on policy issues pertaining to race does not, however, explain why this is so. The mainstream explanation is that the New Right has gained influence on its own, by force of popular pressure, and succeeded in grabbing the policy consensus on race and pulling it rightward. New Rightists themselves argue that increased anti-anti-racist rhetoric is a response to an objective problem or threat (for example, the presence of 'alien cultures' in Britain or of 'reverse racism' in the United States).

The symbolic conflict approach rests upon an alternative explanation, one that focuses less on race than on the political reaction to it by the state/power bloc. In this view, the new racism has been less the cause of the right turn in government policy formation than created by it. Its central claim is that the New Right has gained influence not of its own accord, but rather because its ideas have been useful to government policy-makers in search of new ideological formulations with which to justify the right turn in policy formation that was already under way. In other words, the New Right has had an impact on the political center only because the political center was already moving to the right. The rightward shift of the policy consensus on race matters must be understood, therefore, not as a populist or policy response to an objective problem or threat (that is, the presence of black immigrants or the actions of anti-racists), but rather as a process whereby the state/power bloc has mobilized to call a halt to programs previously regarded as a main vehicle for racial progress and, in the process, to defend relations of racial advantage in the face of challenge.

Such a focus on the symbolic dimensions of policy formation allows for an appreciation of the processes by which political legitimacy is forged during periods such as the present when society is operating in a manner that is at odds with its professed ideals. Although liberal democracies such as the United States and Britain profess a commitment to opportunity and equality, societal constraints have been placed disproportionately on the backs of people of color. In this context, the construction and uses of folk devils such as 'welfare queens' and 'Euro-scroungers' provides a symbolic resolution of this contradiction and renders the abstract ideal consistent with everyday and material reality.

Evaluating the degree of impact that the new racism of the New Right has had on government policy formation serves to remind one that the policy formation process always involves competing narratives, metaphors and discursive practices that seek to bolster one view of what the issue is, why it is there, and how to resolve it. In many ways, the 'problems' in need of policy resolution are created in and through the policy-making process, a counter-intuitive insight that is missed by those who approach the policy arena from a technicist or narrowly empirical perspective. Only with an appreciation of the symbolic dimensions of the policy-making process is it possible to appreciate that the narratives mobilized and metaphors

employed often reveal more about the perspectives and interests of those in the dominant society who are attempting to
solve a 'problem' than the deviants who are the ostensible
focus of the policy-making effort. In this sense, the new racism
of the New Right is as much about an effort to construct a
non-problematic white identity and to justify the operation of
the meritocratic ideal in a context of structural inequity as it is
about combating 'reverse racism' or protecting equal treatment. It is to the broader implications of the meanings mobilized in New Right discourse about race that I now turn.

Conclusion: Challenging the New Racism; Combating the New Right

Race has not declined in significance in the United States or Britain; rather its significance has changed. Race remains an important lens through which current issues and events are perceived and explained, as well as a fundamental dimension of institutional relations of inequality. Although the assertion of the biological inequality of different races is an ideology which has fallen largely into disrepute, race-based symbolism nevertheless remains an important explanatory framework for many present-day issues and challenges, as well as a legitimating ideology for elites.

One reason the continuing significance of race is so often overlooked is because its contours have changed. While civil and political rights for people of color are no longer contested, except at the very fringes of US and British politics, debates relating to the meaning of social equality and the means by which to achieve it are far from resolved. Moreover, as a result of the victory of previous anti-racist struggles in making a public racial language more or less illegitimate in the political cultures under study, the New Right has been forced to appeal to the racial anxieties of relevant social groups without, significantly, drawing upon explicit racial referents. Other social categories (such as crime, immigration and welfare) are employed to evoke race without explicitly addressing it.

These innovations in the expression and social character of racial ideology are what constitute the new racism: the New Right in the United States and Britain has been its key purveyor. The new racism of the New Right constitutes a distinct response to the liberal racial understandings ushered in by popular struggles (in preceding decades and now), as well as to the liberal state reforms instituted to accommodate them. In proposing an alternative set of racial meanings and associated policy recommendations, the New Right has obstructed the road to racial progress and even acted as a vehicle of retreat.

In a narrow sense, the New Right has helped to legitimate the deradicalization of anti-racism. By rearticulating a whole range of liberal racial understandings associated with the postwar consensus, the New Right has advanced the government's retreat from a commitment to racial progress. In a voice claiming deference to abstract democratic values such as freedom and equality of opportunity, the New Right has put into circulation a range of meanings – and a corresponding set of policy proposals – with which relevant social groups (both dominant and subordinate) have been able to rationalize the continued exclusion of people of color from the mainstream of the nation's economic and social life.

Yet in a broader and more meaningful sense, the new racism has been important to the winning of popular support for a much wider agenda of social and economic conservatism. This wider agenda has less to do with the expression of particularistic racist attitudes than with the articulation of conservative assumptions regarding who is deserving and who is undeserving, the nature of equality, the meaning of national/cultural identity, and the proper role of state activity. Thus, the new racism is not a mere cover or smokescreen for conservative views; rather, the New Right's brand of conservatism carries within it a very definite theory of race.

The differences between the new racism of the New Right in the United States and Britain are manifold. This is so both because racial understandings are connected to the specific character of social relations in a given country, and also since the meanings people give to them are infused with and mediated by the symbols provided by a particular political culture. Racial understandings are shaped by social experience, political history, and cultural tradition – in addition to the more typically examined economic factors – and each of these inevitably vary across national boundaries.

Perhaps the most fundamental difference to emerge from my search for key categories of meaning is that British racial ideology is largely exclusionary in character while in the United States it is more inclusionary. In Britain, it is often asserted that black people are in the nation but can never be of the nation. Indeed, the terms 'black' and 'British' appear in British New Right discourse as virtually mutually exclusive. In the United States, on the other hand, and in large part due to the fact that black people have been in the country since its inception, as slaves, racial ideology is more often voiced in terms of debate over the legitimate Constitutional means of inclusion. For example, opposition to the policy of affirmative action is frequently grounded in the argument that the Constitution meant for the nation's laws to be color-blind rather than color-conscious, or for equality to mean individual equality of opportunity, not collective equality of outcome.

Yet the set of racial meanings produced and circulated by the New Right, whether exclusionary or inclusionary in form, has served in both countries to perpetuate and further entrench relations of racial inequality. That is, despite differences in discursive strategies utilized, the New Right in the United States and Britain has mobilized a similar range of meanings on matters pertaining to race, and with comparable effects. Both have attempted to rearticulate previous liberal racial understandings and, in the process, to rationalize the withdrawal of the state from its key role in promoting programs of economic and political justice for people of color.

Moreover, there exists a shared cluster of ideological mechanisms which unite the seemingly disparate categories of meaning identified within New Right racial discourse in the two countries. These mechanisms serve to legitimate existing relations of racial domination by:

1. reifying institutionalized patterns of racial inequality so that they appear above or outside history as natural and/or inevitable;
2. creating a homogeneous unity of the nation over and above divisions of race and class;
3. constructing racialized political enemies as scapegoats for the many and real discontents of relevant social groups;
4. mystifying complex structural sources of social disadvantage via the construction of racialized victims who are themselves blamed for their own subordinate social location; and
5. rationalizing the government's deradicalization of anti-racism.

The interaction of these ideological mechanisms form the basis of what has been characterized throughout as the new racism.

The new racism is not so much an aberration from prevailing ideologies, or the result of the infiltration of individuals with racist ideas aligned with the Far Right, than a modified variant of widespread and generally accepted beliefs already in circulation in the political cultures under study. The search for the key categories of meaning that together constitute the new racism therefore need not be a search for the bizarre, the irrational, or the absurd. Quite the contrary, as this study has revealed, the most basic and apparently common sense underlying cultural and political assumptions have become key stakes of symbolic conflict.

The new racism has enabled New Rightists and their supporters to justify the benefits which they historically have derived, and continue to derive, from institutional relations of racial inequality without, significantly, appearing as mean-spirited racists. It allows them to reconcile their commitment to an idealized version of a liberal-democratic society with their fear of the challenge to their socio-economic and cultural position posed by a militant 'underclass', one that is profoundly racialized in the popular political imagination. It is precisely this combination of supporters' respect for existing institutions and dominant values with the perceived threat to their economic and social status from classes both above and below that produces an authoritarian, and in this case specifically racialized, response. New Right symbolic conflict over the meaning of race provides a legitimate means to rationalize the denial of social rights to people of color as well as to justify supporters' own positions of relative advantage.

It has been wholly in the interest of dominant groups to promote an ideology that allows a defence of an idealized version of both capitalism and democracy while rejecting their historical results (in this case, racial inequality). The new racism functions for the dominant class as an essentially anti-radical, even anti-reformist, ideology. It deflects attention regarding the sources of subordinate groups' anxieties and grievances away from structural or historical explanations, and towards more personalized and racialized categories of explanation. Disaffection is deflected from the targets of power, position and privilege towards those classes lower on the social ladder – the urban poor, the black working class, the chronically unemployed, and immigrant workers. In this way the ideology of race supplants class as an explanation for social phenomena; indeed, it becomes the ideological lens through which class conflict is experienced and lived.

While the new racism was produced first and foremost as a political reaction to anti-racist struggles for equality and justice and the liberal reforms of the state to accommodate them, it is the climate of economic downturn and its associated political dimensions that has rendered the new racism of the New Right particularly potent. The wider economic and political climate has provoked a right turn from above wherein ruling elites have mobilized to provide conditions for profitable capital accumulation during a period of economic contraction and, in the process, to break the mould of the so-called post-war consensus. New Right symbolic conflict over key assumptions associated with this consensus (including liberal racial understandings), and its impact on government policy formation and the construction of beliefs among relevant social groups, has been largely dependent upon this right turn from above to grant it legitimacy.

This insight carries important implications for the study of social movements and social change. The heightened role of the state in actively garnering legitimacy for itself has translated into the historical fact that, in this century, economic downturn has produced, more often than not, ground fertile for the Right. During times of hardship and instability, the ideological forces of hegemony have quite successfully constructed the social world in such a way as to provoke cross-class alliances on the basis of race and other ostensibly non-class identities. The salience of the new racism of the New Right in the past couple decades is but one instance of this more general phenomenon.

Appreciation of the fact that many alternative ways are available for agents to construct consciousness of the social world links up with the insights of the symbolic conflict model offered above. A study of the symbolic dimensions of politics is a study of the construction and uses of key symbols which influence the perception of events, the interpretation of experiences, and the justification of certain courses of action over others. It is a study of the social production of consent; consent not to the instrumental interests of the dominant social bloc but rather to the ideological representations of the social world through which such interests are perceived and judged. Domination of the contested symbolic field has become a significant aim of political action precisely because the power to dominate the drafting of the ideological map of social reality contributes significantly towards specific social outcomes – that is, which group secures instrumental benefits for its particular interests and which group becomes or remains materially and/or culturally dispossessed. The group that dominates the contested symbolic field, a domination which is always temporary and needs constantly to be defended against challenge, is able to control the definition of the 'real' itself – a power of control that is intimately linked with the power to control.

The New Right has sought to dominate the contested symbolic field by rearticulating key categories of meaning associated with the post-war consensus. A central aspect of this process has been the symbolic construction and uses of political enemies, moral allies, and a whole range of social 'problems' in need of particular policy solutions. By selectively emphasizing certain categories of meaning (for example, the allegedly subversive activities of anti-racists) to the exclusion of others (for example, institutional relations of inequality), the New Right has helped to organize popular anxieties and discontents in a manner that legitimates the flow of benefits of government policy away from subordinate groups and toward dominant ones. In this view, legitimation does not involve the simple imposition of ruling ideas from above or even the reality of popular recognition of a set of dominant values. Legitimation is not a factual reality of popular consent to the governed, but rather a process whereby those who govern must continually produce and shape the consent to which they refer themselves.

By creating a set of fundamental beliefs about the causes and consequences of social phenomena, New Right symbolic conflict over liberal racial understandings has served as an important component in making the right turn in government policy formation politically possible. New Right racial ideology has mobilized a set of meanings that has interpreted and framed political events in a manner which has secured a degree of popular support for conservative policies. At the very least, the symbolic struggles of the New Right have helped to build public opposition to liberal policies and to fragment the opposition to conservative ones.

An examination of the effects of the sort of symbolic politics practiced by the New Right indicates the critical role discourse plays in producing and shaping the links between public beliefs and social experience. These links are by no means automatic; they are forged actively by different social groups with opposing material interests at stake. By mediating agents' interpretations and beliefs about social experiences, discourse is crucial to the process of the formation of popular consent (or opposition) to dominant representations of social reality. Discursive forms reinforce certain beliefs to the exclusion of others, and so help to justify certain courses of action over others. Indeed, a change in the categories of meaning utilized carries the power to change the sort of solution pursued.

However, the power of discursive forms to transmute experience is not limitless – it is bounded by a material basis. The discursive turn in much of the contemporary symbolic politics literature is limiting since it neglects this material basis and disconnects the study of symbols from the study of class (that is, how class conflict is constructed ideologically). Discourse is thereby transformed from a mediator of lived experience to a creator of it, a transformation which is important to contest. Just as pornography does not create the rapist; neither does racial discourse create the racist. The creating element lies in the social world and the disposition of subjects, not in the discursive forms themselves. To assert the latter is to mistake the ideological map of the social world for its actual terrain. People bring experiences to discourse just as discourse mediates experiences. It follows that it is important to acknowledge the inherent limitations of the effort to control subordinate groups by ideological rhetoric from above. The effect of growing social inequality must be acknowledged for its potential to expose dominant representations to popular criticism. Thus, while New Right ideas certainly have affected the consciousness of relevant social groups, there is perhaps more ambiguity in popular views than some would suggest. Events such as the Poll Tax demonstration in 1990 in Britain

and the Los Angeles rebellion in 1992 suggest the real potential for popular forces to resist and challenge dominant interpretations of social reality and the relations of material
inequality these interpretations service.

Yet the dialectic between experiences and discourse also
points in the other direction, in the direction of mystification,
thus making it only a potential. This is so since experience is
never so unidimensional that it cannot be recognized in many
alternative forms of expression. One's experience of declining
living standards, for example, can accommodate a whole
range of explanations: the volatility of the international capitalist system, the failure of a political party of leader, the evils
of a scapegoat, or feelings of personal inadequacy. Which alternative is actually taken up in practice depends less upon the
abstract power of a symbol than on the set of material and
political factors which makes a particular symbol so evocative.

By granting concessions to New Right demands, mainstream
political parties (both conservative and liberal) have reinforced the meanings produced and transmitted in New
Right ideology. Far from appeasing the New Right, such concessions have lent right-wingers the increased confidence and
political will to press even harder for their demands. Moreover,
these concessions have sent a powerful message that the New
Right is correct in its interpretations of political events. In so
doing, mainstream political parties unwittingly have facilitated
the growth in power of Far Right groupings such as the militias in the United States or the British National Party which
merely take New Right interpretations to their logical conclusion. Perhaps more common, though, is the way in which
liberal/Left echoes of New Right discourse legitimate power
via the dissemination and circumvention of liberal values and
rhetoric.

The hegemonic project of the New Right in both the
United States and Britain remains just that: a project.
Realization that there are many possible ways to construct the
social world and, by implication, that the New Right's political
response to the disintegration of the post-war consensus is not
the only 'natural' or inevitable one, opens an important analytic and political space for thinking about how to contest the
increasingly salient and normalized New Right brand of
'common sense'. It is useful for those interested in challeng-

ing the New Right and combating the New Racism and the more authoritarian form of democracy that their intersection portends to develop a transformative strategy based on the insights of the symbolic conflict model of New Right politics offered in this book.

First, it is essential for progressives to develop effective anti-racist strategies that respond to and challenge the new forms of racism championed by the New Right. Anti-racist principles based on an abstract liberal universalism (such as color-blindness or-non-racialism) are not up to the task of responding to the new, more indirect and structural forms of racial exclusion that accompany the discursive innovations of the new racism in the post-civil rights era. If anti-racist strategies are focused only on battling conscious attitudes of racial prejudice or the more overt forms of discrimination, then the deeper and more systemic patterns of racial inequality that operate without obvious ill-intent or mean-spirited affect will be left untouched. Rather than offer abstract platitudes or morality plays that ask 'why can't we just all get along', anti-racists need to point to the ways in which relatively mainstream cultural codes operate *in interaction with the present historical context* to obscure and reify continued and patterned relations of racial inequality. Multiculturalist agendas that reduce the anti-racist project to one of inclusion or diversity run the risk of unwittingly colluding in the sanitized public transcript of racial reconciliation that sidesteps structural issues of white power and advantage. And as Daryl Scott has recently pointed out, forms of liberal anti-racism that rationalize the government pursuit of racial equality policies with therapeutic appeals based on pity and damage imagery (by contrast to conservative appeals based on contempt) also unwittingly collude in the triumph of New Right narratives that foreground the need for state-sponsored rehabilitationist efforts to counter the pathologies in communities of color that are the alleged creation of the liberal state, thereby making it difficult to dissuade those who look to the wider gamut of conservative policy initiatives as an effective 'cure'.

It is essential today to challenge those institutional and cultural practices that are fair in form but discriminatory in practice. Many laws exist on the books today that allow individuals to pursue remedy against discrimination. What is at risk are the tools available to act against patterned discrimination and to link past practices to present effects. It is the refusal on the part of actors from across the political spectrum to see race in its historical and societal context that absolves nations such as the United States and Britain of responsibility for coming to terms with their racial legacies. Rather than continue to participate in national debates about race that have been cleansed of any mention of race save disingenuous gestures of rhetorical inclusion, the task today is to challenge the framework of assumptions that evades responsibility to act against patterned discrimination. To do so means articulating and defending vastly different assumptions regarding the meaning of equality, the rights of citizenship, the nature of racism, the role of the state *vis-à-vis* the pursuit of racial equality, and so on. Only then will it be possible to shift the debate from the present focus on fairness, merit and the cultural attributes of the so-called black underclass to national conversations that address and ameliorate the structural realities related to systematically asymmetrical relations of racial power and advantage.

The second task facing those who wish to combat the new racism of the New Right is to take aim at the symbolic dimensions of the conservative agenda. It is up to progressive forces not only to combat the legislative initiatives advocated by the New Right, but also its worldview. Rather than engage in technocratic tussles with conservatives over the specifics of particular policy issues, as the New Democrats and New Labour have done so earnestly, the symbolic conflict model presented above suggests the importance of the discursive struggle to contest exactly what is at issue. It is important for progressive opponents of the New Right to challenge the domain of 'truths' and engage in the cultural sphere and the space of representation, and thereby to strive to move previously uncontested cultural codes into the realm of the contested. Only then will it be possible to create new horizons of possibilities based on an alternative set of categories of meaning – social justuce, egalitarianism, group rights, openness to cultural/racial diversity, and so on – within which opposing forces by necessity will have to articulate their demands and interests.

Such a project of seizing the rules disseminated in New Right discourse, inverting their meaning, and replacing them with representations that redirect the rules against the New

Right's political project, is what is connoted in the sociological literature as the struggle for hegemony. The concept of hegemony introduces the meaningful view that politics involves more than cost-benefit analysis or the individual exercise of rational choice. It is today's conservatives in the United States and Britain that have realized the political capital of struggles in the realm of culture to engage at the level of passions and imaginary identifications. Progressive opponents of the New Right must also operate at these levels if the project of recapturing the forward-looking energy and common sense appeal of conservative tropes is to be successful. Fresh narratives that serve to reconfigure cause and effect, reassign blame and responsibility, and rearticulate identity and memory, must be fashioned in order to contribute to significant reversals at the symbolic level that cannot be coopted or reabsorbed into already existing systems of exclusion.

For a progressive counter-hegemonic project ultimately to work, however, it is necessary to offer more than better stories. Reversing the trend toward a more authoritarian form of democracy that the intersection of the New Right and the new racism portends requires the political will and capacity to address the gross and growing material inequalities that characterize present day U.S. and British society. Absent this will and capacity, an idealist strategy based solely on the offering of progressive counter-stories risks furthering the process whereby the symbolic dimensions of policy formation continues to be orchestrated at the expense of substantive benefits.

Notes

Introduction: The New Right – Storm-Troopers in the Name of Liberty

1. Arthur Miller; quoted in *Observer Review* (15 October 1995) p. 7.
2. Many scholars have elaborated on the breakdown of the post-war consensus in the mid-1970s. For example, see: Andrew Gamble, *The Free Economy and the Strong State* (London: Macmillan, 1988); Thomas Ferguson, 'Party Realignment and American Industrial Structure: The Investment Theory of Political Parties in Historical Perspective', *Research in Political Economy*, vol. 6 (1983); Thomas Ferguson and Joel Rogers, 'The Reagan Victory: Corporate Coalitions in the 1980 Campaign', in Ferguson and Rogers (eds), *Hidden Election: Politics and Economics in the 1980 Presidential Campaign* (New York: Pantheon Books, 1981).
3. A moral panic involves sudden hysteria about particular activities or pre-existing groups thought to engage in them, accompanied by calls for exclusion or suppression. Moral panics are especially useful during those periods of societal transition, such as the present, when the moral boundaries of the national community are being redrawn. For more on the concept of moral panic, see: Stanley Cohen, *Folk Devils and Moral Panics: The Creation of Mods and Rockers* (Oxford: Basil Blackwell, 1987); Philip Jenkins, *Intimate Enemies* (New York: Aldine de Gruyter, 1992); Stuart Hall *et al.*, *Policing the Crisis: Mugging, the State, and Law and Order* (London: Macmillan, 1978).
4. This phrase refers to a book by that title: Murray Edelman, *Constructing the Political Spectacle* (University of Chicago Press, 1988).
5. The concept of race is used here to refer not to a biological reality but to a social construction. Many authors (for example, Robert Miles, *Racism*,1989) place quotation markers around the word 'race' to remind the reader of this point, while others prefer the term 'racialization' (for example, Stephen Small, *Racialised Barriers: The Black Experience in the United States and England in the 1980s* [London: Routledge, 1994] or 'racial' (for example, Howard Winant, *Racial Conditions*, 1994). Although often cumbersome, such detailed attention to the use of language is laudable in its goal not to implicate social scientists in the reproduction of a concept that has been proven invalid. I fully subscribe to this view of race as a social and not a biological construction, although hereafter I do not place markers (quotes) around the word. It is also important to note difficulties associated with the use of the term 'black', as it has a different empirical referent in each country. In the United States, the term is used most often to refer to people of African origin, although I employ the term

274

as a political alternative to the more troublesome 'non-white' construction to include Latinos and other so-called minority groups. At times in the text, especially when I am dealing with specific policy issues such as immigration, I use the term 'black' in the more limited sense in order to distinguish between people of African origin and Latinos, Asians, and others. In Britain, the term 'black' is sometimes used to refer to people of African origin exclusively (Africans and African-Caribbeans), at other times it includes Asians and others; unfortunately there is no consensus among official bodies nor the racialized groups themselves. One of the reasons for such lack of consensus is political; during the height of the burgeoning culture of racialized resistance in Britain, for example, the African, African-Caribbean and Asian communities united under the banner 'black' in their common struggle against racism, while in the relatively more depoliticized (or identity politics) context of the 1980s and 1990s, racialized identity has once again been broken down into respective ethnic and even national identity compartments. In an attempt to reduce the level of confusion on this matter, I half-heartedly use the tepid terms 'people of color' and 'communities of color' to refer to so-called minorities or non-whites, unless I am talking about policies that target particular groups, in which case I use the more specific term (that is, African-Caribbean, Latino, and so on).

6. The phrase 'right turn' comes from a book by that title: Thomas Ferguson and Joel Rogers, *Right Turn: The Decline of the Democrats and the Future of American Politics* (New York: Hill & Wang, 1986). It refers to the abandonment of core post-war liberal commitments: progressive taxation, social welfare programs, business regulation, the protection of labor unions, and programs of positive action for women and people of color which occurred during the early Reagan and Thatcher years.

7. On family and moral issues see: Allen Hunter and Linda Gordon, 'Danger from the Right', *Radical America*, 16 (May–June 1982). On status anxieties see Alan Crawford, *Thunder on the Right* (New York: Pantheon 1980). For an emphasis on intellectual response to the 1960s see: Peter Steinfels, *The Neoconservatives* (New York: Simon & Schuster, 1980); Gary Dorrien, *The Neoconservative Mind: Politics, Culture, and the War of Ideology* (Philadelphia: Temple University Press, 1993). For detail about the role of religious mobilization see: Sara Diamond, *Spiritual Warfare* (Boston: South End Press, 1989). From the perspective of electoral realignment see: Gillian Peele, *Revival and Reaction: The Right in Contemporary America* (Oxford: Clarendon Press, 1984).

8. On race and the electoral right see: Paul Gilroy, *There Ain't No Black in the Union Jack* (London: Hutchinson, 1987); Stuart Hall, 'The Great Moving Right Show', *New Internationalist* (March 1984); Centre for Contemporary Cultural Studies, *The Empire Strikes Back: Race and Racism in 70's Britain* (London: Hutchinson, 1982). On racism and the press see: Paul Gordon and David Rosenberg, *The Press and Black People in Britain* (London: The Runnymede Trust, 1989); Teun van Dijk,

Racism and the Press (London: Routledge, 1991). On the far right see: Michael Billig, *Fascists: A Psychological View of the National Front* (London: Routledge & Kegan Paul, 1978). Important studies of Thatcherism include: Dennis Kavanagh, *Thatcherism and British Politics: The End of Consensus?* (Oxford University Press, 1987); Peter Riddell, *The Thatcher Era and Its Legacy* (Oxford: Basil Blackwell, 1991); and Robert Skidelsky (ed.), *Thatcherism* (London: Chatto & Windus, 1988).

9. Michael Omi and Howard Winant, *Racial Formation in the United States* (New York: Routledge, 1994, 1986).

10. Thomas Edsall with Mary Edsall, *Chain Reaction: The Impact of Race, Rights, and Taxes on American Politics* (New York: Norton, 1992).

11. Stephen Steinberg, *Turning Back: The Retreat from Racial Justice in American Thought and Policy* (Boston: Beacon Press, 1995).

12. Gill Seidel, 'The White Discursive Order: The British New Right's Discourse on Cultural Racism with Particular Reference to the Salisbury Review' (Amsterdam: John Benjamins Publishing Co., 1987); 'Culture, Nation and "Race" in the British and French New Right', in *The Ideology of the New Right*, ed. by Ruth Levitas (Cambridge: Polity Press, 1986).

13. Anna Marie Smith, *New Right Discourse on Race and Sexuality* (Cambridge University Press, 1994).

14. Stephen Small, *Racialised Barriers.*

15. Valuable work has been done in this regard, for example see Paul Gordon and Francesca Klug, *New Right New Racism* (London: Searchlight, 1986).

16. Russ Bellant, 'The Coors Connection: How Coors Family Philanthropy Undermines Democratic Pluralism', (Boston: Political Research Associates, 1990); Russ Bellant, 'Old Nazis, the New Right and the Reagan Administration: The Role of Domestic Fascist Networks in the Republican Party and their Effect on U.S. Cold War Politics', (Boston: Political Research Associates, 1988). Both are now published by South End Press.

17. Anna Marie Smith, *New Right Discourse.*

18. Authors who develop this point include: David Theo Goldberg, *Racist Culture* (Cambridge, Mass.: Blackwell, 1993) and Nancy MacLean, *The Masks of Chivalry* (New York: Oxford University Press, 1994).

19. Katherine Verderey develops a similar argument about the increased salience of nationalism during the period of the exit from communism, in her 'Nationalism and National Sentiment in Post-Socialist Romania', *Slavic Review*, vol. 52, no. 2 (Summer 1993) pp. 179–203.

20. Examples of structuralist accounts include: Mike Davis, *Prisoners of the American Dream* (New York: Verso, 1986); Thomas Ferguson and Joel Rogers, *The Hidden Election: Politics and Economics in the 1980 Presidential Campaign* (New York: Pantheon Books, 1981); Thomas Ferguson and Joel Rogers, *Right Turn: The Decline of the Democrats and the Future of American Politics* (New York: Hill & Wang, 1986); Bob Jessop et al., *Thatcherism: A Tale of Two Nations* (Cambridge: Polity Press, 1988); Paul Hirst, *After Thatcher* (London: Collins, 1989).

21. Ferguson and Rogers; *The Hidden Election* and *Right Term.*

22. Jessop *et al.*, *Thatcherism* For an interesting exchange between these authors and Stuart Hall, see: Stuart Hall, 'Authoritarian Populism: A Reply', *New Left Review*, 151 (1985) pp. 106–13.
23. Jessop. *et al.*, *Thatcherism*, p. 43.
24. This point is related to a distinction between strong versus weak versions of the concept of hegemony; for a discussion of this distinction see: Smith, *New Right Discourse*, pp. 29–40.
25. Stuart Hall, 'The British Left After Thatcherism', *Socialist Review* (March–April 1987) p. 50.
26. Bob Blauner, 'Talking Past Each Other: Black and White Languages of Race', *The American Prospect*, 10 (Summer 1992) pp. 55–64.
27. John Solomos, 'Political Language and Racial Discourse', *European Journal of Intercultural Studies*, vol. 2, no. 1 (1991) pp. 21–34.
28. Credit for the term 'key categories of meaning' is due to Carla Willig, 'AIDS – A Study of the Social Construction of Knowledge', (unpublished doctoral dissertation: Cambridge University, 1991).

1 Race and the Right Turn: The Symbolic Conflict Approach

1. For an elaborated discussion of this point see: Seidel, 'The White Discursive Order'; and 'Culture, Nation and "Race"'.
2. Paul Weyrich, quoted in Flo Conway and Jim Siegelman, *Holy Terror: The Fundamentalist War on America's Freedom in Religion, Politics and Our Private Lives* (New York: Delta, 1982) p. 115.
3. The most recent example of this scholarship is Stephen Steinberg, *Turning Back: The Retreat From Racial Justice in American Thought and Policy* (Boston: Beacon Press, 1995).
4. For an example of the depiction of such a narrative, see Charles Moore, *The Old People of Lambeth* (London: Salisbury Group, 1982).
5. This view is held by New Rightists themselves, such as Adam Meyerson (senior editor of the Heritage Foundation's *Policy Review*), as well as by critical analysts of right-wing social movements, such as Sara Diamond (sociologist and author). These views were communicated to the author in personal interviews.
6. For an example of one whom subscribes to this view, see the work of Ellen Messer-Davidow. This view was communicated to the author in a personal interview.
7. Examples of this view can be found in the work of Ruth Levitas, Gillian Peele, and Anna Marie Smith.
8. Neo-liberalism is based largely upon the free market philosophy of nineteenth century liberalism, as well as the more contemporary *laissez-faire* philosophies of Milton Friedman, Friederich Von Hayek and Ludwig Von Mises. Neo-conservatism derives primarily from the thought of Edmund Burke, especially in Britain. In the United States, neo-conservatism is more of an offshoot of the American classical liberal tradition than genuine European conservatism. For more on the history of American conservatism see: George Nash, *The Conservative*

Intellectual Movement in America since 1945 (New York: Basic Books, 1976).

9. Andrew Gamble, *The Free Economy and the Strong State.*
10. Here I am drawing from Stuart Hall's thesis of 'authoritarian populism'; Stuart Hall, 'The Great Moving Right Show'.
11. Such deflection is at the heart of 'culture of poverty' theories. For an introductory survey of these theories, see Michael Katz, *The Undeserving Poor: From the War on Poverty to the War on Welfare* (New York: Pantheon, 1989).
12. Lewis Carroll, *Alice in Wonderland*; quoted in James Statman 'Exorcizing the Ghosts of Apartheid: Memory, Identity and Trauma in the "New" South Africa', (Washington DC: unpublished conference paper, International Society of Political Psychology, July 1995).
13. The symbolic conflict model is not an alternative to class analysis but an addition to it. That is to say, while class analysis is orientated to the study of instrumental outcomes, or how material benefits are distributed among competing classes in society, the symbolic conflict model is oriented to the study of how such material relationships come to be represented symbolically.
14. Among the most useful examples and/or discussions of what I am labeling the symbolic politics perspective are: Stuart Hall *et al.*, *Policing the Crisis*; Murray Edelman, *The Symbolic Uses of Politics* (Urbana: University of Illinois Press, 1964); Murray Edelman, *Constructing the Political Spectacle*; Pierre Bourdieu, *Language and Symbolic Power*, pt III (Cambridge, Mass.: Harvard University Press, 1991).
15. Paul Weyrich; quoted in Alan Crawford, *Thunder on the Right.*
16. For a useful introductory discussion of the concept of hegemony, see Robert Bocock, *Hegemony* (London and New York: Tavistock, 1986).
17. Such a conception of hegemony as a continual process of struggle is best illuminated in an article by: Stuart Hall, 'The Toad in the Garden: Thatcherism among the Theorists', in *Marxism and the Interpretation of Culture*, ed. by Cary Nelson and Lawrence Grossberg (Chicago: University of Illinois Press, 1988).
18. Bourdieu, *Language and Symbolic Power.*
19. This point is captured by those who focus on the performative nature of identity and language use, a focus which urges that we reject the notion that language is a mediator between subject and object, individual and society, a notion which rests on a false dualism. There is no subjectivity outside of language use, no self outside of society or its power to both constrain and enable thought. Political language does not reflect a fixed 'self' that exists outside of society; rather the self is created through language use, for particular audiences and specific purposes. For an elaborated discussion of these ideas see Michel Foucault, *The Archaeology of Knowledge* (New York: Pantheon, 1972); and 'Prison Talk', interview by J.J. Brochier, in Colin Gordon (ed.) *Power/Knowledge* (New York: Pantheon, 1980) pp. 36–54.
20. Murray Edelman, 'Category Mistakes and Public Opinion' (unpublished essay, 1992).

21. Daniel Bell (ed.), *The New American Right* (New York: Criterion, 1955); *The Radical Right* (New York: Anchor, 1964).
22. Crawford, *Thunder on the Right* p. 127.
23. Ibid. p. 149.
24. Edsall with Mary Edsall, *Chain Reaction.*
25. Gillian Peele, *Revival and Reaction*, pp. 54–79.
26. Russ Bellant, 'The Coors Connection', p. 63. Also see Bellant, 'Old Nazis, the New Right and the Reagan Administration'.
27. Chip Berlet and Jean Hardisty, *Capital Conservatives and Frontier Fascists: The Right-Wing in the United States* (Boston: unpublished synopsis, n.d.).
28. Douglas Frantz and Michael Jonofsky, 'Buchanan Drawing Extremist Support, And Problems, Too', *New York Times* (23 February 1996).
29. This program was screened in January 1984, although it was later the subject of much controversy and successfully challenged in court.
30. David Rose, 'Tory Links with BNP Highlighted by Defection', *Guardian* (5 July 1986).
31. For example, in the first issue of the *Salisbury Review* (Autumn 1982), Powell contributed an essay entitled, 'Our Loss of Sovereignty'. He also wrote an essay for the December 1988 issue entitled 'The UK and Immigration'.
32. Gill Seidel, *The Holocaust Denial: Anti-Semitism, Racism and the New Right* (Beyond the Pale Collective, 1986); 'Culture, Nation and Race in the British and French New Right'; 'Approaches to Discourse, Poetics and Psychiatry' (Amsterdam: John Benjamins, 1987).
33. Frankie Ashton, 'Feminism and the New Right', *New Socialist* (March/April 1988) p. 26.
34. A. Sivanandan, 'From Immigration Control to Induced Repatriation', *Race and Class* (pamphlet no. 5, 1978) p. 139.
35. The tension between these two aspects of ideology – the expressive and the instrumental – has been the subject of much debate. For the first, ideology functions to allay fears, give an outlet for passions, counter feelings of powerlessness, or fulfil an identity function. For the second, ideology serves the interests of the dominant social bloc: to integrate across class, to reinforce observation of social rules, and to deflect opposition from its real target (that is, capitalism). For elaboration of this distinction see: Clifford Geertz, 'Ideology as a Cultural System', in David Apter (ed.), *Ideology and Discontent* (New York: The Free Press, 1964).
36. Credit for this way of formulating the issue is due to Carla Willig, 'AIDS – A Study of the Social Construction of Knowledge'.
37. For a discussion of this point, see the chapter entitled 'Delegation and Political Fetishism' in Pierre Bourdieu, *Language and Symbolic Power*; also see the chapter entitled 'Mass Response to Political Symbols' in Murray Edelman, *The Symbolic Uses of Politics.*
38. For a discussion of the construction and uses of political leaders, see Murray Edelman, *Constructing the Political Spectacle*, pp. 37–65; for a discussion of the relationship between the spokesperson and the group see Pierre Bourdieu, *Language and Symbolic Power*, p. 204.

39. This theme is discussed at length in Stuart Hall, 'The Toad in the Garden: Thatcherism among the Theorists'.

2 The New Right Racial Backlash: A New Racism?

1. Jerry Falwell, 'Moral Majority: A Reaction to Attack on Basic Values', *Conservative Digest* (January 1981) p. 28.
2. Lyndon B. Johnson, 'To Fulfil These Rights', speech delivered at Howard University on 4 June 1965; quoted in *The Moynihan Report and the Politics of Controversy*, ed. by Lee Rainwater and William Yancey (Cambridge, Mass.: MIT Press, 1967) p. 126.
3. The following section was strongly influenced by two articles by A. Sivanandan: 'From Resistance to Rebellion: Asian and Afro-Caribbean Struggles in Britain', (London: Institute of Race Relations, 1986); and 'RAT and the degradation of the black struggle', *Race and Class*, XXVI, 4 (1985) pp. 1–33.
4. Quoted in Sivanandan, 'RAT and the degradation of the black struggle' p. 3.
5. Among these so-called battles were the disturbances at the Brockwell Park Fair (1973), the Carib Club (1974), the bonfire night in Leeds (1975), and the Notting Hill Carnival (1976). In 1981 there were riots in Brixton predominantly involving Afro-Caribbean and Asian youths against the police, followed by similar disturbances in Southall, Liverpool, Manchester and many other British cities. In 1985, Handsworth, Brixton and Tottenham all witnessed disturbances, mostly between West Indian youths and the police.
6. Substantial gains were made in the areas of housing, employment and education. For more information on the anti-racist activities of local authorities see Wendy Ball and John Solomos (eds), *Race and Local Politics* (London: Macmillan, 1990).
7. In the United States, domestic indicators suggested decline as early as the 1960s, but by the mid-1970s decline was certain. Average annual growth in the real Gross National Product (GNP) declined from 4.1 per cent over the period 1960–73 to 2.3 per cent over the period 1973–80. The profits of US firms fell steadily during this same period. Annual net investment in manufacturing plants and equipment, along with productivity, suffered in turn. Double-digit inflation contributed to a domestic economic situation which witnessed the worst business slump since the Great Depression. Internationally, American hegemony in the world economy was slipping. The US share of world GNP dropped from 40 to 26 per cent between 1950 and 1960, and its share of world trade fell from 20 to 16 per cent during that same period. Both shares continued to decline throughout the next two decades so that by 1980 the figures were 21.5 and 11 per cent, respectively. The number of American firms in the world's top fifty industrial companies fell from 42 in 1956, to 32 in 1970, to 23 in 1980. For more detail on the US economic context see Ferguson and Rogers, *Right Turn*, pp. 78–80. In Britain, the economic crisis was and has continued to

be more severe than in the United States, with a greater fall in international influence and comparative domestic economic performance. As in the United States, Britain's economic and structural weaknesses became manifest after the post-war boom. While the economy oscillated between recession and recovery throughout the 1960s, a trend of relative decline clearly had begun. By the time of Thatcher's election in 1979, the economy actually had begun to contract. In the Thatcher administration's first year alone, from December 1979 to December 1980, manufacturing output fell by 15 per cent. About 20 per cent of Britain's manufacturing base was wiped out between 1979 and 1981, so that almost as many manufacturing jobs were lost in the first few years of the 1980s as in the entire fifteen years of deindustrialization between 1966 and 1979 put together. Internationally, the British economy failed to keep pace with the rates of expansion of its major competitors. Britain's position in world manufacturing eroded such that its share fell in output from 9.6 per cent in 1960 to 5.8 per cent in 1975. In the early 1980s, Britain developed a deficit on the manufacturing balance of trade for the first time in industrial history. British labor productivity, output and levels of investment fell considerably below those of its major competitors, in some estimates to little better than half the levels in comparable economies. For more details on Britain's economic decline see: Bob Rowthorn, 'The Past Strikes Back', in Stuart Hall and Martin Jacqnes (eds), *The Politics of Thatcherism*, (London: Lawrence & Wishart, 1983); Andrew Gamble, *Britain in Decline* (London: St Martin's Press, 1982); and John Saville, 'Marxism Today: An Anatomy', *The Socialist Register* (1990).

8. In the United States, unemployment rose from 3.8 per cent between 1965 and 1969, to 5.4 per cent between 1970 and 1974, and then to 7 per cent between 1975 and 1979. Median income fell from a rise of 36 per cent from 1960 to 1969, to 5 per cent between 1969 and 1978. For more on these facets of decline see Ferguson and Rogers, *Right Turn*, pp. 79–80. In Britain, unemployment practically doubled to reach nearly 12 per cent of the labor force in 1980, and in some estimates it reached as much as 20 per cent. Real take-home pay virtually stagnated so that in 1980 it had barely risen above the level it had reached by the beginning of 1974. For adiscussion of these statistics see Andrew Gamble, *Britain in Decline*, p. 18; and John Saville, 'Marxism Today: An Anatomy', p. 45.

9. The mobilization of conservative business interests was marked especially in the United States. Long-standing pro-business organizations such as the National Association of Manufacturers, the National Federation of Independent Business, and the US Chamber of Commerce were revitalized, while new ones such as the Business Roundtable were formed. For more on this see Thomas Ferguson and Joel Rogers, 'The Knights of the Roundtable', *The Nation* (15 December 1979) pp. 620–5. Corporate political action committees, known as PACs, also mushroomed during this period. According to the Federal Election Commission, the number of corporate PACs grew from 89 in 1974, to 433 by the end of 1976, to 784 in 1978, to an incredible 1,512

by 1983. For more on corporate PACs see John Soloma *Ominous Politics: The New Conservative Labyrinth* (New York: Hill & Wang, 1984) p. 69.

10.   This point is demonstrated at length by Ferguson and Rogers (eds), *The Hidden Election*. The authors especially draw attention to sectoral divisions between national versus multinational corporations, as well as labor versus capital-intensive firms. For an elaborated discussion of such business conflict analysis as it relates to the study of the right wing, see: Amy Ansell, 'Business Mobilization and the New Right: Currents in U.S. Foreign Policy', in Ronald Cox (ed.), *Business and the State in International Politics*, (Boulder, Colo.: Westview 1996); Matthew Lyons, 'Business Conflict and Right-Wing Movements in the United States', in Amy Ansell (ed.), *Unraveling the Right* (Boulder, Colo.: Westview, 1997); and Ronald Cox, 'The Military-Industrial Complex and U.S. Foreign Policy: The Political Economy of Business Mobilization', also in Ansell (ed.), *Unraveling the Right*. For additional works that have helped shape my understanding of business conflict analysis, see Thomas Ferguson, *Golden Rule: The Investment Theory of Party Competition and the Logic of Money-Driven Political Systems* (University of Chicago Press, 1995); Bruce Cumings, *The Origins of the Korean War, vol. II, The Roaring of the Cataract 1947–1950* (Princeton University Press, 1990); Thomas Bodenheimer and Robert Gould, *Rollback! Right-Wing Power in U.S. Foreign Policy* (Boston: South End Press, 1989); Mike Davis, *Prisoners of the American Dream: Politics and Economy in the History of the U.S. Working Class* (London: Verso, 1986); David Gibbs, *The Political Economy of Third World Intervention: Mines, Money, and U.S. Policy in the Congo Crisis* (University of Chicago Press, 1991); and Ronald Cox, *Power and Profits: U.S. Policy in Central America* (Lexington: University Press of Kentucky, 1994).

11.   Nowhere is this shift in business sentiment better illustrated than in the Trilateral Commission report entitled *The Crisis of Democracy*. Written by Samuel Huntington, a prominent American neo-conservative thinker, the Report's basic argument was that democracy had overextended itself and was threatening the health of capitalism itself. Such anti-democratic sentiment was all the more significant coming from the Trilateral Commission – a backbone institution of the post-war liberal coalition itself – and is thus suggestive of how the policy preferences of elites adapt and correspond to basic changes in the structure of the economy and British/US industry's strategic position within it. For detailed discussion of the changes that pulled many multinationalists to the right, see: M. Patricia Marchak, *The Integrated Circus: The New Right and the Restructuring of Global Markets* (Montreal and Kingston: McGill–Queen's University Press, 1991), especially pp. 3–14; Ferguson and Rogers, *Right Turn*, ch. 3; and Joseph G. Peschek, *Policy-Planning Organizations: Elite Agendas and America's Rightward Turn* (Philadelphia: Temple University Press, 1987).

12.   On the relationship between big business and the New Right, see Jerome Himmelstein, *To the Right: The Transformation of American Conservatism* (Berkeley: University of California Press, 1990); Russ Bellant, 'The Coors Connection' (Boston: Political Research Associates,

1990); Rogers and Ferguson (eds), *The Hidden Election.* On corporate funding for right-wing organizations and campaigns, see Dan Morgan, 'Conservatives: A Well-Financed Network', *Washington Post* (4 January 1981); and Larry Hatfield and Dexter Waugh, 'Where think tanks get their money', *San Francisco Examiner* (26 May 1992).
13. Will Hutton, *The State We're In* (London: Cape, 1995), p. 172.
14. Ibid., p. 108.
15. Ibid., p. 170.
16. Ibid., p. 172.
17. Edward Wolff, *Top Heavy: A Study of the Increasing Inequality of Wealth in America* (New York: The Twentieth Century Fund Press, 1995) quoted in Richard D. Wolff, 'The New Right's Economics: A Diagnosis and Counterattack', in Ansell *Unraveling the Right.*
18. From B. L. Herlet, 'A Loss of Nerre', *New York Times*, 27 June, 1997.
19. Each of these points is developed at length in Michael Omi, 'We Shall Overturn: Race and the Contemporary Right' (University of California–Santa Cruz: unpublished doctoral thesis, 1987).
20. Omi and Winant, *Racial Formation*, p. 55.
21. Pete Alexander, *Racism, Resistance and Revolution* (London: Cox & Wyman, 1987).
22. Stuart Hall, quoted in Paul Gilroy, 'One Nation Under a Groove: The Cultural Politics of 'Race' and Racism in Britain', in David Theo Goldberg (ed.), *Anatomy of Racism* (Minneapolis: University of Minnesota Press, 1990) p. 265.
23. Martin Barker, *The New Racism: Conservatives and the Ideology of the Tribe* (London: Junction Books, 1982); Gill Seidel, 'Culture, Nation and "Race"'; Pierre-Andre Taguieff, 'The New Cultural Racism in France', *Telos*, 83 (Spring 1990) pp. 109–22; Etienne Balibar, 'Is There a Neo-Racism?', in *Race, Nation, Class: Ambiguous Identities* (London: Verso, 1991); D. Dovidio and J. Gaertner (eds), *Prejudice, Discrimination and Racism* (Orlando, Fla: Academic Press, 1986); David Sears, 'Symbolic Racism', in P. Katz and D. Taylor (eds), *Eliminating Racism*, (New York: Plenum 1988); Roger Wilkins, 'Smiling Racism', *The Nation*, 239 (3 November 1984); J. McConahay, 'Modern racism, ambivalence, and the modern racism scale', in (eds) *Prejudice, Discrimination, and Racism;* Nancy Murray, 'Anti-Racists and Other Demons: the Press and Ideology in Thatcher's Britain', *Race and Class*, 3 (Winter 1986).
24. Jeffrey Prager, 'American Political Culture and the Shifting Meaning of Race', *Ethnic and Racial Studies*, 10 (January 1987) pp. 63–81.
25. Ibid., p. 73.
26. Howard Schuman, Charlotte Steeh and Lawrence Bobo, *Racial Attitudes in America: Trends and Interpretations* (Cambridge, Mass.: Harvard University Press, 1985).
27. Omi and Winant, *Racial Formation.*
28. Frank Reeves, *British Racial Discourse: A Study of British Political Discourse about Race and Race-related Matters* (Cambridge University Press, 1983).
29. This point is illustrated at length in Margaret Wetherell and Jonathan Potter, *Mapping the Language of Racism: Discourse and the Legitimation of Exploitation* (New York: Columbia University Press, 1992).
30. Omi and Winant, *Racial Formation*, p. 117.

31. Steven Rose, R. C. Lewontin and Leon Kamin, *Not In Our Genes: Biology, Ideology and Human Nature* (London: Pantheon, 1984) pp. 66–8.
32. Balibar, 'Is There a Neo-Racism?', p. 9.
33. Murray, 'Anti-Racists and Other Demons'.
34. For elaboration on the history of the term 'new class' see Gary Dorrien, *The Neoconservative Mind*, pp. 13–18, 30–4.
35. In the United States, the recent emergence of journals such as *National Minority Politics* is indicative of this effort at outreach, although it is difficult to evaluate its success. In Britain, publication of *Ethnic Enterprise News* and the inclusion of many articles written by American black neoconservatives in journals such as the *Salisbury Review*, is similarly indicative of the attempt by movement conservatives to reach out to people of color for support.
36. This point is developed at some length by Anna Marie Smith, 'Why Did Armey Apologize? Hegemony, Homophobia and the Religious Right', in Ansell (ed.) *Unraveling the Right.*
37. Barker, *The New Racism.*
38. Ibid., p. 4.
39. Seidel, 'The White Discursive Order'.
40. John Solomos, 'Political Language and Racial Discourse'.
41. Teun van Dijk, *Racism and the Press*; Pierre Taguieff, 'The New Cultural Racism in France'; Wetherell and Potter, *Mapping the Language of Racism.*
42. Wetherell and Potter, *Mapping the Language of Racism*, p. 137.
43. Taguieff, 'The New Cultural Racism in France', p. 117.
44. Paul Gilroy, *There Ain't No Black in the Union Jack.*
45. Anna Marie Smith, *New Right Discourse.*
46. This is the view of Sara Diamond, for example, as communicated to the author in several personal interviews.
47. Omi and Winant, *Racial Formation*, pp. 69–76.
48. Ibid., p. 71.
49. Ibid., p. 75.
50. Thomas Edsall with Mary Edsall, *Chain Reaction.*
51. Stephen Small, *Racialised Barriers.*
52. Wetherell and Potter, *Mapping the Language of Racism*, p. 72.
53. John Thompson, *Ideology and Modern Culture* (Cambridge: Polity Press, 1990).
54. Paul Gilroy, *There Ain't No Black in the Union Jack*, p. 11.
55. For a good survey and discussion of the history of the term racism in academia, see: Stephen Steinberg, *Turning Back.*
56. The term 'American dilemma' is taken from a classic book in the sociology of American race relations by that title: Gunnar Myrdal, *An American Dilemma: The Negro Problem and Modern Democracy* (New York: Harper & Row, 1962, 1944).
57. Wetherell and Potter, *Mapping the Language of Racism*, p. 197.
58. David Wellman, *Portraits of White Racism*, 2nd edn (Cambridge University Press, 1993).

3   The New Right in the United States: Color-Blind Discourse and the Politics of Reverse Racism

1. For an elaborated historical discussion of the US right wing, see Seymour Martin Lipset and Earl Raab, *The Politics of Unreason: Right-Wing Extremism in America, 1790–1977* (University of Chicago Press, 1978); S. M. Lipset, 'The Radical Right', *British Journal of Sociology* (June 1955) pp. 176–209; Bell (ed.), *The New American Right*; S. M. Lipset, 'Three Decades of the Radical Right: Coughlinites, McCarthyites and Birchers', in Daniel Bell (ed.), *The Radical Right* (Garden City: Doubleday, 1963), p. 313–77. Also of importance were the Know-Nothings in the 1850s, the American Protective Association in the late 1880s, and the KKK of the 1920s.
2. Lipset and Raab, *The Politics of Unreason*, p. 361.
3. Kevin Phillips, *The Emerging Republican Majority* (New Rochelle, New York: Arlington House, 1969).
4. Richard Viguerie, 'Editorial Comment', *Conservative Digest* (October 1985) p. 126.
5. Richard Viguerie; quoted in Alan Crawford, *Thunder on the Right*, p. 75. Viguerie also acted as publisher of two key New Right journals, *Conservative Digest* and *New Right Report* (both now defunct). He declared himself bankrupt in 1985 and *Conservative Digest* was bought out by the Unification Church of Revd. Sun Nyung Moon in 1989.
6. *The New Right Takes Aim* (Detroit: UAW National CAP Department, n.d.) p. 11.
7. Other prominent New Rightists during this formative period included: Jesse Helms, Republican Senator (North Carolina) and organizer of The Congressional Club; John T. Dolan (now deceased) of the National Conservative Political Action Committee; Phyllis Schlafly of the pro-family movement and founder of Stop ERA and East Forum; Reed Larson of the National Right to Work Committee; Kathy Teague of the American Legislative Exchange Council; and Paul and Judy Brown of the Life Amendment PAC and American Life Lobby, respectively.
8. For the most comprehensive account of the emergence and issues agenda of the New Christian Right, see: Sara Diamond, *Spiritual Warfare: The Politics of the Christian Right* (Boston: South End Press, 1989); and *Roads to Dominion: Right-Wing Movements and Political Power in the United States* (New York: The Guilford Press, 1995). For another good treatment of this early phase of Christian Right activity see Robert Liebman and Robert Wuthnow, *The New Christian Right* (NY: Aldine, 1983).
9. James Robison, quoted in Dinesh D'Souza, 'Out of the Wilderness: The Political Education of the Christian Right', *Policy Review* (Summer 1987) p. 57.
10. Paul Weyrich; quoted in *The New Right Takes Aim* (Detroit: UAW National CAP Department, n.d.) p. 10.
11. William Lind, *Cultural Conservatism: Toward a New National Agenda* (Washington DC: Free Congress Research and Education Foundation with the Institute for Cultural Conservatism, 1987).

2. Irving Kristol; quoted in Geoffrey Norman, 'The Godfather of Neoconservatism (And His Family)', *Esquire* (13 February 1979) pp. 37–42.
13. The two best general treatments of neoconservatism are: Peter Steinfels, *The Neoconservatives: The Men Who are Changing American Politics* (New York: Simon & Schuster, 1979); and more recently, Gary Dorrien, *The Neoconservative Mind* Also see: Peter Steinfels, 'The Reasonable Right', *Esquire* (13 February 1979) pp. 24–30. Typically included among the ranks of the neoconservatives, despite the attempt by many to eschew being so-labelled, are: Daniel Bell, sociologist (now retired); Robert Nisbet, sociologist; James Q. Wilson, political scientist; Norman Podhoretz, editor of *Commentary*; Irving Kristol, a leading social critic and an editor of *The Public Interest*; Michael Novak, social scientist; Nathan Glazer, sociologist; Samuel Huntington, political scientist; Sidney Hook, philosopher; Midge Decter, writer; Ben Wattenberg, author and former co-editor of *Public Opinion* published by the American Enterprise Institute; and Jeanne Kirkpatrick political scientist and former US Ambassador to the United Nations.
14. Included among the numerous articles on race during this period in *Conservative Digest* alone are: David Brudney, 'Busing: The Rawest Deal', (January 1976) p. 17; Patrick Buchanan, 'Why Reagan Should Veto a Martin Luther King Holiday' (September 1983) p. 28; Orrin Hatch, 'Civil Privileges Act of 1984' (August 1984) p. 33; Joyce Hows, 'Anti-Busing Crusaders Turn Congress Around: Interview with members of NANS' (May/June 1980) p. 33; Patrick McGuigan, 'Brad Reynolds Tells How Conservatives Fight for Civil Rights', (November 1985) pp. 101–8; 'The New Discrimination: A Conservative Digest Poll', (February 1978) p. 13; Michael Novak, 'Allan Bakke: Victim of Discrimination' (January 1978) p. 48; Kevin Phillips, 'The New Racism' (March 1978) p. 15; Thomas Sowell, 'Affirmative Action Just Hasn't Worked; But Trickle-Down Theory is Doing Fine' (October 1981) pp. 18–19; Thomas Sowell, 'What's Wrong With Quotas?' (September 1978); Richard Viguerie, 'Liberals Versus Blacks' (March 1984); Richard Viguerie, 'A True Civil Rights Commission' (May 1984) p. 47; 'What Conservatives Would do for Minorities' (March 1984) pp. 4–5.
15. Among many articles *in Conservative Digest* on race-related topics such as welfare and crime are: Christine Adams, 'Confessions of a Welfare Worker' (September 1982) pp. 24–5; Warren T. Brookes, 'What Welfare Has Done to America's Blacks' (September 1982) p. 23; John Goodman, 'Welfare is Breeding Poverty' (January 1985); Michael Novak, 'Black Abortion: Is It Genocidal?' (February 1977) p. 32; Ronald Reagan, 'The Queen of Welfare' (March 1977) p. 19; Richard Viguerie, 'Conservative Alternatives Beckon Black Families' (July 1984) pp. 46–7.
16. On the role of the anti-busing movement see: Joyce Evelyn Swayne, *Anti-Busing and the New Right: A Rhetorical Criticism of the National Association of Neighborhood Schools* (unpublished doctoral dissertation: Ohio State University, 1981); on anti-integrationist Christian acade-

mies see: David Nevin and Robert Bills, *The Schools That Fear Built: Segregationist Academies in the South* (Washington: Acropolois, 1976).

17. Margaret Quigley and Chip Bertlet, 'Traditional Values, Racism, and Christian Theocracy', *The Public Eye* (December 1992) p. 6.

18. Elliot Abrams, 'The Quota Commission', *Commentary* (October 1972); Louis Henri Bolce and Susan Gray, 'Blacks, Whites, and Race Politics', *The Public Interest* (Winter 1979) pp. 61–75; Carl Cohen, 'Why Racial Preference is Illegal and Immoral', *Commentary* (June 1979) pp. 40–52; Nathan Glazer, 'Is Busing Necessary?', *Commentary* (March, 1972) pp. 39–52; and 'Why Bakke Won't End Reverse Discrimination', *Commentary* (September 1978); Michael Novak, 'Race and Truth', *Commentary* (December 1976) pp. 54–8; Thomas Sowell, 'Affirmative Action Reconsidered', *The Public Interest* (Winter 1976); Ben Wattenberg and Richard Scammon, 'Black Progress and Liberal Rhetoric', *Commentary* (April 1973) pp. 35–44.

19. Nathan Glazer, *Affirmative Discrimination: Ethnic Inequality and Public Policy* (New York: Basic Books, 1975).

20. Important articles on this subject appearing in neoconservative journals during the 1980s include: Walter Berns, 'Let Me Call You Quota, Sweetheart', *Commentary* (May 1981) pp. 48–53; Carl Cohen, 'Naked Racial Preference', *Commentary* (March 1986) pp. 24–39; Chester Finn, 'Affirmative Action Under Reagan', *Commentary* (April 1982); Nathan Glazer, 'The Affirmative Action Stalemate', *The Public Interest* (Winter 1988); Frederick Lynch, 'Surviving Affirmative Action (More or Less)', *Commentary* (August 1990) pp. 44–7; Charles Murray, 'Affirmative Racism: how preferential treatment works against blacks', *New Republic* (31 December 1984); and Philip Perlmutter, 'Balkanizing America', *Commentary* (September 1980) pp. 64–6.

21. *Lincoln Review* served as the nerve center of black conservatism throughout the 1980s. The central idea around which most articles revolve is that the civil rights establishment no longer represents the constituency in whose name it persists in speaking and, as a consequence, had lost the moral high ground. Instead, the black community is presented as a community of individuals, the vast majority of whom, according to *Lincoln Review* contributors, no longer seek a place for themselves on the 'liberal plantation'. Important articles include: Peter Ball, 'Blacks Must Take Responsibility', *Lincoln Review* (Summer 1984); Clint Bolick, 'Civil Rights at the Crossroads', *Lincoln Review* (Summer 1988) pp. 31–7; Walter Bowie Jr., 'It's Not Racism, It's Us', *Lincoln Review* (Fall 1988) pp. 39–47; Allan Brownfeld and J.A. Parker, 'Returning to the Goal of a "Colorblind" American Society', *Lincoln Review* (Summer 1981) pp. 3–22; Orrin Hatch, 'The New Slavery', *Lincoln Review* (Summer 1979) pp. 85–8; William Hough, 'On Being Black in America', *Lincoln Review* (Summer 1984); Clarence Pendleton Jr, 'Affirmative Action and Individual Freedom', *Lincoln Review* (Summer 1986) pp. 23–5; Clarence Thomas, 'Thomas Sowell and the Heritage of Lincoln: Ethnicity and Individual Freedom', *Lincoln Review* (Winter 1988) pp. 7–19; Gregory Wims, 'Blacks and Conservatism: Closer Than We Think', *Lincoln Review* (Fall

1981) pp. 3–5; Nathan Wright Jr, 'Black Conservatism Today', *Lincoln Review* (Summer–Fall 1987) pp. 11–13.

22. For examples of articles that suggest the importance of reaching out to constituencies of color, see: Paul Weyrich, 'Getting Serious About Blacks', *Conservative Digest* (July/August 1989) pp. 11–14; Adam Meyerson, 'Reaching Out to Black Americans', *Policy Review* (Fall 1984); Richard Viguerie, 'Liberals Versus Blacks', *Conservative Digest* (March 1984) p. 9; William Keyes, 'Blacks and Republicans', *Conservative Digest* (July/August 1989) pp. 47–9; William Greider and Harold Logan, 'Why Blacks Are Turning Conservative', *Conservative Digest* (October, 1978) pp. 28–34; Gregory Wims, 'Blacks and Conservatism: Closer Than We Think', *Conservative Digest* (March 1984) p. 12; and J. Perkins (ed.), 'A Conservative Agenda for Black Americans', *Critical Issues* (Washington DC: The Heritage Foundation, 1987).

23. Adam Meyerson, 'Reaching Out to Black Americans', *Policy Review* (Fall 1984) p. 39.

24. This point was communicated to the author during a personal interview with Linda Chavez. Chavez emphasized that action was especially difficult to consider after the embarassment around the Reagan administration's mishandling of the issue of the tax exempt status of Bob Jones University (see Chapter 5).

25. This quote was recorded during a personal interview between the author and Grover Norquist.

26. Frederick Lynch; quoted in: K.L. Billingsley, 'Conservative Republicans hit for affirmative action silence', *Washington Times* (12 February 1995).

27. For an excellent account of the causes and consequences of this period of in-fighting, see Sara Diamond, *Roads to Dominion.*

28. The turn to the so-called culture wars, and the establishment of institutions such as the Center for Cultural Conservatism, was motivated by the belief on the part of leaders such as Weyrich that it is wrong for conservatives to subordinate cultural concerns to economic ones. For an elaborated discussion of the culture wars, see James Davison Hunter, *Culture Wars: The Struggle to Define America* (New York: Basic Books, 1991).

29. The most representative example of the construction and use of such symbols at this time is: Dinesh D'Souza, *Illiberal Education: The Politics of Race and Sex on Campus* (New York: The Free Press, 1991).

30. For a discussion of the racial politics of the paleo-conservatives, see: Sara Diamond, *Roads to Dominion*, p. 272; Chip Berlet (ed.), *Eyes Right! Challenging the Right Wing Backlash* (Boston: South End Press and Political Research Associates, 1995) pp. 37–9; David Cantor, *The Religious Right: The Assault on Tolerance and Pluralism in America* (New York: Anti-Defamation League, 1994) p. 40.

31. This and other quotes from Pat Buchanan can be found in a collection of primary and secondary sources collated and distributed by Political Research Associates (1992).

32. For more on the pro-family, anti-feminist agenda of the right-wing at the 1992 Convention, see: 'Abroad at Home: Merchants of Hate', *New York Times* (21 August 1992).

33. Pat Robertson; quoted in 'Abroad at Home: Merchants of Hate', *New York Times* (21 August 1992). Then Republican Party chairman Rich Bond also made the link between the Democrats and the red menace when he said, 'If the Democrats won this election, Jane Fonda would be sleeping in the White House as a guest of honor at a state dinner for Fidel Castro'.

34. One of the best examples of a book that prematurely heralded the demise of the Christian Right is Michael D'Antonio, *Fall From Grace: The Failed Crusade of the Religious Right* (New Brunswick, NJ: Rutgers University Press, 1992).

35. In 1986, the Moral Majority disbanded and became the Liberty Federation, which itself disbanded in 1989. The Religious Roundtable, a key organization of the Religious Right in the late 1970s and early 1980s, today functions essentially as a letterhead organization only. Christian Voice has been reconstituted with money from the Revd Sun Myung Moon as the secular-oriented American Freedom Coalition, but does not appear to be active under the separate name. For more details on organizational demise and reincarnations, see: Cantor, *The Religious Right*.

36. Sara Diamond, *Roads to Dominion*, p. 2.

37. Thomas Atwood, 'Through A Glass Darkly: Is the Christian Right Overconfident It Knows God's Will?', *Policy Review* (Fall 1990) pp. 44–52. Later that same year, The Heritage Foundation and The Ethics and Public Policy Center sponsored a conference in Washington DC on the topic of Atwood's article.

38. Ralph Reed, 'Casting a Wider Net: Religious Conservatives Move Beyond Abortion and Homosexuality', *Policy Review* (Summer 1993) p. 31. For more on Ralph Reed and the Christian Coalition, see: Jeffrey Birnbaum, 'The Gospel According to Ralph', *Time Magazine* (May 15 1995) pp. 29–35.

39. Ralph Reed; quoted in Sara Diamond, *Roads to Dominion*, p. 250.

40. Richard J. Herrnstein and Charles Murray, *The Bell Curve: Intelligence and Class Structure in American Life* (New York: The Free Press, 1994). Two good sources of critique are: Steven Fraser (ed.), *The Bell Curve Wars: Race, Intelligence, and the Future of America* (New York: Basic Books, 1994); and Russel Jacoby and Naomi Glauberman (eds), *The Bell Curve Debate: History, Documents, Opinions* (New York: Times Books, 1995).

41. The Oregon initiative (now defeated) called for two primary restrictions: for all policies and laws offering protection and access for homosexuals to be eliminated, and for all state and local governments (including schools) to eliminate funding that would 'promote homosexuality'. An almost identical ballot measure was tested in Colorado. It passed, but has since been overturned in the courts.

42. The general lack of action around the 1990/1 Civil Rights Act stands in contrast to activity only a couple of years before when Focus on the Family marshalled its supporters against the 1987-1988 Civil Rights Restoration Act, which Dobson called 'an incredible intrusion into religious liberties'. During the campaign against the Act, Focus on the

Family supporters swamped Congressional switchboards with more
than half a million calls in a single day, according to the *Wall Street
Journal.* The Act none the less eventually passed over Reagan's veto.
For more detail on this, see Cantor *The Religious Right,* p. 77.

43. Around the same time, the Traditional Values Coalition increased the
distribution of their video 'Gay Rights, Special Rights' which is detailed in: 'Hostile Climate: A State by State Report on Anti-Gay Activity
in 1994' (Washington DC: People for the American Way, 1994) p. 13.

44. Christian Right activity against the 'Children of the Rainbow' curriculum for K–6 must be understood against the backdrop of a broader
strategy of running candidates for school boards and waging campaigns to bring God back into the public schools by restoring Bible
readings, ending instruction of new math and sex education, and promoting a rigid code of behavior and expression. In this context, the
Rainbow Curriculum was opposed as an assault on the moral authority
of parents to teach their children about families, and particularly for
its role in allegedly legitimating the gay lifestyle (although only six
pages out of the 443-page curriculum made any reference to gays and
lesbians). The Rainbow Curriculum became a flashpoint when School
District 24 in Queens refused to adopt or revise it, leading to the local
board's suspension of Schools Chancellor Joseph Fernandez, although
the suspension was subsequently reversed. For more detail on the
controversy, see: Terry Golway and Adam Entous, 'Christian Right
vs. Gay Rights: School Board Brawl Looming', *The New York Observer*
(18 January 1993); and 'The Two Faces of the Christian Coalition'
(Washington DC: People for the American Way, 16 September 1994).

45. Racial reconciliation projects teach the virtues of crossing racial lines
for a shared family values agenda, and involves public repentance on
the part of churches for their racist past, as well as the active forging
of new alliances with black church leaders. For a detailed discussion of
the racial reconciliation project of the Promise Keepers, see: Sara
Diamond, 'The Personal is Political: The Role of Cultural Projects in
the Mobilization of the Christian Right', in A. Ansell (ed.), *Unraveling
the Right* (Boulder, Colo.: Westview Press, 1997).

46. The first quote is taken from a special survey conducted by the
Christian Coalition in 1991 and is reported in: 'The Two Faces of the
Christian Coalition' (Washington DC: People for the American Way,
16 September 1994) p. 18. The second quote is taken from John
Wheeler Jr and Paul English, 'Minority myths exploded: poll shows
minorities hold traditional values', *Christian Americans* (October 1993).
The third quote is taken from a speech Reed delivered to a black
church in Niagara Falls, New York: James Perry, 'The Christian
Coalition crusades to broaden rightist political base', *Wall Street Journal*
(19 July 1994). Also, in the Fall of 1993, the Christian Coalition released the results of a poll it had commissioned showing that large
percentages of African-Americans and Latinos oppose abortion, gay
rights, welfare, and affirmative action.

47. For an interesting discussion of the white moral panic, see: Henry A.
Giroux, 'White Panic', in Chip Berlet (ed.), *Eyes Right!,* pp. 82–6.

48. This perspective was put forward in explicit terms by Newt Gingrich himself in his lecture to The Heritage Foundation: 'Building a Conservative Revolution After Reagan' (Washington DC: Heritage Lecture, 1988).

49. A few of the personalities key to the emergence of the New Right remain influential, such as Paul Weyrich, but others such as Howard Phillips and Richard Viguerie are very much on the periphery today. Many attribute this change in status to the fact that such leaders called Reagan a 'useful idiot' and underestimated his handling of the former Soviet Union. It is ironic indeed that many of these leaders were not influential in the 1994 conservative groundswell. Important new leaders include Newt Gingrich and Dick Armey in Congress, grass-roots strategists such as Grover Norquist of the 'Leave Us Alone' coalition and Americans for Tax Reform, and Ralph Reed of the Christian Coalition, as well as conservative Republican Governors such as John Engler (Michigan), Tommy Thompson (Wisconsin), and Christine Whitman (New Jersey).

50. James Atlas, 'The Counter Counterculture', *New York Times Magazine* (12 February 1995) pp. 32–8, 61–5.

51. Bill Clinton; quoted in 'An interview with Adam Meyerson', *Policy Review* (Winter 1994) pp. 14–18.

52. The first issue of the newly-formatted *Policy Review* was published in January/February 1996. The issue focuses on opportunities for the conservative movement to get citizens involved in rebuilding their schools, neighborhoods and communities as part of a vision of creating a vigorous self-governing citizenry. The new statement of mission reads:

> Our mission is to revive the spirit of American citizenship by recovering the core principles of our Founding Fathers and by articulating and advancing the conservative vision of civil society ... Our goal is to stimulate the citizenship movement ... Americans come from all races, all nationalities, all religions. Americans are united in citizenship not by common ancestry but by a common commitment to the political principles of the United States ... We believe that the restoration of civil society is one of the most important challenges and opportunities facing conservatism over the next generation ... Our goal is to rebuild the American Citizenship movement into one of the most significant political and cultural movements of the next generation. (pp. 2, 6)

53. Empower America was founded in 1993 by key leaders of that segment of the conservative movement that is between the Christian evangelical and moderate wings of the Republican Party: Jack Kemp (former Housing and Urban Development Secretary); William Bennett (former Secretary of Education); and former United Nations Ambassador Jeane Kirkpatrick. One of its defining characteristics is the focus on economic growth as opposed to deficit reduction.

54. Geoff Rodkey, *NEWTisms: The Wit and Wisdom of Newt Gingrich* (New York: Pocket Books, 1995).

55. This point of view was communicated to the author by Grover Norquist during a personal interview. For more on Norquist, see Thomas Edsall, 'Right in the Middle of the Revolution', *Washington Post* (4 September 1995).
56. Personal interview with the author.
57. Grover Norquist, *Rock the House* (Washington DC: VYTIS Publishing, 1995) p. 309.
58. Credit for this formulation is due to Dinesh D'Souza; telephone interview with the author.
59. Bolick played a pivotal role in the defeat of the Guinier nomination, along with Paul Weyrich's Coalitions for America and Phyllis Berry Myers at National Empowerment Television. Bolick complained that Guinier 'favors redistributing power and opportunities along racial lines – the antithesis of the Institute's focus on empowering individuals to control their own destinies.' Quoted in: Clint Bolick, 'Clinton's Quota Queen', *Wall Street Journal* (3 April 1994). Clint Bolick is also author of several books; among them: *Unfinished Business: A Civil Rights Strategy for America's Third Century; Changing Course: Civil Rights at the Crossroads;* and *Grassroots Tyranny.*
60. Clint Bolick, 'GOP Can Capture the Civil Rights Issue', *Wall Street Journal* (18 March 1991).
61. 'IJ Launches Effort to Ban Race Preferences', *Liberty and Law* (Winter 1995) p. 1.
62. Robert Woodson; quoted in Dorothy Gaiter, '2 black conservatives are now searching for a new home', *Wall Street Journal* (23 September 1995); also see Robert Woodson, 'The End of Racism? Hardly', *New York Times*, (23 September 1995), op. ed.
63. Donald Lambro, 'Extending a hand from the right', *Washington Times* (20 October 1995).
64. The Center for Equal Opportunity (promotional brochure, 1995). Formerly known as The Center for the New American Community at the Manhattan Institute, the CEO sponsors conferences, supports research, and publishes backgrounders and monographs. The Center publishes the quarterly newsletter *The American Experiment.*
65. Linda Chavez, 'What to do about immigration', *Commentary* (March 1995). In this article, Chavez recommends that skills preferences be made the basis of admissions policy. Clear in her support for legal immigration, Chavez applauds efforts to track down illegal entries, although she opposes efforts to impose new regulations upon business (such as those proposed in Proposition 187) as misguided.
66. Linda Chavez, 'Racial Justice: Changing the Tune', *Legal Times* (26 December 1994).
67. The *Los Angeles Times* (3 November 1994) ran a story demonstrating keen interest in Proposition 187 on the part of the Federation for American Immigration Reform (FAIR), although the organization kept a low political profile because of its purported associations with the Pioneer Fund and other racist and/or extremist organizations. In fact, former INS Commissioner Alan Nelson, one of FAIR's top lobbyists, reportedly helped draft 187 in 1993.

68. Nicholas Lemann, 'Taking Affirmative Action Apart', *New York Times Magazine* (11 June 1995) p. 39.
69. Tom Wood, quoted in Drummond Ayres, Jr, 'Conservatives forge a new strategy to challenge affirmative action', *New York Times* (16 February 1995).
70. This point was communicated to the author by Dinesh D'Souza during a telephone interview (January 1996).
71. During a telephone interview with the author, Dinesh D'Souza defended his view that discriminatory harm exists now almost entirely on the cultural level, making the point that although it is irritating for black people not to get a cab at night in New York City, this harm is quite different from being deprived of a job or the right to free association.
72. D'Souza argues for the repeal of every major civil rights law in the nation, including those that allow blacks to sit at lunch counters and use the same water fountains as everyone else. The federal government would be required to function in a color-blind manner, yet private citizens and institutions (including major corporations) would be free to discriminate.
73. Bob Woodson; quoted in Jack White, 'Dividing Line: The Bigot's Handbook', (e-mail message: 4 October 1995).
74. A handful of black conservatives have been included within the New Right coalition from its very emergence; most notably, Thomas Sowell and Walter Williams. In the 1980s, personalities such as Glenn Loury, Shelby Steele, and Stephen Carter fuelled media attention around black conservatism, although the associated individuals differed in important respects and disavowed being so designated to varying degrees. For more details on the development of black conservatism, see: Deborah Toler, 'Black Conservatives: Part One', *The Public Eye* (September 1993).
75. Among the most important recent books by black conservatives are: Glenn Loury, *One by One from the Inside Out: Essays and Reviews on Race and Responsibility in America* (New York: The Free Press, 1995); Armstrong Williams, *Beyond Blame: How We Can Succeed by Breaking the Dependency Barrier* (New York: The Free Press, 1995); Alan Keyes, *Our Character, Our Future: Reclaiming America's Moral Destiny* (Washington DC: Zondervan, 1996); Alan Keyes, *Masters of the Dream: The Strength and Betrayal of Black America* (New York: William Morrow, 1995); Thomas Sowell, *Race and Culture: A World View* (New York: Basic Books, 1994); Ezola Foster and Sarah Coleman, *What's Right for All Americans: A Fearless Los Angeles School Teacher Challenges the Black Political Establishment* (Washington DC: WRS Publishing, 1995); Robert Woodson, *On the Road to Economic Freedom: An Agenda for Black Progress* (Washington DC: Regnery, 1987); Clint Bolick, *The Affirmative Action Fraud: Can We Restore the American Civil Rights Vision?* (Washington DC: Cato Institute, 1996); Errol Smith, *101 Reasons Not to Be a Liberal* (Washington DC: Saint Clair Rene, 1995); Thomas Sowell, *Migrations and Cultures: A World View* (New York: Basic Books, 1996); Thomas Sowell, *The Vision of the Anointed: Self-Congratulation as a Basis for Social Policy* (New York: Basic Books, 1996).

76. Glenn Loury; quoted in Deborah Toler, 'Black Conservatives: Part One', p. 7. For a similar statement of this argument see Glenn Loury, 'Missing the affirmative action debate', *Washington Times* (4 June 1995).

77. Walter Williams, 'Minority tilt to the political right', *Washington Times* (6 October 1994).

78. Deborah Toler, 'Black Conservatives: Part One'; 'Black Conservatives: Bush's Phantom Coalition', *The New American* (26 February 1991).

79. Project 21 was founded under the auspices of the National Center for Public Policy Research to combat what it regards as the unrepresentative nature of today's black leadership, as reflected by NAACP campaigns in support of Lani Guinier and Dr Joycelyn Elders. Led by a white 23-year-old man from Long Island, Project 21 is establishing chapters in Los Angeles, Houston, and Atlanta, and initiating a lecture series leadership drive on black college campuses. For more on Project 21, see Steven Rubin, 'Black conservatives push bold agenda', *Human Events* (18 March 1994) pp. 228–9; and Trevor Coleman, 'Assault from the right', *Emerge* (February 1994) pp. 48–52.

80. Stephen Craft, quoted in 'Contract with Black America Urged', *USA Today* (31 January 1995).

81. Laurie Kellman, 'Black conservatives push bigger welfare cuts', *Washington Times* (13 January 1995).

82. David Plotz, 'Mr. Righteous', *Washington City Paper* (10 February 1995).

83. Charles Murray, *Losing Ground: American Social Policy 1950–1980* (New York: Basic Books, 1984) p. 223.

84. Paul Weyrich, 'Civil Rights at a Crossroad', *New Dimensions* (July 1991) p. 35.

85. Rush Limbaugh, *The Rush Limbaugh Show* (10 February 1995).

86. Edward Erler, 'The California Civil Rights Initiative: Restoring a Colorblind Constitution' (The Claremont Institute, 6 February 1995), p. 1.

87. Chester Finn, 'Affirmative Action Under Reagan', p. 17.

88. Justice Blackmun; quoted in Alphonso Pinkney, *The Myth of Black Progress* (Cambridge: Cambridge University Press, 1984), p. 151.

89. Glenn Loury, *One By One From the Inside Out*, p. 104.

90. Charles L. Heatherly and Burton Yale Pines (eds), *Mandate For Leadership* (Washington DC: The Heritage Foundation, 1980).

91. Murray, *Losing Ground*, p. 233.

92. Irving Kristol, 'Thoughts on Equality and Egalitarianism', in Colin D. Campbell (ed.), *Income Redistribution* (Washington DC: American Enterprise Institute, 1977) p. 42.

93. Herrnstein and Murray, quoted in David Wellman, 'Minstrel Shows, Affirmative Action Talk, and Angry White Men: Marking Racial Otherness in the 1990s', paper delivered at the American Sociological Association Annual Convention, New York City (August 1996) p. 1.

94. William Henry, *In Defense of Elitism* (New York: Doubleday, 1994).

95. Tom Wood, quoted in *The American Experiment* (Spring 1995) p. 8.

96. Andrew Sullivan, 'Let Affirmative Action Die', *New York Times* (23 July 1995) op. ed.

97. Carl Cohen, 'Why Racial Preference Is Illegal and Immoral', p. 42.

98. Morris B. Abram, 'Fair Shakers and Social Engineers', in (ed.), Russell Nieli, *Racial Preference and Racial Justice* (Washington DC: Ethics and Public Policy Center, 1991) pp. 29–45.

99. Erler, 'The California Civil Rights Initiative', p. 3.

100. The term 'benign neglect' was first coined in this context by Daniel Patrick Moynihan: 'The Negro Family: The Case for National Action', in *The Moynihan Report and the Politics of Controversy*, ed. by Lee Rainwater and William Yancy (Cambridge: MIT Press, 1967).

101. Richard Herrnstein and Charles Murray, *The Bell Curve*; J. Philippe Rushton, *Race, Evolution and Behavior: A Life History Perspective* (New Brunswick, NJ: Transaction, 1995); and Seymour Itzkoff, *The Decline of Intelligence in America: A Strategy for National Renewal* (Westport, Conn.: Praeger, 1995).

102. Tom Morganthau, 'IQ: Is it Destiny?', *Newsweek* (24 October 1994) pp. 53–62.

103. Ibid., p. 50. Also see Charles Lane, 'The Tainted Sources of the Bell Curve', *New York Review* (1 December 1994) pp. 14–19; and Jason De Parle, 'Daring Research or Social Science Pornography?', *New York Times Magazine* (9 October 1994) pp. 46–56, 70, 78–80.

104. Cohen, 'Why Racial Preference is Illegal and Immoral', p. 44. Emphasis added.

105. Linda Chavez, 'Specific Remedies for Specific People', *Washington Post* (4 July 1995).

106. Adam Meyerson, 'Editorial Comment', *Policy Review* (Winter 1991) p. 15.

107. Russell Nieli, 'Ethnic Tribalism and Human Personhood', in Russell Nieli (ed.), *Racial Preference and Racial Justice*, (Washington DC: Ethics and Public Policy Center, 1991) p. 69.

108. William Bradford Reynolds, 'Our Nation's Goal: A Color-Blind Society', *Lincoln Review* (Winter 1984) p. 39.

109. Nathan Glazer, *Ethnic Dilemmas 1964–1982* (Boston: Harvard University Press, 1983) p. 12.

110. Ibid., p. 13.

111. Glenn Loury, 'Individualism Before Multiculturalism', *Commentary* (Spring 1995) p. 92–106.

112. Frederick R. Lynch, 'Surviving Affirmative Action (More or Less)', *Commentary* (August 1990) p. 44.

113. Shelby Steele, *The Content of Our Character: A New Vision of Race in America* (New York: Harper Perennial, 1990) p. 17.

114. Lawrence Mead, 'Social Programs and Social Obligations', *The Public Interest*, 69 (Fall 1982) pp. 31–2.

115. Pat Buchanan, 'Crime and Race: A Reluctance to Acknowledge Reality', *Conservative Digest* (July/August 1989) p. 37.

116. Walter E. Williams, 'The Emperor Has No Clothes', *Moral Majority Report* (17 November 1980).

117. Glenn Loury, 'A New American Dilemma', *The New Republic* (31 December 1984) p. 15.

118. Peter Brimelow; quoted in William Buckley Jr, 'Crime, Race and Reasoning', *Washington Times* (5 January 1993).

119. Dinesh D'Souza, *The End of Racism: Principles for a Multiracial Society* (New York: The Free Press, 1995) p. 268.
120. 'Black Americans Still Trailing Behind', *The Economist*, 314 (3 March 1990) pp. 17–20.
121. Lawrence Mead, 'Social Programs and Social Obligations', *The Public Interest*, 69 (Fall 1982) p. 22.
122. Ibid., p. 19.
123. Nathan Glazer, *Affirmative Discrimination: Ethnic Inequality and Public Policy* (New York: Basic Books, 1975) p. 29.
124. Ben Wattenberg and Karl Zinsmeister, 'The Case for More Immigration', *Commentary* (April 1990) pp. 21–5.
125. During this period, New Right booklets and articles abounded with titles such as: 'Is Humanism Molesting Your Child?', published by the Pro-Family Forum; 'NEA: Ruining Education in America', by Sally Reed (then chairman and executive director of the National Council for Better Education); 'NEA: Bully in the Schoolyard', an editorial in *Conservative Digest*; 'Shutdown the Education Department', by Mary Gray (a freelance writer); 'Education to Remold the Child', by Ruth Feld; 'Secular Humanism in the Schools: an Issue Whose Time Has Come', by Onalee McGraw; *Child Abuse in the Classroom*, by Phyllis Schlafly (anti-gay rights activist and head of the Eagle Forum); and *Blackboard Tyranny*, by Connie Marshner (editor of *The Family Protection Report*, chairman of the Pro-Family Coalition, and director of the Child and Family Protection Institute).
126. Patrick Buchanan, 'Egalitarian education brings us all down', *Conservative Digest* (August 1983) p. 35.
127. Alexander Cockburn, 'Cred Menace', *New Statesman and Society* (24 May 1991).
128. Allan Bloom, *The Closing of the American Mind* (New York: Simon & Schuster, 1987).
129. Allan Bloom, 'Interview with William S. Armistead', *Conservative Digest* (April 1988) p. 26.
130. Dinesh D'Souza, *Illiberal Education*.
131. John Roche, 'Was Everyone Terrified? The Mythology of McCarthyism', *Academic Questions* (Spring 1989) p. 74.
132. Joseph D. Grano, 'Free Speech v. the University of Michigan', *Academic Questions* (Spring 1990) p. 87. The recent upsurge of racism on campus is documented by Mark Chesler and James Crowfout in 'Racism on Campus', in William W. May (ed.), *Ethics and Higher Education* (New York: American Council on Education, 1990). For example, in 1989 alone, racist incidents (including physical assaults on minority students) were reported at 174 campuses nationwide.
133. Irving Kristol, 'The Tragedy of Multiculturalism', *The Wall Street Journal* (31 July 1991) p. 15.
134. Walter Lammi, 'Nietzsche, the Apaches, and Stanford: The Hidden Agenda of Education for Difference', *Academic Questions* (Summer 1991) p. 37.

135. Dinesh D'Souza, quoted in Martin Walker, 'Right, white, and prejudiced', *Guardian* (11 October 1995).

136. Robert Blauner, 'Talking Past Each Other: Black and White Languages of Race', *The American Prospect* (Summer 1992).

137. For a useful discussion of the media panic over illegal aliens in the USA, see Ruth Conniff, 'The War on Aliens: The Right calls the shots', *The Progressive* (October 1993).

138. Arianna Huffington, 'Values vs. origin of newcomers', *Washington Times* (16 June 1995).

139. For examples of this argument, see: Ron Unz, 'Them vs. Unz', *Policy Review* (Winter 1995) pp. 88–96; Nathan Glazer, 'Debate on Aliens Flares Beyond the Melting Pot', *New York Times* (23 April 1995); and Linda Chavez, 'Multicultural Movement Makes Immigration Tougher', *National Minority Politics* (May 1995) p. 7.

140. Ron Unz, 'Immigration or the Welfare State: Which is our real enemy?', *Policy Review* (Fall 1994) p. 37.

141. Peter Brimelow, *Alien Nation: Common Sense about America's Immigration Disaster* (New York: Random House, 1995).

142. Peter Brimelow, quoted in 'Affirmative Action, Immigration: Wedge Issues that need not divide', *Los Angeles Times* (27 February 1995).

143. Patrick Buchanan direct mail, from the files of Political Research Associates.

144. Patrick Buchanan, 'Populist Revolution', *Washington Times* (19 October 1994).

145. Patrick Buchanan; quoted in: Chip Berlet and Margaret Quigley, 'Theocracy and White Supremacy: Behind the Culture War to Restore Traditional Values', in *Eyes Right!*, p. 39.

146. Ibid., p. 37.

147. Patrick Buchanan, 'Time Out on Immigration', *Washington Times* (31 October 1994).

148. Other works that engage in racialized forms of opposition to immigration include: Samuel Francis, *Beautiful Losers: Essays on the Failure of American Conservatism* (St Louis, MO: University of Missouri Press, 1993); Lawrence Auster, *The Path to National Suicide: An Essay on Immigration and Multiculturalism* (Washington DC: American Immigration Control Foundation, 1990); and Humphrey Dalton, *Will America Drown?: Immigration and the Third World Population Explosion* (Washington DC: Scott Townsend, 1993).

149. Jack Kemp and William Bennett, 'The Fortress Party', *Wall Street Journal* (21 October 1994).

150. Linda Chavez; personal interview.

151. Nathan Glazer, *Affirmative Discrimination: Ethnic Inequality and Public Policy* (New York: Basic Books, 1975); Charles Murray, *Losing Ground: American Social Policy 1950–1980* (New York: Basic Books, 1984); William Allen, 'The New Racism is the Old Power Grab', *Conservative Digest* (July/August, 1989) pp. 16–21; Carl Cohen, 'Naked Racial Preference', pp. 24–39.

152. Allan C. Brownfeld and J.A. Parker, 'Editor's Comment', *Lincoln Review* (Summer 1982) p. 6.

153. Carl Cohen, 'Why Racial Preference Is Illegal and Immoral', p. 44.
154. Clarence Pendleton, quoted in 'The New Racists', *Freedom Today* (December 1993) p. 15.
155. Frederick Lynch, 'Surviving Affirmative Action (More or Less)', p. 45.
156. Paul Sniderman and Thomas Piazza, *The Scar of Race* (Cambridge, Mass.: Harvard University Press, 1993).
157. Frederick Lynch, 'Surviving Affirmative Action (More or Less)', p. 46.
158. Philip Perlmutter, 'Balkanizing America'.
159. Leslie Carr, 'Colorblindness and the new racism' (Washington DC: unpublished paper delivered at the 1995 American Sociological Association Annual Convention) p. 5.
160. William Allen, 'The New Racism is the Old Power Grab', p. 17.
161. Patrick B. McGuigan, 'The Racism Scam', *Conservative Digest* (March/April 1989) p. 54.
162. Shelby Steele, *The Content of Our Character*, p. 141.
163. Ernest van den Haag, 'Affirmative Action and Campus Racism', *Academic Questions* (Summer 1989) p. 67.
164. Credit for development of the term 'category mistake' is due to Murray Edelman: 'Category Mistakes and Public Opinion' (Madison, WI: unpublished essay, 1992).
165. Carl Cohen, *Naked Racial Preference*, p. 201.
166. Ibid., p. 211.
167. Allan Brownfeld and J. A. Parker, 'Editor's Comment', *Lincoln Review* (Summer 1982) p. 21.
168. Clarence Pendleton, 'Affirmative Action and Individual Freedom'.
169. Nathan Glazer, *Affirmative Discrimination*, p. 76.
170. Carl Cohen, 'Naked Racial Preference', p. 30.
171. Linda Chavez, 'Minorities can't measure up?', *USA Today* (15 February 1995) p. 11A.
172. Senator Orrin Hatch, 'Civil Privileges Act of 1984', *Human Events* (14 July 1984) p. 33.
173. Alan Keyes, *Masters of the Dream*, p. 123.
174. Thomas Sowell, 'Affirmative Action Reconsidered', *The Public Interest* (Winter 1976) p. 65.
175. This direct mail letter was sent out by the Lincoln Institute on 21 August, 1992. The source is from the files of Political Research Associates in Cambridge, Mass.
176. Patrick McGuigan, 'The Racism Scam', p. 53.
177. Thomas Sowell, 'What's Wrong with Quotas', p. 30.
178. Ibid., p. 30.
179. Charles Murray, 'Affirmative Racism'.
180. Walter Williams, *Freedom Today* (December 1993) p. 15.
181. Rush Limbaugh, *The Rush Limbaugh Show* (14 September 1994).
182. Adam Meyerson, 'Nixon's Ghost: Racial Quotas – May they rest in peace', *Policy Review* (Summer 1995, pp. 4–5).
183. Andrew Sullivan, 'Let Affirmative Action Die', *New York Times* (23 July 1995) op. ed.
184. Nathan Glazer, 'Black and white after 30 years', *Commentary* (Fall 1995) pp. 61–79.

185. The term 'truly disadvantaged' comes from a book by that title: William Julius Wilson, *The Truly Disadvantaged: the Inner City, the Underclass, and Public Policy* (University of Chicago Press, 1987). In this book, Wilson augments earlier arguments against race-based public policy by demonstrating that in practice they often fail to meet the needs of the black underclass, or what he labels the 'truly disadvantaged'.
186. Gwen Richardson, 'Affirmative Action: What do black conservatives think?', *National Minority Politics* (April 1995).

4 The British New Right: A Discourse of Culture, Nation, and Race

1. Cyril Osborne, quoted, in Robert Miles and Annie Phizacklea, *White Man's Country: Racism in British Politics* (London: Pluto Press, 1984) p. 59.
2. Among the best studies of Powellism are: Paul Foot, *The Rise of Enoch Powell* (Harmondsworth: Penguin, 1969); Bill Smithies and Peter Fiddick, *Enoch Powell on Immigration: An Analysis* (London: Sphere, 1969); Tom Nairn, 'Enoch Powell: the New Right', *New Left Review* (May–June 1970), pp. 4–11; Kobena Mercer, 'Powellism: Race, Politics and Discourse',(unpublished doctoral thesis, Goldsmith's College, University of London, 1990); Ken Phillips, 'The Nature of Powellism', in Roger King and Neill Nugent (eds), *The British Right: Conservative and Right Wing Politics in Britain* (Westmead: Saxon House, 1977) pp. 99–132; and Douglas Schoen, *Enoch Powell and the Powellites* (London: Macmillan, 1977).
3. Enoch Powell, quoted in Miles and Phizacklea, *White Man's Country*, p. 2.
4. Enoch Powell, quoted in Paul Gordon and Francesca Klug, *New Right: New Racism* (London: Searchlight, 1986) p. 19.
5. In addition to Members of Parliament such as George Gardiner and Harvey Proctor, leading personalities have included members of various racist pressure groups (such as George Kennedy Young of Tory Action), as well as Conservatives who went on to join rival right-wing parties (such as Stuart Milson, head of the Club's student section in the early eighties, one time member of the now defunct Revolutionary Conservative Caucus, and now a leading member of the British National Party).
6. John Biggs-Davison, quoted in: Robert Copping, 'Monday Club: Crisis and After' (Monday Club pamphlet, 1975).
7. Harvey Proctor, 'Immigration, Repatriation and the CRE' (London: Monday Club pamphlet, 1981).
8. The Monday Club, 'Aims', received 20 October 1995.
9. In 1977, Mrs Thatcher wrote a letter to the Club's then chairman, Sir Victor Raikes, expressing her gratitude for the Club's activity. 'I am, as you know, very grateful for everything that the Monday Club is doing to help us in our efforts to win the next election,' *Monday News*

(February 1977) p. 7. The Club's newsletter, *Monday News* (now *The Journal*) described the election of Margaret Thatcher as heralding a 'new era' for the Monday Club.

10. A group calling itself Western Goals, originating on the West coast of the United States but now active in Britain, was instrumental in facilitating deep splits in the Monday Club during this period. For more on the take-over, see David Rose, 'Far Right Takes Over Monday Club', *Observer* (24 February 1991); and 'Monday Blues', *Searchlight* (March 1991) p. 6.

11. For more on Right Now! and other organizations mentioned above, see 'New Right, New Racism', *Searchlight* (August 1995), pp. 15–16.

12. Gregory Lauder-Frost, quoted in: David Rose, 'Far Right Takes Over Monday Club', *Observer* (24 February 1991).

13. Joy Page, quoted in Jim White, 'Beyond Anybody's Fringe', *Independent* (13 October 1995), pp. 3–5.

14. Editorial, *Free Nation* (January 1983), p. 3. Philip Vander Elst delivered a lecture to the Libertarian Alliance conference in 1991, later published as a Freedom Association reprint, entitled 'A Conservative Critique of Libertarianism', in which he distinguishes the Association's brand of conservatism from libertarian beliefs. He stated, 'The pursuit of liberty can, in certain contexts, be personally, socially and politically self-destructive, particularly when it involves ignorant and immature people, backward cultures, or totalitarian political movements ... ' (p. 2).

15. Angela Ellis-Jones, column in *Free Nation* (October 1987) p. 5.

16. 'New Right Initiatives on Race and Religion', *Searchlight* (September 1990) pp. 18–20.

17. Sian Bees, 'Academics defend BBC against race pressure', *UKPG* (27 June 1994) p. 11.

18. '"Anti-racist" racism of youth education quango', *Freedom Today* (April 1991) p. 5.

19. Gerald Hartup, *Misreporting Racial Attacks* (London: Hampden Trust, 1995) p. 16.

20. Gerald Hartup, 'A tale of bogus race statistics', *Freedom Today* (August 1995) p. 12; 'Association triggers row over CRE ethnic figures', *The Lawyer* (12 September 1995); 'Failure is their business', *Daily Telegraph* (24 August 1995).

21. Gerald Hartup, 'CRE dragging its feet over colour bar homework club', *Freedom Today* (October 1994) p. 7; and 'Race watchdog's silence over political colour bar', *Freedom Today* (December 1992) p. 6.

22. John Bercow, 'No Use Putting on Kid Gloves to Savage Blair', *Forward* (Autumn, 1995) p. 21.

23. Alfred Sherman, 'Why we asked the unasked questions', *The Times* (1 September 1984).

24. Alfred Sherman, quoted in Francesca Klug and Paul Gordon, Boiling into Fascism', *New Statesman* (10 June 1983) p. 12.

25. 'Call for ban on National Front visit', *Guardian* (11 September 1987).

26. Digby Anderson, 'With friends like these ... ', *The Times* (28 November 1986).

27. For more on the Salisbury Group, see: Peter Stothard, 'Who Thinks for Mrs. Thatcher?', *The Times* (31 January 1983); 'Peterhouse Blue', (London: Searchlight pamphlet, 1984); and Gill Seidel, 'The white discursive order: the British New Right's discourse on cultural racism with particular reference to the *Salisbury Review*' (Amsterdam: John Benjamins Publishing Company, 1987).
28. Maurice Cowling (ed.), *Conservative Essays* (London: Cassell, 1978).
29. Charles Moore, *The Old People of Lambeth* (London: Salisbury Group, 1982).
30. Cowling, *Conservative Essays*, p. 44.
31. Cowling, Ibid., p. 149.
32. Roger Scruton, quoted in BBC Report: 'The Conservative New Right in Britain', by Derek Blizard (19 August 1985) p. 26.
33. John Casey, 'One Nation: The Politics of Race', *Salisbury Review* (Autumn, 1982) p. 26.
34. Casey, 'One Nation', p. 18.
35. For a good concise discussion of The Group, see: Peter Popham, 'If you want an opinion, call a historian', *Independent* (13 October 1995); and 'New Right, New Racism', *Searchlight* (August 1995) pp. 15–16.
36. For more on this internal feud, see: 'Telegraph picks Major sceptic', *Guardian* (19 October 1995); 'Editorial Merry-go-round prompts senior Telegraph journalist to quit', *Guardian* (20 October 1995); and 'All my past life has been but a preparation for this hour', *Guardian* (21 October 1995).
37. Roger King and Neill Nugent (eds), *Respectable Rebels: Middle Class Campaigns in Britain in the 1970s* (London: Hodder & Stoughton, 1979). The growth of right-wing organizations lobbying on education and claiming to spring from a groundswell of parental concern is particularly noteworthy, including groups such as the Campaign for Real Education (CRE), Parents for English Education Rights (PEER), the Parental Alliance for Choice in Education (PACE), and the National Council for Educational Standards (NCES).
38. *The Runnymede Trust Bulletin* (November 1994).
39. For more on the conflict between the Federation of Conservative Students and the Conservative Party, see: Ruth Levitas, 'Tory Students and the New Right', *Youth and Policy*, no. 16 (1986).
40. Gordon and Klug, *New Right New Racism*, p. 13.
41. Ray Honeyford, letter to *The Times Educational Supplement* (19 November 1982).
42. Roger Scruton, The Meaning of Conservatism (London: Penguin Books, 1980); quoted in Gordon and Klug, *New Right New Racism*, p. 14.
43. Robin Page, 'To nature, race is not a dirty word', *Daily Telegraph* (3 February 1977); quoted in Barker, *The New Racism*, p. 20.
44. Mary Kenny, *Daily Mail* (6 September 1982); quoted in Gordon and Klug, p. 14.
45. Sally Shreir, 'The Politics of Language', *Salisbury Review* (Summer 1983) p. 12.
46. Clive Ashworth, 'Sociobiology and the Nation', *Salisbury Review* (Summer 1983) p. 9.

47. Ivor Stanbrook, quoted in Barker, *The New Racism*, p. 75.
48. Alfred Sherman, 'Britains' urge', *Daily Telegraph* (9 September 1976).
49. John Page, quoted in Barker, *The New Racism*, p. 20.
50. Editorial, *The Free Nation* (May 1977), my italics.
51. Enoch Powell, 'If West Indians had never come to Britain, would we all be losers?', *Sunday Express* (24 April 1983).
52. John Casey, 'One Nation', p. 24.
53. Enoch Powell, quoted in Barker, *The New Racism*, p. 21.
54. The leaflet was circulated as advertisement for a Monday Club fringe meeting on immigration policy at the 1989 Conservative Party Conference in Blackpool; see: 'Monday Club meet triggers race fury', *New Life* (13 November 1989).
55. Paul Johnson, 'Scarman in flames', *Daily Mail* (14 September 1985).
56. Quoted in Charles Moore, *The Old People of Lambeth*.
57. Moore, *The Old People of Lambeth*, p. 16.
58. Winston Churchill, quoted in *Guardian* (28 April 1994).
59. For more on these and other interventions by Winston Churchill, see *Runnymede Trust Bulletin* (April 1995).
60. 'Campaign against political refugees', *Searchlight* (July 1991) p. 6.
61. Ray Honeyford, 'Multi-Culture "Education"', *Freedom Today* (June 1989).
62. Diane Spencer, 'Multi-ethnic approach condemned', *The Times Educational Supplement* (17 May 1985).
63. Alfred Sherman, 'Schooling by race', *Daily Telegraph* (19 January 1985).
64. Simon Pearce, 'Education and the Multi-racial society', *Monday Club Policy Paper* (May 1985) pp. 4–6.
65. Joanna North (ed.), 'The GCSE: An Examination' (London: Claridge Press, 1987) p. 21.
66. Digby Anderson, 'The English Lesson', *Sunday Telegraph* (23 July 1995).
67. John Casey, *Daily Telegraph* (20 July 1995).
68. Ray Honeyford, 'Attacks on our nation promote racism', *Free Nation* (December 1986).
69. Peregrine Worsthorne, 'Labour's folly over riots and looting', *Sunday Telegraph* (6 October 1985).
70. Alfred Sherman, 'Why Britain can't be wished away', *Sunday Telegraph* (8 September 1976).
71. Ibid.
72. Ibid.
73. Alfred Sherman, 'Britain is not Asia's fiancée', *Sunday Telegraph* (9 November 1979).
74. Enoch Powell; quoted in Paul Gilroy, *There Ain't No Black in the Union Jack* (London: Hutchinson, 1987) p. 43.
75. Peregrine Worsthorne, 'End this silence over race', *Sunday Telegraph* (29 September 1985).
76. 'Yugo-leeches', *Daily Star* (30 May 1994).
77. Enoch Powell, quoted in David Edgar, 'Racism, Fascism and the Politics of the National Front', *Race and Class* (Autumn 1977).

78. Ray Honeyford, 'Multi-ethnic Intolerance', *Salisbury Review* (June 1983).
79. Alfred Sherman, quoted in Paul Gordon and Francesca Klug, 'Boiling into Fascism'.
80. George Gale, column in *Daily Express* (13 June 1978).
81. Harvey Proctor, 'Immigration/Race Relations Policy Committee', *Monday Club Policy Paper* (October 1982).
82. Ronald Butt, 'Britain's Permanent Liberal Government', *Policy Review* (Fall 1979); James Anderton, quoted in Centre for Contemporary Cultural Studies, *The Empire Strikes Back: Race and Racism in 70s Britain* (London: Hutchinson, 1982) p. 9; Peregrine Worsthorne, 'Who can civilise the Yobs', *Sunday Telegraph* (3 November 1985).
83. Donu Kogbara, 'Less Special Pleading', *Sunday Times* (18 April 1993).
84. Ray Honeyford, *Integration or Disintegration? Towards a Non-Racist Society* (London: Claridge Press, 1988).
85. Editorial, *Ethnic Enterprise News* (September/October 1989) p. 5.
86. Russell Lewis, *Anti-Racism: A Mania Exposed* (London: Quartet, 1988).
87. Roger Scruton, 'The paths blocked by anti-racists', *The Times* (16 April 1985).
88. Roger Scruton, 'Who are the real racists?', *The Times* (30 October 1984).
89. Antony Flew, 'The Monstrous Regiment of "Anti-Racism"', *Salisbury Review* (June 1989).
90. Peregrine Worsthorne, column in *Sunday Telegraph* (30 June 1985).
91. Editorial, *Ethnic Enterprise News* (March/April 1989) p. 2.
92. David Edgar, 'Reagan's Hidden Agenda', *Race and Class* (Winter 1981) p. 235.
93. Enoch Powell, quoted in Gordon and Klug, *New Right New Racism*, p. 20.
94. Charles Moore, 'How to spot a racist', *Daily Telegraph* (16 July 1984).
95. Editorial, *Ethnic Enterprise News* (September/October 1989).
96. Antony Flew, *A Future for Anti-Racism?* (London: Social Affairs Unit, 1992) p. 29.
97. Frank Palmer, letter to *London Review of Books* (29 November 1987).
98. Geoffrey Partington, in Dennis O'Keefe (ed.), *The Wayward Curriculum: A Cause for Parent's Concern?'* (London: Social Affairs Unit, 1986) pp. 78–79.
99. Social Affairs Unit press release, 'Preferential Treatment for Racial Minorities is Racist: CRE urged to Condemn Policies of Reverse Racism', (22 November 1984).
100. Harvey Proctor, 'Immigration/Race Relations Policy Committee'.
101. Antony Flew, 'Sense and nonsense about race', *Free Nation* (December 1986).
102. Digby Anderson, 'With Friends like these … '.
103. Kenneth Holland and Geoffrey Parkins, 'Reversing Racism: Lessons from America' (London: Social Affairs Unit pamphlet, 1984).
104. Editorial, *Ethnic Enterprise News* (September/October, 1989) p. 4.
105. Ray Honeyford, 'Multi-Culture "Education"' (June 1989).
106. Antony Flew, *A Future for Anti-Racism?*, p. 27.

107. Ray Honeyford, *Race and Free Speech: Violating the Taboo* (St Albans: Claridge Press, 1992) p. 54.
108. Glory Osaji-Umeaku, *British Race Relations Legislation: How Democratic?* (London: The Abraham and Sarah Foundation, 1992).
109. Andrew Moncur, 'Majority Rights Group Formed', *Guardian* (19 April 1989). Among the leading lights of Majority Rights were Antony Flew, Ray Honeyford, and Roger Scruton, among others.
110. Ray Honeyford, *The Times Educational Supplement* (2 September 1983); 'Multi-Ethnic Intolerance'; 'Multi-Culture "Education"'.
111. Ralph Michael Harrison; quoted in 'New Right New Racism', *Searchlight* (August 1995) p. 16.
112. Derek Laud; 'The Law, Order and Race Relations', *Monday Club Policy Paper* (October 1984) p. 4.
113. Leader, *Daily Mail* (8 October 1985).
114. Editorial, *Daily Telegraph* (17 May 1989).
115. Keith Waterhouse, 'In bed with bigotry', *Daily Mail* (27 February 1989).
116. David Green, 'Sharp division on solution to the crisis of family life', *Independent* (8 July 1993).
117. *The Bell Curve* has been received quite positively by the British New Right, welcoming the controversy as an opportunity to embellish on ideas of freedom and expression central to the anti-'PC' campaign, and to race-stigmatize the Labour Party as the Party of 'quotacrats'. For examples of this reception see: Richard Lynn, 'Is man breeding himself back to the age of the apes?', *The Times* (24 October 1994); Andrew Sullivan, 'Race and IQ – are whites cleverer than blacks?', *Sunday Times* (23 October 1994); Simon Jenkins, 'Cursed by Quotas', *The Times* (19 October 1994). For example, Simon Jenkins uses the controversy to launch an attack on what he refers to as the 'achilles heel' of Tony Blair's 'New Labour' – the politics of the group' – blaming the so-called quotacrats for opening the Pandora's Box of white racial resentment and leading to the publication of biological theories such as the one found in *The Bell Curve*.
118. For commentary on Murray's work in Britain, see Geraldine Bedell, 'An underclass warrior', *Independent on Sunday* (9 January 1994).

5 The New Right and the Racial State

1. Norman C. Amaker, *Civil Rights and the Reagan Administration* (Washington DC: The Urban Institute, 1988) p. 163.
2. Chester Finn, 'Affirmative Action Under Reagan', p. 22.
3. Orrin Hatch, quoted in *In These Times* (23 September 1983) p. 8.
4. Allan C. Brownfeld and J.A. Parker, 'Editor's Comment', *Lincoln Review*, 3.1 (Summer 1982) pp. 3–21.
5. William Bradford Reynolds, quoted in Finn, '*Affirmative Action Under Reagan*', p. 22.
6. William Bradford Reynolds, *In These Times* (28 September 1983) p. 8.
7. Ex-Attorney General Smith, quoted in Finn, '*Affirmative Action Under Reagan*', p. 22.

8. These trends and others are discussed at length in: Michael Omi, 'We Shall Overturn: Race and the Contemporary American Right' (University of California – Santa Cruz: unpublished doctoral dissertation, 1987) p. 133.
9. Ronald Reagan; quoted in Finn, '*Affirmative Action Under Reagan*', p. 27.
10. Orrin Hatch, quoted in Brownfeld and Parker, 'Editor's Comment', *Lincoln Review*, 3.1, p. 9.
11. Finn, '*Affirmative Action Under Reagan*', p. 26.
12. The statistics in this paragraph are taken from: John L. Palmer and Isabel V. Sawhill (eds), *The Reagan Record: An Assessment of America's Changing Domestic Priorities*, An Urban Institute Study (Cambridge, Mass.: Ballinger Publishing Company, 1984) pp. 204–7.
13. Clarence Thomas, 'Thomas Sowell and the Heritage of Lincoln: Ethnicity and Individual Freedom', *Lincoln Review* (Winter 1988), p. 18.
14. Palmer and Sawhill, *The Reagan Record*, pp. 204–5.
15. Ibid.
16. Ibid.
17. Amaker, *Civil Rights*, appendix A.
18. Mary Frances Berry, 'Taming the Civil Rights Commission', *The Nation* (2 February 1985) p. 107.
19. Quoted in Terry Eastland, 'George Bush's Quota Bill: The Dismaying Impact of Griggs', *Policy Review* (Summer 1991) p. 48.
20. Thomas Edsall with Mary Edsall, 'When the official subject is presidential politics, taxes, welfare, crime, rights, or values ... the real subject is RACE', *The Atlantic Monthly* (May 1991) pp. 53–86. The two book-length studies cited are: *Ability Testing* (1982) and *Fairness in Employment Testing* (1989) by the National Research Council.
21. Clint Bolick, 'Time for an Omnibus Civil Rights Bill', *Backgrounder* (30 April 1991) p. 2.
22. Eastland, 'George Bush's Quota Bill', pp. 45, 49.
23. Bolick, 'Time for an Omnibus Civil Rights Bill', p. 6.
24. Women's Equality Poll, conducted by Louis Harris and Peter Harris Research Group (Spring 1995).
25. Patrick Buchanan, 'Affirmative Action Quicksand?', *Washington Times* (23 January 1995) p. 16.
26. William Honan, 'Organized Efforts to End Affirmative Action Grow Nationally', *New York Times* (31 March 1996).
27. Kevin Merida, 'Dole Aims at Affirmative Action', *New York Times* (28 July 1995).
28. Steven Holmes, 'GOP lawmakers offer a ban on federal affirmative action', *New York Times* (28 July, 1995).
29. Jason DeParle, 'Rant/Listen, Exploit/Learn, Scare/Help, Manipulate/Lead', *New York Times Magazine* (28 January 1996) p. 37.
30. Newt Gingrich, quoted in letters to the editor, *Washington Post* (2 August 1995).
31. Steven Holmes, 'Preferences are Splitting Republicans', *New York Times* (29 July 1995).
32. Carl Cohen, 'Race, Lies, and '"Hopwood"', *Commentary* (June 1996) p. 44.

33. Ibid.
34. Steven A. Shull, *A Kinder, Gentler Racism? The Reagan–Bush Civil Rights Legacy* (New York: M.E. Sharpe, 1993).
35. Linda Greenhouse, 'Justices increase workers' burden in job-bias case', *New York Times* (26 June 1993).
36. John F. Dovidio, 'Affirmative Action and Contemporary Racial Bias: Need and Resistance', paper presented at the Annual Meeting of the American Psychological Association, Toronto, Canada (August 1996).
37. David Wellman, 'Minstrel Shows, Affirmative Action Talk, and Angry White Men: Marking Racial Otherness in the 1990s', paper presented to the American Sociological Association Annual Convention, New York (August 1996).
38. Donna Britt, 'Letting statistics do the talking', *The Weekly Journal* (3 August 1995).
39. Ibid.
40. Ibid.
41. Richard Morin and Sharon Warden, 'Americans Vent Anger at Affirmative Action', *Washington Post* (24 March 1995).
42. Peter Kilborn, 'Women and minorities still face Glass Ceiling', *New York Times* (15 March 1995).
43. Ibid.
44. Adolph Reed, Jr, 'Assault on Affirmative Action', in Chip Berlet (ed.), *Eyes Right!*
45. Steven Holmes, 'Income Gap Persists for Blacks and Whites', *New York Times* (23 February 1995).
46. Wellman, 'Ministrel Shows', p. 7.
47. Ibid., p. 8.
48. Edward S. Herman, 'America the Meritocracy', *Z Magazine* (July/August 1996) p. 38.
49. Wellman, 'Ministrel Shows', p. 9.
50. Ibid.
51. Melvin L. Oliver and Thomas M. Shapiro, *Black Wealth/White Wealth: A New Perspective on Racial Inequality* (New York: Routledge, 1995).
52. Wellman, 'Minstrel Shows', p. 9.
53. Britt, 'Letting statistics do the talking'.
54. Herman, 'America the Meritocracy'.
55. Ibid.
56. R.J. Struyk, A. Turner, and M. Fix, *Opportunities Denied, Opportunities Diminished: Discrimination in Housing* (Washington DC: The Urban Institute, 1995).
57. Herman, 'America the Meritocracy' p. 38.
58. Orlando Patterson, 'Affirmative Action, on the Merit System', *New York Times* (7 August 1995).
59. Britt, 'Letting statistics do the talking'.
60. Kevin Merida, 'Study Finds Little Evidence of Reverse Discrimination', *Washington Post* (31 March 1995).
61. Britt, 'Letting statistics do the talking'.
62. Amaker, *Civil Rights*, p. 45.

63. William Bradford Reynolds; quoted in *New York Times* (20 November 1981).
64. David Nevin and Robert E. Bills, *The Schools that Fear Built: Segregationist Academies in the South* (Washington: Acropolis, 1976).
65. Amaker, *Civil Rights*, p. 53.
66. Ibid., p. 48-52.
67. George Bush, quoted in Alexander Cockburn, 'Cred Menace', *New Statesman and Society* (24 May 1991).
68. Reginald Wilson, 'The State of Black Higher Education: Crisis and Promise', in *The State of Black America 1989* (Washington DC: Urban League, 1989) p. 132.
69. Alexander Cockburn, 'Bush and "PC" – A Conspiracy So Immense', *The Nation* (27 May 1991) p. 691.
70. Wilson, 'The State of Black Higher Education', p. 132.
71. Ibid.
72. Alfred Garwood, *Black Americans: A Statistical Sourcebook* (Boulder, Colo.: Numbers and Concepts, 1991) p. 130.
73. Andrew Hacker, 'Affirmative Action: The New Look', *New York Review of Books* (12 October 1989) p. 65.
74. Rochelle Stanfield, 'The Wedge Issue', *Legal Affairs* (1 April 1995), p. 791.
75. Cockburn, 'Bush and "PC"', p. 691.
76. Palmer and Sawhill, *The Reagan Record*, p. 1.
77. Sharon Smith, 'Twilight of the American Dream', *International Socialism*, 54 (Spring 1992) p. 11.
78. Palmer and Sawhill, *The Reagan Record*, p. 97.
79. Ibid.
80. Smith, 'Twilight of the American Dream', p. 11.
81. Kevin Phillips, *The Politics of Rich and Poor: Wealth and the American Electorate in the Reagan Aftermath* (New York: Random House, 1990); quoted in Sharon Smith, 'Twilight of the American Dream', p. 13.
82. 'The 1980s: A Very Good Time for the Very Rich', *New York Times* (5 March 1992). According to statistics compiled by the Congressional Budget Office, the average annual income for the top one per cent rose between 1977 and 1989 by 77 per cent, and for the top fifth by 29 per cent; but the fourth quintile of the population saw their annual income decline by one per cent, and the poorest fifth (where blacks are disproportionately represented) suffered a decline of 9 per cent.
83. The indicators in these two paragraphs are from: Sharon Smith, pp. 12–18.
84. The indicators in this paragraph are from: Roger Wilkins, 'Smiling Racism', *The Nation* (3 November 1984) p. 437.
85. The indicators in this paragraph are taken from the article: 'Black Americans Still Trailing Behind', *The Economist* (3 March 1990) pp. 17–20.
86. Frances Fox Piven and Richard A. Cloward, *The New Class War: Reagan's Attack on the Welfare State and Its Consequences* (New York: Pantheon, 1982) p. 1.

87. Palmer and Sawhill, *The Reagan Record*, p. 187.
88. Smith, 'Twilight of the American Dream', p. 13.
89. Ibid., p. 16.
90. 'Hard Times for Black Americans', *Dollars and Sense* (April 1986) p. 7; quoted in Omi, 'We Shall Overturn', p. 240.
91. 'The War Against the Poor', *New York Times* (6 May 1992).
92. Charles Murray, *Losing Ground: American Social Policy 1950–1980* (New York: Basic Books, 1984); Lawrence Mead, *Beyond Entitlement: The Social Obligations of Citizenship* (New York: The Free Press, 1986); George Gilder, *Wealth and Poverty* (New York: Basic Books, 1981).
93. Marlin Fitzwater, quoted in David Rosenbaum, 'White House Speaking in Code on Riot's Cause', *New York Times* (6 May 1992).
94. Ronald Reagan, 'The Queen of Welfare', *Conservative Digest* (March 1977) p. 19.
95. The statistical breakdown of people receiving welfare for more than five years is: 43 per cent white and other; 34 per cent black; 23 per cent Hispanic. For those receiving benefits for two years or less the breakdown is as follows: 65 per cent white and other; 23 per cent black; 13 per cent Hispanic. For more details on this, see 'People on Welfare, Too, Find a Lot to Criticize', *New York Times* (1 August 1996).
96. Sanford F. Schram, *Words of Welfare: The Poverty of Social Science and the Social Science of Poverty* (Minneapolis: University of Minnesota Press, 1995) p. 132.
97. Jason DeParle, 'Rant/Listen, Exploit/Learn, Scare/Help, Manipulate/ Lead', p. 56.
98. Ibid.
99. Ibid., p. 57.
100. Ibid.
101. Ibid., p. 56.
102. Center on Social Welfare Policy and Law, *Welfare Reform News* (December 1994) p. 7.
103. Center on Social Welfare Policy and Law, *Living at the Bottom* (New York, 1994).
104. James Atlas, 'Clinton signs bill to cut welfare and change with state role', *New York Times* (23 August 1996).
105. Ibid.
106. Mickey Caus, 'Clinton's welfare endgame', *Newsweek* (5 August 1996) p. 65.
107. Ibid.
108. Ibid.
109. Alan Finder, 'Welfare clients outnumber jobs they might fill', *New York Times* (22 August 1996).
110. Schram, *Words of Welfare*, p. 100.
111. According to the INS, 720 461 legal immigrants were admitted in the 1994 fiscal year, down from 914 292 in 1993.
112. Linda Chavez, 'The Myth of Immigrants and Welfare', *USA Today* (3 May 1994) p. 11A.
113. For a history of immigration controls see Robert Miles and Annie Phizacklea, *White Man's Country*; Paul Gordon and Francesca Klug,

British Immigration Control: a brief guide (London: Runnymede Trust, 1985).
114. Roy Hattersley, quoted in Miles and Phizacklea, *White Man's Country*, p. 57.
115. Margaret Thatcher, quoted in *Daily Mail* (31 January 1978).
116. Margaret Thatcher, quoted in *The Times* (1 February 1978).
117. Tony Marlow, quoted in Ruth Brown, 'Racism and Immigration Controls', *International Socialism*, 68 (Autumn 1995) p. 25.
118. Ruth Brown, 'Racism and Immigration Controls', p. 26.
119. Ibid., p. 25.
120. Ibid., p. 26.
121. Ibid., p. 25.
122. Ibid.
123. Ibid., p. 26. Fines imposed by the Carriers' Liability Act are £2000 per passenger. Since 1987, fines totalling £62m have been imposed, see: 'Proposed legislation on asylum', *Refugee Council Briefing Report* (June 1995).
124. Brown, 'Racism and Immigration Controls', p. 27.
125. Ronald Butt, *Sunday Times* (10 February 1980).
126. *Runnymede Trust Bulletin* (November 1992) p. 2.
127. The implications of this practice were underscored in the early 1990s when Kenneth Baker, then Home Secretary, was found in contempt of court for forcibly returning an asylum seeker to Zaire who was subsequently murdered by the same authorities whom he had fled to Britain to escape.
128. Brown, 'Racism and Immigration Control', p. 27. In its study of asylum cases, Amnesty International has accused the British government of systematically violating international law over the detention of asylum-seekers in Britain; for more on this, see *European Race Audit* (London: Institute of Race Relations, December 1994) p. 22. The number of asylum-seekers held in British prisons and immigration detention centers doubled between 1993 and 1995 to more than 600, and many have been detained for up to seventeen months. Three new detention centers were built in 1995 at Gatwick, Heathrow and Stansted airports.
129. *Runneymede Trust Bulletin* (December 1994/January 1995) p. 3.
130. The Home Office has employed private security firms, such as Airline Security Consultants and Group 4, to carry out deportations. Group 4, which already runs Campsfield detention center, has been invited to form the new MUFTI 'riot squads' to control unrest in detention centers and to carry out removals and deportations.
131. Winston Churchill, quoted in 'Broken Promises', *Garavi Gujarat* (5 June 1993).
132. In 1991, the Conservative Party launched a campaign to woo ethnic minority votes. The Party claimed that its values regarding family life and law and order made it the natural choice for ethnic minority voters. Engagements were made among ethnic minority organizations, allowing Conservatives to attempt to play down their reputation as an anti-immigrant party.

133. Charles Wardle, quoted in 'Race Card with a European Dimension', *Runnymede Trust Bulletin* (February 1995). It is interesting to note, as does the Runnymede Trust, that figures published by the Council of Europe show that British citizens have proportionately formed the largest outflow of 'economic migrants' to other EU member states over the past two decades, putting into perspective the furore over the proposed abolition of passport controls.

134. The total of illegal entrants detected and people issued with notices of intention to deport rose to 13 100 in 1994, compared with 10 400 in 1993. There was a drop in the number of people granted asylum during this same period. Of cases considered for asylum, only 825 were recognized as refugees, and some 16 500 were refused asylum or exceptional leave to remain, up from 10 700 in 1993. For more on this, see: 'Big rise in immigrants ordered out', *Daily Telegraph* (12 August 1995).

135. For more on the furore over these proposals, see 'Howard fuels ethnic cleansing', *Caribbean Times* (29 July 1995). Commentators have pointed out that figures that are available suggest that the number of illegal immigrants detected in 1994 was significantly less than that suggested by Howard. For more on this, see: Alan Travis, 'Figures give lie to illegal immigration scares', *Guardian* (26 June 1995).

136. Home Office Report, *The Settlement of Refugees in Britain* (1995).

137. As stipulated by already existing legislation, DSS officers must fill in a form asking the claimant if he or she has come to live in Britain within the past five years and, if so, arrange a full interview to which claimants must bring all travel documents and details of his or her immigration status. 'No to passport checks', *CARF* (May–June 1993). Charity groups were reported to have prepared for a surge in asylum-seekers who were expected to become destitute when their benefits were stopped at the beginning of 1996 under the new rules: Martin Linton, 'Surge in asylum pleas', *Guardian* (20 October 1995).

138. Alan Travis, 'Cabinet split on race issue', *Guardian* (5 October 1995).

139. Gillian Shephard, quoted in Alan Travis, 'Howard "racist" plan alarms industry', *Guardian* (6 October 1995).

140. Roy Hattersley, quoted in: Brown, 'Racism and Immigration Controls', p. 30.

141. Brown, 'Racism and Immigration Controls', p. 32.

142. A. Sivanandan, quoted in Frances Webber, 'European conventions on immigration and asylum', in Tony Bunyan (ed.), *Statewatching the New Europe: a hand book on the European State* (Nottingham: Russell Press, 1993).

143. A. Sivanandan, quoted in 'Europe: Variations on a Theme of Racism', *Race and Class* (January/March, 1991); also see A. Sivanandan, 'The New Racism', *New Statesman and Society* (4 November 1988).

144. Institute of Race Relations, *Policing Against Black People* (London: Institute of Race Relations, 1987) p. vii.

145. Stuart Hall, Chris Critcher, Tony Jefferson, John Clarke, and Brian Roberts, *Policing the Crisis: Mugging, the State, and Law and Order* (London: Macmillan, 1978).

146. Margaret Thatcher; quoted in Paul Gordon and Francesca Klug, *New Right New Racism*, p. 51.
147. Peregrine Worsthorne, *Sunday Telegraph* (12 July 1981).
148. Margaret Thatcher, quoted in *Searchlight* (1 April 1983) p. 6
149. Margaret Thatcher; quoted in James Wightman, 'Hope by Thatcher', *Daily Telegraph* (12 November 1985).
150. Kenneth Baker; communicaton from the Conservative Newsroom filed at the Runnymede Trust (29 October 1991).
151. John Major, 'Back to Basics', *Conservative Party News* (8 October 1993).
152. Paul Wilkinson, 'Police blame cultural gap for rioting', *The Times* (12 June 1995); Bhiku Parekh, 'Bradford's culture clash', *Independent* (12 June 1995).
153. G. Agedah, 'Condon, Mugging and the Black Community', *Nigerian News* (August 1995); 'Condon row', *Searchlight* (August 1995) pp. 6–8; *Runnymede Trust Bulletin* (July/August 1995) p. 1.
154. Jack Straw, quoted in 'Condon row', *Searchlight* (August 1995) p. 6.
155. Institute of Race Relations, *European Race Audit* (March 1995) pp. 1, 4.
156. This investigation is reported in *Police Review* (26 November 1993).
157. The so-called 'sus' laws (abolished in 1981) allowed police officers to search and arrest anyone if criminal intent was suspected. In practice the laws operated in a discriminatory fashion as black people were often singled out as suspicious, without having to demonstrate that such suspicions on the part of the police were reasonable.
158. Vicky Graham, 'Roots of urban disorder still flourishing in inner London', *Police Review* (11 July 1995).
159. Gordon and Klug, *New Right New Racism* p. 48.
160. Douglas Hurd, 'Rivers of Complacency', *Independent* (25 April 1988).
161. Douglas Hurd, 'Races Apart', *Daily Telegraph* (17 May 1989).
162. Ashok Bhat, Roy Carr-Hill and Shushel Ohri, *Britain's Black Population: A New Perspective*, 2nd edn (Aldershot: Brookfields, USA: Gower, 1988).
163. Colin Brown, *Black and White Britain: The Third PSI Study* (London: Heinemann, 1984). Also see Colin Brown and Pat Gay, *Racial Discrimination: Years After the Act* (London, Policy Studies Institute, 1985).
164. Brown, *Black and White Britain*, p. 323.
165. S. Ohri and S. Faruqui, *Racism, Employment and Unemployment* (London: Runnymede Trust Archives, 1988).
166. 'Tory right urges revolt on race contract rule', *Independent* (15 December 1987).
167. John Patten, quoted in D. Lister, 'Writer attacks Left's stance on racism', *Independent* (19 August 1989).
168. John Townend, quoted in *Searchlight* (October 1989).
169. Norman Tebbit, quoted in *Daily Telegraph* (15 January 1990).
170. 'Revival of Loony Left', *The Voice* (15 August 1995).
171. John Taylor, quoted in 'A Black Conservative Dissents', *Guardian* (13 October 1993).
172. The Runnymede Trust, *Trends and Inequalities* (London: Runnymede Trust, 1995).

173. According to the Rowntree report entitled 'Inquiry into Income and Wealth', the poorest 20–30 per cent of the population did not benefit from the economic growth that has occurred since 1977, nothing has 'trickled down'. Instead, this period witnessed a widening of income inequality in a manner that has proven unjust and divisive. For more details on the report, see: 'Trickle-down backed up', *The Economist* (18 February 1995).

174. 'Trickle-down backed up', *The Economist* (18 February 1995).

175. Herman Ousley, 'Commentary', *Municipal Journal* (21–7 July 1995).

176. Ken Jones, *Right Turn: The Conservative Revolution in Education* (London: Hutchinson Radius, 1989).

177. Margaret Thatcher; quoted in *Guardian* (12 October 1985).

178. Chris Searle, 'In Nobody's Ghetto: Beyond Multicultural Education', edited from a speech given to the Conference of the National Anti-Racist Movement in Education (Derby: April 1990) p. 15.

179. Institute of Race Relations, 'Education's new ethnocentric order', *CARF* (March–April 1992) pp. 8–9. According to a 1991 Appeal Court decision in Cleveland which supported a parent who objected to her daughter learning Pakistani (Urdu) and singing nursery rhymes in Punjabi, the right to removal overrides provisions of the Race Relations Act.

180. Institute of Race Relations, 'Racist exclusions', *CARF* (November–December, 1992) p. 9. According to an anonymous survey of London Boroughs carried out by the BBC current affairs program 'First Sight', in one South London borough Afro-Caribbean boys made up 8 per cent of the school population, but nearly 70 per cent of those permanently excluded. According to a South London school governor who is campaigning against the way that exclusions are being carried out,

> Teachers and headteachers are just giving free rein to their racism. Under the 1988 Education Reform Act, power has been taken away from local authorities and delegated to headteachers. The result is that schools are now getting rid of children without much worry that the local authority will be monitoring them with equal opportunities guidelines and the like.

For more on racist exclusions, see: Aubrey Rose, 'Lost boys', *Guardian* (1 August 1995).

181. Baroness Hooper; quoted on BBC program (13 November 1987).

182. *Runnymede Trust Bulletin*, 'Section 11 Funding under Fire', (July/August, 1993) p. 3.

183. Minette Marrin, 'Say "no" to the trendies', *Sunday Telegraph* (23 July 1995).

184. Mark Foster, 'Putting Britain back in the classrooms' mark', *Northern Echo* (19 July 1995).

185. 'We've lost our grip on greatness', *Daily Mail* (21 July 1995).

Selected Bibliography

Secondary Sources

Aho, J., *The Politics of Righteousness: Idaho Christian Patriotism* (Seattle, WA: University of Washington Press, 1990)

Alexander, P., *Racism, Resistance and Revolution* (Bookmarks: Cox & Wyman, 1987)

Allen, T.W., *The Invention of the White Race: Racial Oppression and Social Control* (London: Verso, 1994)

Althusser, L., *Essays on Ideology* (London: Verso, 1984)

Amaker, N.C., *Civil Rights Under the Reagan Administration* (Washington DC: The Urban Institute, 1988)

Amin, K. with C. Oppenheim, *Povety in Black and White: Deprivation and Ethnic Minorities* (London: Runnymede Trust and Child Poverty Action Group, 1992)

Anderson, B., *Imagined Communities: Reflections on the Origin and Spread of Nationalism* (London: Verso, 1983)

Ansell, A., 'Business Mobilization and the New Right: Currents in U.S. Foreign Policy', in Ronald Cox (ed.), *Business and the State in International Politics*, by (Boulder, Colo.: Westview Press, 1996)

—— (ed.), *Unraveling the Right: the New Conservatism in American Thought and Politics* (Boulder, Colo.: Westview, 1997).

——, 'The Color of America's Culture Wars' in *Unraveling the Right.*

—— and J. Statman, 'The War at Wits: Symbolic Conflict and the Makgoba Affair', paper presented to the International Sociological Association Annual Meeting, in conjunction with the South African Sociological Association (Durban, South Africa, 7–11 July 1996)

—— and ——, 'Thawing the 'Thing': On the "Sudden Reemergence" of Racism in the "New' Democracies"', paper presented to the Society for the Psychological Study of Social Issues (Ann Arbor, MI, 31 May–2 June 1996)

Anthias, F. and N. Yural-Davis, *Racialised Boundaries* (London: Routledge, 1992)

Appiah, K.A., 'Racisms', in D.T. Goldberg (ed.), *Anatomy of Racism* (Minneapolis, MN: University of Minnesota Press, 1990)

Arthur, J. and A. Shapiro, *Campus Wars: Multi-Culturalism and the Politics of Difference* (Boulder, Colo.: Westview, 1995)

—— and —— (eds), *Color, Class, Identity* (Boulder, Colo.: Westview, 1996)

Asad, T., 'Multiculturalism and British Identity in the Wake of the Rushdie Affair', *Politics and Society*, vol. 18, no. 4 (1990) pp. 455–80

Ashton, F., 'Feminism and the New Right', *New Socialist* (March/April, 1988)

Atlas, T., 'The Counter Counterculture', *The New York Times Magazine* (12 February 1995)

Balibar, E. and I. Wallerstein, *Race, Nation, Class: Ambiguous Identities* (London: Verso, 1991)

Ball, W. and J. Solomos (eds), *Race and Local Politics* (London: Macmillan, 1990)

Barkan, E., *The Retreat of Scientific Racism: Changing Concepts of Race in Britain and the United States Between the World Wars* (Cambridge University Press, 1992)

Barker, M., *The New Racism: Conservatives and the Ideology of the Tribe* (London: Junction Books, 1982)

——, 'Biology and the New Racism', in D.T. Goldberg (ed.) *Anatomy of Racism* (Minneapolis: University of Minnesota Press, 1990) pp. 18–37

Barkun, M., *Religion and the Racist Right: The Origins of the Christian Identity Movement* (Chapel Hill: University of North Carolina Press, 1995)

Bell, D. (ed.), *The New American Right* (New York: Criterion, 1959)

—— (ed.), *The Radical Right* (New York: Anchor, 1964)

Bellant, R., 'The Coors Connection: How Coors Family Philanthropy Undermines Democratic Pluralism' (Boston: Political Research Associates, 1990)

——, 'Religious Right Rediscovered', *Christian Social Action* (December 1992) pp. 4–8

Berger, J., 'Racial Scars Reopen on U.S. Campuses', *International Herald Tribune* (23 May 1989)

Bergmann, B., *In Defense of Affirmative Action* (New York: Basic Books, 1996)

Berlet, C., 'Civil Liberties', *Shmate*, 11–12 (Summer 1985)

—— (ed.), *Eyes Right! Challenging the Right Wing Backlash* (Boston, Mass.: South End Press, 1995)

——, 'Following the Threads', in Amy Ansell (ed.), *Unraveling the Right* (Boulder, Colo.: Westview, forthcoming 1997)

Berry, M.F., 'Taming the Civil Rights Commission', *The Nation* (2 February 1985)

Bhat, A., R. Carr-Hill and S. Ohri, *Britain's Black Population: A New Perspective*, 2nd edn (Brookfields, USA: Gower, 1988)

Billig, M., *Fascists: A Social Psychological View of the National Front* (London: Routledge & Kegan Paul, 1978)

——, 'Patterns of Racism: Interviews with National Front Members', *Race and Class*, 20 (Autumn 1978)

——, *Ideological Dilemmas: A Social Psychology of Everyday Thinking* (London: SagE, 1986)

Blauner, B., 'Talking Past Each Other: Black and White Languages of Race', *The American Prospect*, 10 (Summer 1992) pp. 55–64

Blizard, D., 'The Conservative New Right in Britain' (BBC Report: 19 August 1985)

Bloom, A., *Prodigal Sons: The New York Intellectuals and their World* (New York: Oxford University Press, 1986)

Blumenthal, S., *The Rise of the Counter-Establishment* (New York: Times Books, 1986)

Bodenheimer, T. and R. Gould, *Rollback! Right-Wing Power in U.S. Foreign Policy* (Boston: South End, 1989)

Bolce, L., G. DeMaio and D. Muzzis, 'The 1992 Republican 'Tent': No Blacks Walked In', *Political Science Quarterly* (Summer 1993) pp. 255–70

Boston, T., *Race, Class, and Conservatism* (New York: Routledge, 1988)

Bourdieu, P., *In Other Words: Essays Towards a Reflexive Sociology* (Cambridge: Polity Press, 1990)

——, *Language and Symbolic Power* (Cambridge, Mass.: Harvard University Press, 1991)

Braham, P., A. Rattansi and R. Skellington (eds), *Racism and Antiracism: Inequalities, Opportunities and Policies* (London: Sage, 1992)

Brown, C., *Black and White Britain: The 3rd PSI Study* (London: Heinemann, 1984)

Brown, Ricardo B., 'Objects of Desire: A Critique of Community and Family in Communitarian Ideology', in A. Ansell (ed.), *Unraveling the Right* (Boulder, Colo.: Westview, 1997)

Brown, Ruth, 'Racism and Immigration Controls', *International Socialism*, 68 (Autumn 1995) pp. 3–36.

Bruce, S., *The Rise and Fall of the New Christian Right: Conservative Protestant Politics in America, 1978–1988* (Oxford University Press, 1990)

——, *The Rapture of Politics: The Christian Right as the United States Approaches the Year 2000* (London: Transaction, 1994)

Bunyan, T., 'Towards an Authoritarian European State', *Race and Class*, vol. 32, no. 3 (January–March 1991) pp. 19–27

Carmines, E.G. and J.A. Stimson, *Issues Evolution: Race and the Transformation of American Politics* (Princeton University Press, 1989)

Centre for Contemporary Cultural Studies, *The Empire Strikes Back: Race, Racism in 70's Britain* (London: Hutchinson, 1982)

Cockburn, A., 'Cred Menace', *New Statesman and Society* (24 May 1991).

Cohen, J. and J. Rogers, '"Reaganism" After Reagan', in by R. Miliband, L. Panitch, and J. Saville (eds) *Socialist Register: Conservatism in Britain and America: Rhetoric and Reality* (London: Merlin, 1987)

Cohen, P., '"It's racism what dunnit": hidden narratives in theories of racism', in J. Donald and A. Rattans (eds), '*Race*', *Culture and Difference* (London: Sage, 1992)

—— and H. Bains, *Multi-Racist Britain* (London: Macmillan, 1988)

Cohen, R., *Frontiers of Identity: The British and the Others* (London: Longman, 1994)

Cohen, S., *Folk Devils and Moral Panics: The Creation of Mods and Rockers* (Oxford: Blackwell, 1987)

Cox, R., 'The Military-Industrial Complex and U.S. Foreign Policy: The Political Economy of Business Mobilization', in A. Ansell (ed.), *Unraveling the Right* (Boulder, Colo.: Westview, 1997)

Crawford, A., *Thunder on the Right: The 'New Right' and the Politics of Resentment* (New York: Pantheon, 1980)

D'Antonio, M., *Fall From Grace: The Failed Crusade of the Christian Right* (New Brunswick, NJ: Rutgers University Press, 1992)

Dallek, R., *Ronald Reagan: The Politics of Symbolism* (London: Harvard University Press, 1984)

David, M., 'Moral and Maternal: The Family in the New Right', in R. Levitas (ed.), *The Ideology of the New Right* (Cambridge: Polity Press, 1986)

Davis, M., 'Reaganomics Magical Mystery Tour', *New Left Review*, 149 (1985)

——, *Prisoners of the American Dream* (New York: Verso, 1986)

Derrida, J., 'Racism's last word', *Critical Inquiry*, no. 12 (1985)

Diamond, S., *Spiritual Warfare: The Politics of the Christian Right* (Boston: South End Press, 1989)

——, 'Rumble on the Right', *Z Magazine* (December 1990)

——, 'Readin', Writin', and Repressin''', *Z Magazine* (February 1991)

——, *Roads to Dominion: Right-Wing Movements and Political Power in the United States* (New York: The Guilford Press, 1995)

——, 'The Personal is Political: The Role of Cultural Projects in the Mobilization of the Christian Right', in A. Ansell (ed.), *Unraveling the Right* (Boulder, Colo.: Westview, 1997)

Dorrien, G., *The Neoconservative Mind: Politics, Culture, and the War of Ideology* (Philadelphia, PA: Temple University Press, 1993)

Dorrien, G., 'Inventing an American Conservatism: The Neoconservative Episode; in A. Ansell (ed.), *Unraveling the Right* (Boulder, Colo.: Westview, 1997)

Dovidio, J.F., *The subtlety of white racism* (Newark: University of Delaware Press, 1977)

——, 'Affirmative Action and Contemporary Racial Bias: Need and Resistance', paper presented at the Annual Meeting of the American Psychological Association, Toronto, Canada (9 August 1996)

—— and S.L. Gaertner, *Prejudice, Discrimination and Racism* (New York: Academic Press, 1986)

Duffield, M., 'New Racism ... New Realism: Two Sides of the Same Coin', *Radical Philosophy*, no. 37 (Summer 1984) pp. 29–34

Dworkin, A., *Right-Wing Women: The Politics of Domesticated Females* (London: Women's Press, 1983)

Eatwell, R., and N. O'Sullivan (eds), *The Nature of the Right: European and American Politics and Political Thought since 1789* (London: Pinter, 1989)

Edelman, M., *The Symbolic Uses of Politics* (Urbana: University of Illinois Press, 1964)

——, *Politics as Symbolic Action: Mass Arousal and Quiescence* (Chicago: Markham, 1971)

——, *Political Language: Words that Succeed and Policies that Fail* (University of Chicago Press, 1977)

——, *Constructing the Political Spectacle* (University of Chicago Press, 1988)

Edgar, D., 'Racism, Fascism and the Politics of the National Front', *Race and Class*, 2 (Autumn 1977)

——, 'Bitter Harvest', in *The Future of the Left*, ed. by James Curran (Cambridge: Polity Press, 1984)

——, 'Dreams of the Volk', *New Socialist*, 45 (January 1987)

——, 'The Neo-Conservatives', *Searchlight* (September 1980)

——, 'Reagan's Hidden Agenda', *Race and Class* (Winter 1981)

Edgar, D., K. Leech and P. Weller, *The New Right and the Church* (London: Jubilee Group, 1985)

Edsall, T., *The New Politics of Inequality* (New York: Norton, 1984).

—— with ——, *Chain Reaction: The Impact of Race, Rights, and Taxes on American Politics* (New York: Norton, 1992, 1991)

—— and ——, 'When the official subject is presidential politics, taxes, welfare, crime, right, or values ... the real subject is RACE', *Atlantic Monthly* (May 1991) pp. 53–86

Edwards, J., *When Race Counts: The Morality of Racial Preference in Britain and America* (New York: Routledge, 1995)

Ehrman, J., *The Rise of Neoconservatism: Intellectuals and Foreign Affairs, 1945–1994* (New Haven, Yale University Press, 1994)

Eisenstein, Z., 'Liberalism, Feminism and the Reagan State', in R. Miliband, L. Panitch and J. Saville (eds), *Socialist Register: Conservatism in Britain and America: Rhetoric and Reality* (London: Merlin, 1987)

——, *The Color of Gender* (Berkeley: University of California Press, 1994)

Epstein, B. and A. Forster, *The Radical Right: Report on the John Birch Society and its Allies* (New York: Vintage, 1967)

Erickson, P., *Reagan Speaks: The Making of an American Myth* (New York University Press, 1985)

Essed, P., *Understanding Everyday Racism* (Newbury Park, CA: Sage, 1991)

Ezekiel, R.S., *The Racist Mind: Portraits of American Neo-Nazis and Klansmen* (New York: Viking, 1995)

Farley, R., *Blacks and Whites: Narrowing the Gap?* (Cambridge, Mass: Harvard University Press, 1984)

Feagin, J.R., 'The Continuing Significance of Race: Antiblack Discrimination in Public Places', *American Sociological Review*, 56 (February 1991) pp. 101–16

—— and M.P. Sikes, *Living with Racism: The Black Middle-Class Experience* (Boston: Beacon, 1994)

—— and H. Vera, *White Racism: The Basics* (New York: Routledge, 1995)

Fekete, L. and F. Webber, *Inside Racist Europe* (London: Institute of Race Relations, 1994)

Ferguson, T. and J. Rogers, 'The Knights of the Roundtable', *The Nation* (15 December 1979) pp. 620–5

—— (eds), *The Hidden Election: Politics and Economics in the 1980 Presidential Campaign* (New York: Pantheon, 1982)

——, *Right Turn: The Decline of the Democrats and the Future of American Politics* (New York: Hill & Wang, 1986)

Fields, B., 'Ideology and Race in American History', in J.M. Kousser and J.M. McPherson (eds), *Region, Race and Reconstruction* (New York: Oxford University Press, 1982)

Fields, B., 'Slavery, race and ideology in the United States of America', *New Left Review*, no. 181 (1990)

Foot, P., *The Rise of Enoch Powell* (London: Penguin, 1969)

Foucault, M., *Archaeology of Knowledge* (London: Tavistock, 1972)

Fraser, S. (ed.), *The Bell Curve Wars: Race, Intelligence, and the Future of America* (New York: Basic Books, 1994)

Frum, D., 'The Conservative Bully Boy', *American Spectator*, vol. 24, no. 7 (July 1991)

Frum, D., *Dead Right* (New York: Basic Books, 1994)

Furgurson, E., *Hard Right: The Rise of Jesse Helms* (New York: Norton, 1986)

Gabriel, J., *Culture, Markets, Racism* (New York: Routledge, 1994)

Gallagher, C., 'White Reconstruction in the University', *Socialist Review*, vol. 24 (1995) pp. 165–87

Gamble, A., *The Free Economy and the Strong State* (London: Macmillan, 1988)

Gamson, W.A., *Talking Politics* (Cambridge University Press, 1992)

——, 'Hiroshima, the Holocaust, and the Politics of Exclusion', *American Sociological Review*, vol. 60, no.1 (February 1995) pp. 1–20

—— and A. Modigliani, 'The Changing Culture of Affirmative Action', *Research in Political Sociology*, 3 (1987) pp. 137–77

Garwood, A., *Black Americans: A Statistical Sourcebook* (Boulder, Colo: Numbers and Concepts, 1991), p. 130

Gates, H.L. (ed.), *'Race', Writing and Difference* (University of Chicago Press, 1986)

Geertz, C., 'Ideology as Cultural System', in *The Interpretation of Cultures: Selected Essays* (New York: Basic Books, 1973)

Gilroy, P., 'Steppin' out of Babylon – race, class and autonomy', in CCCS, *The Empire Strikes Back: Race, Racism in 70's Britain* (London: Hutchinson, 1982)

——, *There Ain't No Black in the Union Jack* (London: Hutchinson, 1987)

——, *Problems in Anti-Racist Strategy* (London: The Runnymede Trust, 1987)

——, 'The End of Anti-Racism', in W. Ball and J. Solomos (eds), *Race and Local Politics* (London: Macmillan, 1990)

——, 'One Nation under a Groove: The Cultural Politics of 'Race' and Racism in Britain', in D.T. Goldberg (ed.), *Anatomy of Racism* (Minneapolis: University of Minnesota Press, 1990) pp. 263–82

——, 'Cultural studies and ethnic absolutism', in L. Grossberg, C. Nelson and P. Treicher (eds), *Cultural Studies* (London: Routledge, 1992)

Gitlin, T., *The Twilight of Common Dreams: Why America is Wracked by Culture Wars* (New York: Henry Holt, 1995)

Goldberg, D.T. (ed.), *Anatomy of Racism* (Minneapolis: University of Minnesota Press, 1990)

——, *Racist Culture* (Oxford: Blackwell, 1993)

Gooding-Williams, R., *Reading Rodney King, Reading Urban Uprising* (New York: Routledge, 1993)

Gordon, L. and A. Hunter, 'Sex, Family and the New Right: Anti-Feminism as a Political Force', *Radical America*, 11–12 (November 1977–February 1978)

Gordon, P., 'New Right, Race and Education – or How the Black Paper Became a White Paper', *Race and Class* (Winter 1988)

——, 'The New Educational Right', *Multicultural Teaching*, 8 (Autumn 1989)

——, 'Citizenship for Some? Race and Government Policy 1979–1989', *Runnymede Commentary* no. 2, (London: Runnymede Trust, 1989)

——, 'A Dirty War: the New Right and Local Authority Anti-Racism', in W. Ball and J. Solomos (eds), *Race and Local Politics* (London: Macmillan, 1990)

—— and F. Klug, 'Boiling into Fascism', *New Socialist* (10 June 1983)

——, and ——, *New Right New Racism* (London: Searchlight, 1986)

—— and D. Rosenberg, *The Press and Black People in Britain* (London: Runnymede Trust, 1989)

Gottfried, P. and T. Fleming, *The Conservative Movement* (Boston: Twayne, 1988)

Gramsci, A., *Selections From the Prison Notebooks*, ed. by Q. Hoare and G.N. Smith (New York: International, 1971)

Gray, J., *Beyond the New Right: Markets, Government and the Common Environment* (London and New York: Routledge, 1993)

Green, D., *The New Right: The Counter-Revolution in Political, Economic and Social Thought* (London: Wheatsheaf 1987)

Greenstein, R., 'Losing Faith in "Losing Ground"', *New Republic* (25 March 1985)

Gunn, S., *Revolution of the Right: Europe's New Conservatives* (London: Pluto, 1989)

Gusfield, J., *Symbolic Crusade* (Chicago: University of Illinois Press, 1963)

——, *The Culture of Public Problems: Drinking and Driving and the Symbolic Order* (University of Chicago Press, 1981)

Hacker, A., 'Affirmative Action: The New Look', *New York Review of Books* (12 October 1989) p. 65

——, *Two Nations: Black and White, Separate, Hostile, Unequal* (New York: Simon & Schuster, 1993)

Hadjor, K.B., *Another America: The Politics of Race and Blame* (Boston, Mass.: South End, 1995)

Hall, S., 'Race, articulation and societies structured in dominance', in *Sociological Theories: Race and Colonialism* (Paris: UNESCO, 1980)

——, 'Cultural studies: Two paradigms', in T. Bennett, G. Martin, C. Mercer and J. Woollacott (eds), *Culture, Ideology and Social Process: A reader* (Milton Keynes: Open University, 1981)

——, 'The Great Moving Right Show', *New Internationalist* (March, 1984)

——, 'Authoritarian Populism: A Reply', *New Left Review*, 151 (1985) pp. 106–13

——, 'Variants of liberalism', in J. Donald and S. Hall (eds), *Politics and Ideology* (Milton Keynes: Open University, 1986)

——, *The Hard Road to Renewal: Thatcherism and the crisis of the left* (London: Verso, 1988)

——, 'The Toad in the Garden: Thatcherism among the Theorists', in Nelson and Grossberg (eds), *Marxism and the Interpretation of Culture* (Chicago: University of Illinois Press, 1988)

——, 'Cultural Identity and Diaspora', in Jonathan Rutherford (ed.), *Identity, Community, Culture, Difference* (London: Lawrence & Wishart, 1990) pp. 222–37

——, 'Ethnicity: Identity and Difference', *Radical America*, no. 23 (1991) pp. 9–20

——, 'The question of cultural identity', in S. Hall, D. Held and A. McGrew (eds), *Modernity and Its Futures* (Cambridge: Polity Press, 1992)

——, 'The West and the Rest: discourse and power', in S. Hall and B. Gieben (eds), *Formations of Modernity* (Cambridge: Polity Press, 1992)

—— and M. Jacques (eds), *The Politics of Thatcherism* (London: Lawrence & Wishart, 1983)

—— et al., *Policing the Crisis: Mugging, the State, and Law and Order* (London: Macmillan, 1978)

Hayes, M., *The New Right in Britain: An Introduction to Theory and Practice* (London: Pluto, 1994)

Hardisty, J., 'Kitchen Table Backlash: The Anti-Feminist Women's Movement', in A. Ansell (ed.), *Unraveling the Right* (Boulder, Colo.: Westview, 1997)

Hilts, P.J. 'Life Expectancy for Blacks in U.S. Shows Sharp Drop', *New York Times* (19 November 1990)

Himmelstein, J.L., '"Reverse Discrimination" and "The Rape of Progress" – Neo-Conservatives on Affirmative Action and Nuclear Power', working paper prepared for the Political Culture and Cognition Seminar of the Center for Research on Social Organization (University of Michigan: November 1980)

——, 'God, Gilder, and Capitalism', *Society*, 18 (September–October 1981)

——, *To The Right: The Transformation of American Conservatism* (Berkeley: University of California Press, 1990)

Hirst, P., *After Thatcher* (London: Collins, 1989)

Hoeveler, J.D. Jr, *Watch on the Right: Conservative Intellectuals in the Reagan Era* (Madison: The University of Wisconsin Press, 1991)

Hofstadter, R., *The Paranoid Style in American Politics* (New York: Vintage, 1967)

Hunter, A., 'In the Wings: New Right Ideology and Organization', *Radical America* (Spring 1981)

——, 'Children in the Service of Conservatism: Parent–Child Relations in the New Right's Pro-Family Rhetoric', *Legal History Program Working Papers*, Series 2 (Madison, WI: Institute for Legal Studies, 1988)

—— and L. Gordon, 'Danger from the Right', *Radical America*, 16 (May–June 1982)

Hutton, W., *The State We're In* (London: Cape, 1995)

Jacoby, R. and N. Glauberman (eds), *The Bell Curve Debate: History, Documents, Opinions* (New York: Times Books, 1995)

Jenkins, P., *Intimate Enemies: Moral Panics in Contemporary Great Britain* (New York: Aldine de Gruyter, 1992)

Jenkins, R. and J. Solomos (eds), *Racism and Equal Opportunity Policies in the 1980s* (Cambridge University Press, 1989)

Jennings, J., *Enemy Within: the Freedom Association, the Conservative Party and the Far Right* (London: Blackrose, 1984)

Jessop, Bob *et al.*, *Thatcherism: A Tale of Two Nations* (Cambridge: Polity Press, 1988)

Jhally, S. and J. Lewis, *Enlightened Racism: The Cosby Show, Audiences, and the Myth of the American Dream* (Boulder, Colo.: Westview, 1992)

Jorstad, E., *The New Christian Right 1981–1988: Prospects for the Post-Reagan Decade* (New York: Edwin Mellen, 1987)

Jones, K., *Right Turn: The Conservative Revolution in Education* (London: Hutchinson Radius, 1989)

Jordon, G. and N. Ashford (eds), *Public Policy and the Impact of the New Right* (London: Pinter, 1993)

Judis, J., 'Something Old, Somethin New', *In These Times* (10 September 1980)

Kavanagh, D., *Thatcherism and British Politics: The End of Consensus?* (Oxford University Press, 1987)

—— and A. Seldon (eds), *The Thatcher Effect: A Decade of Change* (Oxford University Press, 1989)

Kazin, M., 'The Right's Victory and Our Response', *Socialist Review*, 55 (January–February 1981)

Killian, L.M., 'Black Power and White Reactions: The Revitalization of Race-Thinking in the United States', *Annals of the American Academy of Political and Social Science*, 454 (March 1981)

King, D., *The New Right: Politics, Markets and Citizenship* (London: Macmillan, 1987)

King, R. and N. Nugent, *Respectable Rebels: Middle Class Campaigns in Britain in the 1970s* (London: Hodder & Stoughton, 1979)

Klatch, R.E., *Women of the New Right* (Philadelphia, PA: Temple University Press, 1987)

Klug, F. and P. Gordon, 'Election 83: Boiling into Fascism', *New Statesman* (10 June 1983)

Knight, D., *Beyond the Pale: The Christian Political Fringe* (London: Kogan Page, 1981)

Kovel, J., *White Racism: A Psychohistory* (New York: Pantheon, 1970)

Krieger, J., *Reagan, Thatcher and the Politics of Decline* (Cambridge: Polity Press, 1986)

——, 'Social Policy in the Age of Reagan and Thatcher', in R. Miliband, L. Panitch and J. Saville (eds), *Socialist Register: Conservatism in Britain and America: Rhetoric and Reality* (London: Merlin, 1987)

Laclau, E., *Politics and Ideology in Marxist Theory* (London: Verso, 1977)

Lamont, M. and M. Fournier (eds), *Cultivating Differences: Symbolic Boundaries and the Making of Inequality* (University of Chicago Press, 1992)

'Law, Order and the Falklands Spirit, and Repatriation', *Searchlight* (September 1981)

Layton-Henry, Z., *The Politics of Race in Britain* (London: Allen & Unwin, 1984)

——, *The Politics of Immigration: Immigration, 'Race' and 'Race' Relations in Post-War Britain* (Oxford, Blackwell, 1992)

—— and P. Rich (eds), *Race, Government and Politics in Britain* (London: Macmillan, 1986)

Leech, K., 'Moving Right for Jesus', *New Statesman and Society* (25 August 1989)

Liebman, R. and R. Wuthnow, *The New Christian Right* (New York: Aldine, 1983)

Levitas, R., 'New Right Utopias', *Radical Philosophy*, 39 (Spring 1985)

——, 'Tory Students and the New Right', *Youth and Policy*, 16 (1986)

Levitas, R. (ed.), *The Ideology of the New Right* (Cambridge: Polity Press, 1986)

Lipset, S.M., 'The Radical Right', *British Journal of Sociology* (June 1955) pp. 176–209

——, 'Three Decades of the Radical Right: Coughlinites, McCarthyites and Birchers', in D. Bell (ed.), *The Radical Right* (Garden City: Doubleday, 1963) pp. 313–77

—— and E. Raab, *The Politics of Unreason: Right-Wing Extremism in America, 1790–1977*, 2nd edn (University of Chicago Press, 1970, 1978)

Loney, M., *The Politics of Greed: The New Right and the Welfare State* (London: Pluto, 1986)

322   *Bibliography*

Lusane, C., *African Americans at the Crossroad: The Restructuring of Black Leadership and the 1992 Elections* (Boston, Mass.: South End, 1993)

Lyons, M., 'Business Conflict and Right-Wing Movements', in A. Ansell (ed.), *Unraveling the Right* (Boulder, Colo.: Westview, 1997)

MacLean, N., *Behind the Mask of Chivalry: The Making of the Second Ku Klux Klan* (Oxford University Press, 1995)

Marable, M., 'A New Black Politics', *The Progressive* (August 1990)

——, *Speaking Truth to Power: Essays on Race, Resistance, and Radicalism* (Boulder, Colo.: Westview, 1996)

Marx, K., *The German Ideology* (London: Lawrence & Wishart, 1974)

McCarthy, C. and W. Crichlow (eds), *Race Identity and Representation in Education* (New York & London: Routledge, 1993)

McConahay, J.B., 'Modern racism, ambivalence, and the modern racism scale', in J.F. Dovidio and S.L. Gaertner (eds), *Prejudice, Discrimination, and Racism* (Orlando, Fla: Academic Press, 1986)

Mercer, C., 'Fascist Ideology', in J. Donald and S. Hall (eds), *Politics and Ideology* (Milton Keynes: Open University Press, 1986) pp. 208–39

Messer-Davidow, E., 'Dollars For Scholars', in A. Ansell (ed.) *Unraveling the Right* (Boulder, Colo.: Westview, 1997)

Miles, R., 'Marxism Versus the Sociology of "Race Relations"?'', *Ethnic and Racial Studies*, 7 (April 1984) pp. 217–37

——, 'Recent Marxist Theories of Nationalism and the Issue of Racism', *British Journal of Sociology*, 38 (1987) pp. 24–43

——, *Racism* (London: Routledge, 1989)

——, 'Migration Discourse in Post 1945 British Politics', *Migration*, 6 (1989) pp. 31–53

——, *Racism After 'Race Relations'* (London: Routledge, 1993)

—— and Annie Phizacklea, *White Man's Country: Racism in British Politics* (London: Pluto, 1984)

Modood, T., *Racial Equality: Colour, Culture and Justice* (London: Institute for Public Policy Research, 1994)

Morrison, T. (ed.), *Race-ing Justice, En-Gendering Power: Essays on Anita Hill, Clarence Thomas, and the Construction of Social Reality* (New York: Pantheon, 1992)

Murray, N., 'Anti-Racists and Other Demons: the Press and Ideology in Thatcher's Britain', *Race and Class*, 3 (Winter 1986)

Nairn, T., 'Enoch Powell and the New Right', *New Left Review*, vol. 61 (May–June 1970) pp. 4–11

Nash, G., *The Conservative Intellectual Movement in America since 1945* (New York: Basic Books Inc., 1976)

Nevin, D. and R.E. Bills, *The Schools That Fear Built: Segregationist Academies in the South* (Washington: Acropolis, 1976)

Newfield, C. and R. Strickland (eds), *After Political Correctness: The Humanities and Society in the 1990s* (Boulder, Colo.: Westview, 1995)

Nieli, R. (ed.), *Racial Preference and Racial Justice* (Washington DC: Ethics and Public Policy Center, 1991)

Norual, A., *Deconstructing Apartheid Discourse* (Verso, 1996)

Offe, C., 'Democracy Against the Welfare State?: Structural Foundation of Neoconservative Political Opposition', *Political Theory*, 15 (1987) pp. 501–37

Oliver, M.L. and T.M. Shapiro, *Black Wealth/White Wealth: A New Perspective on Racial Inequality* (New York: Routledge, 1995)

Omi, M.A., 'We Shall Overturn: Race and the Contemporary American Right' (unpublished doctoral thesis, University of California at Santa Cruz, 1987)

Omi, Michal and H. Winant, *Racial Formation in the United States* (New York: Routledge, 1994, 1986)

Palmer, J.L. and I.V. Sawhill (eds), *The Reagan Record: An Urban Institute Study* (Cambridge, Mass.: Ballinger, 1984)

Patterson, O., 'Toward a Study of Black America: Notes on the Culture of Racism', *Dissent* (Fall 1989) pp. 476–85

Peele, G., *Revival and Reaction: The Right in Contemporary America* (Oxford: Clarendon, 1984)

——, 'Parties, Pressure Grops and Parliament', in P. Dunleavy, A. Gamble and G. Peele (eds), *Developments in British Politics* (New York: St Martin's, 1990) pp. 69–95

Phillips, Ken, 'The Nature of Powellism', in R. King and N. Nugent (eds), *The British Right: Conservative and Right Wing Politics in Britain* (Westmead: Saxon House, 1977) pp. 99–132

Phillips, Kevin, *The Emerging Republican Majority* (New York: Anchor, 1970)

——, 'The Rise of the Religious Right in America', *International Herald Tribune* (4 March 1988)

——, *The Politics of Rich and Poor: Wealth and the American Electorate in the Reagan Aftermath* (New York: Random House, 1990)

Pinckney, A., *The Myth of Black Progress* (Cambridge University Press, 1984)

Pincus, F. and H.J. Ehrich (eds), *Race and Ethnic Conflict: Contending Views on Prejudice, Discrimination, and Ethnoviolence* (Boulder, Colo.: Westview, 1994)

Piven, F.F. and R.A. Cloward, *The New Class War: Reagan's Attack on the Welfare State and its Consequences* (New York: Pantheon, 1982)

Policing Against Black People (London: Institute of Race Relations, 1987)

Potter, J. and S. Reicher, 'Discourses of community and conflict: The organization of social categories in accounts of a "riot"', *British Journal of Social Psychology*, 26 (1987) pp. 25–40

Prager, J., 'American Political Culture and the Shifting Meaning of Race', *Ethnic and Racial Studies*, 10 (January 1987) pp. 63–81

Quadagno, J., *The Color of Welfare: How Racism Undermined the War on Poverty* (Oxford University Press, 1994)

Quigley, M. and C. Bertlet, 'Traditional Values, Racism, and Christian Theocracy', *The Public Eye* (December 1992)

Rattansi, A. and S. Westwood (eds), *Racism, Modernity and Identity on the Western Front* (Cambridge: Polity Press, 1994)

Reed, A., 'Race and the Disruption of the New Deal Coalition', *Urban Affairs Quarterly* (December 1991) pp. 326–33

—— and J. Bond, 'Equality – Why We Can't Wait', *The Nation* (12 December 1991) pp. 733–7

Reeves, F., *British Racial Discourse: A Study of British Political Discourse about Race and Race-related Matters* (Cambridge University Press, 1983)

Rich, P., 'Conservative Ideology and Race in Modern British Politics', in Z. Layton-Henry and P. Rich (eds), *Race, Government and Politics in Britain* (London: Macmillan, 1986) pp. 45–72

324   *Bibliography*

Riddell, P., *The Thatcher Government* (Oxford: Martin Robertson, 1983)
——, *The Thatcher Era and Its Legacy* (Oxford: Basil Blackwell, 1991)
Rieder, J., *Canarsie: The Jews and Italians of Brooklyn Against Liberalism* (Cambridge, Mass.: Harvard University Press, 1985)
Roediger, D., *The Wages of Whiteness* (New York: Verso, 1991)
Rogers, D., *Contested Truths: Keywords in American Politics Since Independence* (New York: Basic Books, 1987).
Rose, D., 'Tory Links with BNP Highlighted by Defection', *Guardian* (5 July 1986)
——, 'Far Right Takes Over Monday Club', *Observer* (24 February, 1991)
Rose, H. and S. Rose, 'Less than Human Nature: Biology and the New Right', *Race and Class* (Winter 1986)
Rose, Steven, R.C. Lewontin, and L. Kamin, *Not In Our Genes: Biology, Ideology and Human Nature* (London: Pantheon, 1984)
Rose, Susan, 'Gender Education and the New Christian Right', *Society*, 26 (January 1989)
Rosenburg, D., 'Thatcherism and the New Right', *Jewish Quarterly* (Autumn 1989)
Runnymede Trust, *Multi-Ethnic Britain: Facts and Trends* (London, 1994)
——, *New Right: Image and Reality* (London, 1986)
Rusher, W., *The Rise of the Right* (New York: William Morrow, 1984)
Ryan, R. and E. Dixler, 'Reagan's Racial Covenant', *The Nation* (13 October 1984)
Saloma, J.S., *Ominous Politics: The New Conservative Labyrinth* (New York: Hill & Wang, 1984)
San Juan, E., *Racial Formations/Critical Transformations: Articulations of Power in Ethnic and Racial Studies in the United States* (New Jersey: Humanities Press, 1992)
Sayers, S., 'The Dominant Ideology Thesis', *Radical Philosophy* (Spring 1984)
Scarman, Lord, *The Scarman Report: The Brixton Disorders 10–12 April, 1981* (London: Pelican, 1982)
Schmidt, W.E., 'White Men Get Better Deals in Cars, Study Finds', *New York Times* (12 December 1990)
Schoen, D., *Enoch Powell and the Powellites* (London: Macmillan, 1977)
Schram, S.F., *Words of Welfare: The Poverty of Social Science and the Social Science of Poverty* (Minneapolis: University of Minnesota Press, 1995)
Scott, Daryl Micheal, *Contempt and Pity: Social Policy and the Image of the Damaged Black Psyche* (Chapel Hill: University of North Carolina Press, 1997).
Scott, J.C., *Domination and the Arts of Resistance: Hidden Transcripts* (New Haven: Yale University Press, 1990)
Searle, C., 'From Forster to Baker: The New Victorianism and the Struggle for Education,' *Race and Class*, 30.3 (1989)
Seidel, G., *The Holocaust Denial: Antisemitism, Racism and the New Right* (Leeds: Beyond the Pale Collective, 1986)
——, 'Culture, Nation and "Race" in the British and French New Right', in Ruth Levitas (ed.), *The Ideology of the New Right* (Cambridge: Polity Press, 1986)
——, 'The White Discursive Order: the British New Right's Discourse on Cultural Racism with Particular Reference to the *Salisbury Review*' (Amsterdam: John Benjamins, 1987)

Schrag, P., 'Backing Off Bakke: The New Assault on Affirmative Action', *The Nation* (22 April 1996) pp. 11–14

Schuman, H., C. Steeh and L. Bobo, *Racial Attitudes in America: Trends and Interpretations* (Cambridge, Mass.: Harvard University Press, 1985)

Sears, D., 'Symbolic Racism', in P. Katz and D. Taylor (eds) *Eliminating Racism* (New York: Plenum, 1988)

Shull, S.A., *A Kinder, Gentler Racism?: The Reagan-Bush Civil Rights Legacy* (New York: M.E. Sharpe, 1993)

Shupe, A. and W. Stacey, *Born Again Politics and the Moral Majority* (Edwin Mellen, 1982)

Sivanandan, A., 'From Immigration Control to Induced Repatriation', *Race and Class* (pamphlet no. 5, London, Institute for Race Relations, 1978)

——, *A Different Hunger: Writings on Black Resistance* (London: Pluto, 1982)

——, 'Racism Awareness Training and the Degradation of the Black Struggle', *Race and Class*, XXVI, 4 (1985) pp. 1–33

——, 'The New Racism', *New Statesman and Society* (4 November 1988)

——, *Communities of Resistance: Writings on Black Struggles for Socialism* (London: Verso, 1990)

Skidelsky, R. (ed.), *Thatcherism* (London: Chatto & Windus, 1988)

Sleeper, J., *The Closest of Strangers: Liberalism and the Politics of Race in New York* (New York: Norton, 1990)

Small, S., *Racialised Barriers: The Black Experience in the United States and England in the 1980s* (London: Routledge, 1994)

Smith, A.M., *New Right Discourse on Race and Sexuality* (Cambridge University Press, 1994)

——, 'Why Did Armey Apologize? Hegemony, Homophobia and the Religious Right', in A. Ansell (ed.), *Unraveling the Right* (Boulder, Colo.: Westview Press, 1997).

Smith, M.P. and J.R. Feagin (eds), *The Bubbling Cauldron: Race, Ethnicity, and the Urban Crisis* (Minneapolis, MN: University of Minnesota Press, 1995)

Smith, S., 'The Twilight of the American Dream', *International Socialism*, 54 (Spring 1992)

Smitheran-Donaldson G. and T. Van Dijk (eds), *Discourse and Discrimination* (Detroit: Wayne State University Press, 1988)

Sniderman, P.M. and T. Piazza, *The Scar of Race* (Cambridge, Mass.: Harvard University Press, 1993)

Solomos, John, 'Varieties of Marxists Conceptions of 'Race', Class and the State: A Critical Analysis', in John Rex and David Mason (eds), *Theories of Race and Ethnic Relations* (New York: Cambridge University Press, 1986) pp. 84–109

——, 'Institutionalised Racism: Policies of Marginalisation in Education and Training', in Philip Cohen and Harwant Bains (eds), *Multi-Racist Britain* (London: Macmillan, 1988)

——, 'Political Language and Racial Discourse', *European Journal of Intercultural Studies*, vol. 2, no. 1 (1991) pp. 21–34

——, *Black Youth, Racism and the State: the Politics of Ideology and Policy* (Cambridge University Press, 1991)

——, *Race and Racism in Britain*, 2nd edn (London: Macmillan, 1993, 1989)

—— and Les Beck, *Race, Politics and Social Change* (London: Routledge, 1995)

Statman, J.M., 'In the Heroic Vanguard of Normalization: Black Elites and the Creation of the New South Africa' (Dover, Delaware: South African Azanian Student Movement, 1992)

——, 'Exorcizing the Ghosts of Apartheid: Memory, Identity and Trauma in the "New" South Africa' (Washington DC: unpublished conference paper, International Society of Political Psychology, July 1995)

Steinberg, M., 'The Re-Making of the English Working Class?', *Theory and Society*, 20 (April 1991)

Steinberg, Stephen, *The Ethnic Myth: Race, Ethnicity, and Class in America*, 2nd edn (Boston: Beacon, 1989)

——, *Turning Back: The Retreat from Racial Justice in American Thought and Policy* (Boston: Beacon, 1995)

Steinfels, P., *The Neoconservatives: the Men who are Changing America's Politics* (New York: Simon & Schuster, 1979)

——, 'The Reasonable Right', *Esquire* (13 February 1979) pp. 23–44

Struyk, R.J., M.A. Turner and M. Fix, *Opportunities Denied, Opportunities Diminished: Discrimination in Housing* (Washington DC: Urban Institute, 1992)

Studlar, Donley, 'British Public Opinion, Colour Issues and Enoch Powell', *The British Journal of Political Science*, no. 3 (July 1974) pp. 371–81

Swayne, J.E., *Anti-Busing and the New Right: A Rhetorical Criticism of the National Association of Neighborhood Schools*, (unpublished doctoral dissertation: Ohio State University, 1981)

Taguieff, P.A., 'The New Cultural Racism in France', *Telos*, 83 (Spring, 1990) pp. 109–22

Takagi, D.Y., *The Retreat from Race: Asian-American Admissions and Racial Politics* (New Brunswick, New Jersey: Rutgers University Press, 1992)

Taylor, I., 'Law and Order; Moral Order', in R. Miliband, L. Panitch and J. Saville (eds), *Socialist Register: Conservatism in Britain and America: Rhetoric and Reality* (London: Merlin, 1987)

Therborn, G., *What Does the Ruling Class Do When it Rules?* (London: New Left Review, 1978)

Thompson, J.B., *Studies in the Theory of Ideology* (Cambridge: Polity Press,1987)

——, *Ideology and Modern Culture* (Cambridge: Polity Press, 1990)

Tiranti, D., 'The Big Clampdown: Democracy, Freedom and the Rise of the New Right', *New Internationalist*, 133 (March 1984)

Toler, D., 'Black Conservatives: Part One', *The Public Eye* (September 1993)

van Dijk, T., *Racism and the Press* (London: Routledge, 1991)

Verdery, K., 'Nationalism and National Sentiment in Post-socialist Romania', *Slavic Review*, vol. 52, no. 2 (Summer 1993) pp. 179–203

Webber, F., 'From Ethnocentrism to Euro-racism', *Race and Class*, vol. 32, no. 3 (January–March 1991) pp. 11–18

Wellman, D., 'The New Political Linguistics of Race', *Socialist Review*, 16 (May–August 1986) pp. 43–62

——, *Portraits of White Racism*, 2nd edn (Cambridge University Press, 1993)

——, 'Minstrel Shows, Affirmative Action Talk, and Angry White Men: Marking Racial Otherness in the 1990s', paper delivered at the American Sociological Association National Convention, New York City (16 August 1996)

Wetherell, M. and J. Potter, *Mapping the Language of Racism: Discourse and the Legitimation of Exploitation* (New York: Columbia University Press, 1992)

——, H. Stiven and J. Potter, 'Unequal egalitarianism: A preliminary study of discourses concerning gender and employment opportunities', *British Journal of Social Psychology*, 26 (1987), p. 59-71

Whitaker, R., 'Neo-Conservatism and the State', in R. Miliband, L. Panitch and J. Saville (eds) *Socialist Register 1987: Conservatism in Britain and America: Rhetoric and Reality* (London: Merlin, 1987)

Wilkins, R., 'Smiling Racism', *The Nation*, 239 (3 November 1984)

Williams, J. (ed.), *PC Wars: Politics and Theory in the Academy* (New York: Routledge, 1995)

Williams, L., 'Blacks Debating a Greater Stress on Self-Reliance Instead of Aid', *New York Times* (15 June 1986), A24

Willig, Carla, 'AIDS – A Study of the Social Construction of Knowledge' (unpublished doctoral thesis: Cambridge University, 1991)

Wilson, W.J., *The Declining Significance of Race: Blacks and Changing American Institutions*, 2nd edn (Univeristy of Chicago Press, 1980)

——, *The Truly Disadvantaged: the Inner City, the Underclass, and Public Policy* (University of Chicago Press, 1987)

Winant, H., 'Postmodern racial politics', *Socialist Review* (January–March 1990)

——, *Racial Conditions: Politics, Theory, Comparisons* (Minneapolis: University of Minnesota Press, 1994)

——, 'Racial Formation and Hegemony: Global and Local Developments', in A. Rattansi and S. Westwood (eds), *Racism, Modernity and Identity on the Western Front* (Cambridge: Polity Press, 1994) pp. 266–89

Withorn, A., 'Fulfilling Fears and Fantasies: The Role of Welfare in Right Wing Social Thought and Stategy', in A. Ansell (ed.) *Unraveling the Right* (Boulder, Colo.: Westview, 1997)

Wodak, R. and B. Matouschek, '"We are dealing with people whose origins one can clearly tell just by looking": critical discourse analysis and the study of neo-racism in contemporary Austria', *Discourse and Society*, vol. 4, no. 2, (April 1993) pp. 225–48

Wolfe, A., 'The New American Dilemma: Understanding, and Misunderstanding, Race', *The New Republic* (13 April 1992) pp. 30–7

Wolff, E., *Top Heavy: A Study of the Increasing Inequality of Wealth in America* (New York: The Twentieth Century Fund Press, 1995)

Wolff, R.D., 'The New Right's Economics: A Diagnosis and Counterattack' in A. Ansell (ed.), *Unraveling the Right* (Boulder, Colo.: Westview, 1997)

Wrench, J. and J. Solomos, *Racism and Migration in Western Europe* (London: Berg, 1993)

Young, P.D., *God's Bullies: Native Reflections on Preachers and Politics* (New York: Holt, Rinehart & Winston, 1982)

Zizek, S., *Mapping Ideology* (London: Verso, 1994)

Primary (New Right) Sources – The United States

Abrams, E., 'The Quota Commission', *Commentary* (October 1972)

Allen, W.B., 'The New Racism is the Old Power Grab', *Conservative Digest* (July/August 1989) pp. 16–21

Atwood, T., 'Through A Glass Darkly: Is the Christian Right Overconfident It Knows God's Will?', *Policy Review* (Fall 1990) pp. 44–52

Ball, Peter, 'Blacks Must Take Responsibility', *Lincoln Review* (Summer 1984)

Bennett, W.J., 'Why the West?', in W. Lind and W. Marshner (eds), *Cultural Conservatism:Theory and Practice* (Washington DC: Free Congress Research and Education Foundation, 1991) pp. 61–70

——, *The De-Valuing of America: The Fight for Our Culture and Our Children* (New York: Simon & Schuster, 1992)

——, *The Index of Leading Cultural Indicators* (New York: Touchstone, 1994)

Berns, Walter, 'Let Me Call You Quota, Sweetheart', *Commentary* (May 1981) pp. 48–53

Bernstein, Richard, *Dictatorship of Virtue: How the Battle Over Multiculturalism Is Reshaping Our Schools, Our Country, and Our Lives* (New York: Random House, 1994)

Bloom, A., *The Closing of the American Mind* (New York: Simon & Schuster, 1987)

Bolce, L.H. and S. Gray, 'Blacks, Whites, and "Race Politics"', *The Public Interest* (Winter 1979) pp. 61–75

Bolick, C., 'Civil Rights at the Crossroads', *Lincoln Review* (Summer 1988) pp. 31–7

——, *Changing Course: Civil Rights at the Crossroads* (New York: Transaction, 1988)

——, *Unfinished Business: A Civil Rights Strategy for America's Third Century* (Pacific Research Institute for Public Policy, 1990)

——, 'Time for an Omnibus Civil Rights Bill', *Backgrounder* (30 April 1991) pp. 1–14

——, *Grassroots Tyranny: The Limits of Federalism* (Washington DC: The Cato Institute, 1993)

——, *The Affirmative Action Fraud: Can We Restore the American Civil Rights Vision?* (Washington DC: The Cato Institute, 1996)

—— and M.B. Liedl, 'Fulfilling America's Promise: A Civil Rights Strategy for the 1990s', *Policy Review* (June 1990)

Bowie, W., Jr., 'It's Not Racism, It's Us', *Lincoln Review* (Fall 1988) pp. 39–47

Brimelow, P., *Alien Nation: Common Sense about America's Immigration Disaster* (New York: Random House, 1995)

Brookes, W.T., 'What Welfare Has Done to America's Blacks', *Conservative Digest* (September 1982) p. 23

Brownfeld, A.C. and J.A. Parker, 'Returning to the Goal of a "Color Blind" American Society', *Lincoln Review*, 2 (Summer 1981) pp. 3–22

Brudney, D., 'A Black Conservative Champion', *Conservative Digest* (November 1975) p. 45

——, 'Busing: The Rawest Deal', *Conservative Digest* (January 1976) p. 17

Buchanan, P., 'Fashionable Intolerance', *Washington Inquirer* (29 January 1982)

——, 'Egalitarian Education Brings Us All Down', *Conservative Digest* (August 1983) p. 35

——, 'Why Reagan Should Veto a Martin Luther King Holiday', *Conservative Digest* (September 1983) p. 28

——, 'Immigration Reform or Racial Purity?', *Washington Inquirer* (15 June 1984)

——, *Right from the Beginning* (New York: Little, Brown, 1988)

——, 'Crime and Race: A Reluctance to Acknowledge Reality', *Conservative Digest* (July/August 1989) pp. 36–7

Butler, S., M. Sanera and W.B. Weinrod, *Mandate for Leadership II: Continuing the Conservative Revolution* (Washington DC: Heritage Foundation, 1984)

Carter, S.L., *Reflections of an Affirmative Action Baby* (New York: Basic Books, 1991)

'Clarence Pendleton, Chairman, U.S. Civil Rights Commission: An Interview', *Conservative Digest* (July 1986) pp. 83–94

——, *Naked Racial Preference* (New York: Madison, 1995)

——, 'Race, Lies, and "Hopwood"', *Commentary* (June 1996) pp. 39–44

Cohen, C., 'Why Racial Preference Is Illegal and Immoral', *Commentary* (June 1979) pp. 40–52

——, 'Naked Racial Preference', *Commentary*, 81 (March 1986) pp. 24–39

Citrin, J., 'Affirmative Action in the People's Court', *The Public Interest* (Winter 1996) pp. 39–48

D'Souza, D., 'Jerry Falwell is Reaching Millions and Drawing Fire', *Conservative Digest* (December 1986)

——, *Illiberal Education: The Politics of Race and Sex on Campus* (New York: The Free Press, 1991)

——, *The End of Racism* (New York: The Free Press, 1995)

Eastland, T., 'George Bush's Quota Bill: The Dismaying Impact of Griggs', *Policy Review* (Summer, 1991) pp. 45–50

——, *Conservatives in Power: The Task of Governing* (New York: The Free Press, 1992)

——, *Ending Affirmative Action: The Case for Colorblind Justice* (New York: Basic Books, 1996)

—— and W. Bennett, *Counting By Race: Equality from the Founding Fathers to Bakke and Weber* (New York: Basic Books, 1979)

Feulner, E.J., *Looking Back* (Washington DC: Heritage Foundation, 1981)

Finn, C., 'Affirmative Action Under Reagan', *Commentary* (April 1982)

Gilder, G., *Wealth and Poverty* (New York: Basic Books, 1981)

——, 'Whose Economics Really Helps the Poor', *Wall Street Journal* (25 March 1982)

Gingrich, N., 'The Future of the Welfare State', *Conservative Digest* (August 1984)

——, *To Renew America* (New York: HarperCollins, 1996)

Glazer, N., 'The Limits of Social Policy', *Commentary* (September 1971)

——, 'Is Busing Necessary', *Commentary* (March 1972) pp. 39–52

——, *Affirmative Discrimination: Ethnic Inequality and Public Policy* (New York: Basic Books, 1975)

——, 'Why Bakke Won't End Reverse Discrimination', *Commentary* (September 1978)

——, 'The Affirmative Action Stalemate', *The Public Interest* (Winter 1988)

Goodman, J., 'Welfare Is Breeding Poverty', *Conservative Digest* (January 1985)

Greider, W. and H.J. Logan, 'Why Blacks Are Turning Conservative: Liberal Policies are Frustrating Upward-Bound Blacks', *Conservative Digest* (October 1978) pp. 29–31

Hatch, Orrin Senator, 'The New Slavery', *Lincoln Review* (Summer 1979) pp. 85–8

Hatch, O. Senator, 'In the Mainstream: Affirmative Action Blatant Illegal Racism', *Conservative Digest* (July 1980) pp. 14

——, 'Civil Privileges Act of 1984', *Conservative Digest* (August 1984) p. 33

Heatherly, Charles L. (ed.), *Mandate for Leadership: Policy Management in a Conservative Administration* (Washington DC: Heritage Foundation, 1981)

—— and B.Y. Pines, *Mandate for Leadership III: Policy Strategies for the 1990s* (Washington DC: Heritage Foundation, 1989)

Henry, W.A., *In Defense of Elitism* (New York: Doubleday, 1994)

Herrnstein, R.J., and C. Murray, *The Bell Curve: Intelligence and Class Structure in American Life* (New York: The Free Press, 1994)

Hough, W., 'On Being Black in America', *Lincoln Review* (Summer 1984)

Hows, J., 'Anti-Busing Crusaders Turn Congress Around: Interview With Member of NANS', *Conservative Digest* (May/June 1980) p. 33

Keyes, W.A., 'Blacks and Republicans: The GOP is Looking the Wrong Way', *Conservative Digest* (July/August 1989) pp. 47–9

Keyes, A., *Masters of the Dream: The Strength and Betrayal of Black America* (New York: Wiliam Morrow, 1995)

——, *Our Character, Our Future: Reclaiming America's Moral Destiny* (Washington DC: Zondervan, 1996)

Kling, Bill, 'To Be Young, Black and Conservative', *Conservative Digest* (January 1984) pp. 20–1

Kristol, I., 'About Equality', *Commentary* (November 1972)

——, 'What is a Neo-Conservative?', *Newsweek* (19 January 1976)

——, 'Thoughts on Equality and Egalitarianism', in C.D. Campbell (ed.), *Income Redistribution* (Washington DC: American Enterprise Instititue, 1977) pp. 35–42

——, *Two Cheers for Capitalism* (New York: Basic Books, 1978)

——, 'Looking back on Neoconservatism: Notes and Reflections', *American Spectator* (March 1979)

Lind, W. and W. Marshner, *Cultural Conservatism: Toward a New National Agenda* (Washington DC: Free Congress Research and Education Foundation with Institute for Cultural Conservatism, 1987)

—— and —— (eds.), *Cultural Conservatism: Theory and Practice* (Washington DC: Free Congress Research and Education Foundation and Center for Cultural Conservatism, 1991)

Loury, G., *One by One from the Inside Out: Essays and Reviews on Race and Responsibility in America* (New York: The Free Press, 1995)

Lynch, F.R., 'Surviving Affirmative Action (More or Less)', *Commentary* (August 1990) pp. 44–7

——, *Invisible Victims: White Males and the Crisis of Affirmative Action* (New York: Praeger, 1991)

—— and W.R. Beer, 'You Ain't the Right Color, Pal: White Resentment of Affirmative Action', *Policy Review* (January 1990)

Marshner, C., *Blackboard Tyranny* (New Rochelle, New York: Arlington House, 1978)

McGraw, O., *Secular Humanism and the Schools: The Issue Whose Time has Come* (Washington, DC: Heritage Foundation, 1976)

McGuigan, P.B., 'Brad Reynolds Tells How Conservatives Fight For Civil Rights', *Conservative Digest* (November 1985) pp. 101–8

——, 'The Racism Scam: How Liberal Black Leaders Perpetuate Dependence', *Conservative Digest* (March/April 1989) pp. 53–5

Mead, L.M., 'Social Programs and Social Obligations', *The Public Interest* , 69 (Fall 1982) pp. 17–32

Mead, L.M., *Beyond Entitlement: The Social Obligations of Citizenship* (New York: The Free Press, 1985)

——, *The New Politics of Poverty: The Non-Working Poor in America* (New York: Basic Books, 1993)

Meyerson, A., 'Reaching Out to Black Americans', *Conservative Digest* (January 1985) p. 23

Murray, Charles, 'Affirmative Racism: How Preferential Treatment Works Against Blacks', *The New Republic* (31 December 1984) pp. 18–23

——, *Losing Ground: American Social Policy 1950–1980* (New York: Basic Books 1984)

——, 'Admitting Success', *New Republic* (4 February 1985)

——, 'White Welfare, White Families, "White Trash"', *National Review* (28 March 1986)

'The New Discrimination: A Conservative Digest Poll', *Conservative Digest* (February 1978) p. 13

Norquist, G., *Rock the House* (Washington DC: VYTIS, 1995)

Novak, M., 'Race and Truth', *Commentary* (December 1976) pp. 54–8

——, 'Allan Bakke: Victim of Discrimination', *Conservative Digest* (January 1978) p. 48

Pendleton, C., 'Guess Who's Coming to Dinner With the White Folks?', *Conservative Digest* (July 1988)

Pendleton, C.M. Jr., 'Affirmative Action and Individual Freedom', *Lincoln Review*, 7 (Summer 1986) pp. 23–5

Perkins, J. (ed.), *A Conservative Agenda for Black Americans*, 2nd edn (Washington DC: Heritage Foundation, 1990)

Perlmutter, P., 'Balkanizing America', *Commentary* (September 1980) pp. 64–6

Phillips, Kevin, 'The New Racism', *Conservative Digest* (March 1978) p. 15

——, 'Ghetto Conservatism', *Conservative Digest* (May 1978)

Pines, B.Y., *Back to Basics: The Traditionalist Movement that is Sweeping Grassroots America* (New York: William Morrow, 1982)

Podhoretz, N., *Breaking Ranks: A Political Memoir* (New York: Harper & Row, 1979)

——, 'New Vistas for Neoconservatives', *Conservative Digest* (January/February 1989)

'Power Back to the People: Conservative Caucus is organizing the grassroots to get the country back on the right track', *Conservative Digest* (February 1976) pp. 6–10

Rasberry, William, 'Forced Busing has Failed', *Conservative Digest* (September 1975) pp. 39–40

——, 'Pride and Prejudice', *Conservative Digest* (July/August 1989)

Ravitch, D., *The Schools We Deserve: Reflections on the Educational Crisis of Our Times* (New York: Basic Books, 1985)

Reagan, R., 'The Queen of Welfare', *Conservative Digest* (March 1977) p. 19

Reed, R., 'Casting a Wider Net: Religious Conservatives Move Beyond Abortion and Homosexuality', *Policy Review* (Summer, 1993)

Reed, S.D., *NEA: Propaganda Front of the Radical Left* (Washington DC: National Council for Better Education, 1984)

——, 'The NEA: Ruining Education in America', *Conservative Digest* (January 1985) p. 16

'Rev. Falwell 'Reasonable' Man, Says New NBC President; And Feds Continue Race Count', *Conservative Digest* (August 1981) p. 36

Robertson, P. Rev, 'The Wealth of Black Families', *Conservative Digest* (June. 1987) pp. 35–41

Rodriguez, G., 'The New Civil Rights Movement: Economic Empowerment', *Heritage Lectures* (1990)

Scott, O., 'Lessons from the British Schoolmarm', *Conservative Digest* (May/June 1989)

Smith, E., *101 Reasons Not to Be a Liberal* (Washington DC: Saint Clair Rene, 1995)

Sowell, T., 'A Black Conservative Dissents', *Conservative Digest* (November 1976)

——, 'Affirmative Action Reconsidered', *Public Interest*, 42 (Winter 1976)

——, 'Are Quotas Good for Blacks?', *Commentary* (June 1978) pp. 39–43

——, 'What's Wrong with Quotas', *Conservative Digest* (September 1978)

——, 'Myths About Minorities', *Commentary* (August 1979) pp. 33–7

——, 'Affirmative Action Just Hasn't Worked; But Trickle-Down Theory is Doing Fine', *Conservative Digest* (October 1981) pp. 18–19

——, 'Weber and Bakke, and the Presuppositions of Affirmative Action', in W.E. Block and M.A. Walker (eds), *Discrimination, Affirmative Action and Equal Opportunity* (Vancouver: Fraser Institute, 1981)

——, *Civil Rights: Rhetoric or Reality?* (New York: Quill, 1984)

——, *Preferential Politics: An International Perspective* (New York: William Morrow, 1990)

——, *Race and Culture: A World View* (New York: Basic Books, 1994)

——, *Migrations and Cultures: A World View* (New York: Basic Books, 1996)

——, *The Vision of the Anointed: Self-Congratulation as a Basis for Social Policy* (New York: Basic Books, 1996)

Steele, S., *The Content of Our Character* (New York: Harper, 1990)

Steinfels, P., 'Neocons: Friend of Foe?', *Conservative Digest* (September 1979) pp. 22–3

'Stop the MLK Holiday Bill!', *Conservative Digest* (September 1983) p. 26

'Strangers at our Gate: Immigration in the 1990s' (New York: Manhattan Institute, 1994)

Tapscott, M., 'Compassion in America: How Much Longer Will the Poor Suffer the Establishment's Welfare Failures?', *Conservative Digest* (September 1982)

Thomas, C., 'Thomas Sowell and the Heritage of Lincoln: Ethnicity and Individual Freedom', *Lincoln Review* (Winter 1988) pp. 7–19

'Time for an Omnibus Civil Rights Bill', *The Backgrounder* (Washington DC: Heritage Foundation, 1990)

Viguerie, R.A., *The New Right: We're Ready to Lead* (Falls Church, VA: Viguerie, 1981)

——, *The Establishment vs. the People: Is a New Populist Revolt on the Way?* (Chicago: Regnery Gateway, 1984)

——, 'Liberals Versus Blacks', *Conservative Digest* (March 1984)

——, 'A True Civil Rights Commission', *Conservative Digest* (May 1984) p. 47

——, 'Conservative Alternatives Beckons Black Families', *Conservative Digest* (July 1984) pp. 46–7

Wattenberg, B.J. and R.M. Scammon, 'Black Progress and Liberal Rhetoric', *Commentary* (April 1973) pp. 35–44

—— and K. Zinsmeister, 'The Case for More Immigration', *Commentary* (April 1990) pp. 19–25

Weyrich, P., 'Guess Who Is Coming to the Party?', *Conservative Digest* (November 1985)

——, 'What Conservatives Are Looking for from the Next President', *Conservative Digest* (January 1986)

——, 'Getting Serious About Blacks', *Conservative Digest* (July/August 1989) pp. 11–14

——, 'A Conservative Manifesto for the 1990s', *Crisis* (July/August 1990) pp. 43–7

——, 'Cultural conservatism and the conservative movement', in W. Lind and W. Marshner (eds), *Cultural Conservatism: Theory and Practice* (Washington DC: Free Congress Research and Education Foundation, 1991) pp. 19–32

'What Conservatives Would Do for Minorities', *Conservative Digest* (March 1984) pp. 4–5

Whitaker, R. (ed.), *The New Right Papers* (New York: St Martins, 1982)

Williams, A., *Beyond Blame: How We Can Succeed by Breaking the Dependency Barrier* (New York: The Free Press, 1995)

Williams, W.E., 'Ted Kennedy is Not the Black Man's Friend', *Conservative Digest* (December 1979) p. 42

——, 'Many So-Called Leaders of Blacks are Spouting Lots of Nonsense about Blacks', *Moral Majority Report* (17 November 1980)

——, *The State Against Blacks* (New York: McGraw-Hill, 1982)

Will, G., 'Are "Ethnic Review Courts" Next?', *Conservative Digest* (February 1978) p. 38

——, 'Prejudice Against Excellence', *Conservative Digest* (July/August 1989)

Wims, G., 'Blacks and Conservatism: Closer Than We Think', *Lincoln Review* (Fall 1981) pp. 3–5

Woodson, R., *On the Road to Economic Freedom: An Agenda for Black Progress* (New York: Regnery, 1987)

——, 'Is the Black Community a Casualty of the War on Poverty?', *Heritage Lectures* (1990)
——, 'Conservatives and civil rights', in W. Lind and W. Marshner (eds), *Cultural Conservatism: Theory and Practice* (Washington DC: Free Congress Research and Education Foundation, 1991) pp. 195–202
Wright, N. Jr., 'Black Conservatism Today', *Lincoln Review* (Summer–Fall 1987) pp. 11–13.

Primary (New Right) Sources – Britain

Anderson, D. (ed.), *Educated for Employment?* (London: Social Affairs Unit, 1982)
——, 'Ripe for a British Moral Majority', *The Times* (15 October 1985)
——, 'Our debt to the Victorians', *The Times* (15 April 1986)
——, 'With friends like these ...', *The Times* (28 November 1986)
—— and G. Frost (eds), *Hubris: The Tempting of Modern Conservatives* (London: Centre for Policy Studies, 1992)
——, *Of Virtue: Moral Confusion and Social Disorder in Britain and America* (London: Social Affairs Unit, 1992)
Ashworth, C., 'Sociobiology and the Nation', *Salisbury Review* (Summer 1983)
'The Asian Housing Success Story: Academics Belittle Asian Achievements' (London: Social Affairs Unit, 29 March 1985)
Boyson, Rhodes (ed.), *1985: An Escape from Orwells 1984* (Middlesex: Chruchill, 1975)
'Breaking the Spell of the Welfare State' (London: Social Affairs Unit, 1981)
Brown, A., 'Trials of Honeyford' (London: Centre for Policy Studies, 1985)
——, 'Problems in Multicultural Education' (London: Centre for Policy Studies, 1985)
Buckmaster, C., 'Education and the Permissive Society' (London: Monday Club,1982)
——, 'A Manifesto for Education' (London: Monday Club, 1983)
Butt, R., 'Britain's Permanent Liberal Government', *Policy Review* (Fall 1979)
——, 'Who thinks for the church?', *The Times* (12 April 1984)
——, 'No faith in this cure for poverty', *The Times* (5 December 1985)
Casey, J., 'One Nation: The Politics of Race', *Salisbury Review* (Autumn 1982)
Copping, R., 'The Monday Club – Crisis and After' (Current Affairs Information Service, 1975)
Courtney, A., 'The Enemies Within' (London: Monday Club, 1983)
Cowling, M. (ed.), *Conservative Essays* (London: Cassell, 1978)
Cox, C. and J. Marks, 'The Right to Learn' (London: Centre for Policy Studies, 1982)
—— and R. Tingle, 'The New Barbarians', *Salisbury Review* (October 1986)
—— and others, *Whose Schools? - A Radical Manifesto* (London: Hillgate Group, 1986)
Crowther, I., 'Mrs. Thatcher's Idea of the Good Society', *Salisbury Review* (Spring 1983)
Dale, D., 'Denying Homes to Black Children' (London: Social Affairs Unit, 1984)

——, 'The New Ideology of Race', *Salisbury Review* (October 1985)

Ellis-Jones, A., 'Toryism and the Family', *Free Nation* (October 1987)

Flew, A., *The Politics of Procrustes: Contradictions of Enforced Equality* (London: Temple Smith, 1981)

——, *Education, Race and Revolution* (London: Centre for Policy Studies, 1984)

——, 'Race Relations Industry', *Salisbury Review* (Winter 1984)

——, 'Three Concepts of Racism', *Salisbury Review* (October 1986)

——, 'Sense and Nonsense about Race', *Free Nation* (December 1986)

——, 'The Monstrous Regiment of "Anti-Racism"', *Salisbury Review* (June 1989)

——, *A Future for Anti-Racism?* (London: The Social Affairs Unit, 1992)

Gray, J., 'The Politics of Cultural Diversity', *Salisbury Review* (September 1988)

Griffiths, B., 'Monetarism and Morality', (London: Centre for Policy Studies, 1985)

Hartup, G., *Misreporting Racial Attacks* (London: Hampden Trust, 1995)

Hiskett, M., 'Choice in Rotten Apples: Bias in GCSE and Examining Groups' (London: Centre for Policy Studies, 1985)

——, 'Schooling for British Muslims: Integrated, Opted Out or Denominational' (London: Social Affairs Unit, 1989)

Holland, K. and G. Parkins, 'Reversing Racism: Lessons from America' (London: Social Affairs Unit, 1984)

Honeyford, R., 'Multi-ethnic Intolerance', *Salisbury Review* (Summer 1983)

——, 'Teacher and Social Worker – an inevitable conflict', *Salisbury Review* (Spring 1984)

Honeyford, Ray, 'Education and Race – an Alternative View', *Salisbury Review* (Winter 1984)

——, 'Attacks on Our Nation Promote Racism', *Free Nation* (December 1986)

——, 'The Swann Fiasco', *Salisbury Review* (April 1987)

——, *Integration or Disintegration?: Towards a Non-Racist Society* (London: Claridge Press, 1988)

Honeyford, Ray, 'Multi-culture "Education"', *Freedom Today* (April 1989)

——, *Race and Free Speech:Violating the Taboo* (St Albans: Claridge Press, 1992)

'Hong Kong Revolt Crumble', *Race and Immigration Bulletin*, 236 (June 1990)

Howell, D. MP, 'The Conservative Tradition and the 1980s' (London: Centre for Policy Studies, 1980)

'Immigration – an Untenable Situation' (London: Monday Club, 1981)

Jeffery, B., *John Redwood and Popular Conservatism* (London: Tecla, 1995)

Joseph, Sir K., 'Monetarism is Not Enough' (London: Centre for Policy Studies, 1976)

Kogbara, D., 'Less Special Pleading', *Sunday Times* (18 April 1993)

Laud, D., 'The Law, Order and Race Relations' (London: Monday Club, 1984)

Lawlor, S., *Opting Out: A Guide to Why and How* (London: Centre for Policy Studies, 1988)

Lawson, N. MP, 'The New Conservatism' (London: Centre for Policy Studies, 1980)

Levy, D., 'The Politics of Welfare', *Salisbury Review* (October 1985)

Lewis, R., *Anti-Racism: A Mania Exposed* (London: Quartet, 1988)

Marsland, D. and N. Seaton, *The Empire Strikes Back: The 'Creative Subversion' of the National Curriculum* (York: Campaign for Real Education, 1994)

McIntosh, J., F. Naylor and L. Norcross, 'The ILEA After the Abolition of the GLC' (London: Centre for Policy Studies, 1983)

Minogue, K., 'This talk of race is nonsense', *Sunday Telegraph* (24 April 1988)

Mishan, E.J., 'Not by Economics Alone', *Salisbury Review* (Summer 1983)

——, 'What Future for a Multi-Racial Britain?', *Salisbury Review* (June 1988)

Moore, C., *The Old People of Lambeth* (London: Salisbury Group, 1982)

——, 'Brixton – the old community', *Daily Telegraph* (24 March 1982)

——, 'How to spot a racist', *Daily Telegraph* (16 July 1984)

——, 'Anti-racist road to British apartheid', *Daily Telegraph* (15 July 1985)

Moore, P., 'Tradition and Worship', *Salisbury Review* (Summer 1983)

North, J., 'The Politics of Forgiveness', *Salisbury Review* (July 1986)

—— (ed.), *The GCSE: An Examination* (London: Claridge Press, 1987)

O'Keefe, D. (ed.), *The Wayward Curriculum: A Cause for Parent's Concern?* (London: Social Affairs Unit, 1986)

——, 'The Real Racism', *Salisbury Review* (March 1989)

Osaji-Umeaku, G., *British Race Relations: How Democratic?* (London: The Abraham and Sarah Foundation, 1992)

Palmer, F. (ed.), *Anti-racism: An Assault on Education and Value* (London: Sherwood Press, 1986)

Pearce, S., 'Education and the Multi-Racial Society' (London: Monday Club, 1985)

Portillo, M., *Clear Blue Water* (London: Conservative Way Forward, 1994)

Powell, E., *Freedom and Reality* (London: Cox & Wyman, 1969)

——, *Still to Decide* (London: Cox & Wyman, 1973)

——, *No Easy Answers* (London: Sheldon, 1973)

——, 'Our Loss of Sovereignty', *Salisbury Review* (Autumn, 1982)

——, 'The UK and Immigration', *Salisbury Review* (December, 1988)

'Preferential Treatment for Racial Minorities is Racist: CRE urged – Condemn Policies of Reverse Racism' (London: Social Affairs Unit, 1984)

Proctor, H., 'Immigration, Repatriation and the CRE' (London: Monday Club, 1981)

——, 'Education and the Multi-Racial Society' (London: Monday Club,1985)

'Race Relations and the Commission for Racial Equality' (London: Monday Club, n.d.)

Ropke, W., 'The Conditions and Limits of the Market', *Freedom Today* (June 1989)

Savery, J., 'Anti-Racism as Witchcraft', *Salisbury Review* (July 1985)

——, 'Strictly Anti-Racist on Fantasy Island', *Salisbury Review* (April 1987)

Scruton, R., *The Meaning of Conservatism* (London: Penguin, 1980)

——, 'Who are the real racists?', *The Times* (30 October 1984)

——, 'The paths blocked by anti-racists', *The Times* (16 April 1985)

——, 'Sense and Censorship', *Salisbury Review* (April 1986)

——, *Power to the Parents: Reversing Educational Decline* (London: Sherwood Press, 1987)

——, 'The Left Establishment', *Salisbury Review* (December 1988)

——, A. Ellis-Jones and D. O'Keefe, *Education and Indoctrination* (London: Sherwood Press, 1985)

Seldon, A., 'The Litmus Paper' (London: Centre for Policy Studies, 1980)

Shreir, S., 'The Politics of Language', *Salisbury Review* (Summer 1983)

Sherman, A., 'Why Britain can't be wished away', *Daily Telegraph* (9 September 1976)

——, 'Why We Asked the Unasked Questions', *Daily Telegraph* (1 September 1984)

Swerling, S., 'Who's Getting at Our Kids?' (London: Monday Club, 1972)

——, 'Some Uncivil Liberties: A Critical Look at the NCCL' (London: Monday Club, 1983)

Thatcher, M., 'The Moral Basis of a Free Society', *Daily Telegraph* (16 May 1978)

Thomas, H., 'Why the task of Mrs. Thatcher's government has only just begun', *Daily Telegraph* (30 May 1983)

Tingle, R., 'Anglicans and Racism', *Free Nation* (December 1986)

Utley, T.E., 'A Free Market is Not Enough', *Daily Telegraph* (10 January 1977)

——, 'Terrorism and Tolerance' (London: Centre for Policy Studies, 1985)

——, 'A Tory View of Freedom and the State', *Free Nation* (October 1986)

Vander Elst, P., 'Reflections on Thatcherism', *Freedom Today* (June 1989)

Waddington, P.A.J., 'Are the Police Fair?' (London: Social Affairs Unit Research Report 2, 1983)

Waterhouse, K., 'In bed with bigotry', *Daily Mail* (27 February 1989)

Worsthorne, P., 'Who Can Civilise the Yobs?', *Daily Telegraph* (9 September 1976)

——, 'End this silence over race', *Sunday Telegraph* (29 September 1985)

——, 'Labour's folly over riots and looting', *Sunday Telegraph* (6 October 1985)

Young, G.K., 'Chaos or Compulsion', *Race Today* (December 1970)

Index